# Useful Symbols

| | | | |
|---|---|---|---|
| **Ab** | Improper abbreviation. Spell out. | **,/** | Insert comma. |
| **Agr** | Faulty agreement. | **;/** | Insert semicolon. |
| **Amb** | Ambiguous construction. | **:/** | Insert colon. |
| **Ap** | Omission or misuse of apostrophe. | **"/** | Insert quotation marks. |
| **Ca** | Faulty pronoun case. | **./** | Insert period. |
| **Cap** | Capitalize. | **?/** | Insert question mark. |
| **Ch** | Poor choice of word. | **!/** | Insert exclamation point. |
| **Cl** | Lack of clarity. | **−/** | Insert dash. |
| **Coh** | Lack of coherence. | **( )/** | Insert parentheses. |
| **D** | Faulty diction. Check dictionary. | **[ ]/** | Insert brackets. |
| **Div** | Improper division of word. | **∧** | Omitted word(s). |
| **Dng** | Dangling modifier. | | Delete. |
| **Frag** | Fragmentary sentence. | **◡** | Close up. |
| **Glos** | Check glossary. | **∼** | Transpose. |
| **Gr** | Faulty grammar. | **#** | Separate; leave space |
| **Id** | Faulty idiom. | **?** | Do you mean this? |
| **Ital** | Italicize. | | Is this right? |
| **K** | Awkward construction. | **X** | Obvious error. |
| **L** | Faulty level of diction. | | |
| **Lc** | Use lower case. | | |
| **Log** | Faulty logic. | | |
| **MM** | Misplaced modifier. | | |
| **Ms** | Improper manuscript form. | | |
| **No ¶** | No paragraph indention. | | |
| **¶** | Begin new paragraph. | | |
| **¶ U** | Paragraph lacks unity. | | |
| **¶ Coh** | Paragraph lacks coherence. | | |
| **Pass** | Poor use of passive. | | |
| **P** | Error in punctuation. | | |
| **//** | Faulty parallelism. | | |
| **Ref** | Faulty pronoun reference. | | |
| **Rep** | Weakening repetition. | | |
| **S** | Poor sentence structure. | | |
| **Sp** | Error in spelling. | | |
| **Sub** | Poor subordination. | | |
| **T** | Wrong tense of verb. | | |
| **Tr** | Transpose words or phrases. | | |
| **Trans** | Faulty transition. | | |
| **W** | Wordiness. | | |
| **WO** | Poor word order. | | |
| **WW** | Wrong word. | | |

! shouldn't be making this mistake of this point in the coarse

!! I'm really displeased

# A RHETORIC AND COMPOSITION HANDBOOK

### Richard M. Weaver
*Late of the College of the University of Chicago*

Revised with the assistance of Richard S. Beal

(original title: *A Rhetoric and Handbook*)

QUILL

New York                    1974

Copyright © 1957, 1967 by Holt, Rinehart and Winston, Inc.

All rights reserved. No part of this book may be reproduced or utilized in any form or by any means, electronic or mechanical, including photocopying, recording or by any information storage and retrieval system, without permission in writing from the Publisher. Inquiries should be addressed to William Morrow and Company, Inc., 105 Madison Avenue, New York, N.Y. 10016.

Library of Congress Catalog Card Number: 81-19928
ISBN 0-688-05239-8 (pbk.)

Printed in the United States of America

1 2 3 4 5 6 7 8 9 10

Acknowledgment is made for permission to use material quoted on the following pages:

*page 10*—From *Rich Land, Poor Land* by Stuart Chase. Copyright 1936 by Stuart Chase. Used by permission of McGraw-Hill Book Company.

*page 18*—From "You Can't Write Writing" by Wendell Johnson. Reprinted by permission from ETC: *A Review of General Semantics*, Vol. I, No. I; copyright 1943, by the International Society for General Semantics.

*page 32*—From *Words and their Ways in English Speech* by James Bradstreet Greenough and George Lyman Kittredge. New York: The Macmillan Company.

*page 35*—From "Labor, Leisure, and Liberal Education" by Mortimer J. Adler, by permission of *The Journal of General Education*, Pennsylvania State University Press.

*page 37*—From "On the Aims and Instruments of Scientific Thought" from *Lectures and Essays* by William Kingdon Clifford. London: Macmillan and Company, Ltd.

*page 37*—From *Physics: Its Laws, Ideas, and Methods* by Alexander Kolin. Copyright 1950 by Alexander Kolin. Used by permission of McGraw-Hill Book Company.

*page 38*—From *Why Men Fight* by Bertrand Russell. New York: Appleton-Century-Crofts, Inc.

*page 38*—From *Men of Art* by Thomas Craven. Copyright 1931 by Simon and Schuster, Inc.

*page 39*—From *A Rhetoric of Motives* by Kenneth Burke, Englewood Cliffs, N.J. Prentice-Hall, Inc.

*page 41*—From *Modern Democracy* by Carl L. Becker. New Haven, Conn.: Yale University Press.

*page 47*—Reprinted by permission of Dodd, Mead & Company, Inc., from *This Green World* by Rutherford Platt. Copyright 1942 by Dodd, Mead & Company, Inc.

*page 50*—From *Politics* by Aristotle. New York: Oxford University Press.

*page 52*—From "The Community College" by Sigurd Rislov. Used by permission of the author.

*page 53*—From *The Study of Man* by Ralph Linton. Copyright 1936, by D. Appleton-Century Company, Inc. Reprinted by permission of Appleton-Century-Crofts, Division of Meredith Publishing Company.

*page 57*—From "Riveting a Skyscraper," *Fortune* Magazine, October, 1930. Courtesy of *Fortune* Magazine.

*page 61*—From *Studies in Words* by C. S. Lewis. New York: Cambridge University Press.

*page 62*—From *Heritage from Hamilton* by Broadus Mitchell. New York: Columbia University Press, 1957.

*page 64*—From "Popular Songs vs. the Facts of Life" by S. I. Hayakawa. Reprinted by permission from ETC: *A Review of General Semantics*, Vol. XII, No. 2; copyright 1955, by the International Society for General Semantics.

"My Ideal," copyright © 1930 by Famous Music Corporation. Copyright © renewed 1957 by Famous Music Corporation. (　　) "The Man I Love," copyright 1924 by New World Music Corporation. Used by permission. (　　) "My Heart Stood Still," copyright 1927 by Harms, Inc. Used by permission. (　　) "You Were

Meant For Me," lyrics by Arthur Freed; melody by Nacio Herb Brown. Copyright © 1929 Robbins Music Corporation, copyright renewal 1957 Robbins Music Corporation, New York, N.Y. Used by permission copyright proprietor.

page 67—From *The Mirror of the Sea* by Joseph Conrad. By permission of the Trustees of the Joseph Conrad Estate and Messrs. J. M. Dent and Sons, Ltd.

page 72—From p. 37 *You Can't Go Home Again* by Thomas Wolfe. New York· Harper & Row, 1940.

page 74—From *The Death of a Moth and Other Essays* by Virginia Woolf, copyright 1942 by Harcourt, Brace & World, Inc., and reprinted with their permission and with the permission of Leonard Woolf and the Hogarth Press, Ltd.

page 78—From *The Great Gatsby* by F. Scott Fitzgerald. New York: Charles Scribner's Sons.

page 80—From *The Bostonians* by Henry James. Dial Press edition, copyright 1945.

page 81—From pp. 101–103, *The Web and the Rock* by Thomas Wolfe. Copyright 1937, 1938, 1939 by Maxwell Perkins as Executor. Reprinted by permission of Harper & Row, Publishers.

page 83—From *Babbitt* by Sinclair Lewis. Harcourt, Brace & World, Inc., New York.

page 84—From *The Prussian Officer* by D. H. Lawrence. Reprinted courtesy of D. H. Lawrence Estate and William Heinemann, Ltd.

page 84—From *Starling of the White House* by Thomas Sugrue. Copyright © 1946 by Simon and Schuster, Inc., and reprinted by their permission.

page 84—From *Erik Dorn* by Ben Hecht. New York, 1921: C. P. Putnam's Sons. Reprinted by permission of Putnam's & Coward-McCann.

page 85—From *Let Us Now Praise Famous Men* by James Agee and Walker Evans by permission of Houghton-Mifflin Company.

page 89—From *The Conspirators, A Study of the Coup d'Etat* by D. J. Goodspeed. Copyright © 1962 by D. J. Goodspeed. Reprinted by permission of the Viking Press, Inc., and The Macmillan Company of Canada, Ltd.

page 99—From *Travels With Charley in Search of America* by John Steinbeck. Copyright © 1961, 1962 by The Curtis Publishing Co., Inc., © 1962 by John Steinbeck. Reprinted by permission of The Viking Press, Inc.

page 103—From *Yankee Lawyer* by Arthur Train. New York: Charles Scribner's Sons.

page 142—From the Proposal for a League to Enforce Peace—Negative—Courtesy of Carnegie Endowment for International Peace.

page 146—From *Minority Report* by H. L. Mencken. © Copyright 1956 by Alfred A. Knopf, Inc. Reprinted by permission.

page 153—Reprinted with permission of The Macmillan Company from "Right and Wrong" from *The Case for Christianity* by C. S. Lewis, copyright The Macmillan Company 1952; and with permission of the Executors of C. S. Lewis and Geoffrey Bles Ltd.

page 191—From *U.S. Foreign Policy* by Walter Lippmann. Boston: Little Brown and Company and *Atlantic Monthly* Press.

page 191—From "The Chinese Character," *Selected Papers*. By permission of George Allen and Unwin, Ltd.

page 203—From *The South Old and New* by Francis Butler Simkins. Copyright 1947 by Alfred A. Knopf, Inc. Reprinted by permission.

page 204—From "Thomas Paine," *Damaged Souls* by Gamaliel Bradford. Boston: Houghton-Mifflin Company.

page 204—From "Writers: Enemies of Social Science" by Lyman Bryson. Reprinted with permission of *Saturday Review*.

page 209—From *The Medical Follies* by Morris Fishbein, M.D. New York: Boni and Liveright.

page 209—From *Fighting Years* by Oswald Garrison Villard. New York: Harcourt, Brace & World, Inc.

page 210—From "Fenimore Cooper's Literary Offenses" in *How to Tell a Story and Other Essays* by Mark Twain. Reprinted by permission of Harper & Row, Publishers.

page 211—From *The Universe and Dr. Einstein* by Lincoln Barnett. Copyright 1948 by Harper & Brothers and Lincoln Barnett, copyright 1950 by Lincoln Barnett. Reprinted by permission of William Sloane Associates.

*page 212*—From *The Promise of American Life* by Herbert Croly. New York: The Macmillan Company.

*page 214*—From *The Meaning of a Liberal Education* by Everett Dean Martin. New York: W. W. Norton & Company, Inc.

*page 215*—From *The Americans* by Hugo Munsterberg. Reprinted by permission.

*page 216*—From *The Road to Serfdom* by Friedrich A. Hayek. Chicago: The University of Chicago Press. Copyright 1944 by the University of Chicago.

*page 217*—From *The Economic Consequences of the Peace* by John Maynard Keynes. New York: Harcourt, Brace & World, Inc. Copyright 1920 by Harcourt, Brace & Company, Inc.

*page 218*—From *My Several Worlds* by Pearl S. Buck by permission of The John Day Company, Inc., publisher.

*page 218*—From *Rhetoric* by Aristotle, translated by W. Rhys Roberts. Oxford: The Clarendon Press.

*page 219*—From *Japan: An Attempt at Interpretation* by Lafcadio Hearn. New York: The Macmillan Company.

*page 221*—From *The Meaning of a Liberal Education* by Everett Dean Martin. W. W. Norton and Company, Inc.

*page 222*—From "Main Speech" from *One Man's Meat* by E. B. White. New York: Harper and Row, Inc.

*page 225*—From *Opinions of Oliver Allston* by Van Wyck Brooks. New York: E. P. Dutton & Co., Inc., publishers.

*page 226*—From *Middletown* by Robert S. and Helen Merrell Lynd. New York: Harcourt, Brace and Company, Inc.

*page 231*—From Ernest Nagel's section in Chapter 4, "Science and the Humanities," of *Education in the Age of Science*, edited by Brand Blanshard, Basic Books, Inc., Publishers, New York, 1959.

*page 232*—From "Science Has Spoiled My Supper" by Philip Wylie, by permission of the author. This article appeared in *The Atlantic Monthly*, April, 1954.

*page 245*—From *The Managerial Revolution* by James Burnham. New York: The John Day Company, Inc.

*page 246*—From *Arkansas* by John Gould Fletcher. Chapel Hill: The University of North Carolina Press.

*page 247*—From "English Liberty in America" from *Character and Opinion in the United States* by George Santayana. London: Constable and Company, Ltd.

*page 249*—From "Play in Poetry" by Louis Untermeyer. Reprinted by permission of Harcourt, Brace and Company, Inc.

*page 255*—From *Our America* by Waldo Frank. Courtesy of the author and Liveright Publishing Corporation, copyright 1947, Waldo Frank.

*page 255*—From *The Age of Innocence* by Edith Wharton. Copyright, 1920, D. Appleton and Company. Reprinted by permission of the publishers, Appleton-Century-Crofts, Inc.

*page 257*—From "Newport and the Robber Baronesses" by John Peale Bishop. New York: Charles Scribner's Sons.

*page 258*—From "Hacienda," from *Flowering Judas* by Katherine Anne Porter. New York: Harcourt, Brace & World, Inc.

*page 263*—From *The Conservative Mind* by Russell Kirk. Chicago: Henry Regnery Company.

*page 263*—From "The American Magazine." Copyright 1919 by Alfred A. Knopf, Inc. and renewed 1947 by H. L. Mencken. Reprinted from *Prejudices: First Series*, by H. L. Mencken, by permission of the publisher.

*page 268*—From *Business Be Damned* by Elijah Jordan. New York: Henry Schuman, Inc.

*page 269*—From *The Book of Daniel Drew* by Bouck White. New York: Doubleday & Company, Inc. Used by permission of T. Paul Kane.

*page 269*—From *Heaven Trees* by Stark Young. New York: Charles Scribner's Sons.

*page 269*—From "The Future of Man" by C. P. Snow by permission of *The Nation*.

# Preface

## to the Second Edition

When Richard Weaver died in April, 1963, he was at work on two books. One, *Visions of Order*, was already in press and appeared in 1964; it was the third of three volumes which represent his significant legacy to the study of rhetoric and the part it has played and should play in men's lives. The other was his revision of the present text, a revision only partially completed at the time of his death.

The two books, the one a forceful, scholarly statement of a moral philosophy, evolved in response to what he saw as the cultural crisis of our time, and the other a textbook in composition, are less widely separated than one might assume. For Richard Weaver's composition text is perhaps one of the few in recent years which was undertaken less from a belief that another such text presenting somewhat different materials —or much the same material somewhat differently—might bring about an "improvement" in the writing of students who used it, than from a deep conviction that an understanding of rhetoric and its uses was truly indispensable to the health of a culture. In his chapter on "The Cultural Role of Rhetoric" in his *Visions of Order*, Weaver argues that "society cannot live without rhetoric," for the end of living is not only cognition but also activity. And dialectic, supremely in favor in our time, can serve only cognition, can tell man only how the terms and propositions he uses are related. Rhetoric, in contrast, serves action. It alone is our means of telling man what to do. Only an education concerned to bring together the dialectician and the rhetorician, the thinker and the doer, can be a valid education. To whatever extent he could make it so, Weaver saw his text as an effort to restore rhetoric to the attention he believed it must be given in our time.

Such are the convictions, I think, out of which Weaver's text grows. They explain the emphasis, in his Preface to the First Edition, upon what the writer *can* do in preference to admonitions about what he should avoid, and they explain the emphasis upon argument and persuasion over other forms of discourse. They explain, of course, his introduction of some material from traditional rhetoric only rarely included in such texts in 1957, when his first edition was published, though now more familiar fare. They explain, in part at least, the rigor of his text. For it is a rigorous text which makes far fewer concessions to easy informality, either in substance or style, than a good many of our composition texts have recently made. But rigor is acceptable in some quarters today, and Weaver was striving for control of substance rather than ease or wide appeal.

Some comment on my own relation to this revision is in order. Having admired certain aspects of the text, and being invited to discuss its revision with the author in early 1962, I did so, and ended by agreeing to make specific suggestions about the readings to accompany the text, and to read the manuscript as it was revised. I agreed, I might add, with some real trepidation, for Richard Weaver's resoluteness was more calculated to inspire awe than ease. But through extended correspondence, I came to learn not only about the depth of his commitment to his subject and to the projected revision, but also a good deal about his essential kindness. When he died, the majority of the readings were more or less agreed upon, and the initial chapters of the rhetoric were nearly ready to be sent on to me for reading.

After inevitable delays, I undertook to put the manuscript in final order, and to revise those sections upon which Weaver had not yet worked. Though I have replaced and sometimes expanded some illustrative selections, somewhat further revised the readings, reworked certain parts of the Handbook and Glossary, and attended to a variety of mechanical considerations, whatever contribution I have made is confined to such details. The structure and substance of the text are Richard Weaver's, and it has seemed to me that they should remain so.

This revision could not have been completed without the cooperation of several people. It would have been impossible without the help of Mr. Kendall Beaton, Richard Weaver's brother-in-law, through whose efforts the portions of the manuscript were eventually gathered and passed on to me. Professor Robert Saitz, of Boston University, provided much assistance in reworking the Handbook and Glossary; and Professor Joseph Zaitchik of Massachusetts State College at Lowell contributed heavily in checking many sections of the manuscript and making numerous suggestions. Finally, I owe much to the patient assistance of Mrs. Dorothy Cook, of Boston University, who devoted many hours to checking permissions and handling all necessary correspondence.

R. S. B.

*Boston University*
*March 1967*

# Preface

## to the First Edition

This text has been written on the assumption that there is no substitute for rhetorical fundamentals in the teaching of writing. If any special appeals are needed to win the interest of the students, these are better supplied by the teacher in passing than by the textbook, whose subject is principles. It has been recognized, at the same time, that many students arrive at college with limited preparation and doubtful motivation, and that it is easy to pitch a book concerned with the principles of an art above the level at which they must begin work. An earnest attempt has been made to keep the language simple and to avoid complex theoretical discussions which have little bearing upon freshman writing.

It appears to this author that too many current texts take a negative approach. The long lists of "Do not's," the correction charts, and a general tone suggesting that the student is at every moment going to do something wrong tend to freeze students who under a different kind of treatment might warm up and, after a few inevitable mistakes, discover that they like to express themselves in English. The present work therefore takes the affirmative attitude toward writing in the sense that it stresses the features of successful composition rather than the penalties and the ignominy that lie in wait for breakers of rules. The author feels that this is the only way in which composition and rhetoric can be restored to the place they anciently, and rightfully, held in the curriculum. That such a restoration would be in the interest of American students and citizens is one of the book's underlying conceptions.

There are two particulars of substance in which this book represents a departure from the majority of texts now in use. The first is the extended treatment given to argumentation, together with a discussion of the now almost totally neglected "topics" of persuasion. This special emphasis is in a way a concession to the times. Never before have so many pleas been made to the individual for an active citizenship. Active citizenship in the essential sense requires an understanding of the laws of evidence, the ability to criticize lines of argumentation, and some skill in making arguments in return. The "continuing debate" which is democracy cannot proceed unless a significant number of our people have an adequate grounding in logic and persuasion. At the same time, the enormous amount of propaganda which today assails every individual in a modern nation makes it more necessary than ever before to arm him with effective means of discrimination and criticism. A knowledge of how arguments are made and of the relative strength of different kinds of arguments is the best equipment for dealing with propaganda at any level. Though the introduction of the "topics" into a textbook of freshman English is a fairly radical innovation, it is felt that these topics are justified by their proved value in helping students to assay the arguments of others and to find substance for arguments of their own.

A second departure from the more usual practice appears in the section on "Grammar." The author believes with I. A. Richards that language is "inescapably normative." Although there has been no disposition here to shy away from rules, something of the method of descriptive linguistics has been introduced into those parts concerned with definitions and the explanation of functions. The assumption is that descriptive accounts of standard usages provide, in a good many instances, a more complete or more realistic statement of those usages than do the dogmatic-sounding assertions found in some traditional grammars. Of course, behind every question of usage lies a question of efficiency and expressiveness. Majority preference does not necessarily make a use right; but objective accounts of how language is actually employed can uncover opportunities and expose the narrowness of ill-considered rules. It is hoped that the bringing together of these methods on a practical level will make the learning of grammar seem less artificial to the student.

The book of readings has been arranged according to forms and methods rather than according to subject matter. Selections have been made primarily for their value as models of expression, but there has been some attempt to mingle the old and the new in order to show the essential continuity of serious thinking.

Every book of this kind owes something to its forerunners. I could not hope to acknowledge my indebtedness to all who have furnished useful suggestions and leads. There is a great mass of generally familiar material used in the teaching of college composition upon which everyone draws consciously or unconsciously. But I wish to mention, as books that I have studied with strong interest and real appreciation of their value, Donald Davidson's *American Composition and Rhetoric,* Cleanth Brooks and Robert Penn Warren's *Modern Rhetoric,* John M. Kierzek's *The Macmillan Handbook of English,* Guy B. Woods and W. Arthur Turner's *The Odyssey Handbook and Guide to Writing,* and Easley S. Jones's *Practical English Composition.* Finally, I owe a great debt for inspiration and knowledge to my colleagues on the English Staff of the College of the University of Chicago who in the past decade have worked out a uniquely valuable course in fundamental English composition.

R. M. W.

*College of the University of Chicago*
*January 15, 1957*

# To the Student

Composition and rhetoric have always had a key role in education, although approaches to them have varied greatly, and until recently the study of "rhetoric," in any formal sense, has been out of favor for some years. This text assumes that although the ways in which we learn to write effectively may differ, some disciplined attention to those rhetorical principles common to all good writing is useful for all students.

This text also assumes that an approach to writing should be positive, and that composition and rhetoric have a subject matter which can be taught. While providing the kind of information necessary to achieve correctness, the text tries principally to open up some of the possibilities of expression and communication. It assumes that writing can be a creative process, in which attention is focussed as little as practical on what ought *not* to be done, and as much as possible on what *can* be done; and that this process will be aided if the course can teach something useful about invention, disposition, and style.

Invention means simply finding something to say. From one point of view, rhetoric cannot teach one what to say; it is merely a formal discipline like logic. It teaches *how,* but not *what.* When the subject is viewed in its true scope, however, it appears that given a certain end, or a purpose that one wishes to accomplish, there are principles for discovering subject matter. Rhetoric cannot tell one in abstraction whether to write on the great Chicago fire, or photosynthesis, or how to bake a cake. But given the topic and the end in view for the writing, it can give one a scheme for finding relevant things to say about the topic. This aspect of rhetoric is particularly stressed in the section on argumentation, where there is discussion of the means of finding or inventing effective arguments.

The second item in the subject matter of rhetoric is disposition, or organization. Once a topic has been settled on, and the significant points have been selected for presentation, what is the most effective order in which to put them before the reader? This question also has to be answered with reference to purpose. But if the objective in writing is clear, it can be demonstrated that one order is more effective than another. It is a part of the art of rhetoric to analyze the various methods of organization as they bear upon the resources of the writer, the occasion for which he is writing, and the capacity and attitude of the audience he expects to reach. The subject of disposition or ordering is dealt with most directly in the section on exposition, although all of the "Forms of Discourse" must take it into consideration. The student will find, moreover, that problems of organization appear not merely in connection with his paper as a whole, but also in the construction of single paragraphs and even single sentences.

Finally, a complete rhetoric must address itself to the matter of style.

Style is a combination of all the elements, large and small, that make the difference between writing which is dull, inert, and unpleasing to read, and writing which is clear, lively, energetic, and capable of affecting us by its very form. Obviously there is no one best style for all writers, or for all occasions, though there are certain principles of expression which are rarely absent from any truly effective style. The student is advised to aim at a style which will incorporate these principles while giving opportunity for the special lines of interest and ways of thought and feeling which make him an individual person. The chapters on the sentence and diction illustrate many ways in which sentence form and vocabulary can contribute to a strong and effective style. The student bent on improving his style is not necessarily trying to become a literary man; he is trying to become a forceful writer. A course in rhetoric can bring to his attention many methods and devices which he would be a long time discovering on his own. The study of style should begin to open up for him the immense resources of the language he has inherited.

Composition should be a rigorous course, but it is important to see wherein its rigor lies. Language exists in the form of a set of symbols—letters, words, and phrases. Any course which teaches the use of a set of symbols makes some demand upon the intellect. Most people regard this as normal in the case of mathematics, but for some reason do not do so in the case of language. Yet language *is* another system of symbolic expression, and it requires something of the same precise thinking as does mathematics. Indeed, the comparison between linguistic and mathematical expression can be carried further. And it might be claimed that, of the two, language is the more difficult. In mathematics, most symbols are invariant in meaning and most quantities are definite. In the symbols of language there are numberless gradations of meaning, of relationship, and of tone which must be taken into account if one's expression is to be exact and forceful.

It is no mystery that mathematics and composition are often regarded as the two taskmasters of the liberal arts curriculum, both requiring close concentration and continuing alertness. Their relative difficulty, however, is a testimony to their value—to the fact that they are doing something for us.

The time-tested principle that reward is in proportion to effort will be borne out in the course in English composition. The investment may be considerable, but the dividends are proportionately large. To write well, one must be alive at every point of one's being, with the result that composition, more than any other subject, is a training of the whole man. The wise student will therefore regard this course as a welcome proving-ground for his abilities.

# Contents

## Part One
## General Problems of Composition   1

## Part Two
## The Forms of Discourse   21

## Part Three
## Special Problems of Composition   161

## Chapter Six     The Sentence                                                163

## Chapter Seven     The Paragraph                                            201

## Part Four
## A Concise Handbook   303

# Part One

## General Problems of Composition

# Chapter One

## Organization

### FINDING A SUBJECT

What to write about is the first problem of a student who must periodically submit a theme or essay. This question arises not from actual lack of material but from failure to take the right view of the material one has. A short reflection should convince the student that he thinks about many things; and a solution to the problem will be found partly at least in an examination of what he already has in mind. One of the great revelations of education comes when we perceive that there is no such thing as a naturally uninteresting subject. Anything can be interesting if one knows enough about it. A certain amount of imagination is required and a certain focusing of the view, of course, but there is no reason why a small thing should be of small interest, or why a familiar one should be devoid of rich possibilities. A piece of chalk, which the student sees daily as one of the "uninteresting" appurtenances of the classroom, provided the English scientist T. H. Huxley with material for a fascinating lecture on geology and evolutionary theory. The automobile is an exceedingly commonplace object in American life, yet with the right approach it becomes a subject of commanding interest to the economist, to the engineer, or to the prospective vacationer. Perhaps few things arouse so little thought as the table salt, yet when salt is considered in relation to living organisms, in connection with certain historical movements, or with regard to its industrial uses, it is suddenly transformed into a subject of extraordinary interest. These are examples of ordinary objects capable of imaginative treatment; and it is precisely this kind of connection which the student must make between his stock of knowledge and its opportunities for development and interpretation. The point to be borne in mind is that if the writer will but make an effort to become interested in a subject, it will yield far more than casual acquaintance may have suggested. Real interest starts when we begin to look at things in the right way.

In the practical work of finding subject matter we can locate three areas from which the college student can draw material for his papers. The first of these is the experience of his life, or his background. Every person can speak with information and authority about the experiences which have gone into making him what he is. Although many young people at the beginning of college have not grown accustomed to reflect upon their personal histories, a little practice should soon enable them to recognize potential subject matter. Our memories naturally cluster about certain vivid or evocative experiences, which form chapters in our lives. The teachings of parents; our feeling about some influential person, such as an unusual neighbor, an athletic coach, or a pastor; our first contact with a new environment; our first experience with job-holding; or the occasion of our learning some important truth about human nature, all have possibilities for the kind of presentation which will interest others.

Here are some examples of topics from this first area of interest:

| | |
|---|---|
| Skeletons in My Closet | Escape from Authority |
| Noises in the Night | Why Parents Are Necessary |
| The Day My World Changed | Home Town Thoughts |
| A Summer's Reading | Learning the Hard Way |
| Early Ambitions | A World I Never Made |

The second area from which the student can readily draw is the college world. To some extent the college community reproduces on a small scale the world at large. It has its varied interests and professions, its diverse types of people, its controversial ideals, its exciting or unexpected happenings. An awareness of what goes on around one in this new environment will uncover many challenging topics: the differences in backgrounds and aspirations of students, the ever-present issue of academic freedom, the problems of student discipline, the influence of social and honorary organizations—these are only a few of the subjects open to systematic investigation. Here are some specimen topics drawn from this second area.

Lecture and Class Discussion: A Comparison
Advantages and Disadvantages of the Honor System
The Influence of Intercollegiate Athletics on the Student Body
What Parents Expect of College
First Experiences in Dormitory Living
Does College Education Encourage Class Consciousness?
Compulsory Class Attendance
The Uses of the College Library
Are Teachers Interested in Students?
Comparing College with My Expectations
The Economic Problems of an Average College Student
Public vs. Private Colleges

Finally, as a third area, there is the world of local, national, and international affairs with which the student, by virtue of his college training, finds that he has ever-increasing contact. This is a world in which we all have a certain duty to become interested, and students of relatively mature age and background may wish to draw their topics chiefly from this general area. It is true that topics from such fields sometimes defy by their very scope successful treatment in a short paper; others require more detailed or concrete information than many first-year students have. Yet after these allowances have been made, there remain many problems about which students can write effectively. The question of local and federal educational support, of military training, of book and motion picture censorship, of the political influence of the press, of trends in religious beliefs are close enough to the student to encourage opinions whose full presentation may take the form of a theme. Such topics as the following are capable of satisfactory treatment in a paper of moderate length.

The Beat Generation
Movies, Television, and Morals
Is War Murder?
The Prospects of World Peace
Should Gambling be Legalized?
What I Have Seen of the Effects of Divorce
The Changing American City
Is Individualism on the Wane?
Politics in College
Local Government in My Home Town
Who Are the Leaders of Opinion?
Military Science as a Part of Education
Students and Civil Rights

All of these are offered as examples of the kind of material which, without being trivial, is readily available to the student. In these areas of personal experience and background, of present environment, and of large and inescapable social problems, the enterprising writer can find more than enough to satisfy his assignments. If he finds that in some instances he must perform some investigation or even assume an initial interest in a subject, he should realize that both processes are normal parts of education. Whenever we write a paper, we are to some extent teaching ourselves about the subject. We are either acquiring more facts or seeing more clearly the relationships of the facts we know.

## LIMITING A SUBJECT

After the writer has determined the area of experience or observation from which he will draw his material, he has to delimit a subject. This delimiting of a subject is essential if the paper is to convince a reader that it is "about" something. There are a few types of writing, such as articles in encyclopedias, which develop their subjects without exploiting any special angle of interest. Even these, however, are planned to be as concise and informative as possible, and similarly, the usual theme, essay, or article has a definite purpose which requires a directed appeal. Actually the step of delimitation consists of taking a subject with several potentialities and seizing one of these with a specific audience or a specific occasion in view. Thus we can say that a *true* subject is a general subject narrowed in scope until it suits an occasion, whose demands the writer must train himself to judge. When he has thought about the expectations of the audience and has measured his own knowledge or has estimated the knowledge he can readily acquire, he has made a start toward writing the paper.

Let us look for a moment at what occurs in the process of delimiting or focusing on a subject. "The New World" is a subject, but an exceedingly large and undefined one, and a writer would have difficulty in arousing interest in anything so general, to say nothing of his trouble in making an approach. "Native Peoples of the New World" would be somewhat more specific and would provide a focus of interest, but it remains unwieldy. "The Indian Tribes of North America" would reduce the scope yet further, but would leave one still with a large subject, suitable for book-length treatment. We should have to continue this process of delimitation until we reached something like "Early Contacts with the Indians in the Settlement of New England" or "Tribal Customs of the Navahos" before arriving at a subject manageable within the limits of a fairly long essay or capable of arousing specific interest.

Or again, let us suppose that a student is interested in writing on baseball. Since a little thought shows him that this is a large subject, his first need is to define his own interest in it, or the special interest of the audience he desires to inform. Possibly his interest will be in how the game is played, and his paper will be essentially an account of a process. A different paper of considerable interest could be written on the origin of baseball and the early development of the game. Another kind of paper could be written on baseball as a spectacle, with attention to the crowded bleachers, the rivalry of the teams and players, and all else that goes to make a game exciting. Still another kind of paper could be written about its social and psychological effects, both upon the players and the American public which follows it in great numbers. Each of these approaches takes the general subject "baseball" and relates it to a special interest, which furnishes the writer with a principle of selection.

The same procedure of drawing upon a special source of interest can be followed when the writer is dealing with some material object, say a canoe. The real or supposed history of its invention is a possible subject. Types of canoes and materials from which they have been made is another. The means of operating a canoe and the uses to which canoes have been put offer still further possibilities.

In each of these instances the process of focusing is essentially a process of finding a guiding purpose in the writing. Too often the beginner supposes it is enough merely to sit down "to write." But the resolve to write presumes an interest in communicating something. It is therefore important at the outset to ask oneself why the projected piece of communication is required. It may be needed to clarify one's own thoughts upon a subject, or to impart facts about the subject to others, or to inspire in others definite attitudes toward the subject. There is no true subject without an angle of interest, and every good piece of writing is guided by serving such an interest.

The subjects here used as illustrations have been simple, but the procedure is the same for all. Whether one is writing of baseball, or the French Revolution, or the novel, or the principles of business administration, the first thing·to do is to focus the subject in the light of a purpose.

**Exercise:** *From the general topics in the following list, determine limited subjects which you think could be treated in a paper of 600–1000 words.*

| | |
|---|---|
| Cities | Music |
| Fishing | Timepieces |
| Race Relations | Scenic Wonders |
| Games of Chance | Scholarship |
| Gardening | Industrial Progress |
| War | Political Parties |
| The Profession of Medicine | The Study of History |
| Newspapers | Slang |
| The American Revolution | Commercial Airlines |
| Eugenics | Publicity |

# PRINCIPLES OF ORDERING

## General Parts

After the topic has been so restricted that the focus of interest is clear, the writer turns his attention to the order of its development. Sometimes the nature of the subject will suggest a particular sequence; sometimes the sequence is suggested by the kind of effect one wishes to achieve; but we shall look first at what may be thought of as the general parts of any discourse. By general parts we mean three stages of development which are so regularly present that they may be expected in any type of writing whose purpose is to explain or inform. They are dictated by the need of communicating. These three stages are simply the beginning, the middle, and the end. The principle that these should appear in a composition would be too obvious to bear repeating were it not frequently ignored. The very word "composition," meaning an arrangement of component parts, implies order and relationship. How are these general parts related to each other?

Most of us, probably, have listened to speeches which were nothing more than prolonged beginnings, the speaker having become so absorbed in making his contact with the audience that he failed to do justice to the promised subject matter of the speech. Sometimes a piece of discourse will be nothing more than a middle, in the sense that it has content but tells us little about why the author chose to offer it, or what he expects to accomplish by means of it. Another may be nothing more than an end, in that the author neglects both to prepare for the subject and to give the supporting material of his point. Thus he does little more than dwell on his conclusion and hope for the best. All of such examples, whether oral or written, are faulty compositions because the author has not taken into account this essential structure. The inclusive pattern of beginning, middle, and end is a remedy for lack of balance and completeness.

The beginning is an especially strategic part of any piece of writing, since it is the attention-getter. It is here that the author reveals whether he is seeing his subject in the light proper to enlist the interest of prospective readers. It is here also that he gives some indication of the level of his treatment. If he has thought enough about his subject and has realized in what way his interest is a communicable one, the chances are increased that he will make an effective beginning, one which will carry his readers through the critical first sentences. The beginning always has to a certain extent the task of justifying the subject, or of explaining why the writer is writing upon this subject. Even with assigned papers, it is usually necessary to make some gesture in this direction. As a general rule, this is best done indirectly, or in a way incidental to the announcement of the forthcoming subject matter. But always in beginnings, the writer has to alert himself to what may be called the writing situation, which includes the nature of his subject, his own knowledge of the subject, the knowledge he can assume on the part of the audience, and, of course, his guiding purpose. When he surveys the situation in this manner, he is many times more likely to make a meaningful start than when he launches abruptly into his core material.

It is in the middle or "body" that the writer actually gets down to the task which he has set out to perform, since this part contains what may be broadly described as the matter, or the proof. Subjects vary so much that it is impossible to indicate here in any specific way what the development of this part will be. But in general, if the beginning makes an appropriate introduction and tells with what the piece of writing is going to deal, the middle does the actual dealing, whether the substance be a description, a narration, or an argument. It is enough to see here, then, that the middle is devoted to the essential content of the composition, and it is in this part that the heavy work of presentation must be done.

The end of the paper is hardly less strategic than the beginning, for here the writer gets a chance to restate in compact form what he has said or to re-emphasize his specific points or applications. The criticism made of some papers, that they do not conclude but merely stop, is a serious one, for it means that the writer has thrown away one of his best chances of impressing his audience. Endings have, by virtue of their position, a kind of prominence, and if the writer will use this natural advantage, while adding to it other means of rhetorical emphasis, he can make his ending a memorable and effective part of his paper. But if he uses this part to ramble on or to introduce fresh considerations which cannot be disposed of there, he will probably spoil the good effects he has achieved. Like the beginning, the ending is peculiarly a "contact" part with an audience, and any fumbling will not remain concealed from the reader, who is by now expecting a well selected and ordered review of the substance and purpose of the paper.

## Organization in Relation to Subject Matter

The sequence of beginning, middle, and ending constitutes a pattern looking toward the reader's needs. But within this general pattern there are other patterns which respond to the requirements of the subject matter itself. When we turn our attention to the substance to be dealt with, we find that most pieces of writing follow either a *natural* or a *logical order*.

### Natural Order

*Natural order* is inherent in the subject of the writing and is generally impossible to miss or confuse. When a writer follows this order, he is simply taking a pattern which already exists in the object or the event which he has chosen to discuss.

Descriptions of physical objects and of processes belong to this first class because the pattern exists independently of the writer, and there is seldom good reason for departing from it. The structure of an object which is to be described will impose an order upon the description. Though one has the choice of passing from side to side, or bottom to top, or from outer to inner, and so on, the fact remains that one follows a pattern present in the object itself. The paragraph below illustrates natural order, which is determined by the spatial layout of the subject.

> The Thirteen Colonies were divided, by topographical conditions as well as by political affiliations, into three groups, whose interests were by no means identical. The dividing lines were the Hudson River and the Potomac River and Chesapeake Bay. The four New England Colonies had a population of less than 750,000, and were engaged in agriculture and ocean commerce, with the beginnings of some struggling manufactures; the Middle Colonies had a population of not quite 1,000,000; they were almost wholly agricultural and furnished the food supplies; the four Southern Colonies, with more than 1,000,000, were also agricultural,

but their chief product was tobacco (the cotton planting being then only just introduced and the cotton gin not yet invented), and the greater part of this was raised for export.

—Francis Vinton Greene, *The Revolutionary War
and the Military Policy of the United States*

Similarly, organization may be determined by a sequence in time. If you are describing a process which has a number of steps, you naturally follow the steps as they occur. If you were describing how to start an automobile, you would begin with the first step and go on consecutively to the last in the operation. Any change in this order would probably create confusion. The same is true of accounts which present a historical sequence. Here is a passage organized according to stages of time.

Cattle invaded the grass where the buffalo had long grazed. The grass and the buffalo thrived together. But the steers were too many. They checked the vitality of the grass; their paths became gullies; they gave the grass no rest. Sheep—too many of them—cut to the heart of the grass with their sharp mouths and killed it outright. Forests in the headquarters of the canyons were cut down. Plows ripped the sod loose all over the great plains. Huge areas were burned over to expose minerals or "improve" the range. Some authorities believe that fire was the most destructive of all the enemies of the grass. The plants of the virgin sod were mostly perennials. They depend less on seed for spreading than on new buds. This gives them great flexibility  Both fire and overgrazing destroy the equilibrium.

When grass goes, erosion begins. No less than 165 million acres of grass now stand utterly devastated or seriously depleted. The great dust storms of recent years are not a chance phenomenon but the culmination of a long tragic process. After a storm, the fine silt scattered over the fields is impenetrable to water. Even heavy rains promptly run off. That is why rain in the Dust Bowl, which looks like a godsend, often means so little. Sometimes a single storm will remove several inches of soil, first the loam and fine sand, then the coarse sand. Finally the wind may take all soil down to hardpan and so create true desert conditions. Sand dunes begin to roll as on a beach. Good land beyond is covered by the marching dunes.

—Stuart Chase, *Rich Land, Poor Land*

### Logical Order

*Logical order,* on the other hand, is a thought-out order. It is always the product of analysis. The writer is faced with a large number of ideas on a subject, some big, some small, some highly relevant, others less so. His task is to work out a pattern of relationship for them. His only guide is their meaning in reference to what he wants to say. He must *arrange* an order in relation to the governing thought.

This kind of order is required for the explaining of ideas and the making of arguments. Here one has nothing external against which to check the correctness of one's organization. Instead, the writer must see to it that the development is from the general to the specific, from one statement to another statement that is implied by it, or according to some point of interest that he has made clear. Let us suppose that a student has been asked to write a paper on why the United States abandoned its historic isolationism. Plainly, with this subject he is in the realm of ideas, and his basic pattern will have to be one of related reasons. We might therefore expect him to arrive at something like the following.

I. Why the United States abandoned its historic isolationism
   A. Because of the change in international relations resulting from technology and invention
   B. Because of instability produced by nationalistic economic policies
   C. Because of military danger in a world at war

Obviously this is a different kind of progression from the spatial and temporal patterns illustrated above. Here items, "A," "B," and "C" are related to "I" as causes. They are ordered according to an estimate, though not necessarily the only possible estimate, of their influence on the effect.

For further illustration, let us say that a student is writing on the topic "Why Freedom of the Press Is Essential to Democratic Government." In thinking about this topic, too, he will discover that his organization must express a logical structure in which one idea is dependent upon another. He therefore finds his plan taking the form of a series of statements which grow out of one another, moving toward the conclusion he set out to prove.

I. Why freedom of the press is essential to democratic government
   A. Democratic government cannot function without an informed public
   B. There can be no informed public without a free discussion of issues
   C. There can be no free discussion of issues without a free press presenting all the points of view

The order here is logical because each statement implies or makes necessary the following one. Logic is a working out of implied relationships. There is always a *reason* why one thing comes before or after another.

In pursuing a natural order, there is no problem in making the plan seem right, since a kind of inevitability is imposed by the external configuration of the subject. In writing a paper based on logical order, however, we must often strive to give the plan an inevitability by making the reasoning sufficiently strong, or the analysis perfectly clear. A reader will usually desire to know why the order chosen is preferred to the other orders. It is part of the writer's job to make him feel that from the point of view which has been taken, the sequence that appears is the most reasonable.

## THE OUTLINE

As we draw near the actual work of writing, we begin to think about the part-to-part arrangement of the paper. At this point many teachers of composition insist upon an outline. Outlines are not, however, useful to all writers in the same degree. An outline is felt by some to be too rigid and to interfere with the free development of the subject matter. Some writers can get along well enough with a rough sketch of what they plan to do. For the majority of us, however, something more complete is advisable. An outline is helpful because it gives a kind of skeletal view of the subject. It keeps us from straying and it preserves the right proportions by showing just how much development should be given to each part of the topic. It is easy for one to become so absorbed in a favorite aspect of a subject that he emphasizes it at the expense of the others. The result may give a false impression of one's purpose in writing. A logical outline can serve as a checkrein on this tendency. Even though we sometimes feel that an outline is hampering us with its rigidity, this rigidity may be the very thing to prevent us from running on carelessly and distorting the emphasis our paper ought to have.

Outlines usually appear either as topic outlines or sentence outlines. In the topic outline the writer uses single words and phrases to indicate his headings. In the sentence outline he uses full sentences for the headings, including the subordinate ones. Mixing of the two types is illogical. The outline should be consistently a topic outline or a sentence outline. The sentence type is better when the subject must be outlined in considerable detail. The topic outline will do if headings need only be sketched in.

We may now look at the process of outlining and compare the two kinds.

Let us suppose that a student has decided to prepare a paper on the advantages of living in a suburban community. Clearly this is a case of writing in which there exists no natural object he can turn to for a pattern of organization. The advantages he is to discuss will exist in his own thought and feeling. He must study these to see which advantages should come first and which later. Let us imagine that he is struck most forcibly by the economic advantages, and next by the greater opportunities for social life and cooperation. After he has thought over the relative force of the various appeals, he might determine an order like this.

ADVANTAGES OF LIVING IN A SUBURBAN COMMUNITY

    I. Economic advantages
       A. Less expensive housing
       B. More convenient shopping facilities

II. Social advantages
   A. Greater opportunity to know neighbors as individuals
   B. Closer contact with community organizations

III. Advantages of health and recreation
   A. Freedom from congestion and noise of city
   B. Space for gardening, games, and other exercise
   C. Ready access to countryside

The value of any outline lies in its system of coordination and subordination. We can see from the outline above that headings I, II, and III are conceived as having approximately equal importance, and that they will accordingly demand roughly equal space in the treatment. We see likewise that "A" or "Less expensive housing," under "I" or "Economic advantages," is only a part of "I," and therefore gets only part of the treatment reserved for the general heading. But at the same time it gets a treatment roughly equal to that of "B," because "B," or "More convenient shopping facilities," is but another part with the same rank. In this way any complete outline assigns ranks of importance to the various phases of the subject which mill around in one's mind and so gives the entire paper a kind of structure which might otherwise be lacking.

A sentence outline will differ from this only in that each heading and subheading will be in full sentence form and can therefore accommodate more details. Below is the same subject outlined with full sentences.

ADVANTAGES OF LIVING IN A SUBURBAN COMMUNITY

I. The economic advantages alone are important
   A. Housing is generally less expensive
   B. Local business centers make shopping convenient

II. There are attractive social advantages
   A. The typical inhabitant of a suburban community gets to know his neighbors as individuals
   B. He also has more contact with community organizations

III. The advantages of health and recreation are especially important for men with families
   A. Living is free from the noise and congestion of the city
   B. It is easy to obtain space for gardening, games, and other healthful exercise
   C. Access to the countryside is a simple matter

This example shows the basic requirements of outlining and its usefulness in giving us the logical organization of a subject in skeletal form, which enables us to see the relative size and the relationship of the parts. If it is to fulfill this purpose, the parts of the outline must add up to the whole subject; those parts designated as equal in rank, such as "I" and "II" or "A" and "B," must cover matters of approximately equal importance; and there must be no serious overlapping of parts. When an outline meets these requirements of coordination and subordination, we have a logical scheme for our paper, whatever the subject may be.

Outlines are not made for their own sake, and even when they are of use, they can be followed too rigorously or unimaginatively. If in the course of developing a paper one discovers new ideas that seem essential to the subject, it may be advisable to revise part of the outline or even to go back and make an entirely new outline. A change in one's estimate of the material that has been gathered also may make these alterations necessary. Nothing is lost, of course, when an outline is changed for the better. The object is to produce a well-written paper with a progression that anyone can grasp.

We turn now to some other means of attaining this end.

## BASIC MEANS TO CLARITY

### Unity and Coherence

The outline is a general aid in achieving the basic means to clarity, which are unity and coherence.

The requirement of unity demands that all the material be about one definite thing or idea. Every part of a unified composition has some bearing upon the central subject. There are no irrelevancies or excursions into side issues. Everything concerns the principal idea. We are conscious that the writer has stuck to his purpose. Although an outline will help you to determine whether the material originally selected has this unity of idea, you must ask yourself again and again whether each part really belongs to the subject you have chosen. The stricter you are in deciding what belongs and what does not, the less cleaning up will be required in the later stages of writing.

Coherence is related to unity, but it brings in the additional factor of order. If we can say that unity means a general relationship of all the parts, we can say that coherence means an arrangement of the parts for a progressive development. It is possible to think of a mass of material which would have a high degree of unity but a low degree of coherence. Such material would all have reference to the same thing, but it would lack organization. For example, a spectator's report of a football or a basketball game would have unity if all the statements pertained to the game. But if he were in a state of high excitement, they might have this unity without having the coherence necessary to enable us to follow what had happened. They would not reflect sequence, or an explanation by cause and effect, or any other pattern of development. The same might be true of a report of a battle, or of an account of a meeting, or of a visit to the doctor, or any other body of material which needs to be organized before it can be communicated. Coherence may be likened to a thread along which the separate facts or ideas are strung. It is not enough for these to be all of a general subject; they must also be placed in an order.

Unity and coherence together form the basic test of intelligibility. They relate to the general scope and pattern of the composition, and above anything else they show whether the writer has enough control of his material to write clearly.

## Proportion

Even in the preliminary ordering of the paper, the writer has to give some attention to proportion. He has to determine how much space is to be given to each main topic and to each subtopic. He must offer an adequate treatment of the whole subject while preserving the right degree of importance among the parts. Here the standard plan of beginning, middle, and end will not be of much guidance, because the length of topics and subtopics will differ according to the nature of the subject and the occasion. But the topic or sentence outline can be of real help, since the length at which a given topic or subtopic must be outlined is a fair index to the length of treatment which it will require. A good outline can therefore serve as an initial check upon disproportionate development. Anyone who writes out of sudden inspirations or fits of interest is prone to expand parts without regard to their contribution to the main point he has set out to make. A paper developed in this way loses its unity and misplaces its emphasis.

Since no general rule regarding proportioning can be given, we can say only that a paper has the right proportion of parts when it has answered every question which is reasonably proper to its purpose and level of treatment. An effective way to apply this test is to put yourself in the reader's place and imagine the questions that might arise in his mind. If the paper is one of explanation, he may ask whether the *what, when, where,* and *how* have been dealt with in sufficient detail. A paper on the origin of trial by jury might be expected to give much space to the *when* and the *how;* a paper on the future of electronics might be expected to give much space to *what* electronics is, and so on, with the guiding purpose always exerting a heavy influence upon one's judgment of what is enough for a given point.

Proportioning is carried out within the scale set for the piece of writing, which may vary almost without limit. If one were writing a 1,000 word paper on "Fishing in Florida," one might give, say, 100 words to the subtopic "Fishing for Tarpon." But if one were doing an article of 5,000 words on the same subject, the account of fishing for tarpon would get 500 words without changing the relative proportion of the parts. It is the part-to-whole relationship which tells us whether the treatment of a subtopic has been too little or too much.

If a part is allowed to develop beyond its function, it calls into question what the paper is really discussing. If it is not given the space which its importance requires, it will likely leave unanswered questions of the sort pointed out above. Due proportion is really part of the logic of the paper, and it is of critical value in making clear the intent and meaning. Proportioning carries out the idea originally proposed by the writer's conception of its unity and coherence.

## Visible Transitions

The need of proportion underlies the fact that nearly every piece of writing has parts which must be joined to one another. Even though the elementary principles of arrangement which have been described help one to pass from part to part, there is usually need for further help at important points. Let us remember that "transition" signifies passage, or a going across from one place to another.

A writer who has had little experience with the reactions of readers is likely to neglect transitions for two reasons, which need to be recognized. He may become so immersed in his material that he forgets the comparative ignorance of the reader. Because he has worked at it with some care and knows where the various details fall into place, he assumes that the reader will have an equal familiarity with the material. Consequently he may fail to bring out the relationships or lines of reasoning which provide coherence. Every writer has to realize that for the time being he is an expert upon the subject he has chosen to present. He has brought together the facts and has organized them into a meaningful pattern in his own mind. The odds are great that the potential reader has not done this. Probably the reader knows few if any of the facts, and since he has not been thinking about the subject, he has felt no need of organizing it. He is one who has to be told something new and has to be told it in a way which will make the understanding of it simple. All this means that those connections which are obvious and clear to the writer will have to be put down in express form for the benefit of the reader, who is waiting to be informed.

In the second place, even if the writer is discussing a subject which is more or less familiar to everyone, it is likely that he will seek to make his own point regarding it, which requires an appropriate order of parts. Therefore, even in those cases where he can assume a fair degree of knowledge, he cannot assume a knowledge of this special organization which reflects his purpose in writing. The reasoning of the paper particularly must be made clear by connecting words and phrases.

These facts tell us why skillful writers are careful to use transitional expressions, or "signposts." Such expressions keep the progression moving steadily by informing the reader how much has been covered thus far, how the part in hand relates to the foregoing, and what is to be expected in the succeeding development. A coherent piece of writing has a kind of organic unity, with each part growing out of the preceding part and into the next. Often such connection has to be indicated between single sentences. Between paragraphs it is usually imperative to mark the passage of thought. English has a large stock of "signpost" terms—words like *besides, consequently, however, nevertheless, thus*—which tell the reader in what way the composition is developing. By their meaning they serve as direction-givers, and although an excessive use of them may cause a paper to seem overwritten or too self-consciously written, the beginning writer is more likely to employ too few of them than too many. A longer list of such visible markers of transition will be found in Chapter 7. You should acquaint yourself with this list, learn to know the specific meanings of the different terms, and use them to keep the progress of your thought in full view of the reader.

## Repetition and Restatement

While it is true that repetition is sometimes a sign of a limited vocabulary and that restatement is often an indication of a lack of ideas, it is by no means true that all repetition is a fault. Professional writers often make effective use of these devices. Repetition of a key word can keep the reader attentive to the development of its meaning and the applications that are being made. If a writer is dealing with the subject "democracy," this word may appear a number of times, along with "democratic" and "democrat." Repetition often also serves as an effective device for achieving emphasis. It is a sound principle that people who are learning something for the first time must be told not once, but twice, and often three times. A writer who develops his work on this principle, by repeating key words, by pausing at certain intervals to sum up or to paraphrase what he has been saying, is aware of the importance of impressing new material upon the mind of the reader. Repetition can also be used effectively by the writer who wishes to persuade by appealing to the emotions of his readers. One cannot fail to be moved by the powerful repetitions in Winston Churchill's speech after Dunkirk.

> We shall go on to the end, we shall fight on the seas and oceans, we shall fight with growing confidence and growing strength in the air, we shall defend our island, whatever the cost may be, we shall fight on the beaches, we shall fight on the landing grounds, we shall fight in the fields and in the streets, we shall fight in the hills; we shall never surrender. . . .

Repetition and restatement are also excellent transitional devices, serving as links between sentences and between paragraphs. Because extensive use of formal transitional markers often results in "self-conscious" writing, the good writer makes an effort to introduce a variety of linking devices, including repetition and restatement. Notice how smoothly Wendell Johnson moves from sentence to sentence and from paragraph to paragraph.

This discussion is not designed to take the place of a textbook for the teaching of effective communicative writings, but it is offered in the hope that a brief statement of a few simple principles upon which such writing is based might serve at least to raise the question as to why these principles are not more adequately taught by English instructors.

The first of these principles has already been given in the statement that clearness depends upon, and can be measured in terms of, the degree of agreement between the writer and his readers as to what the words of the writer represent. Simply by striving for a high degree of such agreement, the writer discovers, in some measure, his ingenuity in achieving it. He discovers the usefulness of conditional and quantifying terms, the confusion created by leaving out significantly differentiating details, the degree to which the meaning of a term varies from context to context, and the kinds of differences he must allow for among his readers' habits of interpreting words. He learns to rely less on the dictionary and more on the linguistic habits of the people for whom he writes. He discovers that literary posing, pleasurable as it may be, usually can be enjoyed only at the expense of effective communication—that Chesterton's paradoxes or Paul de Kruif's chronic astonishment are more titillating than informative. He discovers that there are various levels of abstraction, and that if he goes systematically from lower to higher levels he can use so-called abstract words and still be reasonably clear.

Above all, perhaps, he discovers the basic significance of order, or relations, or structure, or organization. This matter of structural relationships has wide ramifications, and no writer ever exhausts it, but the student quickly grasps some of its more obvious aspects, if he is striving for agreement between himself and his reader. It does not take him long to understand that the organization of what he writes should correspond to the organization of what he is writing about if the reader is to follow him readily. The graduate students with whom I work frequently have difficulty organizing their descriptions of experimental techniques or procedures, and I have found that it is more helpful to refer them to a cookbook than to a textbook on composition. By examining a cookbook they see at once that the organization of a description of procedure is determined simply by the order of the events that make up the procedure. First you do a, and then b, and then c, and you write it in that order because you do it in that order. This simple principle of order is fundamental in practically all descriptive, narrative, and expository writing, and it is obvious to anyone who is attempting to be considerate of the reader.

One might suppose that graduate students would know this, but in spite of the years they have spent in English courses most of them seem not to have learned much about it. The more significant fact is that, as a rule, they learn quite readily to apply this simple principle, once it is clearly explained and demonstrated to them. In this case, certainly, one can make a tree that either God or the English teachers forgot to make.

One aspect of organization that seems to have eluded practically all graduate students is that involved in the making of transitions. Even those who have been taught how to lay beads in a row have not been taught how to string them. Just as the order of what one writes is determined by the order of the parts or events involved in what one is writing about, so the

ways in which transitions are made in the writing are determined by the ways in which the parts or events are related in the realities one is describing, narrating, or explaining. The ability to move from one sentence or paragraph or chapter to the next, in such a way as to blend them into a unified whole, is largely dependent upon an understanding of the reasons for going from one to the next, of why one statement should follow another instead of the reverse, of why one should say, "It follows, then," rather than "But." And these reasons are found in the character of the relations existing among the details of that about which the writing is being done. This becomes obvious to one who is not trying to write writing, but who is attempting, rather, to write-about-something-for-someone.
—Wendell Johnson, *You Can't Write Writing*

It is worthwhile to keep in mind that clearness achieved through repetition is usually worth more than elegance achieved through variation. A writer's good sense will ordinarily tell him when repetition reaches the point of monotony, or when the simple recurrence of a sound becomes a distraction. And, correspondingly, the tone of a passage will nearly always tell the reader whether the author is repeating deliberately—for the purpose of achieving unity, coherence, or emphasis—or carelessly.


## Vocabulary

The writer who hopes to hold his readers must of course pay attention to vocabulary. The levels of usage in English will be discussed in some detail in the chapter on "Diction"; here we are concerned only with pointing out some mistakes and excesses that should be avoided even at the beginning.

It often happens that because of a writer's special interest in a subject his vocabulary will be larger and more technical than that of his audience. There are some subjects, moreover, which cannot be presented without using special terms. These cases raise a problem of how to be clear in communicating to the general reader. In some instances the difficulty may be removed by finding familiar equivalents for the more specialized terms. But there are other instances in which a technical word or phrase is so closely associated with an object or a process that to omit mention of it would be to leave the reader uninformed. When it is necessary to use a specialized or unusual term, one can often simplify matters by taking time to define it. Time taken to define is seldom wasted in any piece of informative writing, and in many situations it will make the difference between success and failure in communication. With some audiences, for example, the term *retort* as used in chemistry would mean little until the user of the word had given some description and some idea of the use of the apparatus. With some audiences, *oligarchy* would be an obstacle to understanding, which the alert writer would get over by a simple definition and illustration.

The kernel of this advice is, do not expect too much of your reader in the way of vocabulary. It is safer to underestimate than to overestimate his acquaintance with your terms, especially if you are dealing with a subject that has developed special names for things.

In general, bear in mind that most papers assigned in college are to be written on the level of serious discussion. Your instructor will not wish you to pose as more learned, literary, or sophisticated than you are. On the other hand, he will not be pleased if you adopt a slipshod, colloquial, or inaccurate vocabulary. You should try for a tone which is serious without being stiff, informal without being cheap or careless, and effective without obvious straining for effect. The vocabulary you use is a principal means of achieving the right level and setting the right tone. You should try first of all for exactness, frequently consulting a dictionary about words which are new in your vocabulary or words which people seem to use in loose senses. You should also strive for an adequate range of vocabulary to get into your writing the shades of meaning that careful treatment of a subject usually demands. Finally, your vocabulary normally should reflect, as you advance in your courses, a growing acquaintance with the terms in which scientific and literary subjects are discussed by the educated world.

### Simplicity

One of the greatest obstacles to clearness is the unjustified fear of being simple. Some writers compose as if they were ashamed of being direct. They seem to feel that what they are setting down is not writing unless it is filled with polysyllabic words and wordy phrases. This belief is usually a mistaking of pretentiousness for profundity and of complicatedness for skill. It results in vagueness, needless elaboration, and artificiality of tone. Sometimes courage is required to be simple when everyone else is being pretentious, but to do so pays in the long run. Resolve at the beginning to rid yourself of any feeling that simplicity in itself is a sign of lack of knowledge or mastery, for in most instances the very opposite is true. Obviously some subjects demand a more complex treatment than others; and some, for reasons which we have mentioned, cannot be presented without some special vocabulary. Yet in the expression of thought simplicity is often the mark of mastery. An involved style and an inflated vocabulary are more often the sign of awkwardness than of real skill. There is a difference between simplicity and simple-mindedness. Simplicity may be the outcome of hard thinking about a subject, whereas involved and difficult writing may be only a cover-up for inadequate information and failure to think the matter through. For most purposes of communication you will find that a style which is simple, direct, and to the point serves best.

# Part Two

# The Forms of Discourse

There is a traditional division of writing into forms of discourse. The four principal forms are commonly labelled exposition, description, narration, and argumentation.

Exposition is the form which explains a subject. Its purpose is to make the reader understand. This kind of writing, consequently, is practiced whenever it is necessary to tell what a thing is, how it functions, how its parts are related to each other, and how it is related to other things. It has little purpose beyond clarifying such matters. When a piece of writing leaves us with a clear idea of what something is or how it works, it satisfies the objectives of exposition. An article setting forth the structure of the government of the United States, or the germ theory of diseases, or the nature of the escapement mechanism of a watch would thus be expository in that it would convey an accurate and coherent explanation of these subjects. The expositor addresses himself to the intellect; he does not try to move or influence, and he does not strive to impress, except with the completeness and fidelity of his statement. A large majority of the lectures given in college are examples of exposition, since they present information in an organized way; and the simple directions we give our fellows about doing things or going places are elementary examples of the same form.

Because it is used to transmit knowledge by explanation, this is perhaps the most widely used of all the forms of discourse; and because some communication of facts and ideas enters into most pieces of writing, it combines rather freely with the other forms.

Most description is distinguished from exposition in that its primary function is to make us see things, or to perceive the special quality of them. Whereas exposition makes us see in the sense of understanding, description makes us see in the sense of visualizing. Roughly speaking, description focuses upon the appearance of an object and exposition upon the nature of it. In description, we see vividly and concretely; we perceive the object with a kind of fullness for which exposition does not strive. Thus a description of a house would be expected to make much of its individual or characteristic appearance—of the way it looks—and less of the strictly analyzable aspects such as size, material of construction, and architectural plan. Similarly, a description of a countryside would be less concerned with those features which make a topographical study and more concerned with the various particularities of visible outline and coloring and local atmosphere. Description, because it is interested in the special appearance of its object—whether it be a farmhouse, or the Empire State Building, or the Bay of Naples—often dwells on aspects which are unique; but exposition normally confines itself to the general and the definable. Hence description leaves us with an idea of its nature or its arrangement. Because of this connection with the senses and with imagery, much descriptive writing is classified as "creative." Descriptions are sometimes written to be presented alone; but very often they too combine with other forms of discourse and are contributing parts of a larger whole.

Narration is a form of discourse which presents events in a related series. It tells of an action or a group of actions in such a way as to give what is popularly recognized as a "story." Students sometimes apply the name "story" to any piece of writing which shows progression, but narrative in the true sense is limited to events in time. Like description, it departs from exposition in the direction of the more concrete and hence the more vivid. Although modern fiction makes use of many specially devised techniques of narration, narrative in its essential meaning is but a sequence of events so arranged as to take the reader from a beginning to an end while giving a lively sense of actuality. Narration therefore exhibits its method in the ordering of the parts of an action just as description exhibits its method in the characterizing of features and qualities. Like description again, narration is directly concerned with the evoking of pictures, but whereas description puts its pictures in a framework of space, narration puts its pictures in a framework of time. From the psychological point of view, narration is probably the most elementary form of discourse, inasmuch as almost everyone is born with some ability to tell a story.

Argumentation is distinguished from the other three forms of discourse in that its function is to prove. It might be said, of course, that exposition "proves" by asserting facts and their relationships, that description "proves" that things appear in such and such a way, and that narration "proves" that a set of events occurred in the order and manner related. The proof offered by argumentation, however, differs from these in definite respects.

First, its methods of proof have been reduced to a science, known as logic, whereby one can say with some exactness whether a given statement has been established or made good by the evidence offered in support of it. Logical proofs are never mere matters of opinion. There is no rule for telling whether or not an object has been fully described, but there are rather precise rules, as we shall see later, for determining whether or not a statement made in argument has been substantiated. The methods of argumentation are a body of scientifically analyzed processes, which must be followed strictly to yield a correct result.

Second, argumentation is frequently concerned with matters of policy. Matters of policy are distinguished from matters of fact in that they deal with what ought to be done rather than what is true of a situation by the standard of fact. For example, it is one thing to prove that women constitute more than one half of the population of the United States; it is a different thing to prove that women should be allowed to vote. The first statement can be settled by the methods that apply to any question of fact; but the second must be settled with reference to what one considers desirable. Argumentation accordingly embraces the field in which men deliberate about choices, and therefore it demands a combination of logic and rhetoric, which will be treated in detail in the section on argumentation.

An extended argument often includes passages of exposition, description, and narration.

Today there is a tendency to ignore these traditional distinctions and to attempt to reclassify the forms of discourse with reference to contemporary fashions in publishing. However, there is enough inherent difference in the four forms to justify learning them, although we should feel free to use them in varying proportion according to the needs of a specific writing task. Modern forms such as the feature article, the profile, the interview, and so forth have not supplanted exposition, description, narration, and argumentation; they have only used these basic forms in new combinations. An awareness of their natural differences enables us to work more securely and to detect the sources of certain faults likely to crop up in composition. A piece of exposition, for instance, can be marred by the injection of critical and evaluative statements which might be suitable or even necessary in argumentation. And argumentation, although it may employ exposition, description, and narration, must duly observe the purposes of these. Carelessness about the different ends served by the forms of discourse can diminish the effectiveness of any piece of writing.

Furthermore, the forms of discourse are important tools of analysis when we are doing reading of the active and critical kind. They enable us to see the lines of the writer's intention and to judge his over-all success. Indeed, a recognition of the form of discourse which predominates often gives us the key to the structure and purpose of a composition.

We turn now to a more detailed study of the aims and methods of the forms of discourse.

# Chapter Two

# Exposition

## DEFINITION

Definition is the kind of exposition most natural to begin with, because it lies at the base of all writing whose aim is to explain. We have described exposition as a means of producing understanding. But whether or not we understand is determined finally by whether or not we can define. The minimal requirement of all expression is that the speaker or writer know what he is talking about. It goes without further saying that he cannot know what he is talking about unless he can tell what it is; in other words, unless he can define. We shall presently discover, however, that telling what a thing is may be considerably more complicated than just giving a name and perhaps supplying a few synonyms. Nevertheless, the essential step of telling what a thing is constitutes the first step in making clear; and this is why we begin our study of exposition by examining the process of defining.

Definition is essentially a process of limitation, as the origin of the term itself makes evident. Our term *definition* is derived from the combination *de* + the verb form *finire*, which means to limit or to set bounds. We see this concept in our everyday use of "definite" and "indefinite." Thus a "definite" period means a limited one; a "definite" subject is one that is made distinct from other subjects by having its boundaries clearly drawn, and of course "indefinite" describes the opposite of this condition. Actually, then, what the definer does is to conceive and state his subject in such a way that it has clearly marked boundary lines and so cannot be confused with any other subject. Figuratively speaking, definition builds a fence around whatever is being defined, which separates it from everything else in the world. The success of the fence in keeping out the rest of

25

the world measures the success of the definition. Accordingly, if we are defining democracy, we do not wish it to be confused with other forms of government which may bear resemblance to it; if we are defining amateur athletics, we wish to leave it clearly marked off from the world of non-amateur athletics. Similarly, if we are defining an object, say a helicopter, we shall have to draw a distinct line between it and the various other types of aircraft. Definition then aims to circumscribe its subject for the purpose of clear identification. Once a subject has been defined, it can thenceforward be treated in a fixed sense.

The student may already be aware that several different kinds of explanations are referred to as "definitions." There are the definitions one finds in a dictionary; there are simple, one-sentence definitions, such as "a triangle is a geometric figure with three sides and three angles"; and there are essay-like treatments of terms ranging in length all the way from a paragraph or so to many pages. The function of limiting the meaning of a term appears in all of these, but variations in form and purpose cause us to recognize three main types: "dictionary" definitions, logical or formal definitions, and extended definitions.

### Dictionary Definitions

A *dictionary definition* is a historical survey of the term being defined and is, consequently, the most inclusive of the three types. It gives not only the most common current meaning but also past meanings, meanings which have grown specialized through use in some particular trade, profession, or field of learning, meanings peculiar to one level of usage, such as slang, and figurative or poetical meanings. All standard dictionaries list these meanings according to some method and so endeavor to give a full account of every term, with the changes of meaning it has undergone and the special applications it is capable of in different areas of expression.

The word "magazine" may serve as an illustration. Originally "magazine" meant a storehouse or place of deposit. Later its meaning was narrowed to indicate the room of a ship where gunpowder was stored. Today, by a transfer of meaning, it signifies a periodical which contains a store of articles, stories, poems, and the like; and there have grown up also a few more or less specialized meanings. These are the changes in meaning the word has undergone. In an unabridged dictionary you will find this kind of inventory of practically every important word.

In making distinctions between the kinds of definitions, it needs to be borne in mind that the dictionary definition follows the word rather than the object which the word signifies; that is to say, it furnishes a chronicle of the term as part of our vocabulary and does not go beyond the record of its usage to insist upon any special connection. It is right to say, therefore, that the dictionary defines words rather than things. Things, in which we must include concepts, are properly the subjects of logical and extended definitions.

## Logical Definitions

*Logical* (also called *formal*) *definition* takes one of the received or established meanings of a term and expresses this in a rigid formula. The formula is made possible by the fact that any term to be definable must have a general aspect and at least one particular aspect. A logical definition is composed by putting the two together. If, for instance, we say that man is a "rational animal," we are combining the general aspect "animal" and the particular aspect "rational" to mark man off from all other creatures. In this way the term undergoing definition is located with reference to one genus or class, in this instance "animal," and next with reference to other members of the same class by the distinguishing attribute "rational." Hence we say that a logical definition includes a generic aspect and a particular or individuating aspect. To express this in still another way, the logical definition first identifies the thing extensively, or with a group larger than itself, and then intensively, or with a property or a set of properties peculiar to itself. The process is roughly comparable to identifying a man through the name "Henry Smith," except that here the order of the two parts is reversed. The complete name tells us that he belongs to the "Smith" family or "class," and that by virtue of being "Henry" he is distinguishable from John, Susan, Jane, and other members of the Smith family. Likewise in defining an object or a concept, we must know its family and we must also know the property or special character which makes it an individual member of that family.

We shall illustrate the process of constructing a logical definition by taking something that is familiar and determining its generic and particular aspects. Suppose we use as our *definiendum* or "term-to-be-defined" *overcoat*. The first step, as we have just been noting, is to determine the general kind of thing *overcoat* is. The class in which it is placed should not be too broad or too narrow; perhaps we can agree that *overcoat* belongs to the class "clothing" or "apparel." Therefore the first part of our definition will be "an article of clothing." Since this comprises a rather large class, however, we must take some pains to mark *overcoat* off from other members of the class. We shall probably have to point out that it is usually heavy in comparison with other articles of clothing, that it is worn on the outside of other clothes, and that it is designed for protection against cold. Now in "article of clothing" we have given its general aspect, and in the details about weight, manner of use, and purpose we have given its individuating aspects. The extent to which this process of individuation must be carried depends, of course, upon how much needs to be done to distinguish the overcoat from other articles of clothing which resemble it or might be confused with it by someone who has to rely solely upon our definition. The aim obviously is to make the details restrictive enough without being too restrictive. If the details are not restrictive enough, such things as gowns and robes might be included; if they are too restrictive—if, for instance, we had said that an overcoat is made of wool—we would be excluding many things which belong within the definition, since overcoats are made of cotton, fur, and other materials. The purpose, as we stated at the beginning, is to build the fence right where it will divide the world of overcoats from everything else. The fence is sufficient only when we have found the smallest genus which will give the kind of thing being defined and when we have made the proper demarcation within the genus.

We now see that the formula of logical definition mentioned earlier consists of the following:

$$definiendum = \text{genus} + \text{differentia}$$

Genus and differentia are only technical names for the two aspects which we introduced at the beginning, genus signifying family or class, and differentia (plural: differentiae) signifying the group of distinguishing particulars. The formula is actually an equation, since the genus and differentia added together must exactly equal the term to be defined. Thus we can say that man is a rational animal and that a rational animal is a man.

With this formula in mind, let us try another logical definition, taking this time a concept, "democracy." As before, our definition will consist of the genus of this term with enough particulars to identify it within the genus. We begin then by saying that "democracy" belongs to the class "forms of government." There are many forms of government, however, and to complete the definition we add the differentia "characterized by rule by the people." With the formula thus satisfied, we have said what democracy essentially is and so have given it a logical or formal definition.

**Exercise:** *Analyze these definitions until you can recognize the genus and differentia present in each.*

1. A classic is a work which gives pleasure to the minority which is intensely and permanently interested in literature.

   —Arnold Bennett

2. Religions are the expression of human nature's eternal and indestructible metaphysical need.

   —Jacob Burckhardt

3. Any arrangement of acts and events is comic which gives us, in a single combination, the illusion of life and the distinct impression of a mechanical arrangement.

   —Henri Bergson

4. The people is any majority told by the head.

   —Edmund Burke

5. Hence we see what is the nature and office of a slave; he who is by nature not his own but another's man, is by nature a slave; and he may

be said to be another's man who, being a human being, is also a possession.

—Aristotle

6. The orator is a good man skilled in speaking.

—Quintilian

7. I call therefore a complete and generous education that which permits a man to perform justly, skillfully, and magnanimously all the offices, both public and private, of peace and of war.

—John Milton

8. Home is the place where, when you have to go there, they have to take you in.

—Robert Frost

We have seen that a logical definition has a preciseness which enables us to express it as a formula. But it is important to guard against the following types of errors in constructing this kind of definition.

1. *The defining part should not include the term being defined because this makes the definition circular.* Nothing is accomplished, for example, by defining "agriculturalist" as "one who engages in agriculture" or "courageous" as "the state or quality of having courage." It may be objected that dictionaries not infrequently do include the term being defined, or a variant of it, in the defining part; but this is another type of definition, and you will usually find that the term is qualified or elaborated in such a way that simple circularity is avoided. Thus if "poverty" is defined as "the state of being poor or without means," the qualifying phrase "without means" takes us outside the term itself and its variant forms. Furthermore, a dictionary will usually amplify the definition by the inclusion of synonyms, which also break the circularity.

2. *Do not define a term negatively unless some idea of privation is essential to its meaning.* It is proper to define "spinster" as a woman who has never had a husband, but it would not be proper to define "lion" as an animal which is not a tiger. A lion is not determined by its not being a tiger, but a spinster is determined by the fact of her never having had a husband. Negative definitions are satisfactory, accordingly, only when some idea of negation is a necessary part of the differentia.

3. *A logical definition should not be figurative.* Although some of the world's most widely quoted definitions do employ figures, logical definition is a strict mode of exposition which sticks to a core of literal meaning. For instance, Karl Marx's "religion is the opiate of the people" is not a satisfactory logical definition.

**Exercise:** *Criticize the definitions given below by the rules just stated. Determine whether the genus and the differentia are satisfactory. Look for examples of circular definition and for the use of figurative or non-literal expression. In each case point out the inadequacy.*

1. An automobile is a self-propelled vehicle.
2. Common law is law which is not statutory.
3. Vacation is a period in which one does not work.
4. Affluence is the condition of being affluent.
5. Bread is the staff of life.
6. A circle is a line whose every point is equidistant from a center.
7. Collectivism is a theory of society by which the means of production are collectively owned and operated.
8. A desert is a tract of land characterized by absence of water and vegetation.
9. The eyes are the windows of the soul.
10. Literature is anything printed in a book.

**Exercise:** *After this practice in criticizing logical definitions, select six of the terms listed below and try constructing such definitions of your own. Afterward, check your definitions by the rules we have been applying.*

| | |
|---|---|
| 1. culture | 11. ambition |
| 2. labor | 12. faith |
| 3. poetry | 13. free enterprise |
| 4. radicalism | 14. honor |
| 5. fair play | 15. intelligence |
| 6. militarism | 16. courage |
| 7. school | 17. internationalism |
| 8. knife | 18. social science |
| 9. success | 19. politics |
| 10. mass production | 20. progress |

It is useful to learn to compose logical definitions because this type lies at the heart of all definition. In both the dictionary definition and the extended definition it is usually necessary to say somewhere what the term means in its strictest conception. We have seen how the logical definition does this by using a genus and a differentia as a means of location. Through these, both the upper and the lower limits are marked off and so the theory of definition as a process of limitation is carried out.

## Extended Definitions

### Function

The other types of definition are carried out through a more flexible or informal means of development, and this is especially true of the *extended definition*, which may serve a number of purposes. Sometimes the writer will present an extended definition simply because he feels that the true meaning of the term is distorted in the public mind. Many people feel thus today with regard to frequently used terms like "freedom" or "propaganda." These words have been employed so carelessly and have been used so much for political purposes that one can scarcely risk the use of them without a fresh demarcation of their boundaries. The extended definition in such case would be a redefinition serving to remove confusions and to make the content more precise through the kind of elaboration which is possible with this type. In another situation, a writer will present an extended definition of a term because he senses a need for fuller understanding. Its general meaning may be clear enough, but people may have lost sight of some of the things which it properly includes. An extended definition of "citizenship" which emphasizes the duties in addition to the privileges might be an instance of this kind, since there has been a general tendency to think more about what citizenship confers upon us than about what it demands. Furthermore, a writer will sometimes present an extended definition in order to set up an ideal meaning in contrast with the meaning which merely reflects existing facts. Philosophers and advocates of political reform often find it needful to state what a term means as an ideal conception rather than as a generalization about a present situation. There would be a great difference between defining, say, "international law" as an ideal and defining the sort of international law which has existed in the world since 1919. In the first instance, the definer would be dealing with what ought to be; in the second, with what actually was or is.

Virtually all extended definitions tend to be *ad hoc,* or directed toward a special end, in that the writer is trying, in addition to making his meaning clear, to effect some change of conception or attitude in the reader. That is the very purpose of extending the definition. Dictionary definitions and logical definitions are merely informative, but most extended definitions are written to change people's minds about the thing being defined.

## Methods of Development

We have already noted that extended definitions may vary in length from a paragraph to entire chapters or essays. Often it will be found that they develop the ideas expressed in the logical definition, particularly those in the differentia. A thing undergoing definition may be marked off from other members of its class by reference to its cause or manner of origin, effect, material, size, shape, appearance, or mode of operation. The choice of which particular to stress naturally depends upon the object defined. Some things are best identified or individuated by the way in which they originate, some by the effects they produce, others by peculiarities of form or appearance. Many definitions in chemistry, for example, confine themselves to telling how a compound is produced. Many instruments cannot be defined satisfactorily without a clear explanation of their use. And since these different particulars are best elaborated in different ways, we find that there are a number of ways of extending a definition. Among other useful methods are comparison and contrast, illustration and example, enumeration of parts, and explanation of purpose. The pattern of extended definition can be varied in many ways, inasmuch as one can utilize practically any combination of methods in making the definition clear.

But even before these methods are brought into use, a writer will occasionally find it valuable to point to the *derivation* of a term. Derivations sometimes bring to light fundamental though partly obscured significances of a word which are influential in controlling its meaning. This is true because in some instances the original concept behind the term tends to accompany it in its later history, so that to recall a word in its first or primitive meaning is to recapture some essential idea for which it stands. Observe in the definition quoted below how Richard C. Trench brings out a core meaning of "classic" by giving an account of its derivation.

> We call certain books "classics." We have indeed a double use for the word, for we speak of the Greek and Latin as the "classical" languages, and the great writers in these are "the classics"; while at other times you hear of a "classical" English style, or of English "classics." Now "classic" is connected plainly with "classis." What then does it mean in itself, and how has it arrived at this double use? The term is drawn from the political economy of Rome. Such a man was rated as to his income in the third, such another in the fourth, and so on; but he who was in the highest was emphatically said to be of *the* class, "classicus"—a class man, without adding the number, as in that class superfluous; while all the others were "infra classem." Hence, by an obvious analogy, the best authors were rated as "classici," or men of the highest class; just as in English we say "men of rank" absolutely, for men who are in the highest ranks of the state.
>
> —Richard C. Trench, *On the Study of Words*

*a. Comparison and Contrast*    Because definition is a process of drawing a line between what a term includes and what it excludes, there always arises a need for *elimination*. And since the process of elimination always involves a contrast between what the term is and what it is not, *comparison and contrast* is a useful expository device in definition. An attempt to define *prose*, for example, makes inevitable some contrast with *poetry*. The definer would probably point out that prose is unmetered and unrhymed discourse, that it normally has a more relaxed rhythm than poetry, and that it rarely makes as liberal a use of metaphor. Experimental verse of the modern age has undermined some of these differences, but as long as the two are distinguishable kinds of composition, some kind of elimination through contrast would be necessary to define either of them.

A clear example of this method will be seen in the following definition of slang. Since the line between slang and the better accredited forms of speech is not clear in the minds of most people, the authors of the definition find it needful to contrast slang with the more proper or "legitimate" level of speech.

> A peculiar kind of vagabond language, always hanging around on the outskirts of legitimate speech, but continually straying or forcing its

way into the most respectable company, is what we call *slang*. The prejudice against this form of speech is to be encouraged, though it usually rests on a misconception. There is nothing abnormal about slang. In making it, men proceed in precisely the same manner as in making language, and under the same natural laws. The motive, however, is somewhat different, for slang is not meant simply to express one's thoughts. Its coinage and circulation come rather from the wish of the individual to distinguish himself by oddity or grotesque humor. Hence slang is seldom controlled by any regard for propriety, and it bids deliberate defiance to all considerations of good taste.

Slang is commonly made by the use of harsh, violent, or ludicrous metaphors, obscure analogies, meaningless words, and expressions derived from the less known or less esteemed vocations or customs. But the processes involved are strikingly linguistic. In fact, slang may almost be called the only living language, the only language in which these processes can be seen in full activity.

—James Bradstreet Greenough and George Lyman Kittredge,
*Words and Their Ways in English Speech*

We should observe here that the resemblance between slang and the other kinds of speech is stressed first. Slang is made in the same way as other language, and it obeys the same basic laws. Consequently, there is nothing about slang that could be called "abnormal." But now the contrasting features are introduced. Slang is distinguished from the other speech by the motive of its use and by its indifference to standards of taste and propriety. Those who employ it are seeking originality or effectiveness and are willing to forego the "respectability" which standard usage assures. Furthermore, slang takes its origin from things obscure, unusual, or of little esteem; and because it works to bring such things into the world of discourse, it is a creative expression, or the only "living language." By means of two points of resemblance and four of difference, the authors succeed in drawing the line between slang and standard speech.

We have seen that it is sometimes necessary to make an extended definition because the current or generally received definition is partial or misleading. We naturally incline to think of things according to their everyday appearances, although a really sound definition may place such appearances in quite a subordinate place. For example, the average person tends to think of *wealth* as signifying a large sum of money. To the political economist, however, who is concerned with how wealth came into being, how it is distributed, how it is symbolized, and how it affects the condition of a society, the term has a far more comprehensive and abstract meaning than this. Therefore considerable discussion may be required to define the meaning which economics gives to this seemingly simple term. A definition of this kind of the term "wages," utilizing the method of comparison and contrast, may be seen in the following passage.

As used in common discourse "wages" means a compensation paid to a hired person for his services; and we speak of one man "working for wages" in contradistinction to another who is "working for himself." The use of the term is still further narrowed by the habit of applying it solely to compensation paid for manual labor. We do not speak of the wages of professional men, managers or clerks, but their fees, commissions, or salaries. Thus the common meaning of the word wages is the compensation paid to a hired person for manual labor. But in political economy the word wages has a much wider meaning, and includes all returns for exertion. For, as political economists explain, the three agents or factors in production are land, labor, and capital, and that part of the produce which goes to the second of these factors is by them styled wages.

Thus the term labor includes all human exertion in the production of wealth, and wages, being that part of the produce which goes to labor, includes all reward for such exertion. There is, therefore, in the politico-economic sense of the term wages no distinction as to the kind of labor, or as to whether its reward is received through an employer or not, but wages means the return received for the exertion of labor as distinguished from the return received for the use of capital, and the return received by the land-holder for the use of land. The man who cultivates the soil himself receives his wages in its produce, just as, if he uses his own capital and owns his own land, he may also receive interest and rent; the hunter's wages are the game he kills; the fisherman's wages are the fish he takes. The gold washed out by the self-employing gold-digger is as much his wages as the money paid to the hired coalminer by the purchaser of his labor, and, as Adam Smith shows, the high profits of retail store keepers are in large part wages, being the recompense of their labor and not of their capital. In short, whatever is received as the result or reward of exertion is "wages."

—Henry George, *Progress and Poverty*

In Mortimer J. Adler's "Labor, Leisure, and Liberal Education" we can see a more extended example of how one can delimit a meaning through contrast and elimination. Adler begins by denoting education as a process for the improvement of men. But there are two ways in which this improvement can be conceived: we can improve men in those faculties which all men share in common, or we can improve them with respect to their individual talents and functions. The first kind of education—the liberal education—aims at a betterment of the human being as such; the second aims at producing more highly skilled workers or functionaries. Pursuing the distinction further, he notes that liberal education has results intrinsic to the person, whereas specialized or non-liberal education has extrinsic effects in the form of products or services.

It follows then that liberal education is education for leisure—and for the "free man." Specialized education is training for labor—and for the "slave." But once this criterion is clearly established, Adler is able to include in liberal education not only the traditional disciplines but also those things which contribute to physical and moral excellence. For although the specialized and extrinsic have been eliminated, there remains within the boundary of liberal education much that is non-intellectual—whatever contributes to the excellence of man as a member of the class "human beings."

By developing his definition through comparison and contrast, the author has ruled out what is sometimes improperly confused with liberal education while retaining what is sometimes unfairly excluded from it.

Let me begin where anyone has to begin—with a tentative definition of education. Education is a practical activity. It is concerned with means to be employed or devised for the achievement of an end. The broadest definition with which no one, I think, can disagree is that education is a process which aims at the improvement or betterment of men, in themselves and in relation to society. Few will quarrel with this definition because most people are willing to say that education is good; and its being good requires it to do something that is good for men. The definition says precisely this: that education improves men or makes them better.

All the quarrels that exist in educational philosophy exist because men have different conceptions of what the good life is, of what is good for man, of the conditions under which man is improved or bettered. Within that large area of controversy about education, there is one fundamental distinction that I should like to call to your attention.

There seem to be two ways in which men can be bettered or improved: first, with respect to special functions or talents and, second, with respect to the capacities and functions which are common to all men. Let me explain. In civilized societies, and even in primitive societies, there is always a rudimentary, and often a very complex, division of labor. Society exists through a diversity of occupations, through different groups of men performing different functions. In addition to the division of labor and the consequent diversity of functions, there is the simple natural fact of individual differences. So one view of education is that which takes these individual and functional *differences* into consideration and says that men are made better by adjusting them to their occupations, by making them better carpenters or better dentists or better bricklayers, by improving them, in other words, in the direction of their own special talents.

The other view differs from this in that it makes the primary aim of education the betterment of men not with respect to their differences but with respect to the *similarities* which all men have. According to this theory, if there are certain things that all men *can* do, or certain things that all men *must* do, it is with these that education is chiefly concerned.

This simple distinction leads us to differentiate between specialized education and general education. There is some ground for identifying specialized education with vocational education, largely because specialization has some reference to the division of labor and the diversity of occupations, and for identifying general education with liberal education because the efforts of general education are directed toward the liberal training of man as *man*.

There is still another way of differentiating education in terms of its ends. . . . An educational process has an *intrinsic* end if its result lies entirely within the *person* being educated, an excellence or perfection of his person, an improvement built right into his nature as a good habit is part of the nature of the person in whom a power is habituated. An *extrinsic* end of education, on the other hand, lies in the goodness of an *operation*, not as reflecting the goodness of the operator but rather the perfection of something else as a result of the operation being performed well.

Thus, for example, there can be two reasons for learning carpentry. One might wish to learn carpentry simply to acquire the skill or art of using tools to fabricate things out of wood, an art or skill that anyone is better for having. Or one might wish to learn carpentry in order to make good tables and chairs, not as works of art which reflect the excellence of the artist, but as commodities to sell. This distinction between the two reasons for learning carpentry is connected in my mind with the difference or distinction between liberal and vocational education. Thus carpentry is the same in both cases, but the first reason for learning carpentry is liberal, the second vocational.

All of this, I think, leads directly to the heart of the matter: that vocational training is training for work or labor; it is specialized rather than general; it is for an extrinsic end; and ultimately it is the education of slaves or workers. And from my point of view it makes no difference whether you say slaves or workers, for you mean that the worker is a man who does nothing but work—a state of affairs which has obtained, by the way, during the whole industrial period, from its beginning *almost* to our day.

Liberal education is education for leisure; it is general in character; it is for an intrinsic and not an extrinsic end; and, as compared with vocational training, which is the education of slaves or workers, liberal education is the education of free men.

I would like, however, to add one basic qualification at this point. According to this definition or conception of liberal education, it is not restricted in any way to training in the liberal arts. We often too narrowly identify liberal education with those arts which are genuinely the liberal arts—grammar, rhetoric and logic and the mathematical disciplines—because that is one of the traditional meanings of liberal education. But, as I am using the term "liberal" here, in contradistinction to "vocational," I am not confining liberal education to intellectual education or to the cultivation of the mind. On the contrary, as I am using the phrase, liberal education has three large departments, according to the division of human excellences or modes of perfection. Physical training or gymnastics in the Platonic sense, if its aim is to produce a good co-ordination of the body, is liberal education. So also is moral training, if its aim is to produce moral perfections, good moral habits or virtues; and so also is intellectual training, if its aim is the production of good intellectual habits or virtues. All three are liberal as distinguished from vocational. This is not, in a sense, a deviation from the conception of liberal education as being concerned only with the mind, for in all three of these the mind plays a role. All bodily skills are arts; all moral habits involve prudence; so the mind is not left out of the picture even when one is talking about moral and physical training.

—Mortimer J. Adler, "Labor, Leisure, and
Liberal Education"

*b. Example and Illustration*   Sometimes definitions are best developed through *example and illustration*. This method may be especially helpful when the term is either unusually difficult or unusually abstract. The following definition adds illustration to comparison and contrast to make clear the meaning of a very abstract concept. The object is to arrive at a definition of "theoretical exactness." The author first develops the contrasting idea "practical exactness" and then presents an illustration of what he set out to define, namely "theoretical exactness." By these means a conceptual ideal is made concrete for the reader.

The word "exact" has a practical and a theoretical meaning. When a grocer weighs you out a certain quantity of sugar very carefully, and says it is exactly a pound, he means that the difference between the mass of the sugar and that of the pound weight he employs is too small to be detected by his scales. If a chemist had made a special investigation, wishing to be as accurate as he could, and told you that this was exactly a pound of sugar, he would mean that the mass of sugar differed from that of a certain standard piece of platinum by a quantity too small to be detected by *his* means of weighing, which are a thousandfold more accurate than the grocer's. But what would a mathematician mean, if he made the same statement? He would mean this. Suppose the mass of a standard pound to be represented by a length, say a foot, measured on a certain line; so that half a pound would be represented by six inches, and so on. And let the difference between the mass of the sugar and that of the standard pound be drawn upon the same line to the same scale. Then, if that difference were magnified an infinite number of times, it would still be invisible. This is the theoretical meaning of exactness; the practical meaning is only very close approximation; *how* close depends upon the circumstances.

—William Kingdon Clifford,
"On the Aims and Instruments of Scientific Thought,"
from *Lectures and Essays*

Here is a further example in which the abstract concept "science" is made both clear and vivid through a series of striking illustrations followed by a short passage of generalization.

If you ask a physicist how fast a falling blue glass marble, released from rest, will move 1 sec. after its release, he will give you the answer without looking it up in a table or performing a measurement. How does he know it? He knows it from the generalization that (neglecting air resistance) all objects (blue marbles, green marbles, as well as grand pianos) fall at a specific locality with the same acceleration (known to him from experiments) and from the further generalization that the velocity after falling 1 sec. is numerically equal to the acceleration.

If you ask him, "How much will I weigh if I stand on a tower whose height is equal to the earth's radius?" he will say, "You will weigh one fourth of what you weigh on the earth's surface." How does he know it? Nobody has ever built such a tower, and nobody ever weighed objects at such a height. He knows it from the generalization that the weight of a body decreases in inverse proportion to its distance from the earth's center.

If you ask a chemist what will happen if a new hormone you have just synthesized is heated at a temperature of 5000 C., he will tell you without hesitancy that it will decompose into its original constituents, although he had never heard of the hormone before. Again, this answer is based on a generalization, namely, that all chemical compounds decompose before they reach a temperature of 5000 C.

We can infer from these examples that science is a collection of generalizations. The aim of any science is to establish a set of general statements (laws) from which the answer to any particular question could be obtained.

This aim may not sound very worth while. There is a large store of professed generalizations, such as "At night all cats are gray" or "Still waters run deep," on which we seldom like to rely. As we shall see presently, however, the generalizations of science, unlike the aforementioned ones, are not inspired by the imagination of a poetic mind but are carefully established by methods which inspire in us confidence in their validity.

—Alexander Kolin, *Physics: Its Laws, Ideas, and Methods*

*c. Enumeration of Parts*    Sometimes a definition is best made by enumerating the parts of an object, or by listing the factors which produce an effect. "Patriotism" is a term which would tempt many people to be wordy, irrelevant, or too subjective. In the definition below Bertrand Russell succeeds in increasing our understanding of patriotism by listing and explaining its active ingredients.

Patriotism is a very complex feeling, built up out of primitive instincts and highly intellectual convictions. There is love of home and family and friends, making us peculiarly anxious to preserve our own country from invasion. There is the mild instinctive liking for compatriots against foreigners. There is pride, which is bound up with the success of the community to which we feel that we belong. There is a belief, suggested by pride, but reinforced by history, that one's own nation represents a great tradition and stands for ideals that are important to the human race. But besides all these, there is another element, at once nobler and more open to attack, an element of worship, of willing sacrifice, of joyful merging of the individual life in the life of the nation. This religious element in patriotism is essential to the strength of the State, since it enlists the best that is in most men on the side of national sacrifice.

—Bertrand Russell, *Why Men Fight*

*d. Combined Methods*    Sometimes, in a definition no longer than a paragraph, a writer will successfully combine a number of methods. Below is a definition of artistic "Impressionism," by Thomas Craven, in which the author draws upon enumeration of features, comparison and contrast, and cause and effect. The result defines Impressionism and also places it in the general context of our life:

The term Impressionist, broadly speaking, means precisely what it says: an eyeful of nature; an instantaneous vision of the world, or of that very small pocket of the world which may be grasped instantaneously; a glimpse of externals; a sensational record of appearances. We may gather at once that it is opposed to classic art, that it places the simple act of vision above imagination, sight above knowledge, fidelity to natural appearances above a conception of humanity and a criticism of life. From the remotest beginnings of painting, as far back as one cares to go, artists have been occupied with the facts of life, with faces, figures, scenes, and events—things accessible to the eye—but never, when men of brains and beliefs, have they treated these facts as isolated fragments to be mechanically recorded in the manner of the camera. When painting was really an important art, as well understood and as widely circulated, let us say, as the art of fiction during the last century; when it was a common language embodying collective beliefs and enlisting the powers of great minds, there were no Impressionists. But gradually, for reasons I have already given, painting declined, and, in the words of MacColl, "the absence of a religion, of an architecture, or a court or a caste of patrons, left individual inspiration to its own fires, languors, and eccentricities." I do not wish to imply that Western civilization is going to the devil, that because painting has languished, the spirit of art is dead, or, with religion a-mouldering in the grave, there is nothing in modern life worth painting. My point of view is that the office once held by painting has been usurped by other arts which have adapted themselves to new conditions. Whether it will regain that office is not for me to say, but certain it is that it will never again become a considerable factor in the lives of men as long as it continues to illustrate abstruse psychological theories and to sacrifice the larger centers of human interest to technical exercises.

—Thomas Craven, *Men of Art*

As another example of complex method, let us look at Kenneth Burke's definition of "the mystic soldier," the man who finds his supreme gratification in an activity which inspires most people with horror or repugnance. Burke first describes the nature of his inner craving, then details the sources that give him satisfaction, and then suggests his effect upon a world which has vastly increased the means of destruction. Through the device of an extended definition, he compels us to see this frightening personality and his role in the unleashing of war.

Thus, too, there is the mysticism of war. There are those for whom war is a vocation, to whom the thought of the universal holocaust is soothing, who are torn with internal strife unless, in their profession as killers, they can commune with carnage. The imagery of slaughter is for them the way of mortification. As leaders, they are not mere "careerists," looking for a chance to let their friends in on government contracts at a high figure. They are mystic soldiers, devout—and killing is their calling. What of them?

They find solace in the thought of the great holocaust; they love the sheer hierarchical pageantry, the Stoicism of the disciplinary drill, the sense of unity in the communal act of all the different military orders marching in step, or the pious contemplation of the parade made static and "eternal," in the design of a military burying grounds, with its motionlessly advancing rank and file of graves.

What of *these* votaries, when their motives are hierarchically amplified, and empowered, with the great new weapons? And what of the fragments of such dedication, among the petty officials and journalistic hacks who know nothing of this quiet, deep-lying terror, but would do their lowly bit toward its unleashing, in daily pronouncements and bureaucratic finaglings that add steadily to the general ill will throughout the world?

—Kenneth Burke, *A Rhetoric of Motives*

## EXERCISES

**Exercise A**    *Choose one of the terms below and study its origin and development in one or more unabridged dictionaries. Then write a short definition of the term employing the "historical method."*

1. boycott
2. scruple
3. rifle
4. bunk
5. romance
6. colonel
7. mob
8. lynch
9. corporation
10. atomic
11. senate
12. infant

**Exercise B**    *Write a strict logical definition of each of the following terms.*

1. genius
2. army
3. attorney
4. window
5. real estate
6. river
7. jazz
8. pin
9. radar
10. pathology

**Exercise C**    *Write an extended definition of approximately 400 words of one of the following. Compose your definition in such a way as to anticipate partial or mistaken understandings.*

1. mathematics
2. salesmanship
3. temperance
4. leadership
5. social fraternities
6. censorship
7. urban renewal
8. public opinion
9. civil defense
10. liberal education

**Exercise D**    *Using comparison and contrast, write a definition of one of the following pairs.*

1. high school and college
2. generosity and wastefulness
3. manslaughter and murder
4. faith and conviction
5. exaggeration and lying
6. popular and classical music
7. servility and respect
8. wisdom and prejudice
9. vocation and avocation
10. pure and applied science

**Exercise E**    *Choose some term appearing in current political discussion which you feel is a source of misunderstanding. Using any combination of the methods we have discussed, write an extended definition clarifying its meaning.*

**Exercise F** *Study the following passage and discuss the methods by which Becker arrives at his definition of democracy.*

Democracy, like liberty or science or progress, is a word with which we are all so familiar that we rarely take the trouble to ask what we mean by it. It is a term, as the devotees of semantics say, which has no "referent" —there is no precise or palpable thing or object which we all think of when the word is pronounced. On the contrary, it is a word which connotes different things to different people, a kind of conceptual Gladstone bag which, with a little manipulation, can be made to accommodate almost any collection of social facts we may wish to carry about in it. In it we can as easily pack a dictatorship as any other form of government. We have only to stretch the concept to include any form of government supported by a majority of the people, for whatever reasons and by whatever means of expressing assent, and before we know it the empire of Napoleon, the Soviet regime of Stalin, and the Fascist systems of Mussolini and Hitler are all safely in the bag. But if this is what we mean by democracy, then virtually all forms of government are democratic, since virtually all governments, except in times of revolution, rest upon the explicit or implicit consent of the people. In order to discuss democracy intelligently it will be necessary, therefore, to define it, to attach to the word a sufficiently precise meaning to avoid the confusion which is not infrequently the chief result of such discussions.

All human institutions, we are told, have their ideal forms laid away in heaven, and we do not need to be told that the actual institutions conform but indifferently to these ideal counterparts. It would be possible then to define democracy either in terms of the ideal or in terms of the real form —to define it as government of the people, by the people, for the people; or to define it as government of the people, by the politicians, for whatever pressure groups can get their interests taken care of. But as a historian I am naturally disposed to be satisfied with the meaning which, in the history of politics, men have commonly attributed to the word—a meaning, needless to say, which derives partly from the experience and partly from the aspirations of mankind. So regarded, the term democracy refers primarily to a form of government by the many as opposed to government by the one— government by the people as opposed to government by a tyrant, a dictator, or an absolute monarch. This is the most general meaning of the word as men have commonly understood it.

In this antithesis there are, however, certain implications, always tacitly understood, which give a more precise meaning to the term. Peisistratus, for example, was supported by a majority of the people, but his government was never regarded as a democracy for all that. Caesar's power derived from a popular mandate, conveyed through established republican forms, but that did not make his government any the less a dictatorship. Napoleon called his government a democratic empire, but no one, least of all Napoleon himself, doubted that he had destroyed the last vestiges of the democratic republic. Since the Greeks first used the term, the essential test of democratic government has always been this: the source of political authority must be and remain in the people and not in the ruler. A demo-

cratic government has always meant one in which the citizens, or a sufficient number of them to represent more or less effectively the common will,
freely act from time to time, and according to established forms, to appoint
or recall the magistrates and to enact or revoke the laws by which the community is governed. This I take to be the meaning which history has impressed upon the term democracy as a form of government.

—Carl L. Becker, *Modern Democracy*

## ANALYSIS

We are by now familiar with the principle that definition draws a
boundary around something that is conceivable as a whole. Normally in
our thinking we tend to take in things as wholes before we proceed to
examine them further, and this is the reason for placing definition before
analysis in a study of the means of exposition. But once we have grasped
something as a whole, the next step is to look for its parts or its internal
divisions. Here is the point at which we make use of analysis. Analysis is a
process by which we separate any whole into its components. Derivatively
the word signifies a loosening, the root idea being that if we "loosen"
something which is bound together as a whole, it will fall into the parts
which are its constituents. If we untie a cord that binds a bundle of sticks,
or if we take the screws out of a timepiece, we allow the parts to become
separable, and such actions form a rough analogy of what we do when we
analyze anything, including general ideas. The analysis always deals with
a whole having parts. It does not create them but finds them and calls
attention to them; it discerns them.

Once the nature of the analytical process is understood, it will readily
be seen that analysis is one of the most common, as it is one of the most
necessary, operations of thought. Indeed, it could be said that wherever a
problem exists, there exists also a call for analysis. To understand the
nature of a firearm, one makes an analysis which distinguishes the parts.
To understand how to fill a fountain pen, one analyzes the steps of a process. The president of a company must analyze for the stockholders the
factors behind a rise or fall in the company's income. A government official
must analyze the methods of flood control employed by his agency. A
college examiner must analyze the performance of students with reference
to their previous preparation and other circumstances. A judge must
analyze the points presented by the plaintiff and defendant. Clearly this
list could be extended without limit, so that we are justified in saying that
there is perhaps no more common necessity in our lives than the power of
correct analysis.

### Partition and Classification

Though all analysis is a process of taking apart, there is some value in
recognizing two types, which are distinguished as *partition* and *classification*. *Partition* is the type of analysis employed when the object is habitu-

ally thought of as a unit, so that the analysis resembles more or less the taking apart of a single mechanism or anything that usually functions as a whole. The analysis of the government of the United States into the legislative, judicial, and executive departments would be, for example, the partition of a unit. An analysis of a television set, or a casting rod, or an ice skate would similarly be partition.

*Classification,* on the other hand, is the separation into groups of objects which are habitually thought of as existing severally or individually. Thus human beings are thought of as existing individually even though they make up the unit "mankind." Books are generally thought of as separate entities, although all the books in any one place may be said to compose a library. What classification therefore does is to take these individual things and place them in larger groups, and it is these groups which are regarded as the real components of the unit. In this way all mankind can be classified into groups on the basis of race, of political affinity, of type of religion, of level of culture, and so on. The difference between partition and classification is perhaps mainly rhetorical in that with partition the emphasis remains upon the whole, and with classification the emphasis is upon the parts or groups into which the single individual may be placed. Or, to put this in a slightly different way, partition begins with the whole and works toward the part; classification begins with the single parts and looks for larger categories into which they may be placed.

Both types may be illustrated if we take as our subject of analysis the newspaper. If we are interested in analyzing the contents of one single issue, we make a partition and accordingly proceed to determine the several distinct parts of the unit. With the ordinary type of newspaper such division will give us a news section, a section of editorial and general comment, a society section, a sports section, a financial and commercial section, and an advertising section. This partition is possibly not complete, and in the layout of the paper some parts may overlap owing to the exigencies of space; yet it would provide a reasonably satisfactory division of the contents. On the other hand, if we are making a classification of all newspapers, we would take this paper as one of many which are to be placed in like groups on the basis of some resemblance. We might therefore group them according to extent of circulation, physical size, political views, journalistic style, and so forth. In this instance we have taken individuals and arranged them in classes.

We might also note in passing that newspapers themselves perform an analysis by classification in the section generally headed "Classified Advertising." In this section a relatively large number of small single advertisements are classified with reference to what they are offering or seeking. So we commonly find such groups as "Help Wanted," "Household Goods for Sale," "Apartments for Rent," "Business Opportunities," and so on. Although this represents a rather loose type of classification, it illustrates the underlying principle.

### Requirements of Analysis

The requirements of sound analysis are simple in outline. First, *one must determine a clear basis of division.* Everything depends upon this, for an analysis cannot be made unless we know upon what line things are being divided.

Next, *one must follow the basis of division consistently.* To follow an analysis half through upon one basis of division and then to shift to another results in confusion.

Finally, *one must carry out the division until it has accounted for everything.* Naturally an analysis is not complete if some parts of the original unit have not been separated out, and if our principle of division will not allow us to accommodate them, the chance is that we have chosen the wrong principle at the beginning.

To illustrate the necessity of these requirements, let us suppose that a student must make an analysis of the works of John Milton. This will be an analysis by classification, inasmuch as the works exist as separate units and the first step will be to determine a principle upon which to classify. He might decide to divide them simply into poetry and prose. This would be satisfactory because the basis is definite, and the result is exhaustive. Again, with a different object in view, he might divide them according to subject matter. Then he would have a division consisting of theology, history, political and social reform, education, and one or two others. Or, with still another object in view, he might divide them according to periods of the author's life, in which case the division would be works of early period, works of middle period, and works of late period.

| A. | B. |
|---|---|
| *Basis of division: literary form* | *Basis of division: subject matter* |
| Poetry | Theology |
| Prose | History |
| | Political and social reform |
| | Education |
| **C.** | Other |

*Basis of division: periods of author's life*
Works of early period
Works of middle period
Works of late period

But he could not, in a correct analysis, shift from one basis of division to another. He could not, for example, have an analysis consisting of works of early period, works of middle period, and poetry, because Milton wrote poetry in each of the periods of his life and therefore poetry would overlap the divisions made on the basis of age. Similarly, he could not have prose, poetry, and theology, because it can be argued that Milton dealt with theology in both his prose and his poetry, and theology would therefore overlap the other two. The function of the clear basis of division is to separate parts, and obviously this cannot be done with overlapping. That is why the first concern in analysis is to determine a basis of division which will make clear the distinct parts.

**Exercise:**    *Determine two or more different bases of division for each of the following.*

1. A church congregation
2. A science laboratory
3. A neighborhood drug store
4. A YMCA
5. An airport

6. An orchestra
7. A theatrical company
8. A corporation
9. A weekly magazine
10. A student association

**Exercise:**    *Choose one of the following subjects and write a paper of 500–750 words in which you first offer a logical definition and then make an analysis.*

1. Intramural athletics
2. The Federal Reserve System
3. Registration at your college or university
4. Preventive medicine
5. Engineering
6. The tariff system
7. Collective bargaining

8. Meteorology
9. The study of philosophy
10. Examinations
11. Wildcat oil drilling
12. The ROTC
13. Extracurricular activities
14. The grading system

We have stressed the point that analysis is performed upon some whole which must be regarded as constituted of parts. It is clear that different interests in a subject will lead to different visualizations of its make-up, and this means that analysis will in most cases have some special approach to its subject. The particular approach will determine the principle of division to be employed. We have found this already in our discussion of the different purposes for which the works of Milton can be classified. To take another instance, a given segment of a population could be analyzed according to a number of different professional interests. An anthropologist might be interested in a division according to ethnic groups, a public health official according to physical welfare, a salesman according to income brackets, a minister according to religious affiliation, and so on. And correspondingly with regard to simple objects: a pocket knife might be analyzed according to the different parts that make up the whole, according to the different materials that went into its manufacture, or according to the different uses to which it can be put. In every case the analysis will reflect some governing interest in the object. Analysis is made so that we can better understand the organization of the whole, but that understanding is a response to some felt need. The need will determine the line of our partition or classification.

**Exercise:**    *Suggest a basis of division for each of the following subjects and state the interest it would reflect. Then write an essay of classification in which the interest is the guiding purpose.*

| | |
|---|---|
| 1. Automobiles | 11. Campus traditions |
| 2. Mystery novels | 12. Purposes in going to college |
| 3. Dogs | 13. Civic organizations |
| 4. Aquatic sports | 14. Political parties |
| 5. High school organizations | 15. Television or radio programs |
| 6. Shoppers | 16. Churchgoers |
| 7. Gardens | 17. Firearms |
| 8. Summer jobs | 18. Subway riders |
| 9. Women's hats | 19. College teachers |
| 10. Children's books | 20. Smokers |

It is important to keep in mind that the way we visualize the structure or grouping of a unit is a natural response to some interest we have in it. Indeed, analysis which is carried out merely for the sake of analysis is justly ridiculed as pedantry. However, once the interest has been recognized, the analysis itself should be a strictly intellectual operation. In the process of distinguishing parts, one must firmly set aside emotionalism and try to see objectively what is there. Nearly all analysis is performed as a prior operation, whose object is to put us in position to do something with the parts or with the relationship we can show to exist among them. That makes it all the more necessary not to allow feeling to intrude and deceive us about these matters. Analysis itself, once the problem has been set up, becomes a work of scientific examination in which, as with all scientific undertakings, objective attention to the facts is necessary. Even if one expects later to use the results of an analysis for something that has emotional or persuasive aims, the end will be served best by being coldly objective in the analytical stage. You may hate war, but if you allow this feeling to affect your analysis of the causes of war, you only leave yourself in a poor position to deal with the causes. When a physician is analyzing our condition, or an economist is analyzing the causes of a depression, we trust him to be strictly impersonal. The value of his analysis, or the measure of its further usefulness, rests upon this faithfulness to what is verifiable. In the same way, if you are engaged in discussion, and emotion causes you to make a faulty analysis, you are less able to continue your discussion intelligently. That is why we insist that a writer, even after he has been impelled to make an analysis by a feeling of interest in a subject, must practice a disciplined detachment while he is taking the subject apart.

The habit of dispassionate analysis is most valuable. The successes of modern science rest in a very large part upon careful analyses of physical phenomena; a physicist analyzing the structure of the atom, a chemist analyzing the elements of a compound, and a biologist analyzing the anatomy of an organism are all carrying on this work of separating into parts for the purpose of further knowledge and, in many cases, of practical application. The same method is desirable when one is dealing with matters that are not physical. We find that careful and detached analysis puts us in better position to understand and usually to do something effective about the problem which is facing us. A student failing in his studies may find that an honest analysis of how he spends his time will enable him to see the source of his difficulties. A student having difficulty with a certain course may find that analyzing the course into its different parts is the necessary step toward mastering it. And, more broadly speaking, all of our hope that the evils of society can be overcome through rational effort rests upon the assumption that by analysis we can succeed in understanding these evils in their true nature.

Not all analysis calls for such a rigorous process of division; nor is the usefulness of analysis limited to highly serious matters. "Informal" or "literary" analysis shows a more casual organization and approach. It divides its subject into parts, but does not attempt a complete or precisely discriminating segmentation. There are some subject matters which practically defy a definitive analysis and some in which the order or division may not be from great to small or from important to less important but may be in accordance with the idea that prompted the analysis. Because such ideas are various, we can expect many patterns in informal analysis. Here the object is to communicate ideas and information in the light of a certain interest and without the stern logical division of formal analysis.

In the selection that follows we have an example of a subject which requires "informal" treatment. The author relates his analysis to the problem of seeing. He is concerned with the questions of how much variety of color we can perceive in the out of doors and how adequately we can describe the varieties.

The exposition begins with a discussion of the primary colors which can be seen. The next phase of the treatment takes up the shades of green in leaves. Then the different colors in the bark of trees are listed. Finally some different colors produced by differing intensities of light are described. In the last two paragraphs the author takes up directly the problem which is behind the analytical excursion. Variety in color is so great that we may never hope to describe all the differences, but we can share with the artist his delight in its "infinite gradations."

Color is always to be seen in the countryside whenever there is light. That includes the dullest day of winter, and overcast and stormy days of every season. The brightest primary colors are always present as well as the most delicate hues. You might suppose that bright red is not a year round color. Let us see. In the June meadow burns the flame red of the devil's paintbrush and the scarlet of wild strawberries. The next month, on the edge of the woods, a wood lily will fling out its red vibrations. In August, at the foot of the hill, along the brook flare glossy rubies of honeysuckle and bittersweet nightshade berries. Later in August the cardinal flower throws out a sharp band from the long end of the spectrum. In September, the Jack-in-the-pulpit fruits and Russula mushrooms are among the countless objects that flash the long red waves of light. In October, the leaves of the red maples, sassafras and sumac will surrender their chlorophyll and throw off scarlet vibrations instead of green. In early winter the climbing bittersweet and the fruit of the cranberry tree will flare from the hedge rows. All through the winter there is no brighter scarlet than the tips of Cladonia lichens called "British soldiers," or the twigs of the red osier dogwood, or the winter buds of willows, red maples and blueberries.

You can see through the seasons a similar succession of yellow, purple, blue, green or any other color or hue you may look for. Color is no seasonal phenomenon; there is always more of it.than most of us ever see.

Exploring for bright color the year round brings undreamed-of surprises. When you accustom your mind's eye to detect hues, the beauty of the world we live in becomes a revelation. I used to consider that green leaves are all about the same green tone. That is so far from the fact that it is often possible to tell the species of a tree from its distinctive shade of green. Birches are yellow green; poplars, gray green. Sugar maple leaves are a bright rich green above and silvery green beneath. When the wind blows the whole tree gleams with silver. The elm leaves are a polished dark bluish green; the cherry is similar but even glossier. The locust presents a beautiful duotone effect, with lighter and darker green leaves on the same twig. The ash is a dark blue green. The American beech has foliage of clear bright green. Poison ivy starts as bronze red and turns to polished green as sparkling, if it is growing in full sunlight, as though covered with cellophane.

Each conifer, too, has its distinctive shade of green. The white pine is well named not only for its white wood but also for the accents of white light which play through its needles. This effect is due in part to a light blue tint, almost white, in the lines of the breathing pores on the under side of each needle and in part to highlights from the polished surface of the needles. Other species of pine are on the dark side. The three common species of pine native in the eastern United States are named after the tones of their green needles; red, white and black. The famous cultivated variety of spruce, known as blue spruce, has beautiful blue green needles. The hemlock is a dark yellow green and very lustrous.

Among herbaceous plants one of the loveliest shades of green is found in the leaves of clover. The surface is dull, with a bluish tone mottled with light blue angular check marks. In contrast, the mullein is as gray as a woolly blanket, but when you hold it up to the sun the transmitted light is clear yellow green. Of all the bright greens in the world there is none brighter than the pleated leaves of lady's-slipper and Clintonia. They have a high polish in contrast with the blue green of honeysuckle leaves which have a beautiful rich suède finish. Bloodroot leaves, when they first appear in early spring, are unique not only for their fantastic design but also because they are a lovely blue green. And the exquisite flowers shoot up on dynamic straight stems through the heart-shaped base.

A vast array of unseen color will suddenly flare when you look for the hues in bark. I used to think that all bark, with the exception of white birch, was a nondescript grayish or brownish tone. That was before I really *looked* at bark and discovered not only a variety of hues of one color but also many different colors. That of the yellow birch is glistening yellow. Sweet birch bark and the younger bark of cherry are maroon. The younger bark in the upper branches of Scotch pine is such a bright orange that the species can be identified by this feature. The white in white oak bark gives the bole its distinctive gray tint by which it can be identified from all other species of oaks. The barks of the American beech and of the red maple are smooth battleship gray. The deeply sculptured bark of the black locust has bright yellow streaks in its fissures. The Osage orange bark is orange, although the name is a coincidence, as the tree is named after its fruit and not its bark. There is a distinct difference in the whites of the two white birch trees: the gray birch is a cold silvery white; the paper birch is a warmer buff white, due to the orange inner bark just below the surface.

So mobile is color outdoors that it changes with every intensity of light. Perhaps this is one reason why certain seasons of the year are considered to be rather drab or colorless. November is the darkest month of the year. Then the sky is frequently overcast and the noon sun is closer to the horizon. The snow which builds up intensities of light in winter has not yet arrived. In these days of reduced illumination, reds turn purple. This is seen in the colors of lichens, twigs of dogwoods or buds of red maple and willow. Yellow turns olive green. Bright green becomes bluish. Look at the foliage of conifers, club-mosses and evergreen ferns in November. Blue turns deeper blue, witness the bloom on the canes of brambles and the metallic blue of the fluted shafts of the scouring rushes. The orange in the carpet of fallen leaves, in catkins, seeds, grasses, and the November hues of hay-scented ferns turns brownish. Brown is a degraded orange. It is produced when the pigments that give off the light waves of orange act as a sort of brake to reduce their intensity—or the same effect is produced when the original source light is of low intensity.

Conversely, outdoor hues are entirely changed by increased illumination. Red appears as purplish pink; yellow becomes warmer; green grows bluer; blue, purpler; and orange, reddish. Violet remains violet but of a paler tint.

This is one reason why it is difficult to discuss precisely the colors of things. Objects which have not changed their color natures take on different hues when the atmospheric illumination varies. All such changes are optical illusions; they are of the psychological nature of color which is so fluid as it plays on the sensitive nerve ends in our eyes.

This fact makes color in the outdoors one of the least known and least understood of nature's phenomena. The terminology for color is incomplete and inaccurate. We speak in generalities, dividing this vast array of hues, tints and tones under a few key labels like red, yellow, green, blue, orange. Violet, purple and magenta are ambiguous words. Even the botanists with all their striving for precision of expression have never finally agreed on a way of describing colors accurately. In the *Manual of Botany* by the great Asa Gray most of the hues from pink to violet are simply called "purple." But if a quality as elusive as color cannot be accurately described, at least it can be felt and the comparison of tones, tints and hues made and enjoyed on the spot while you look at the objects. In this way one can learn to think in terms of color and feel an artist's thrill over its infinite gradations.

—Rutherford Platt, *This Green World*

## EXERCISES

**Exercise A**    *Study the example of analysis given below. Note the bases of division. Observe the order in which the parts are presented and the means by which they are related to the whole. Are there other bases of division or orders of presentation the authors could have used equally well for their purposes?*

[1] The true forms of government, therefore, are those in which the one, or the few, or the many, govern with a view to the common interest; but governments which rule with a view to the private interest, whether of the one, or of the few, or of the many, are perversions. For the members of a state, if they are truly citizens, ought to participate in its advantages. Of forms of government in which one rules, we call that which regards the common interests, kingship or royalty; that in which more than one, but not many, rule, aristocracy; and it is so called either because the rulers are the best men, or because they have at heart the best interests of the state and of the citizens. But when the citizens at large administer the state for the common interest, the government is called by the generic name—a constitution. And there is a reason for this use of language. One man or a few men may excel in virtue; but as the number increases it becomes more difficult for them to attain perfection in every kind of virtue, though they may in the military virtue, for this is found in the masses. Hence in a constitutional government the fighting men have the supreme power, and those who possess arms are the citizens.

Of the above-mentioned forms, the perversions are as follows: of royalty, tyranny; of aristocracy, oligarchy; of constitutional government, democracy. For tyranny is a kind of monarchy which has in view the interest of the monarch only; oligarchy has in view the interest of the wealthy; democracy, of the needy: none of them the common good of all.

—Aristotle, *Politics*

[2] Employed in this sense, zoology, like botany, is divisible into three great but subordinate sciences, morphology, physiology, and distribution, each of which may, to a very great extent, be studied independently of the other.

Zoological morphology is the doctrine of animal form or structure. Anatomy is one of its branches; development is another; while classification is the expression of the relations which different animals bear to one another, in respect of their anatomy and their development.

Zoological distribution is the study of animals in relation to the terrestrial conditions which obtain now, or have obtained at any previous epoch of the earth's history.

Zoological physiology, lastly, is the doctrine of the functions or actions of animals. It regards animal bodies as machines impelled by certain forces, and performing an amount of work which can be expressed in terms of the ordinary forces of nature. The final object of physiology is to deduce the facts of morphology, on the one hand, and those of distribution on the other, from the laws of the molecular forces of matter.

—T. H. Huxley, *Discourses Biological and Zoological*

[3] There are four classes of Idols which beset men's minds. To these for distinction's sake I have assigned names, calling the first class *Idols of the Tribe;* the second, *Idols of the Cave;* the third, *Idols of the Market-place;* the fourth, *Idols of the Theatre.*

The formation of ideas and axioms by true induction is no doubt the proper remedy to be applied for the keeping off and clearing away of idols. To point them out, however, is of great use, for the doctrine of Idols is to the Interpretation of Nature what the doctrine of the refutation of Sophisms is to common Logic.

The Idols of the Tribe have their foundation in human nature itself and in the tribe or race of men. For it is a false assertion that the sense of man is the measure of things. On the contrary, all perceptions as well of the sense as of the mind are according to the measure of the individual and not according to the measure of the universe. And the human understanding is like a false mirror, which, receiving rays irregularly, distorts and discolours the nature of things by mingling its own nature with it.

The Idols of the Cave are the idols of the individual man. For every one (besides the errors common to human nature in general) has a cave or den of his own, which refracts and discolours the light of nature, owing either to his own proper and peculiar nature, or to his education and conversation with others, or to the reading of books, and the authority of those whom he esteems and admires, or to the differences of impressions, accordingly as they take place in a mind preoccupied and predisposed or in a mind indifferent and settled, or the like. So that the spirit of man (according as it is meted out to different individuals) is in fact a thing variable and full of perturbation, and governed as it were by chance. Whence it was well observed by Heraclitus that men look for sciences in their own lesser worlds and not in the greater or common world.

There are also Idols formed by the intercourse and association of men with each other, which I call Idols of the Market-place on account of the commerce and consort of men there. For it is by discourse that men associate, and words are imposed according to the apprehension of the vulgar. And therefore the ill and unfit choice of words wonderfully obstructs the understanding. Nor do the definitions or explanations, wherewith in some things learned men are wont to guard and defend themselves, by any means set the matter right. But words plainly force and overrule the understanding, and throw all into confusion, and lead men away into numberless empty controversies and idle fancies.

Lastly, there are Idols which have immigrated into men's minds from the various dogmas of philosophies and also from wrong laws of demonstration. These I call Idols of the Theatre, because in my judgment all the received systems are but so many stage-plays, representing worlds of their own creation after an unreal and scenic fashion. Nor is it only of the systems now in vogue or only of the ancient sects and philosophies that

I speak, for many more plays of the same kind may yet be composed and in like artificial manner set forth, seeing that errors the most widely different have nevertheless causes for the most part alike. Neither again do I mean this only of entire systems, but also of many principles and axioms in science, which by tradition, credulity, and negligence have come to be received.

But of these several kinds of Idols I must speak more largely and exactly, that the understanding may be duly cautioned.

—Francis Bacon

[4] Since the turn of the century, a new educational institution has appeared in America. During the past twenty years, it has grown at an accelerated pace and there are reasons for believing that it will become standard equipment in the nation's public school program.

This institution is the public two-year college, sometimes called a junior college, a community college, or just plain college. The typical community college is a local organization, either district or county. Nine tenths of its students live within a 35-mile radius. There are no fraternities or sororities and usually no dormitories. It boasts small classes, emphasis on teaching, a comprehensive advisory and counseling program for its students, and a personal student-teacher relationship. It undertakes three major functions.

First and paramount is its program of lower-division, freshman-sophomore, courses paralleling the state university and other senior institutions. Students planning to specialize in any of the regular or academic professional areas, such as law, medicine, dentistry, engineering, teaching, business, psychology, physics, chemistry, botany, can begin college in their own community and transfer with comparable advanced standing to senior institutions for completion of their training without loss of time or credits. About 35 per cent of the full-time students in community colleges complete advanced work at a senior institution.

Second, it provides terminal training for students who are not going to be baccalaureate candidates but who want and need more education than high school provides. For these there are such alternatives as trade courses in airframe and aircraft engine mechanics, auto mechanics, radio and television servicing, metal shop, machine shop, or courses for the semiprofessional technician in the various branches of engineering or in laboratories. Some terminal students take business courses, secretarial training, or agriculture. Others take regular lower-division college courses in order to be more knowledgeable persons with broader intellectual and emotional horizons, whatever their occupations.

Besides these two services for the college-age population, the community college attempts to be an educational and cultural reservoir for the adult population of the area. This is its third function and it does this in several ways. One is by providing evening courses for people already employed or in business. The content of such courses is determined by the nature of the group for which they are operated and by interests and wants of the population. There may be classes in modern world problems, history, psychology, philosophy, economics, or whatever interest and facilities warrant. Many of the adults in these classes are college graduates who either want to take those courses which their degree requirements excluded, or want to retake some they once had in order to renew acquaintance with an area of worth to them. Others are without academic degrees, but wish to drink deeper at the Pierian spring.

Another primarily adult service of the community college is to act as a focal point for cultural activities. Do those with musical ability wish to cultivate their talents? The college organizes a chorus, an orchestra, or produces an opera with a local cast. Are there people willing to put forth a concerted effort to make better sense out of current affairs? A college-community forum is organized and leading figures in contemporary problems are brought in to present their views and discuss possible solutions. Comparable assistance can be given to amateur thespians, writers, artists, both in performance and appreciation.

This triadic obligation—to the university-bound student, to the terminal student, and to the adult—is, of course, not assumed by every two-year college. Some have a highly specialized objective to which all else is legitimately subordinate. What has been described is what appears to be the emerging pattern for the typical public two year college.

—Sigurd Rislov, "The Community College"

[5] The fact that the content of any culture can be analyzed and placed in such compartments, perhaps with the aid of an occasional *tour de force*, has led certain writers to attach more importance to these arbitrary divisions than they really deserve. One writer speaks of the "universal patterns" in culture which are thus revealed. Actually, there are no universal patterns, only a series of universal needs which each society has met in its own way. These needs can be grouped under three headings, biological, social, and psychic. The *biological needs* are those which derive from man's physical characteristics. They include such things as the need for food and shelter, for protection from enemies, whether human or animal, and the need for reproduction to perpetuate the species. These needs are common to men and animals and are of a particularly immediate and pressing sort. Unless the culture provides adequate techniques for meeting them, neither the individual nor the group can survive. At the same time these needs are more closely related to the natural environment than any others, and the specific form in which they present themselves may be largely determined by it. Thus the type of food and shelter required by the members of a society will vary with the region in which they live. It will not be the same for Polynesians and Eskimos. The natural environment will also have a strong effect, through the materials which it offers, upon the techniques which a society develops for meeting these needs. There are areas in which no food crops can be raised, areas without metallic ores, and so on.

The *social needs* of human beings arise from man's habit of living in groups. Similar needs must be present, in rudimentary form, for all gregarious animals, but the close interdependence of the members of a human society gives them a much greater importance for man. The first and most vital of these needs is that of preserving the solidarity of the group. Closely connected with these are the needs for reducing friction between individuals and minimizing open clashes, for training individuals for special statuses in the social system, and for coordinating their activities and providing the group with leadership and direction. These needs are only remotely influenced by the natural environment and present themselves to all societies in very much the same form. At the same time, their effective solution depends more on the adequate training of the individual and his conditioning to social life than upon anything else, so that a great number of workable solutions are possible.

Lastly, there are the *psychic needs,* which are extremely difficult to define but real nevertheless. One of the most important functions of any culture is to keep a majority of the people who share it happy and contented. All human beings have desires for favorable responses from other individuals, for things which are unattainable (or for easy roads to attainment), and for psychological escapes. In the long run the satisfaction of these needs is probably as important to the effective functioning of a society as that of the needs of the other two categories, although they are less immediate and pressing. However, these needs are in themselves vague and general, being given point by the individual's cultural conditioning, and the responses to them which various cultures provide are almost infinitely varied. Depending on his training, the individual can obtain a warm sense that he is looking well and exciting admiration by wearing a bone through his nose, a new loin-cloth, or the latest products of a fashionable tailor. He can escape from reality equally well by immersing himself in a game of chess, hiring a medicine man to make a charm, or anticipating a better social status in his next incarnation. Utility imposes fewer restrictions upon this aspect of culture than on any other with the possible exception of language, and the diversity of forms is correspondingly great.

—Ralph Linton, *The Study of Man*

**Exercise B**    *Select one of the following and develop a paper of 600–800 words.*

1. Review the way in which you spend your time. Then write a paper analyzing a typical week's expenditure.

2. Select some important political figure or some celebrity from the entertainment world. Write an analysis of his points of appeal to the public.

3. Write an analysis of the basic topographical features of your state.

4. Write an analysis by classification of the public eating places in your city or near your campus.

5. Analyze the subjects you have studied in high school and college, using as your basis of division their appeal to you or their difficulty for you. Develop the analysis in the form of a paper.

## EXPOSITION OF PROCESS

One of the most common needs in expository writing is to divide a process into a series of distinct steps. This requires an analytical organization which follows a natural order. If the process is a simple one, the steps can be easily distinguished. A very generalized pattern would consist of: gathering the necessary materials, beginning the process, following the steps in the process, and then completing the work. If the writer is thinking clearly about his subject, usually a time order will impose itself. Where more complicated processes are the subject, the different steps may require their own internal organization. For example, it might be useful to discuss different materials or various methods, and it is sometimes necessary to call attention to mistakes that can be made. A complete and well-written analysis of a process leaves the reader satisfied as to *how it is done*.

The account below of "making tappa" is an exposition of a process that most of us have never heard of, yet the author, Herman Melville, enables a reader to follow it very easily. He has discerned the natural stages of the process, and he has divided his exposition accordingly, allowing us to fix our attention upon one at a time. Notice how careful he is to bring in at just the right places various relevant facts, such as the source of the material, the place where it is given the initial water treatment, and the nature of the tool used in beating it. Notice also how he helps us to visualize the unfamiliar by referring to such familiar things as wrapping paper, corduroy, and the gold-beating process, and how he keeps the time sequence before us very carefully by the use of words such as *when, then, after, now,* and *until.* This sequence is so clearly maintained that we are not distracted by his discussion of the making of the mallet, or by his reference at the end to an earlier stage in which dye is sometimes applied.

Although the whole existence of the inhabitants of the valley seemed to pass away exempt from toil, yet there were some light employments which, although amusing rather than laborious as occupations, contributed to their comfort and luxury. Among these, the most important was the manufacture of the native cloth, — "tappa," — so well known, under various modifications, throughout the whole Polynesian Archipelago. As is generally understood, this useful and sometimes elegant article is fabricated from the bark of different trees. But, as I believe that no description of its manufacture has even been given, I shall state what I know regarding it.

In the manufacture of the beautiful white tappa generally worn on the Marquesan Islands, the preliminary operation consists in gathering a certain quantity of the young branches of the cloth-tree. The exterior green bark being pulled off as worthless, there remains a slender fibrous substance, which is carefully stripped from the stick, to which it closely adheres. When a sufficient quantity of it has been collected, the various strips are enveloped in a covering of large leaves, which the natives use precisely as we do wrapping-paper, and which are secured by a few turns of a line passed round them. The package is then laid in the bed of some running stream, with a heavy stone placed over it, to prevent its being swept away. After it has remained for two or three days in this state, it is drawn out, and exposed, for a short time, to the action of the air, every distinct piece being attentively inspected, with a view of ascertaining whether it has yet been sufficiently affected by the operation. This is repeated again and again, until the desired result is obtained.

When the substance is in a proper state for the next process, it betrays evidences of incipient decomposition; the fibers are relaxed and softened, and rendered perfectly malleable. The different strips are now extended, one by one, in successive layers, upon some smooth surface—generally the prostrate trunk of a cocoa-nut tree—and the heap thus formed is subjected, at every new increase, to a moderate beating, with a sort of wooden mallet, leisurely applied. The mallet is made of a hard heavy wood resembling ebony, is about twelve inches in length, and perhaps two in breadth, with a rounded handle at one end, and in shape is the exact counterpart of one of our four-sided razor-strops. The flat surfaces of the implement are marked with shallow parallel indentations, varying in depth on the different sides, so as to be adapted to the several stages of the operation. These marks produce the corduroy sort of stripes discernible in the tappa in its finished state. After being beaten in the manner I have described, the material soon becomes blended in one mass, which, moistened occasionally with water, is at intervals hammered out, by a kind of gold-beating process, to any degree of thinness required. In this way the cloth is easily made to vary in strength and thickness, so as to suit the numerous purposes to which it is applied.

When the operation last described has been concluded, the new-made tappa is spread out on the grass to bleach and dry, and soon becomes of a dazzling whiteness. Sometimes, in the first stages of the manufacture, the substance is impregnated with a vegetable juice, which gives it a permanent color. A rich brown and a bright yellow are occasionally seen, but the simple taste of the Typee people inclines them to prefer the natural tint.

—Herman Melville, *Typee*

A justly admired example of description of a process is the passage below on riveting structural steel. The writer has made the process clear by the simple device of following the rivet. Its course is marked out in clear stages by the different operations that have to be performed. First, the heater heats the rivet to the desired temperature. Then he passes it to the catcher, who deftly receives it in his tin can. The catcher then places it in the prealigned hole, and the bucker-up presses his dolly bar against the capped end. The gun man then goes to work on the other end with his pneumatic hammer. A great deal of subsidiary detail is brought in to describe more fully the process of riveting, but all of it is clearly associated with these stages of the rivet's progress from the keg to its place in the steel beam.

Although, as we have noted, the more strictly technical or scientific descriptions are little concerned with evoking qualities, some descriptions of processes are directed in part at least to the arousing of attitudes. "Riveting a Skyscraper" was written for the general readership of *Fortune Magazine*. Obviously the author wants to convey to his readers a sense of the danger and skill involved in the riveter's job, but he does this indirectly and subtly. "The catcher's position," we are told, "is not exactly one which a sportsman catching rivets for pleasure would choose"—and the understatement makes us aware of the ever present possibility of a fatal accident. The rivet is thrown through the air with such precision that its course is referred to as a "trajectory"—a term usually employed to describe the paths of projectiles. The short emphatic sentence "And the tin can clanks" suggests that the catcher is so skillful that he cannot miss. And the foreman's "Well, he's not supposed to [miss]" is a very effective summing up of the workers' calm, professional attitude. Such details are woven in to arouse our respect for the poise and the skill of the riveters.

The actual process of riveting is simple—in description. Rivets are carried to the job by the rivet boy, a riveter's apprentice whose ambition it is to replace one of the members of the gang—which one, he leaves to luck. The rivets are dumped into a keg beside a small coke furnace. The furnace stands on a platform of loose boards roped to steel girders which may or may not have been riveted. If they have not been riveted there will be a certain amount of play in the temporary bolts. The furnace is tended by the heater or passer. He wears heavy clothes and gloves to protect him from the flying sparks and intense heat of his work, and he holds a pair of tongs about a foot and a half long in his right hand. When a rivet is needed, he whirls the furnace blower until the coke is white-hot, picks up a rivet with his tongs, and drives it into the coals. His skill as a heater appears in his knowledge of the exact time necessary to heat the steel. If he overheats it, it will flake, and the flakes will permit the rivet to turn in its hole. And a rivet which gives in its hole is condemned by the inspectors.

When the heater judges that his rivet is right, he turns to face the catcher, who may be above or below him or fifty or sixty or eighty feet away on the same floor level with the naked girders between. There is no means of handing the rivet over. It must be thrown. And it must be accurately thrown. And if the floor beams of the floor above have been laid so that a flat trajectory is essential, it must be thrown with considerable force. The catcher is therefore armed with a smallish, battered tin can, called a cup, with which to catch the red-hot steel. Various patented cups have been put upon the market from time to time but they have made little headway. Catchers prefer the ancient can.

The catcher's position is not exactly one which a sportsman catching rivets for pleasure would choose. He stands upon a narrow platform of loose planks laid over needle beams and roped to a girder near the connection upon which the gang is at work. There are live coils of pneumatic tubing for the rivet gun around his feet. If he moves more than a step or two in any direction, he is gone, and if he loses his balance backward he is apt to end up at street level without time to walk. And the object is to catch a red-hot iron rivet weighing anywhere from a quarter of a pound to a pound and a half and capable, if he lets it pass, of drilling an automobile radiator or a man's skull 500 feet below as neatly as a shank of shrapnel. Why more rivets do not fall is the great mystery of skyscraper construction. The only reasonable explanation offered to date is the reply of an erector's foreman who was asked what would happen if a catcher on the Forty Wall Street job let a rivet go by him around lunch hour. "Well," said the foreman, "he's not supposed to."

There is practically no exchange of words among riveters. Not only are they averse to conversation, which would be reasonable enough in view of the effect they have on the conversation of others, but they are averse to speech in any form. The catcher faces the heater. He holds his tin can up. The heater swings his tongs, releasing one handle. The red iron arcs through the air in one of those parabolas so much admired by the stenographers in the neighboring windows. And the tin can clanks.

Meantime the gun-man and the bucker-up have prepared the connection—aligning the two holes, if necessary, with a drift pin driven by a pneumatic hammer—and removed the temporary bolts. They, too, stand on loose-roped boards with the column or the beam between them. When the rivet strikes the catcher's can, he picks it out with a pair of tongs held in his right hand, knocks it sharply against the steel to shake off the glowing flakes, and rams it into the hole, an operation which is responsible for his alternative title of sticker. Once the rivet is in place, the bucker-up braces himself with his dolly bar, a short heavy bar of steel, against the capped end of the rivet. On outside wall work he is sometimes obliged to hold on by one elbow with his weight out over the street and the jar of the riveting shaking his precarious balance. And the gun-man lifts his pneumatic hammer to the rivet's other end.

The gun-man's work is the hardest work, physically, done by the gang. The hammers in use for steel construction work are supposed to weigh around thirty pounds and actually weigh about thirty-five. They must not only be held against the rivet end, but held there with the gun-man's entire strength, and for a period of forty to sixty seconds. (A rivet driven too long will develop a collar inside the new head.) And the concussion to the ears and to the arms during that period is very great. The whole platform shakes and the vibration can be felt down the column thirty stories below. It is common practice for the catcher to push with the gun-man and for the gun-man and the bucker-up to pass the gun back and forth between them when the angle is difficult. Also on a heavy rivet job the catcher and the bucker-up may relieve the gun-man at the gun.

The weight of the guns is one cause, though indirect, of accidents. The rivet set, which is the actual hammer at the point of the gun, is held in place, when the gun leaves the factory, by clips. Since the clips increase the weight of the hammer, it is good riveting practice to knock them off against the nearest column and replace them with a hank of wire. But wire has a way of breaking, and when it breaks there is nothing to keep the rivet set and the pneumatic piston itself from taking the bucker-up or the catcher on the belt and knocking him into the next block.

—"Riveting a Skyscraper"
from *Fortune Magazine*

# OTHER METHODS OF EXPOSITION

## Comparison and Contrast

Because of their fundamental nature, definition and analysis enter into most pieces of exposition. In making any subject clear, one always needs to tell what it is, and one often needs to take it up in some part-by-part order. However, these means are often supplemented by other means. An exposition may develop by *comparison and contrast*. When we compare and contrast two or more items, we shed light on resemblances and differences; and we often come to understand a thing more fully by perceiving what it is like and what it is unlike. It adds to our knowledge to understand in what ways a republic and a democracy compare and differ, or to see what pure and applied mathematics have in common and how they differ. We do not have to be equally interested in both items under comparison; we can compare A and B primarily for the purpose of clarifying B. If we are studying twentieth-century poetry, for example, we will be in a better position to understand contemporary poetic techniques if we examine closely a few nineteenth-century poems. In Moses Coit Tyler's description of the early settlers of New England we can see how comparison and contrast is skillfully used for such a purpose.

Tyler begins by dividing all Englishmen of the first half of the seventeenth century into two broad classes: the disciples of things as they are and the disciples of things as they ought to be. Then he subdivides each of these classes into two groups or subclasses according to whether their motives were noble or base. There were, in the first broad class, those who opposed change because they believed it would do more harm than good. But there were also those who resisted it out of "torpor," "frivolity," "cowardice," and other ignoble tendencies. Notice that Tyler has here taken up the respectable group first, the mean or contemptible one second.

But when he turns to the second broad class, he reverses this order. Here he begins with the people who are impelled by bad motives—the "crackbrained," "the shallow," and those who hoped to profit personally from the overthrow of an order. Having dismissed these with appropriate descriptions, the author can now turn to what he is primarily interested in, the character of the Puritan settlers of New England, or the nobly inspired advocates of things as they ought to be. We can see them more clearly because they have been contrasted with their contemporaries. By reserving his real subject until last, Tyler gives it the emphasis natural to a final position and also leaves himself free to deal with it at length.

> The personal traits of the original New-Englanders were in many ways remarkable. To know these people we need to know the people from whom they came. The English race has been described as one having practical sagacity rather than ideas; as being weighted by grossness of fibre, sluggishness, animal instincts, earthly preferences; as caring more for dull precedents than for brilliant intuitions; as making whatever progress it achieves by feeling its way safely step by step, rather than by projecting its way boldly from the beginning with the easy infallibility of abstract reasoners. There is some truth in this description; but it is far from being the whole truth. Especially far is it from being the whole truth if applied to the English people as they were in the first half of the seventeenth century. At that time, though they were apparently divided into many classes, they were really divided into only two:—first, the disciples of things as they are; second, the disciples of things as they ought to be. Without

doubt, in the first of these two classes were included vast numbers of thoughtful and noble natures, who with intelligent deliberation accepted things as established notwithstanding their faults, rather than encounter the frightful risk of having all things unsettled, and of making them worse in the very attempt to make them better; but in this class, likewise, were included the still larger number of those whose natures were neither noble nor thoughtful, and whose conservatism was only the expression of their intellectual torpor, their frivolity, their sensualism, their narrowness, or their cowardice. As to the second class, it certainly included many base persons also, many crackbrained and shallow persons, multitudes who shouted and wrangled for change, impelled to it by all sorts of contemptible motives,—aimless discontent, curiosity, lust, lawlessness, folly, cruelty, ambition, hope of pillage amid the wreck of other people's possessions. Nevertheless in this class, if anywhere, were to be found those men, whether many or few, in whom at that time centred for the English-speaking race the possibility of any further progress in human society; the men who not only dared to have ideas, but dared to put them together and to face the logical results of them; who regarded their own souls, and truth, more than they did gold, or respectability, or bodily comfort, or life; who had a high and stout confidence that as God in wisdom had made the world, so man by increasing in wisdom might improve his own condition in the world; and who proposed then and there, if possible, to bring all things in religion and in politics to some genuine test, in which nothing foolish should be retained because it was old, and nothing wise rejected because it was new. At no other time, probably, has there been in England a greater activity of brain directed toward researches into the very roots of things, than there was during that time; and never in England has the class of persons just described been larger in numbers, wider in the range of its individual peculiarities, more heterogeneous, more resolute, or more hopeful.

It was principally out of this second class, this vast, loosely connected, and deeply excited class of Englishmen in the seventeenth century—the Englishmen who were not sluggish, were not living for physical comfort, were not ruled by animal instincts, were not tied to precedents, were not afraid of ideas—that the twenty-one thousand people came who between 1620 and 1640 populated New England. Primarily, then, these first New-Englanders were thinkers in some fashion; they assumed the right to think, the utility of thinking, and the duty of standing by the fair conclusions of their thinking, even at very considerable cost. Of course among them were representatives of all degrees of intellectual radicalism, from the wealthy, reputable, and moderate non-conformists of Massachusetts Bay, down to the lowly and discreet separatists of Plymouth, and still further down to that inspired concourse of crotchety and pure-hearted enthusiasts, the Anabaptists, Antinomians, Quakers, Ranters, and Seekers, who found their first earthly paradise in Rhode Island. But the one grand distinction between the English colonists in New England and nearly all other English colonists in America was this, that while the latter came here chiefly for some material benefit, the former came chiefly for an ideal benefit. In its inception New England was not an agricultural community, nor a manufacturing community, nor a trading community: it was a thinking community; an arena and mart for ideas; its characteristic organ being not the hand, nor the heart, nor the pocket, but the brain.

—Moses Coit Tyler, *A History of American Literature,*
*1607–1765* (1878)

## Illustration and Example

*Illustration* and *example* can forward a general exposition much as they do a definition. By bringing in real or hypothetical instances, a writer enables his reader to visualize facts and their relationships better than many words of abstract statement might do. Effective writers often make use of the technique of following up a generalization by citing one or more illustrative particulars. Thus, if we have made a general statement about the study habits of college seniors, we would do well to offer several representative examples.

It is difficult to argue with an illustration or an example. If these are well chosen, they present a kind of self-evidence of what one is talking about. Even hypothetical examples share the same value, for they are constructed on the basis of real cases.

In the paragraph below, C. S. Lewis is explaining the difficulty of defining, or determining, criteria for "bad" literature. He offers a series of brief examples to show how works which have been widely regarded as great achievements have had the very qualities which are supposed to produce "badness." Each example has the effect of torpedoing one of the rules.

> Dr. I. A. Richards first seriously raised the problem of badness in literature. And his singularly honest wrestling with it shows how dark a problem it is. For when we try to define the badness of a work, we usually end by calling it bad on the strength of characteristics which we can find also in good work. Dr. Richards began by hoping he had found the secret of badness in an appeal to stock responses. But Gray's *Elegy* beat him. Here was a good poem which made that appeal throughout. Worse still, its particular goodness depended on doing so. This happens again and again. The novel before you is bad—a transparent compensatory fantasy projected by a poor, plain woman erotically starving. Yes, but so is *Jane Eyre.* Another bad book is amorphous; but so is *Tristram Shandy.* An author betrays shocking indifference to all the great political, social, and intellectual upheavals of his age; like Jane Austen. The solution of the problem is, I suspect, still far away.

—C. S. Lewis, *Studies in Words*

## Cause and Effect Relationships

An exposition may also be developed through examination of *cause and effect* relationships. Again, it is a natural habit of our thinking to understand the nature of a thing by finding out what caused it or by studying its effects. One purpose of exposition is to clarify relationships, and cause and effect relationships are frequently of the first importance. Because exposition is addressed to the understanding, it can make considerable use of this basic means of enlightenment.

In the following selection, the author makes use of comparison and contrast as well as cause and effect analysis for the purpose of explaining the economic philosophy of Alexander Hamilton. In order to do this, Mitchell compares Hamilton with his arch rival Thomas Jefferson, and he relates the viewpoints of both men to their backgrounds. Mitchell then is in an excellent position to examine Hamilton's economic policies.

While more words have been spoken and written on this [question of strict or loose interpretation] than on any other constitutional theme, the cabinet opinions offered to President Washington by Jefferson and by Hamilton may stand for the remainder. The two are poles apart. Jefferson averred that "To take a single step beyond the boundaries . . . specially drawn around the powers of Congress, is to take possession of a boundless field of power, no longer susceptible of any definition. . . . Certainly no such universal power was meant to be given to them. It was intended to lace them up straightly within the enumerated powers. . . ." On the other hand, it appeared to Hamilton "that this *general principle* is *inherent* in the very definition of government, and *essential* to every step of the progress to be made by that of the United States; namely, that every power vested in a government, is, in its nature, SOVEREIGN, and includes . . . a right to employ all the means requisite, and fairly applicable, to the attainment of the *ends* of such power, and which are not precluded by restrictions and exceptions specified in the constitution, or not immoral, or not contrary to the essential ends of political society."

Whence came this contradiction of views? It did not descend from difference in learning, though Jefferson's knowledge of political philosophy, from classical times, was superior to Hamilton's. The economic historian may be allowed to fix it in the contrasting experience of these statesmen. Jefferson grew up on an agrarian frontier, in a locality yet visited by Indians—tame ones, to be sure, but with the smack of the farther wilderness about them. His school and college mates were sons of farmers. In France he enjoyed the friendship of physiocrats who found all true wealth springing from land, and who opposed to the meddling of mercantilists the free law of nature. His beloved home on a mountaintop was isolated; the fields that spread below formed a domain nearly self-sufficient. In such environment government could be minimal.

Hamilton spent all his life in seaports which lived upon traffic. The means of wealth were man-made, like shops and ships; the instruments by which these operated were social, like credit. His was an environment of people, interdependent, bound by conventional ties. Here public controls and services were essential. Jefferson's background was rural, where dwelt rights. Hamilton's was urban, lively with interests. Hamilton was a man of the industrial revolution which was emerging, not of the agricultural revolution which had preceded. He was bourgeois, not a country gentleman. This mundane explanation of the divergence of leaders may be extended to embrace the sections of America which they represented, the more thickly settled and diversified North, and the sparsely populated South specialized to extracting from the soil.

Given their distinct environments, we may particularize for each man within his setting. Hamilton for more than a decade had "considered that . . . a bank is not a mere matter of private property, but a political machine of the greatest importance to the State." While yet a soldier in the Revolution he had urged on Duane and Morris a more ambitious bank than the one Morris established. The years of disrupted credit and currency had further impressed him with the need for a handmaiden of the Treasury. He rejected the Bank of North America as unequal to the function he envisioned. His report of December, 1790, proposing the Bank of the United States, opened with persuasive pages unobstrusively instructing Congress in the uses of banks in general and particularly for this country. His pains were not misplaced, as the reaction of Jefferson and others demonstrated. Jefferson, much abroad, was unfamiliar at first hand with the vexations in America with which Hamilton contended.

To Hamilton a corporation was a useful expression of governmental authority, the sponsorship of law necessary to enlist private enterprise. Hamilton was a corporate man. To Jefferson a corporation was economically repugnant and constitutionally illicit.

—Broadus Mitchell, *Heritage from Hamilton*

## EXERCISES

**Exercise A**  *Write a comparison and contrast theme on one of the following:*

Two political parties
Two or more ideologies
Two cities or states
Two historical figures (presidents, generals, religious leaders, etc.)
Two professions or skills
My view of life and my grandfather's
My reaction to college and my roommate's
My religious beliefs and my friend's

**Exercise B**  *Write a theme in which you make use of cause and effect analysis.*

Why this course (or another course) is difficult for me
Why I am superstitious
Why the United States became involved in Vietnam
Why people don't do enough reading
Why Goldwater was defeated
Why we lost the football (baseball, hockey, etc.) game

**Exercise C**  *Write a theme in which you make extensive use of illustration.*

College teachers
Good citizenship
Books I like to read
Movies I enjoy
Television commercials
What my parents taught me
Upperclassmen
Courage
Courtesy

**Exercise D**    *Analyze the methods of exposition used in the following selection.*

Because I have long been interested in jazz—its history, its implications, its present developments—I also listen to some extent to popular songs, which are, of course, far from being the same thing. My present subject is an attempt to examine, from a semantic point of view, the words of popular songs and jazz songs in order to discover their underlying assumptions, orientations, and implied attitudes.

First, let me clarify the distinction between popular songs and jazz. In "true" jazz, as the jazz connoisseur understands the term, the basic interest in the part of both musician and listener is in the music as music. Originality and inventiveness in improvisation are highly prized, as are the qualities of instrumentation and of rhythm. Popular music, on the other hand, stands in about the same relationship to jazz as the so-called "semi-classics" stand in relation to Bach, Beethoven, and Brahms. Just as the musical ideas of the classics are diluted, often to a point of insanity, in the "semi-classics," so are the ideas of jazz (and of semi-classics) diluted in popular music—diluted, sweetened, sentimentalized, and trivialized.

Now the contrast between the musical sincerity of jazz and the musical slop of much of popular music is interestingly paralleled in the contrast between the literary sincerity of the words of blues songs (and the blues are the basic source of jazz inspiration) and the literary slop in the majority of popular songs. The words of true jazz songs, especially the Negro blues, tend to be unsentimental and realistic in their statements about life. (In saying "Negro blues," I should add that most of these are written by Negroes, but some have been written by whites under Negro inspiration.) The words of popular songs, on the other hand, largely (but not altogether) the product of white song-writers for predominantly white audiences, tend towards wishful thinking, dreamy and ineffectual nostalgia, unrealistic fantasy, self-pity, and sentimental clichés masquerading as emotion.

We have been taught—and rightly—to be more than cautious about making racial distinctions. Hence let me hasten to explain that the differences between (predominantly Negro) blues and (predominantly white) popular songs can, in my opinion, be satisfactorily accounted for without "racial" explanations. The blues arise from the experiences of a largely agricultural and working-class Negro minority with a social and cultural history different from that of the white majority. Furthermore, the blues—a folk music which underwent urbanization (in New Orleans, Chicago, New York, Memphis, Kansas City, and elsewhere)—developed in an economic or market situation different from that in which popular songs, aimed at mass markets through mass entertainment media, developed. With these cultural and economic conditions in mind, let me restate the thesis of this paper, using this time the terminology of general semantics: The blues tend to be *extensionally* oriented, while popular songs tend to exhibit grave, even pathological *intensional* orientations.

Perhaps I can make my thesis come to life by discussing a specific area of emotion about which songs are written, namely, love in the light of what Wendell Johnson calls the IFD disease—the triple-threat semantic disorder of Idealization (the making of impossible and ideal demands upon life), which leads to Frustration (as the result of the demands not being met), which in turn leads to Demoralization (or Disorganization, or Despair). What Johnson says in *People in Quandaries* is repeatedly illustrated in the attitudes toward love expressed in popular songs.

First, in looking forward to love, there is an enormous amount of unrealistic idealization—the creation in one's mind, as the object of love's search, of a dream girl (or dream boy) the fleshly counterpart of which never existed on earth:

Will I ever find the girl in my mind,
The girl who is my ideal?

Every night I dream a little dream,
And of course Prince Charming is the theme,
The he for me . . .

Next, of course, one meets a not-altogether-unattractive person of the other sex, and the psychological process called *projection* begins, in which one attributes to a real individual the sum-total of the imaginary perfections one has dreamed about:

I took one look at you,
That's all I meant to do,
And then my heart stood still . . .

You were meant for me, and I was meant for you.
Nature fashioned you and when she was done,
You were all the sweet things rolled up in one . . .
I confess, the angels must have sent you,
And they meant you just for me.

Wendell Johnson has commented frequently on what he calls a prevalent belief in magic. Some of his clients in his speech clinic at the University of Iowa, he says, will do no drills, perform no exercises, read no books, carry out no recommendations; they simply seem to expect that now that they have come to THE right speech clinic their stuttering will somehow magically go away. The essence of magic is the belief that you don't have to do anything—the right magic makes all effort unnecessary.

Love is depicted in most popular songs as just this kind of magic. There is rarely an indication in the accounts of love-euphoria commonly to be found in these songs that, having found the dream-girl or dream-man, one's problems are just beginning.

—S. I. Hayakawa, "Popular Songs vs. the Facts of Life"

## EXPOSITORY DESCRIPTION

Between exposition and description proper there is a kind of middle ground, which is sometimes called expository or technical description. Like other expository writing, it is addressed to the understanding. Its purpose is to make us perceive the nature of an object. It is often concerned with spatial features and time sequences, but these are presented as matters of fact which we must know in order to grasp the nature of the object being described. The presentation is analytical, and there is no attempt to appeal to the feelings.

Expository description has many uses in science and business. The descriptions of organisms, of mechanisms, and of various kinds of systems all have an expository end in view. When exposition is the dominant purpose, it is right to distinguish this kind of writing from the description which has an esthetic purpose.

The latter differs from expository description in being more subjective and more literary. It does not merely point out and list; it also evokes the special character of its object, and sometimes it seeks to leave a single dominant impression. Technical description does a literal job of setting down what is there in terms whose reference can be checked or verified; literary description, while using the factual nature of the object as a starting point, moves quite freely into the realm of imagination and feeling. The essential distinction is one of purpose, because an object can be described by either method, the first being directed to the understanding and the second largely to the emotional part of our nature. A technical description of a modern automobile engine would be an exceedingly dry and tedious affair to most of us, calling for concentrated attention to the parts and their relationships. But a description of the same engine in a full-page advertisement in a leading magazine generally includes suggestive and evaluative terms and may even remind one of the emotional effect of poetry.

To observe this difference, consider the three descriptions of oceans which follow. The first, taken from an encyclopedia, has the limited purpose of conveying information. Every fact is definite, and every statement is capable of scientific ascertainment. The other two, which are taken from literary works, present little which is factual in this sense; everything is used to create a feeling about the subject. The purpose is to develop an attitude in the reader.

> ATLANTIC OCEAN, the body of water lying between the eastern coasts of the Americas and the western coasts of Europe and Africa, and

extending from the Arctic Basin to the Great Southern Ocean. Its greatest breadth, attained in lat. 25° N., is 4500 miles; but between Cape S. Roque in Brazil and Cape Palmas its breadth is only 1600 miles. Its superficial extent, not including the inland seas, is 23,215,000 square miles or 10,588,000 square miles in the north Atlantic Ocean and 12,267,000 in the south Atlantic. The mean depth of the north Atlantic is 2,047 fathoms; of the south Atlantic 2,067 fathoms.

—*Encyclopedia Americana*

There is one knows not what sweet mystery about this sea, whose gently awful stirrings seem to speak of some hidden soul beneath; like those fabled undulations of the Ephesian sod over the buried evangelist, St. John. And meet it is, that over these sea-pastures, wide-rolling, watery prairies and Potters' Fields of all four continents, the waves should rise and fall, and ebb and flow unceasingly; for here, millions of mixed shades, drowned dreams, somnambulisms, reveries; all that we call lives and souls, lie dreaming, dreaming, still; tossing like slumberers in their beds; the ever-rolling waves made so by their restlessness.

To any meditative Magian rover, this serene Pacific once beheld, must ever after be the sea of his adoption. It rolls the midmost waters of the world, the Indian Ocean and the Atlantic being but its arms. The same waves wash the new-built moles of the California towns, but yesterday planted by the recentest race of men, and lave the faded but still gorgeous skirts of Asiatic lands, older than Abraham; while all between float milky-ways of coral isles, and low-lying, endless, unknown Archipelagoes, and impenetrable Japans. Thus this mysterious, divine Pacific zones the world's whole bulk about; makes all coasts one bay to it; seems the tide-beating heart of earth. Lifted by those eternal swells, you needs must own the seductive god, bowing your head to Pan.

—Herman Melville, *Moby Dick*

For all that has been said of the love that certain natures (on shore) have professed to feel for it, for all the celebrations it has been the object of in prose and song, the sea has never been friendly to man. At most it has been the accomplice of human restlessness, and playing the part of dangerous abettor of world-wide ambitions. Faithful to no race after the fashion of the kindly earth, receiving no impress from valor and toil and self-sacrifice, recognizing no finality of dominion, the sea has never adopted the cause of its masters like those lands where the victorious nations of mankind have taken root, rocking their cradles and setting up their gravestones. He—man or people—who, putting his trust in the friendship of the sea, neglects the strength and cunning of his right hand, is a fool! As if it were too great, too mighty for common virtues, the ocean has no compassion, no faith, no law, no memory. Its fickleness is to be held true to men's purposes only by an undaunted resolution, and by a sleepless, armed, jealous vigilance, in which, perhaps, there has always been more hate than love. *Odi et amo* may well be the confession of those who consciously or blindly have surrendered their existence to the fascination of the sea. All the tempestuous passions of mankind's young days, the love of loot and the love of glory, the love of adventure and the love of danger, with the great love of the unknown and vast dreams of dominion and power, have passed like images reflected from a mirror, leaving no record upon the face of the mysterious sea. Impenetrable and heartless, the sea has given nothing of itself to the suitors for its precarious favors. Unlike the earth, it cannot be subjugated at any cost of patience and toil. For all its fascination that has lured so many to a violent death, its immensity has never been loved as the mountains, the plains, the desert itself have been loved. Indeed, I suspect that, leaving aside the protestations and tributes of writers who, one is safe in saying, care for little else in the world than the rhythm of their lines and the cadence of their phrase, the love of the sea, to which so many men and nations confess so readily, is a complex sentiment wherein pride enters for much, necessity for not a little, and the love of ships—the untiring servants of our hopes and self-esteem —for the best and most genuine part.

—Joseph Conrad, *The Mirror of the Sea*

We can see from this comparison that expository or technical or scientific description is bound to certain methods which are determined by its end. It has to be objective, which is a way of saying that it must respect the object as it is. It is usually complete because it has the duty of conveying information. It is generally systematic or schematic because its details must communicate an order. Lastly, it is abstract because it tends toward the general and away from the concrete and specific. Its object is not to convey the unique aspects of what is described, even though the object is a particular one. Technical description will render it in such a way that its features are made commensurable with those of other objects, or expressible in general terms. A house, presented with all its details, might impress us as having a unique or individual appeal; but a technical description of a house would be concerned only with those matters of design, size, and materials which make it comparable—in the abstract—with all other houses.

A convenient way to see the different principles on which technical and literary description operate is to think of the distinction between the anatomy and the physiognomy of a human face. The anatomy is concerned with those features found in all faces, and it makes a standard scientific report on frontal lobe, cheekbones, nose, oral cavity, and so on. This is a technical description of a human face. But physiognomy begins where anatomy leaves off, for it is concerned with those configurations which are peculiar to the face being studied. It concentrates upon the individuality of the structure in such a way as to leave a particular impression of the person being described. Consequently its attention is focused upon the special modifications of those features which anatomy lists, since these modifications are what give any person his individual cast of countenance. This then is the type of description which tries to leave a unique impression by selecting whatever departs from the general or the normal. In a broad way, all literary description, regardless of its object, is of a physiognomy; and it therefore contrasts with scientific description, which sticks to the general and the systematic.

Technical or scientific description, although it often looks simple when it is done well, is actually one of the hardest tests of a writer. It calls especially for two things which most of us are prone to shun: an attentive study of what is actually there, and a choice of words which will convey this without distracting associations. Here a comparison with analysis is possible. We saw that a successful analysis depends in part upon a writer's suppression of his own attitude or feeling. Likewise in the writing of a technical or scientific description, much depends upon our ability to see the object just as it exists and to express it in a literal vocabulary. The aim of the technical description is to adhere as closely as possible to the outline of the object being described, after planning some order of presentation. A close examination, a clear organization of treatment, and a vocabulary chosen for the adaptation of its terms to the object are the necessary means to the writing of technical or scientific description.

The most significant aspect of technical description is that little if anything of the qualitative is given. Qualities are connected with our feelings about things, and science is not concerned with feelings. Therefore language which might have the effect of repelling or attracting the reader does not suit the strict purpose of technical description. A scientific description of primitive man, for example, should not make us either recoil with aversion from this subhuman type or admire his supposed virtues; its purpose is to depict as carefully as possible the appearance and habits of a prehistoric member of the human race. A technical description of a machine gun is not designed to fill us with remorse over the number of lives it has taken or to move us to admiration for the triumphs of technology which have made its invention possible. Both of these would be issues quite apart from the problem of a business-like technical description. Technical or scientific description is a description of limited objectives. The demands within those objectives will often require great concentration and ingenuity on the part of the writer. But he has taken the first step when he has made the necessary exclusion of those qualities which belong to literary or artistic description, where it is proper to deal in impressions and to address oneself to the emotions.

How difficult it is to explain adequately even a simple object in words may be discovered by taking something like a penknife or a corkscrew and imagining that you have to describe its form and function to someone who has never heard of it. You will probably find that you must acquire a much more definite knowledge of it through close observation. Moreover, putting this knowledge into simple and precise words will strain your vocabulary to the limit. But the experience is worthwhile, for there will always be a need for presenting such subjects in language.

**Exercise:**    *Write an expository description of 300–600 words of one of the following:*

1. A pencil sharpener
2. A cigarette lighter
3. A traffic light
4. A carpenter's plane
5. The heating system of a house
6. The gymnasium on your campus
7. A transistor
8. An adding machine
9. A washing machine
10. A power mower
11. A dump truck
12. A tennis court
13. A vacuum sweeper
14. A Diesel engine
15. An auditorium

# Chapter Three

# Description

The aim of description is to make us see with a certain fullness of detail which produces some impression on our feelings. It focuses upon surfaces and appearances. It gives us a sense of the color, life, and variousness of its subject, even when that happens to be a fairly simple thing. Description of this kind is often thought of in connection with running brooks, and woodland flowers; and while these are certainly susceptible of realistic and moving description, so are slums, battlefields, and unattractive human beings. The essential technique will remain the same, whether the purpose is to fill us with pleasure and reverence or with horror and disgust. Certain details will be selected, certain words will be chosen, and a certain order will be followed so that the writer will be saying in effect: this is the way it seemed to me and this is the way it would seem to you. The seeming of the object is indeed the matter of this kind of writing, and that is why we call description an art. Art is concerned with the way in which things can appear to our developed faculties of perception and evaluation; and while it does not ignore the factual aspects, it uses them for its own purposes.

## POINT OF VIEW

Point of view is one of the means of organizing a description. By establishing a perspective, point of view gives the writer a standard for selection and control. He will not wish, in any case, to report everything; but his point of view will center the focus upon what he can report from a certain position. He presents not a miscellany of facts, but a series of visual and other details as they might appear to an observer in his place. This conforms, of course, with our natural experience in seeing and in collecting our impressions. By limiting his account to what can be seen from where he is standing, the writer gives his description, in addition to an organization, a naturalness and a credibility.

The point of view should always be clearly indicated, whether directly or indirectly. Consider the following passage, in which Thomas Wolfe describes a trucking warehouse in a great city.

> Out of his front windows George could see nothing except the somber bulk of the warehouse across the street. It was an old building, with a bleak and ugly front of rusty, indurated brown and a harsh webbing of fire escapes, and across the whole width of the facade stretched a battered wooden sign on which, in faded letters, one could make out the name—"The Security Distributing Corp." George did not know what a distributing corporation was, but every day since he had come into this street to live, enormous motor vans had driven up before this dingy building and had backed snugly against the worn plankings of the loading platform, which ended with a sharp, sheared emptiness four feet above the sidewalk. The drivers and their helpers would leap from their seats, and instantly the quiet depths of the old building would burst into a furious energy of work, and the air would be filled with harsh cries:
>
> "Back it up, deh! Back it up! Cuh-*mahn!* Cuh-*mahn!* Givvus a hand, youse guys! Hey-y! *You!*"
>
> They looked at one another with hard faces of smiling derision, quietly saying "Jesus!" out of the corners of their mouths. Surly, they stood upon their rights, defending truculently the narrow frontier of their duty:
>
> "Wadda *I* care where it goes! Dat's *yoeh* lookout! Wat t'hell's it got to do *wit* me?"
>
> They worked with speed and power and splendid aptness, furiously, unamiably, with high, exacerbated voices, spurred and goaded by their harsh unrest.
>
> —Thomas Wolfe, *You Can't Go Home Again*

The opening phrase of this description definitely establishes the point of view. The details then follow a clear progression: first the "somber bulk" of the warehouse, then the "bleak and ugly front" and the "webbing of fire escapes" on to the sign "The Security Distributing Corp." Finally it drops down to the loading platform, with its "sharp, sheared emptiness." Next, attention is directed to the activity that goes on: drivers and helpers backing up their trucks and beginning the work of loading and unloading with loud cries and jeers. This is the *pattern* "George Webber" sees as he looks down from his front windows.

With a different kind of situation it may be most useful to follow a moving point of view. Then one sees through the eyes of an observer who is making a tour of what is to be described. By this method Washington Irving gave a vivid description of the home of Baltus Van Tassell as it appeared to Ichabod Crane in "The Legend of Sleepy Hollow."

It was one of those spacious farmhouses, with high-ridged but lowly-sloping roofs, built in the style handed down from the first Dutch settlers; the low projecting eaves forming a piazza along the front, capable of being closed up in bad weather. Under this were hung flails, harness, various utensils of husbandry, and nets for fishing in the neighboring river. Benches were built along the sides for summer use; and a great spinning-wheel at one end and a churn at the other, showed the various uses to which this important porch might be devoted. From this piazza the wondering Ichabod entered the hall, the center of the mansion and place of usual residence. Here rows of resplendent pewter, ranged on a long dresser, dazzled his eyes. In one corner stood a huge bag of wool ready to be spun; in another, a quantity of linsey-woolsey just from the loom; ears of Indian corn, and strings of dried apples and peaches, hung in gay festoons along the wall, mingled with the gaud of red peppers; and a door left ajar gave him a peek into the best parlor, where the claw-footed chairs and dark mahogany tables shone like mirrors; andirons, with their accompanying shovel and tongs, glistened from their covert of asparagus tops; mock oranges and conch-shells decorated with mantelpiece; strings of various colored birds' eggs were suspended above it; a great ostrich egg was hung from the center of the room, and a corner cupboard, knowingly left open, displayed immense treasures of old silver and well-mended china.

—Washington Irving, "The Legend of Sleepy Hollow"

Here the point of view shifts with the movement of Ichabod Crane. First he sees the house from some distance. Next he takes a careful look at the piazza, or front porch. Then he enters the central hall and finally goes far enough to get "a peek into the best parlor." The reader understands that he is moving with Ichabod and will see what the latter sees in his progress toward and into the house.

Virginia Woolf's "The Death of the Moth," a piece of description more tinctured with the subjective, derives much of its power from its consistent point of view.

In this fine sketch the moth becomes for the author a representative part of animated nature. Her attention is fixed upon it in the midst of watching various signs of nature's activity outside her window. What inspires that also inspires the moth; it is a communicant of the energy of the world. All of this leads to reflection upon the forms that life can take. Further watching leads, however, to an awareness that not all is well with the moth. Although alive, it appears to be stricken; it struggles and becomes quiet; and this action is oddly matched by a quiescence of the activity outside the window. It now appears that the moth is dying, and the triumph of so great a power over so insignificant a victim fills the author with wonderment. The moth in its final posture of death is made to testify to a universal feeling about death.

The descriptions of the movements of the moth, while precise in themselves, serve as starting points for free association upon the great themes of life and death. Outward description is thus made instrumental to inner feelings and to reflection.

Moths that fly by day are not properly to be called moths; they do not excite that pleasant sense of dark autumn nights and ivy-blossom which the commonest yellow-underwing asleep in the shadow of the curtain never fails to rouse in us. They are hybrid creatures, neither gay like butterflies nor sombre like their own species. Nevertheless the present specimen, with his narrow hay-coloured wings, fringed with a tassel of the same colour, seemed to be content with life. It was a pleasant morning, mid-September, mild, benignant, yet with a keener breath than that of the summer months. The plough was already scoring the field opposite the window, and where the share had been, the earth was pressed flat and gleamed with moisture. Such vigour came rolling in from the fields and down beyond that it was difficult to keep the eyes strictly turned upon the book. The rooks too were keeping one of their annual festivities; soaring round the tree tops until it looked as if a vast net with thousands of black knots in it had been cast up into the air; which, after a few moments sank slowly down upon the trees until every twig seemed to have a knot at the end of it. Then, suddenly, the net would be thrown into the air again in a wider circle this time, with the utmost clamour and vociferation, as though to be thrown into the air and settle slowly down upon the tree tops were a tremendously exciting experience.

The same energy which inspired the rooks, the ploughmen, the horses, and even, it seemed, the lean bare-backed downs, sent the moth fluttering from side to side of his square of the window-pane. One could not help watching him. One was, indeed, conscious of a queer feeling of pity for him. The possibilities of pleasure seemed that morning so enormous and so various that to have only a moth's part in life, and a day moth's at that, appeared a hard fate, and his zest in enjoying his meagre opportunities to the full, pathetic. He flew vigorously to one corner of his compartment, and, after waiting there a second, flew across to the other. What remained for him but to fly to a third corner and then to a fourth? That was all he could do, in spite of the size of the downs, the width of the sky, the far-off smoke of houses, and the romantic voice, now and then, of a steamer out at sea. What he could do he did. Watching him, it seemed as if a fibre, very thin but pure, of the enormous energy of the world had been thrust into his frail and diminutive body. As often as he crossed the pane, I could fancy that a thread of vital light became visible. He was little or nothing but life.

Yet, because he was so small, and so simple a form of the energy that was rolling in at the open window and driving its way through so many narrow and intricate corridors in my own brain and in those of other human beings, there was something marvellous as well as pathetic about him. It was as if someone had taken a tiny bead of pure life and decking it as lightly as possible with down and feathers, had set it dancing and zigzagging to show us the true nature of life. Thus displayed one could not get over the strangeness of it. One is apt to forget all about life, seeing it humped and bossed and garnished and cumbered so that it has to move with the greatest circumspection and dignity. Again, the thought of all that life might have been had he been born in any other shape caused one to view his simple activities with a kind of pity.

After a time, tired by his dancing apparently, he settled on the window ledge in the sun, and, the queer spectacle being at an end, I forgot about him. Then, looking up, my eye was caught by him. He was trying to resume his dancing, but seemed either so stiff or so awkward that he could only flutter to the bottom of the windowpane; and when he tried to fly across it he failed. Being intent on other matters I watched these futile attempts for a time without thinking, unconsciously waiting for him to resume his flight, as one waits for a machine, that has stopped momentarily, to start again without considering the reason for its failure. After perhaps a seventh attempt he slipped from the wooden ledge and fell, fluttering his wings, on to his back on the window sill. The helplessness of his attitude roused me. It flashed upon me that he was in difficulties; he could no longer raise himself; his legs struggled vainly. But, as I stretched out a pencil, meaning to help him to right himself, it came over me that the failure and awkwardness were the approach of death. I laid the pencil down again.

The legs agitated themselves once more. I looked as if for the enemy against which he struggled. I looked out of doors. What had happened there? Presumably it was midday, and work in the fields had stopped. Stillness and quiet had replaced the previous animation. The birds had taken themselves off to feed in the brooks. The horses stood still. Yet the power was there all the same, massed outside indifferent, impersonal, not attending to anything in particular. Somehow it was opposed to the little hay-coloured moth. It was useless to try to do anything. One could only watch the extraordinary efforts made by those tiny legs against an oncoming doom which could, had it chosen, have submerged an entire city, not merely a city, but masses of human beings; nothing, I knew had any chance against death. Nevertheless after a pause of exhaustion the legs fluttered again. It was superb this last protest, and so frantic that he succeeded at last in righting himself. One's sympathies, of course, were all on the side of life. Also, when there was nobody to care or to know, this gigantic effort on the part of an insignificant little moth, against a power of such magnitude, to retain what no one else valued or desired to keep, moved one strangely. Again, somehow, one saw life, a pure bead. I lifted the pencil again, useless though I knew it to be. But even as I did so, the unmistakable tokens of death showed themselves. The body relaxed, and instantly grew stiff. The struggle was over. The insignificant little creature now knew death. As I looked at the dead moth, this minute wayside triumph of so great a force over so mean an antagonist filled me with wonder. Just as life had been strange a few minutes before, so death was now as strange. The moth having righted himself now lay most decently and uncomplainingly composed. O yes, he seemed to say, death is stronger than I am.

—Virginia Woolf, "The Death of the Moth,"
from *The Death of the Moth and Other Essays*

## SCALE

Closely related to the point of view is the *scale* upon which a writer of description presents his detail. Clearly it would be absurd to include in a description detail too small to be perceived from the point of view which has been taken. A house at a distance of a mile will appear only as an outline and some surfaces; and one does not jump from these to the number of the front steps and the shape of the door posts as though both orders of details were visible at the same time. One simply obeys the limits imposed by the point of observation. Thus from a great distance one reports the larger aspects, and these form a standard by which one decides what can go into the description. Naturally the same principles hold for details seen at a near distance. In most descriptions, the scale of details must be consistent; that is to say, the writer should set a scale and continue throughout with details of roughly the same size as those with which he began.

It is not impossible, however, to change one's scale in the course of a description if this is done according to plan and with due notice to the reader. But here again a certain principle of consistency must be observed, for one will go by graduated steps from the larger to the smaller, or from the smaller to the larger. There must be no jumping from large scale to small scale, such as would confuse the reader, but a progressive change of scale which varies according to the nearness' of the object. The following description by Mark Twain of an approaching Mississippi River steamboat has been justly admired for its handling of details in this fashion.

Assembled there, the people fasten their eyes upon the coming boat as upon a wonder they are seeing for the first time. And the boat *is* a rather handsome sight, too. She is long and sharp and trim and pretty; she has two tall, fancy-topped chimneys, with a gilded device of some kind swung between them; a fanciful pilot-house, all glass and "gingerbread," perched on top of the "texas" deck behind them; the paddle-boxes are gorgeous with a picture or with gilded rays above the boat's name: the boiler deck, the hurricane deck, and the texas deck are fenced and ornamented with clean white railings; there is a flag gallantly flying from the jack-staff; the furnace doors are open and the fires glaring bravely; the upper decks are black with passengers; the captain stands by the big bell, calm, imposing, the envy of all; great volumes of the blackest smoke are rolling and tumbling out of the chimneys—a husbanded grandeur created with a bit of pitch pine just before arriving at a town; the crew are grouped on the forecastle; the broad stage is run far out over the port bow, and an envied deck-hand stands picturesquely on the end of it with a coil of rope in his hand; the pent steam is screaming through the gauge-cocks; the captain lifts his hand, a bell rings, the wheels stop; then they turn back, churning the water foam, and the steamer is at rest. Then such a scramble as there is to get aboard, and to get ashore, and to take in freight and to discharge freight, all at one and the same time; and such a yelling and cursing as the mates facilitate it all with! Ten minutes later the steamer is under way again, with no flag on the jackstaff and no black smoke issuing from the chimneys. After ten more minutes the town is dead again, and the town drunkard asleep by the skids once more.

—Samuel L. Clemens, *Life on the Mississippi*

In summary, scale must always be taken into account in the writing of description, but one has a choice between the single scale with the fixed point of view and the constantly changing scale if the observer or the object is shifting position.

Exercise: *Write an imaginative description of one of the following sub- jects. Follow some order in the presentation of your details and avoid confusing the reader with abrupt changes of scale. Remember that this kind of description shows the object as it appears from some position which has been made clear.*

1. A busy intersection
2. A factory district of your town (or of any town)
3. The stadium on a Saturday afternoon
4. A typical corner drugstore
5. The most pretentious house in town
6. The family doctor
7. A streamlined passenger train
8. A lakeside resort
9. The view from an observation tower
10. An army post

## DOMINANT IMPRESSION

Sometimes a writer will desire to describe a subject in such a way that a single aspect or characteristic will dominate the impression which the description gives. There is an important amount of psychological truth in descriptions of this kind because we tend to recall a person or a thing through some outstanding quality that distinguishes it. Whenever we think of the subject, we tend to think of it through the medium of this special impression it has made. Accordingly, one might see New York City under the dominant aspect of crowds and congestion, or an old friend through some amiable mannerism, or the family car through some pecu- liarity which use has caused it to develop. In order to leave this dominant impression in a description, the writer makes the details center around this special attribute, and they combine to bring out the salient feature or the special "felt" quality of the object. To recognize elements which will combine in this way for a single effect naturally requires some sensitivity and imagination. The elements will be found to some extent by a perceptive study of the object itself, but the selection and presentation of them must depend upon our feeling or mental state—must express our reaction to the character of the thing described.

The need to produce a dominant impression through description is common to a wide range of writing. Such description will be found in studies of characters and scenes in serious novels; it will be found also in such "practical" pieces of writing as advertisements and radio scripts.

Study the passage below, in which F. Scott Fitzgerald describes in a few sentences a young woman of the jazz age, floating along on the surface of its materialism and aimlessness.

> For Daisy was young, and her artificial world was redolent of orchids and pleasant, cheerful snobbery and orchestras which set the rhythm of the year, summing up the sadness and suggestiveness of life in new tunes. All night the saxophones wailed the hopeless comment of the "Beale Street Blues," while a hundred pairs of golden and silver slippers shuffled the shining dust. At the gray tea hour there were always rooms that throbbed incessantly with this low, sweet fever, while fresh faces drifted here and there like rose petals blown by the sad horns around the floor.
>
> Through this twilight universe Daisy began to move again with the season; suddenly she was again keeping half a dozen dates a day with half a dozen men, and drowsing asleep at dawn with the beads and chiffon of an evening dress tangled among the dying orchids on the floor beside her bed. And all the time something within her was crying for a decision. She wanted her life shaped now, immediately—and the decision must be made by some force—of love, of money, of unquestionable practicality—that was close at hand.
>
> —F. Scott Fitzgerald, *The Great Gatsby*

**Exercise:**   *Select one of the following and write a description which aims at a single dominant effect.*

1. A dull Sunday afternoon
2. Autumn woods
3. A Christmas festival
4. A village character
5. A television addict

6. A college dance
7. A supersalesman
8. A lunch wagon
9. A sale in a bargain basement
10. A country fair

## THE LANGUAGE OF DESCRIPTION

We have been stressing the fact that the writer of literary description is adding a dimension not present in scientific or technical description. This dimension enters when the writer begins to visualize for us, or to make the objects vivid. The distinction between an abstract and colorless description and a vivid description of the same object shows itself in some deep-lying differences in the language itself, which will be considered more fully in the chapter on "Diction." Here it is necessary to point out that some words have association with our sensory experience and for this reason call to mind things that are "life-like." Indeed, "vivid" means "living," and one of the first differences that we mark in the material we read is just this one between the thin and lifeless, and the full-blooded and real.

For the purposes of writing we must recognize that certain classes of terms are qualitatively of the first kind and certain others of the second. A practical way to distinguish between the two is to ask ourselves if an expression recalls something that we have seen, or touched, or tasted, or smelled, or heard. If the expression recalls any one of these sensations, it belongs to the class which can make objects seem actual and appear with the depth of something that we have experienced. Such expressions as "green," "bitter," or "prickly" will call up sensations which anyone must have felt. Sometimes a single expression will call up a variety of sensations; "blood," for example, is a word which might bring up experiences transmitted through sight, touch, taste, and smell. It is such expressions which give a dimension of reality to imaginative description.

In the opposite group of expressions are those which describe without bringing the memory of a sensation. Such expressions as "just," "impossible," "extensive," "lateral," "prior," and the like belong to this class. Even when we feel that they do arouse some sensation, it is likely to be slight or accidental. They do not carry a burden of necessary sensory association. Writings that we react against as "dry" nearly always have a great proportion of such expressions, which are empty of vivid content. They are not meaningless, but when we think about the meaning of them, we have to use our reason rather than our memory and imagination. Since description of the kind we are discussing now appeals to the senses, it cannot afford a heavy use of such terms. It works through the word of sensory attachment, or through the image-bearing term.

In proportion then as description makes us feel the substance or the living quality of an object, it uses a vocabulary associated with the less intellectual and with the more sensory areas of experience. A certain effort of the intellect is required to call an apple "ellipsoid," because this modifier is at least partly conceptual, but to call an apple "red" or "sweet" involves mainly a recollection of the senses. The same difference is seen between saying "the water is cold" and "the water is 40° F." We call up instantly a remembrance of coldness, but we have to think for a second about what 40° F. signifies. Now, since the purpose of literary description is to create an image of something, we must rely for success upon those terms whose content registers immediately. The successful piece of description creates a kind of photoplay in the mind. Joseph Conrad has expressed this principle for writers in his preface to *The Nigger of the Narcissus:* "All art, therefore, appeals primarily to the senses, and the artistic aim when expressing itself in written words must also make its appeal through the senses, if its highest desire is to reach the secret spring of responsive emotions."

In attempting to make description vivid, however, you are likely to be struck with the difficulty of avoiding overused modifiers. There are many modifiers which have quite obvious sensory connections but which have been employed so many times that their sharpness has been lost. This is especially true when they are modifiers conventionally applied to a familiar range of subjects, as "blue" to the sky, "bright" to the sun, "sleepy" to a small town, and so on. One soon finds that the avoidance of these and the discovery of other modifiers which will be both applicable and fresh is the real task of the writer of description. It requires a continual sorting over of the resources of our vocabulary until we are satisfied that we have something which is usable but not stale. Beyond this, however, there is another step; after we have escaped mere triteness, we have to discover the individuating modifier—the term which, though taken from standard vocabulary, gives the impression of belonging uniquely to the object which it modifies. Often the individuating effect is achieved not through the discovery of single apt terms but rather through the shading of them by qualification and juxtaposition. The writer may thus be using words somewhat as an artist uses paints, to blend with or to offset one another. When successful, this is the highest type of description, inasmuch as it not only makes us see the object, as all good description should do, but also gives us that sense of individuality which is the final convincing attribute of anything that is to be considered "real."

The following passage from Henry James, one of the great masters of this order of description, repays close study.

The little straggling, loosely clustered town lay along the edge of a blue inlet, on the other side of which was a low, wooded shore, with a gleam of white sand where it touched the water. The narrow bay carried the vision outward to a picture that seemed at once bright and dim—a shining, slumbering summer-sea, and a far-off circling line of coast, which, under the August sun, was hazy and delicate. Ransom regarded the place as a town because Doctor Prance had called it one; but it was a town where you smelt the breath of hay in the streets and you might gather black-berries in the principal square. The houses looked at each other across the grass—low, rusty, crooked, distended houses, with dry, cracked faces and the dim eyes of small-paned, stiffly sliding windows. Their little door-yards bristled with rank, old-fashioned flowers, mostly yellow; and on the quarter that sloped back from the sea the fields sloped upward, and the woods in which they presently lost themselves looked down over the roofs.
—Henry James, *The Bostonians*

The subject of the description is a small seacoast resort town, and James succeeds in making it peculiarly credible and real, partly through employment of the less conventional modifier and partly through a crafts-man's use of the more conventional ones. For example, "straggling" and "loosely-clustered" are hardly conventional terms to apply to a town, and consequently they give the impression of being found for this particular one. The phrase "gleam of white sand where it touched the water" is a sharply rendered perception. To call the sea "shining" is no novelty, but this somewhat trite modifier is compensated for by "slumbering summer-sea," in which the compound "summer-sea" gives a definite impression caught and crystallized. One must note too that "August sun" is a particular kind of sun, and the "hazy and delicate" line of coast contains just enough paradox to set us thinking about it if we are reading the passage attentively. Approximately the same can be said for the clauses "where you smelt the breath of hay in the streets" and "you might gather blackberries in the principal square." These tell us that it is a town in name but a town into which the country intrudes quite freely. "Rusty," "crooked," and "distended" are modifiers not often used to describe houses; therefore they possess freshness. The "dry, cracked faces" and the "dim eyes of the small-paned, stiffly sliding windows" are further details which only an observation at once precise and imaginative would see. The dooryards are described for us chiefly through a vivid impression of "old-fashioned flowers, mostly yellow," in which the color in the visual image is the highlighting detail. At the close, the description returns to the scale of the beginning, in which objects are given a somewhat more distant and generalized appearance.

In the following description by Thomas Wolfe we are given a powerfully vivid rendering of a boy's world. The description contains dozens of sensory images—visual, auditory, olfactory, tactile: "the feel of soft tar in the streets"; the feeling when you hold "a baseball in your hands for the first time in the spring"; the sight of "apple blossoms drifting to earth"; "the strong, clean, pungent smell of good tobacco"; "the drone of voices from the classroom." These are images out of the experience of any boy who has walked on hot asphalt streets, played baseball in the spring, and sat in a classroom on the last day of school.

> This street held for him a universe of joy and magic which seemed abundant for a thousand lives. Its dimensions were noble in their space and limitless surprise. Its world of houses, yards, and orchards and its hundred people seemed to him to have the incomparable grandeur of the first place on earth, the impregnable authority of the center of the universe.
>
> In later years, George plainly saw that the world in which he lived had been a little place. All of the dimensions of the street had dwindled horribly. The houses that had seemed so imposing in their opulence and grandeur, the lawns that were so spacious, the backyards and the vistaed orchards that went on in limitless progressions of delight and new discovery that never had an end—all this had shrunken pitifully, incredibly, and now looked close, and mean, and cramped. Yet even then, years later, the street and all its million memories of a buried life awoke for him with the blazing and intolerable vividness of a dream. It was a world which he had known and lived with every atom of his blood and brain and spirit, and every one of its thousand images was rooted into the structure of his life forever, as much a part of him as his inmost thoughts.

At first it was just the feel of the grass and the earth and the ground under your naked feet in May when you were going bare foot for the first time and walking gingerly. It was the cool feel of the sand up through your toes, and the feel of the soft tar in the streets and walking on a wall of concrete blocks, and the feel of cool, damp earth in shaded places. It was the feel of standing on the low edge of a roof or in a barn loft opening or on the second story of a house that was being built and daring another boy to jump; and looking over, waiting, knowing you must jump; and looking down, and waiting, daring, taunting, with a thudding heart, until you jumped.

And then it was the good feel of throwing a small, round, heavy stone through the window of a vacant house when the red and ancient light of evening was blazing on its windows; and it was like feeling a baseball in your hands for the first time in the spring, and its round and solid weight at the end of your arm and the way it shot away like a bullet the first time when you threw it with a feeling of terrific power and speed and it smacked into the odorous, well-oiled pocket of the catcher's mitt. And then it was like prowling round in dark, cool cellars, thinking you would come upon a buried treasure any moment, and finding rows of cobwebbed bottles and the rusty frame of an old bicycle.

Sometimes it was like waking up on Saturday with the grand feeling of Saturday morning leaping in your heart, and seeing the apple blossoms drifting to earth, and smelling sausage and ham and coffee, and knowing there would be no school today, no dreadful, morning, schoolhouse bell today, no thudding heart, and pounding legs, and shuddering nerves and bolted and uneasy food, and sour, distressful coffee in your guts, because there would be no school today and it was golden, shining, and triumphant Saturday.

And then it was like Saturday night, and joy and menace in the air, and everyone waiting to get out on the streets and go "uptown," and taking a hot bath, and putting on clean clothes and eating supper, and going uptown on the night-time streets of Saturday, where joy and menace filled the air about you, and where glory breathed upon you, and yet never came, and getting far down towards the front and seeing Broncho Billy shoot the bad men dead three times until the last show of the night was over, and a cracked slide was shone on the screen which said "Good Night."

Then it was like Sunday morning, waking, hearing the bus outside, smelling the coffee, brains and eggs, and buckwheat cakes, feeling peaceful, sweetly happy, not exultant as on Saturday, a slumberous, drowsy, and more mournful joy, the smell of the Sunday newspapers, and the Sunday morning light outside, bright, golden, yet religious light, and church bells, people putting on good clothes to go to church, and the closed and decent streets of Sunday morning, and going by the cool side where the tobacco store was, and the Sunday morning sports inside who didn't have to go to church, and the strong, clean, pungent smell of good tobacco, and the good smell and feel of the church, which was not so much like God as like a good and decent substance in the world—the children singing, "Shall we gather at the River the Bew-tee-ful the Bew-tee-ful R-hiv-er!"—and the drone of voices from the classrooms later on, and the dark walnut, stained-glass light in the church, and decent, never-gaudy people with good dinners waiting for them when they got home, and the remote yet passionate austerity of the preacher's voice, the lean, horselike nobility of his face as he craned above his collar saying "heinous"—and all remote, austere, subdued, and decent, as if God were there in walnut light and a choker collar; and then the twenty-minute prayer, the organ pealing a rich benison, and people talking, laughing, streaming out from the dutiful, weekly, walnut disinfection of their souls into bright morning-gold of Sunday light again, and standing then in friendly and yet laughing groups upon the lawn outside, and streaming off towards home again, a steady liquid Sunday shuffle of good leather on the quiet streets—and all of it was good and godly, yet not like God, but like an ordered destiny, like Sunday morning peace and decency, and good dinners, money in the bank, and strong security.

—Thomas Wolfe, *The Web and the Rock*

Wolfe had a great lust for life, and he possessed the power of giving a second dimension to his experience. The first comes through the simple recording of what he sees and feels; but the second proceeds from his very intensity and produces something like a vision. Such writing belongs of course to description for literary effect.

## EXERCISES

**Exercise A** *Write an analysis of one of the following descriptive passages.*

[1] The room displayed a modest and pleasant color-scheme, after one of the best standard designs of the decorator who "did the interiors" for most of the speculative-builders' houses in Zenith. The walls were gray, the woodwork white, the rug a serene blue; and very much like mahogany was the furniture—the bureau with its great clear mirror, Mrs. Babbitt's dressing-table with toilet articles of almost solid silver, the plain twin beds, between them a small table holding a standard electric bedside lamp, a glass for water, and a standard bedside book with colored illustrations—what particular book it was cannot be ascertained, since no one had ever opened it. The mattresses were firm but not hard, triumphant modern mattresses which had cost a great deal of money; the hot water radiator was of exactly the proper scientific surface for the cubic contents of the room. The windows were large and easily opened, with the best catches and cords, and Holland roller shades guaranteed not to crack. It was a master-piece among bedrooms, right out of Cheerful Modern Houses for Medium Incomes. Only it had nothing to do with the Babbitts, nor with any one else. If people had ever lived and loved there, read thrillers at midnight and lain in beautiful indolence on a Sunday morning, there were no signs of it. It had the air of being a very good room in a very good hotel. One

expected the chambermaid to come in and make it ready for people who would stay but one night, go without looking back, and never think of it again.

Every second house in Floral Heights had a bedroom precisely like this.

—Sinclair Lewis, *Babbitt*

[2] They had marched more than thirty kilometers since dawn, along the white, hot road, where occasional thickets threw a moment of shade, then out into the glare again. On either hand, the valley, wide and shallow, glittered with heat; dark green patches of rye, pale young corn, fallow and meadow and black pine woods spread in a dull, hot diagram under a glistening sky. But right in front the mountains ranged across, pale blue and very still, snow gleaming gently out of the deep atmosphere. And towards the mountains, on and on, the regiment marched between the rye fields and the meadows, between the scraggy fruit trees set regularly on either side of the high road. The burnished, dark green rye threw off a suffocating heat, the mountains drew gradually nearer and more distinct. While the feet of the soldiers grew hotter, sweat ran through their hair under their helmets, and their knapsacks could burn no more in contact with their shoulders, but seemed instead to give off a cold, prickly sensation.

—D. H. Lawrence, *The Prussian Officer*

[3] He was the sort of man who wipes his feet on the door mat before entering the house, whether it is raining or not. Sometimes he had to go and search for the mat, which had been kicked aside, but this neither disturbed nor deterred him. His voice was so soft that it seemed to come from an immaterial source, like the sounds in dreams. Yet it carried across a room without difficulty and left a memory wherever it was placed. His eyes were never without the molecular arrangement which causes a twinkle. Their centers could become hard and their lenses caught everything that moved, but the twinkle never did more than recede a little during these interruptions. His attitude was that of an ego perfectly attuned to its surroundings. He considered any man to be God's greatest handiwork, and therefore worthy of his complete attention at any and all times. In this judgment there was neither selection nor differentiation; intellect, morals, charm, were minor variations in the external mechanism; the internal part, the center and motivation, was changeless and common to all. He bowed as solemnly to a seven-year-old girl as he did to a seventy-year-old lady; he listened intently to fools; he kept wise men from stumbling when they forgot absently to step up at a curb.

—Thomas Sugrue, *Starling of the White House*

[4] The employees of the editorial room—a loftlike chamber crazily crowded with desks, tables, cabinets, benches, files, typewriters; lighted by a smoke-darkened sun and the dim glow of electric bulbs—were already launched upon the nervous routine of their day. An excited jargon filled the place which, with the air of physical disorder as if the workers were

haphazardly improvising their activities, gave the room a vivid though seemingly impermanent life.

On the benches against a peeling wall sleepy-faced boys with precocious eyes kept up a lazy hair-pulling, surreptitious wrestling bout. They rose indifferently in response to furiously repeated bellows for their assistance—a business of carrying typewritten bits of paper between desks a few feet apart; or of sauntering with eleventh-hour orders to the perspiring men in the composing room.

In the forward part of the shop a cluster of men stood about the desk of an editor who in a disinterested voice sat issuing assignments for the day, forecasting to his innumerable assistants the amount of space needed for succeeding editions, the possible development in the local scandals. His eye unconsciously watched the clock over his head, his ear divided itself between half a dozen conversations and a tireless telephone. With his hands he kept fumbling an assortment of clippings, memoranda, and copy.

Oldish young men and youngish old men gravitated about him, their faces curiously identical. These were the irresponsible-eyed, casual-mannered individuals, seemingly neither at work nor at play, who were to visit the courts, the police, the wrecks, the criminals, conventions, politicians, reformers, lovers, and haters, and bring back the news of the city's day. A common almost racial sophistication stamped their expression. They pawed over telephone books, argued with indifferent, emotionless profanity among themselves on items of amazing import; pounded nonchalantly upon typewriters, lolled with their feet upon desks, their noses buried in the humorous columns of the morning newspapers.

—Ben Hecht, *Erik Dorn*

[5] All over Alabama, the lamps are out. Every leaf drenches the touch; the spider's net is heavy. The roads lie there, with nothing to use them. The fields lie there, with nothing at work in them, neither man nor beast. The plow handles are wet, and the rails and the frogplates and the weeds between the ties: and not even the hurryings and hoarse sorrows of a distant train, on other roads, is heard. The little towns, the county seats, house by house white-painted and elaborately sawn among their heavy and dark-lighted leaves, in the spaced protections of their mineral light they stand so prim, so voided, so undefended upon starlight, that it is inconceivable to despise or to scorn a white man, an owner of land; even in Birmingham, mile on mile, save for the sudden frightful streaming, almost instantly diminished and silent, of a closed black car, and save stone lonesome sinister heelbeats, that show never a face and enter, soon, a frame door flush with the pavement, and ascend the immediate lightless staircase, mile on mile, stone, stone, smooth charted streams of stone, the streets under their lifted lamps lie void before eternity. New Orleans is stirring, rattling, and sliding faintly in its fragrance and in the enormous richness of its lust; taxis are still parked along Dauphine Street and the breastlike, floral air is itchy with the stilettos and embroiderings above black blood drumthroes of an eloquent cracked indiscoverable cornet, which exists only in the imagination and somewhere in the past, in the broken heart of Louis Armstrong; yet even in that small portion which is

the infested genitals of that city, never free, neither of desire nor of waking pain, there are the qualities of the tender desolations of profoundest night. Beneath, the gulf lies dreaming, and beneath, dreaming, that woman, that id, the lower American continent, lies spread before heaven in her wealth. The parks of her cities are iron, loam, silent, the sweet fountains shut, and the pure façades, embroiled, limelike in the street light are sharp, are still.

—James Agee and Walker Evans,
*Let Us Now Praise Famous Men*

**Exercise B**    *By using words which recall sensory experience, write a vivid description of one of the following. Remember that a description is often richer if it appeals to more than one sense.*

1. A hot August afternoon
2. An old attic
3. Inside a repair garage
4. A Midwestern cornfield
5. A beauty shop
6. An airport
7. A crowd at a boxing match
8. Mountains in winter
9. A student lounge
10. An ice-skating party
11. The audience at a political speech
12. First signs of spring
13. Thanksgiving dinner
14. A neighborhood playground
15. The family breakfast table

**Exercise C**

1. Write a description of a person, place, or scene avoiding as far as possible the subjective kind of modifier. Your aim should be to achieve an effect through the use of objective detail.

2. Write a description using as a model the method and style of Thomas Wolfe.

3. Take some very familiar object or scene and describe it in such a way as to bring out unsuspected features of interest.

4. Write a description of a person in which you proceed from physical or external features to the "inner" man or the personality.

5. Write a description in which you make extended use of a comparison. The comparison might appear at the beginning and at the end, or it might be mentioned several times.

# Chapter Four

# Narration

Narrative writing deals with events in a series. Its function is to tell us *what happened.* Therefore we say that the subject matter of narrative is action.

## TIME ORDER

The art of telling a story in simple form is something that comes to most of us naturally. Even a small child is usually able to give an account, though halting and incomplete, of his experiences. He will say that he went to the country to visit his grandfather, and that he saw the cows, and they had ice cream for dinner, and he skinned his knee while playing in the yard. This artless recital has some essential features of narrative. In fact, narrative writing ranges all the way from such a short and simple type of relation to large-scale examples such as the history of an epoch and complex examples such as one may encounter in the modern novel. All are characterized by a series of connected events in a period of time.

Time order is of course a natural order, and the key to the structure of a narrative is sequence. Usually this sequence is simple. In an auto-biographical narrative you would expect to begin with the time and place of your entrance into the world. Next would follow childhood impressions and the adventures of boyhood; then your special interests and activities in school, and finally perhaps the maturing of your intention to go to college. A systematic account of a battle would likely begin with the plans of the opposed generals, move on next to the reports of reconnais-sance parties, and then to the first contact of the armies and the maneuvering for position. The story of the actual fighting would keep clear the sequence of major events, and the account might conclude with the final operations of the victorious side. The narrative account of a natural disaster, say a flood or a fire, would similarly move through an order of time; from the first discovery that something had "broken loose," through the more spectacular or serious stages, to a final report of what could be learned only at the end, the number of lives lost or the amount of damage done. In this way time order serves as a framework for facts that have a consecutive relation.

Although an order of time is essential to narrative, the order is not always simple and straightforward, as in the events described above. The reader must be given a clear understanding of the sequence of time, but there are often good reasons for presenting events out of natural sequence. Some narratives, both fictional and real, begin at the point of a crucial incident and then take us back to explain what led to the incident. In this kind of narrative pattern, the events might follow thus: 4, 5, 6, 1, 2, 3, 7, 8, 9, 10. Here the story begins with event number four, probably because it is felt to have some special significance in the unfolding of the whole series. Then after progression from four through six, the story takes us back to the beginning to show us what the crucial event developed out of—to give us the narrative background. Such a plan might begin by showing us an inventor just about to abandon his efforts when he hits on the hoped-for discovery, or two lovers about to break up when they find the source of their misunderstanding, or an explorer confronted with the greatest peril of his trip, which he must survive if he is to go on. Again, if there are ten significant episodes in the life of a captain of industry, the story might begin with episode two, in which we see him starting as a stockroom clerk, or with episode four, in which we see him resolutely forging ahead, or with episode ten, in which we see him at the height of his success. Generally speaking, such rearrangements are for the purpose of capturing attention; we might be slow in grasping the significance of episodes one to three unless we had episode four to focus the interest of the narrative. The motion picture has made us familiar with the altered time sequence through its use of the flashback to bring in supporting detail and to sharpen the dramatic point of the action. In the hands of a capable writer the time order is flexible, and may be arranged in almost any way.

The passage below entitled "Petrograd 1917" narrates the arrival of Lenin in that city near the beginning of the Russian Revolution. One of its striking features as composition is the maintenance of a perfect time order despite the necessity of including a good deal of background material. The events in their order may be succinctly listed as follows:

1. The Stockholm Express arrives in Petrograd.
2. Lenin, followed by other exiles, steps down from the train.
3. A large party of officials is waiting to greet him.

4. Madame Kollontai presents him with a bouquet, and there are handshakes and embraces.
5. The crowd passes into the waiting room, where Lenin is given an official greeting by Chkeidze, the president of the Petrograd Soviet.
6. Lenin responds by addressing not Chkeidze, but the crowd outside.
7. He amazes the reception committee by speaking of the Russian Revolution as the beginning of a "world-wide socialist revolution," but the crowd senses the impulse of his remarks.

Yet this undeviating time order does not make the writing seem mechanical. By the skillful use of varied beginnings and transitional devices the author has made the narrative organic, so that the events flow into one another. And the circumstantial detail is brought in at appropriate places where it never appears to get in the way of the flow.

PETROGRAD 1917

It was early spring and the evenings were still cold in Petrograd. On the platform of the Finland Station the members of the reception committee huddled in their overcoats and shuffled their feet as they waited for the train. The Stockholm Express was very late, but it arrived at last with a squealing of brakes and clouds of cheap coal smoke. Carriage doors opened and passengers began to dismount, their coat collars turned up against the chill.

A short man in a long coat and round fur cap stepped down to the platform, then turned to help a woman off the train. The waiting group started forward, and from somewhere down by the engine a band struck up the 'Marseillaise.' As the two travellers moved arm in arm towards the exit, the glow from the station lights illumined the man's face. His wide mouth, broad nose, and high forehead rather suggested a middle-aged Socrates, as did his little twinkling eyes peering out from under bushy eyebrows. At first glance, it seemed above all a good-humoured face, filled with laughter, and only those who watched it intently for a long time ever began to feel that there was something sinister in its perpetual silent mirth. It was, in any case, a face soon to become familiar to millions.

Vladimir Ilich Ulianov, better known in Russian *émigré* circles and the anti-Tsarist underground by the cover name of Lenin, had come back to Petrograd. By the old Julian calendar, the date was 3 April, 1917, and the Russian Revolution was already five weeks old.

Waiting to greet Lenin were members of the Central Committee of the Bolshevik Party, a few personal friends, and some Left-wing political leaders. The small man with the reddish beard and nervous Gallic gestures was Kamenev, a 'Right-wing' Bolshevik; the tall woman holding the bouquet of flowers was Madame Alexandra Kollontai, a socialist agitator; and close behind Madame Kollontai was Raskolnikov, representing the mutinous sailors of the 'Red' Kronstadt naval base. Besides his wife, Krupskaya, Lenin had with him about forty exiles, of whom at least two, Zinoviev and Sokolnikov, were already famous names in the revolutionary movement.

Madame Kollontai thrust the bouquet into Lenin's hands. He stood holding it awkwardly, but without the least self-consciousness, while his eyes darted shrewdly from face to face with the utmost good nature. After the handshakes and embraces, everyone turned and went into the station.

The former imperial waiting-room was very cold. Over the empty fireplace on the far wall was a bare patch which had recently been covered by the embossed insignia of the Romanoffs—a double-headed eagle clutching a sceptre in its claws. Through the open doors a searchlight could be seen playing upon the façade of the building. Chkeidze, the president of the Petrograd Soviet and no friend of the Bolsheviks, was waiting to greet Lenin officially. It was an awkward moment, but Chkeidze fumbled through it with a few conventional words about 'closing the ranks of democracy.' When Lenin spoke in reply, he did not address Chkeidze at all, but turned to the crowd assembled outside.

'Dear comrades,' he began, 'soldiers, sailors, and workers—'

His guttural voice boomed out to reach the mass of people jammed in the doorway and piled up in the square beyond. Just as later he would appeal to the proletariat of the belligerent nations over the heads of their governments, so now he addressed himself to the crowd rather than to their elected representatives. This was the authentic Leninist note. These were the people he talked to.

He spoke of the revolution the workers had made, and praised them for it. Then he went on to say that the 'robber imperialist war' would generate civil conflicts throughout Europe, bringing down the capitalist order in ruin and ushering in the 'world-wide socialist revolution.'

The reception committee listened to him in amazement, for this was not how any of them interpreted the events taking place in Russia. Although they were all Marxists, not even the most ardent socialist among them believed that Russia was ready for socialism. Eventually, of course, a socialist system would be established, but this upheaval they were living through was surely only the beginning, the bourgeois stage, the necessary preliminary to the 'world-wide socialist revolution.' They listened to Lenin's words with growing bewilderment and did not understand him.

But Lenin, after all, was not talking to them. He was talking to the Dark People, the huddled crowd outside. And they understood—if not the meaning of the words themselves, at least the spirit behind them. Russia had found her Robespierre.

—Major D. J. Goodspeed, *The Conspirators,*
*A Study of the Coup d'Etat*

## MOTIVE

We see clearly that some kind of time order is necessary before we can understand the connected series of events which make up a narrative. A further necessary element is motive. There are accounts of processes in which the element of motive is absent or is at a minimum, but these, strictly speaking, belong to exposition. All narrative which concerns the actions of human beings has to introduce the idea of motive or purpose in

the minds of the characters. If a motion picture opens with a scene showing someone walking down the street, you instantly try to grasp the story
by asking, What is his object? Is he coming home from work? Is he on the
way to market? Is he looking over a town in which he is a stranger? Not
until some possible answer is found to the question are you able to follow
the events at all. So it is with any situation involving a story: the Jones
boys, who usually disturb the neighborhood with their noise, are suspi-
ciously quiet this afternoon; Mr. Weber, who has not been late for work
in twenty years, showed up at the office this morning at 10:35; Washington
County, which has always voted Republican, went Democratic in the last
election. A narrative about any of these would depend upon an understanding of motive; that is, upon explanation of why the actors proceeded
as they did. These are people in situations to which they are responding,
and the object of the response—what the persons involved desire to do at
that time—gives us the master key to the action. In narrative, consequently, there is always present a *why*, which must be answered satisfactorily before the account of events can proceed very far. What is true
of a situation involving a single action is true also when we turn to very
large segments of human affairs: we find that some indication of motive is
necessary if they are to have the kind of connectedness which makes a
story. Even history cannot be written without a constant ascription of
motives to kings, generals, parliamentary leaders, and peoples. The element of motive or purpose must be inferred to make the story of any
human action complete. For example, there is a limit to what can be
drawn from the following catalogue of dates and occurrences.

| | |
|---|---|
| June 28, 1914 | Gavrilo Prinzip shot and killed the Archduke Francis Ferdinand, heir apparent to the Hapsburg crown. |
| July 5 | Austrian and German officials conferred at Potsdam. |
| July 23 | Austria presented an ultimatum to Serbia. |
| July 28 | Austria declared war. |
| July 29 | Russia began mobilization. Germany declared war on Russia. |
| August 2 | German troops occupied Luxembourg, and Germany declared war on France. |
| August 4 | German troops crossed the border of Belgium. |
| August 5 | The British government announced that a state of war existed between Great Britain and Germany. |

But now let us see how a trained historian weaves this into a narrative.

On June 28, 1914, the murder of the Archduke Francis Ferdinand at
Serajevo set light to a powder trail which within a brief span exploded the
European magazine in a series of detonations. Exactly one month later
Austria-Hungary declared war on Serbia, whose appeal to her ally and
protector led Russia to order a partial mobilization on her southern front.
The same day, July 29, an Imperial Council at Potsdam decided on war

against Russia, and, as a corollary, against France, although hoping to bargain for Britain's neutrality. While the chancelleries of Europe argued at cross purposes, the military tide swept them off their feet. On July 31 Russia ordered a general mobilization, and Germany, taking equivalent steps, sent a 12 hours' ultimatum. Austria, seeking belatedly to temporize, was dragged in the train of her more determined ally. By noon on Aug. 1 a state of war existed between Russia and Germany, and next day German troops entered French territory. At 7 P.M. came Germany's ultimatum to Belgium demanding an unopposed passage. On Aug. 3 Germany's formal declaration of war on France followed, and on Aug. 4 her troops crossed the Belgian frontier, for the sanctity of which England stood guarantor. At midnight, in reply, England entered the war, while the Belgian populace, rising to resist the German invaders, sounded the death-knell of gladiatorial wars and inaugurated the new warfare of peoples.

—B. H. Liddell Hart, "World War I," from
*The Encyclopaedia Britannica*

In this paragraph we see not only what is happening but we see also why it is happening. We see nations acting out of motives of ambition, rivalry, and fear; we understand events which, taken on the surface, might seem unrelated or extraordinary. We understand that Austria acts because she feels she must have satisfaction for the assassination of the heir to the throne, that Russia acts because her ally Serbia is threatened by Austria, that Germany acts out of a policy predetermined for the event of a general European war, and that France acts in response to German action. Finally we see Britain coming in because she is the guarantor of Belgian neutrality, which has been violated by the movement of the German armies. Admittedly it is not a very pretty story, but it is narrative as far as the connection of events goes, the author having placed these in a context of meaning. The difference between the bare calendar of happenings which we first looked at and this account of the beginning of World War I is an illustration of the part that motive has in making a story coherent.

## CONFLICT

Another element present in nearly all narrative is *conflict*. We have explained that a story is made up of a connected series of actions with a meaning. Now this meaning nearly always arises out of some opposition of forces which stimulates our interest in how the situation will "come out." Human interest in all types of conflict is very basic. We know that if a fight breaks out on a street, a crowd will gather immediately; we see people going to athletic contests in tens of thousands; we note the keen attention with which people follow a close political battle; and even much of our small talk concerns the rivalries, the competitions, and the successes of our friends. All of these contain the element of conflict which promises an issue.

The conflicts in which human beings engage are chiefly of three kinds. In one kind man is struggling against nature. This may assume the form of a mariner battling against the sea, of a young scientist seeking the means to control some disease, or of a farmer struggling to wrest a living from the soil. All of these represent conflict of man with some part of his environment.

In the second type of conflict man is struggling against man. Conflicts of this kind appear in war, in business, in society. The struggle between Tories and patriots at the time of the Revolution is an example of this. The story of a financial tycoon seeking control of a railroad empire would be an example from the business world. The struggle of a newcomer to win recognition in a conservative society or the fight made by Huckleberry Finn against the influence of civilization exhibits conflict in the social world.

The third form is inner conflict, the individual struggling against himself. In this case the contending forces may be courage and fear, honesty and temptation, selfishness and generosity, and the like. Shall the ambitious young lawyer become party to a deal which, by dubious means, would make him a million dollars or shall he heed his conscience and be content with a modest livelihood? Inner conflicts such as these often furnish the plots of short stories and novels.

Regardless of the form which the narrative may take—history, novel, short story, myth, fairy tale—there will be present this opposition of forces giving rise to tension. The reason that most people prefer stories, or accounts in story form, is that an opposition of forces creates suspense. Our interest is sustained until the question "Who won?" is answered. A good narrative therefore always arises out of a situation in which such factors are present.

## POINT OF VIEW

In narrative as in descriptive writing, there is need for adopting a *point of view*. One does not jump about aimlessly in telling a story any more than in writing a description; the reader must know from what angle he is expected to follow things. And the action must be told in such a way that we understand the relation of the narrator to the story.

The most generally used point of view in narrative is the *omniscient*. "Omniscience" means the condition of knowing everything. Here it applies to everything about the series of events, and, furthermore, "everything" means everything relevant. Nearly all historians and many writers of fiction adopt the omniscient point of view. This enables them to include anything that could have been seen by any observer at any time. When a historian prepares to write about an event, he does an extensive amount of research, reading the accounts left by many participants and eyewitnesses, digesting other contemporary sources, and studying official records. When he has done all this, he assumes that he has a reasonably complete knowledge of all the particulars; and when he writes, he presents the entire event as passing under his view. And while his knowledge of it can never be actually complete, it will go far beyond what any one person could have experienced. Therefore it takes on a certain character of omniscience. An account of the siege of Yorktown or the storming of the Bastille or the Haymarket riot could thus be presented out of many sources so as to appear in an over-all view. A newspaper reporter sent to cover a fire or an accident would ordinarily follow a similar method; he would interview those involved and would talk to eyewitnesses until he was able to produce a general picture of it—more than would be possible for anyone relying solely upon his own observation.

In stories the writer will sometimes choose the omniscient point of view because it enables him to move about freely. The writer of fiction who adopts this point of view is able to include not only everything that could have been seen by any observer at any time but also the feelings and thought processes of the characters. Instead of confining himself to what one person might have seen, the writer takes the liberty of relating all the details, regardless of who experienced them. By this means he can tell all about events which occurred to different people at the same time. He has full freedom in his selection of detail and can look down like a god on the imaginative world he has created.

Another technique of presentation, much favored by modern writers of fiction, is the *limited* point of view, or *selective omniscience*. By this method the writer consciously holds himself to what one person might have seen or experienced. Sometimes that person is the chief character of the story—the *center of consciousness*—so that we see the action through the eyes of the one principally involved. Sometimes he is a person having but a slight connection with the story—a minor character or even an "innocent bystander"—though he must be someone in a position to see, and perhaps evaluate, the significant happenings. When the narrator—not the author, but the *persona* who relates the events—tells his own intellectual and emotional reactions in the first person, the narration is given from the *subjective* point of view. When the narrator prefers to be an unthinking and unfeeling camera, or a "fly on the wall," his narration is *objective*. It is usually more difficult to relate a story from the limited and objective points of view, but there are certain artistic advantages in the convincingness of the situation, the immediacy of the events, and the presentation of detail.

An interesting example of both point of view and conflict will be seen in the excerpt below from Edmund Gosse's *Father and Son*. The point of view, which is consistently maintained, is that of a small child looking up to his father. The conflict is between the child's idea of his father's omniscience and certain of his experiences which undermine that idea.

Like most small children at the outset of life, he regarded his parents, and especially his father, as knowing everything. Finding that his father could state something which the child knew to be untrue came as a great revelation, an "appalling discovery." Finding later that he could deceive his father completed the destruction of the idea that his parent was all-wise. The point of view helps to emphasize the significance of such minor incidents to a child, and the conflict is resolved in the child's discovery that he had become an individual.

. . . My Father and Mother, in their serene discipline of me, never argued with one another, never even differed; their wills seemed absolutely one. My Mother always deferred to my Father, and in his absence spoke of him to me, as if he were all-wise. I confused him in some sense with God; at all events I believed that my Father knew everything and saw everything. One morning in my sixth year, my Mother and I were alone in the morning-room, when my Father came in and announced some fact to us. I was standing on the rug, gazing at him, and when he made this statement, I remember turning quickly, in embarrassment, and looking into the fire. The shock to me was as that of a thunderbolt, for what my Father had said *was not true*. My Mother and I, who had been present at the trifling incident, were aware that it had not happened exactly as it had been reported to him. My Mother gently told him so, and he accepted the correction. Nothing could possibly have been more trifling to my parents, but to me it meant an epoch. Here was the appalling discovery, never suspected before, that my Father was not as God, and did not know everything. The shock was not caused by any suspicion that he was not telling the truth, as it appeared to him, but by the awful proof that he was not, as I had supposed, omniscient.

This experience was followed by another, which confirmed the first, but carried me a great deal further. In our little back-garden, my Father had built up a rockery for ferns and mosses, and from the water-supply of the house he had drawn a leaden pipe so that it pierced upwards through the rockery and produced, when a tap was turned, a pretty silvery parasol of water. The pipe was exposed somewhere near the foot of the rockery. One day, two workmen, who were doing some repairs, left their tools during the dinner-hour in the back-garden, and as I was marching about I suddenly thought that to see whether one of these tools could make a hole in the pipe would be attractive. It did make such a hole, quite easily, and then the matter escaped my mind. But a day or two afterwards, when my Father came in to dinner, he was very angry. He had turned the tap, and, instead of the fountain arching at the summit, there had been a rush of water through a hole at the foot. The rockery was absolutely ruined.

Of course I realized in a moment what I had done, and I sat frozen with alarm, waiting to be denounced. But my Mother remarked on the visit of the plumbers two or three days before, and my Father instantly took up the suggestion. No doubt that was it; mischievous fellows had thought it amusing to stab the pipe and spoil the fountain. No suspicion fell on me; no question was asked of me. I sat there, turned to stone within, but outwardly sympathetic, and with unchecked appetite.

We attribute, I believe, too many moral ideas to little children. It is obvious that in this tremendous juncture, I ought to have been urged forward by good instincts, or held back by naughty ones. But I am sure that the fear which I experienced for a short time, and which so unexpectedly melted away, was a purely physical one. It had nothing to do with the emotions of a contrite heart. As to the destruction of the fountain, I was sorry about that, for my own sake, since I admired the skipping water extremely, and had no idea that I was spoiling its display. But the emotions which now thronged within me, and which led me with an almost unwise alacrity, to seek solitude in the back-garden, were not moral at all, they were intellectual. I was not ashamed of having successfully—and so surprisingly—deceived my parents by my crafty silence; I looked upon that as a providential escape, and dismissed all further thought of it. I had other things to think of.

In the first place, the theory that my Father was omniscient or infallible was now dead and buried. He probably knew very little; in this case he had not known a fact of such importance that if you did not know that, it could hardly matter what you knew. My Father, as a deity, as a natural force of immense prestige, fell in my eyes to a human level. In future, his statements about things in general need not be accepted implicitly. But of all the thoughts which rushed upon my savage and undeveloped little brain at this crisis, the most curious was that I had found a companion and a confidant in myself. There was a secret in this world and it belonged to me and to a somebody who lived in the same body with me. There were two of us, and we could talk with one another. It is difficult to define impressions so rudimentary, but it is certain that it was in this dual form that the sense of my individuality now suddenly descended upon me, and it is equally certain that it was a great solace to me to find a sympathizer in my own breast.

—Edmund Gosse, *Autobiography*

## FOCUS OF INTEREST

We have seen that a narrative is made up not of just any series of actions but of a series which has a meaning as a whole. Like a piece of exposition, it has a unity, but unlike exposition, it cannot derive this unity from the objective features of what is related. If we are writing an exposition of a mechanism or an organization, the features of the thing itself tell us where to begin and where to end, but what tells us where to begin narrating a series of actions? This question may be answered by the phrase "focus of interest." The unity of a narrative is supplied by a kind of human interest in what is happening, or in what may be broadly termed "plot." It is plot which gives dramatic significance to the action, and accordingly the plot determines the limits of the narrative.

Focus of interest has some relationship to point of view, especially to the limited or personal point of view. If the story is being presented through the eyes of a chief character, the action must answer the question foremost in his mind, "How am I going to meet the problem created by this situation?" The story is not concluded until the reader's curiosity is satisfied with a credible answer. If an observer is telling the story, he centers interest upon how things "came out" for the one principally involved. Even in a narrative which is written from the omniscient point of view, we have a focus of interest determined by some conflict whose issue we are eager to know. It is that which gives dramatic and structural unity to histories, incidents, anecdotes, and the like. In the following narrative by Plutarch of the famous encounter between Antony and Cleopatra our interest is sustained by a desire to see which one will get the better of the other. The story has a beginning, a middle, and an end determined by our interest in this question.

Such being his temper, the last and crowning mischief that could befall him came in the love of Cleopatra, to awaken and kindle to fury passions that lay still and dormant in his nature and to stifle and finally corrupt any elements that yet made resistance in him, of goodness and a sound judgment. He fell into the snare thus. When making preparation for the Parthian war, he sent to command her to make her personal appearance in Cilicia to answer an accusation, that she had given great assistance, in the late wars, to Cassius. Dellius, who was sent on this message, had no sooner seen her face, and remarked her adroitness and subtlety in speech, but he felt convinced that Antony would not so much as think of giving any molestation to a woman like this; on the contrary she would be the first in favor with him. So he set himself at once to pay his court to the Egyptian, and gave her his advice, "to go," in the Homeric style, to Cilicia, "in her best attire," and bade her fear nothing from Antony, the gentlest and kindest of soldiers. She had some faith in the words of Dellius, but more in her own attractions, which, having formerly recommended her to Caesar and the young Cnaeus Pompey, she did not doubt might prove yet more successful with Antony. Their acquaintance was with her when a girl, young and ignorant of the world, but she was to meet Antony in the time of life when women's beauty is most splendid, and their intellects are in full maturity. She made great preparation for her journey, of money, gifts, and ornaments of value, such as so wealthy a kingdom might afford, but she brought with her her surest hopes in her own magic arts and charms.

She received several letters, both from Antony and from his friends, to summon her, but she took no account of these orders; and at last, as if in mockery of them, she came sailing up the river Cydnus, in a barge with gilded stern and outspread sails of purple, while oars of silver beat time to the music of flutes and fifes and harps. She herself lay all along, under a canopy of cloth of gold, dressed as Venus in a picture, and beautiful young boys, like painted Cupids, stood on each side to fan her. Her maids were dressed like Sea Nymphs and Graces, some steering at the rudder, some working at the ropes. The perfumes diffused themselves from the vessel to the shore, which was covered with multitudes, part following the galley up the river on either bank, part running out of the city to see the sight. The market-place was quite emptied, and Antony was at last left alone sitting upon the tribunal; while the word went through all the multitude, that Venus was come to feast with Bacchus, for the common good of Asia. On her arrival, Antony sent to invite her to supper. She thought it fitter that he should come to her; so, willing to show his good humor and courtesy, he complied, and went. He found the preparations to receive him magnificent beyond expression, but nothing so admirable as the great number of lights; for on a sudden there was let down altogether so great a number of branches with lights in them so ingeniously disposed, some in squares and some in circles, that the whole thing was a spectacle that has seldom been equalled for beauty.

The next day, Antony invited her to supper, and was very anxious to outdo her as well in magnificence as contrivance; but he found he was altogether beaten in both, and was so well convinced of it, that he was himself the first to jest and mock at his poverty of wit, and his rustic awkwardness. She, perceiving that his raillery was broad and gross, and savored more of the soldier than the courtier, rejoined in the same taste, and fell into it at once, without any sort of reluctance or reserve. For her actual beauty, it is said, was not so remarkable that none could be compared with her, or that no one could see her without being struck by it, but the contact of her presence, if you lived with her, was irresistible; the attraction of her person, joining with the charm of her conversation, and the character that attended all she said or did was something bewitching. It was a pleasure merely to hear the sound of her voice, with which, like an instrument of many strings, she could pass from one language to another; so that there were few of the barbarian nations that she answered by an interpreter; to most of them she spoke herself, as to the Aethiopians, Troglodytes, Hebrews, Arabians, Syrians, Medes, Parthians, and many others, whose language she had learnt; which was all the more surprising because most of the kings her predecessors scarcely gave themselves the trouble to acquire the Egyptian tongue, and several of them quite abandoned the Macedonian.

Antony was so captivated by her, that, while Fulvia his wife maintained his quarrels at Rome against Caesar by actual force of arms, and the Parthian troops, commanded by Labienus (the king's generals having made him commander-in-chief), were assembled in Mesopotamia, and ready to enter Syria, he could yet suffer himself to be carried away by her to Alexandria, there to keep holiday, like a boy in play and diversion, squandering and fooling away in enjoyments that most costly, as Antiphon says, of all valuables, time.

—Plutarch, *Lives of Illustrious Men*

The very expression "focus of interest" tells us that narrative is selective. A narrative is never a perfectly complete account of an action, just as a description is never a complete picture of a person or scene. Both are compelled by the nature of art to choose according to a purpose. Just as description tries to find those details which will render an object vivid and impressive, so narrative tries to find details which will make an action seem significant and real. It is sometimes said that narrative aims at the illusion of reality. But this has to be achieved in a certain way. For example, the battle of Waterloo has occurred once and for all; it will never be reproduced in its totality. Anything like a complete account of it, which would include the actions important and unimportant, of each individual soldier, would run to countless volumes. But by making an artistic selection of these details, so that the broad character of the action is represented, we can create a story which, while actually an abstract of the total detail of the battle, is truthful in what it presents. This is, indeed, the only kind of truth for narrative and descriptive writing. But if the task is performed with skill and fidelity, it will be a higher and not a lower order of truth than a mere catalogue of facts. Contrary to the impression held by some, facts never speak for themselves, and a collection of facts is no more a story than a pile of bricks is a house. It is necessary to select them and to put them in some frame of meaning before they will stick together. Often some have to be left out owing to limitation of space, and many may have to be left out as irrelevant. What is created with the remainder is not a distortion, but a true rendering of what has significance for us as human beings interested in the point of the story.

The sharp focus of interest which controls the selection of detail in this brief selection from John Steinbeck suggests clearly the sort of intense significance an effective writer can give to a simple personal experience.

Sunday morning, in a Vermont town, my last day in New England, I shaved, dressed in a suit, polished my shoes, whited my sepulcher, and looked for a church to attend. Several I eliminated for reasons I do not now remember, but on seeing a John Knox church I drove into a side street and parked Rocinante out of sight, gave Charley his instructions about watching the truck, and took my way with dignity to a church of blindingly white ship lap. I took my seat in the rear of the spotless, polished place of worship. The prayers were to the point, directing the attention of the Almighty to certain weaknesses and undivine tendencies I know to be mine and could only suppose were shared by others gathered there.

The service did my heart and I hope my soul some good. It had been long since I had heard such an approach. It is our practice now, at least in the large cities, to find from our psychiatric priesthood that our sins aren't really sins at all but accidents that are set in motion by forces beyond our control. There was no such nonsense in this church. The minister, a man of iron with tool-steel eyes and a delivery like a pneumatic drill, opened up with prayer and reassured us that we were a pretty sorry lot. And he was right. We didn't amount to much to start with, and due to our own tawdry efforts we had been slipping ever since. Then, having softened us up, he went into a glorious sermon, a fire-and-brimstone sermon. Having proved that we, or perhaps only I, were no damn good, he painted with cool certainty what was likely to happen to us if we didn't make some basic reorganizations for which he didn't hold out much hope. He spoke of hell as an expert, not the mush-mush hell of these soft days, but a well-stoked, white-hot hell served by technicians of the first order. This reverend brought it to a point where we could understand it, a good hard coal fire, plenty of draft, and a squad of open-hearth devils who put their hearts into their work, and their work was me. I began to feel good all over. For some years now God has been a pal to us, practicing togetherness, and that causes the same emptiness a father does playing softball with his son. But this Vermont God cared enough about me to go to a lot of trouble kicking the hell out of me. He put my sins in a new perspective. Whereas they had been small and mean and nasty and best forgotten, this minister gave them some size and bloom and dignity. I hadn't been thinking very well of myself for some years, but if my sins had this dimension there was some pride left. I wasn't a naughty child but a first rate sinner, and I was going to catch it.

I felt so revived in spirit that I put five dollars in the plate, and afterward, in front of the church, shook hands warmly with the minister and as many of the congregation as I could. It gave me a lovely sense of evildoing that lasted clear through till Tuesday. I even considered beating Charley to give him some satisfaction too, because Charley is only a little less sinful than I am. All across the country I went to church on Sundays, a different denomination every week, but nowhere did I find the quality of that Vermont preacher. He forged a religion designed to last, not predigested obsolescence.

—John Steinbeck, *Travels with Charley*

## EXERCISES

**Exercise A**   *From your own life select some significant experience or group of experiences which has a considerable degree of unity, so that you think of it as a kind of "chapter." Relate this in the form of an autobiographical narrative of 1000–1200 words, using the first-person point of view. Write it so that the focus of interest is clear for your reader, and remember that a certain amount of individuating detail will probably be necessary to make the experience seem real.*

**Exercise B**   *Select some well-known building or other point of interest within traveling distance of your campus and visit it. Write a paper combining narration and description in which you relate the incidents of the trip and present a detailed picture of the scene you visited.*

**Exercise C**   *Choose some outstanding event from American history. Read up on the subject in the library, taking notes. From the data you have collected, write a relatively short (1000–1500 words) account of the history of the event. Any of the topics below would do, and they will suggest others.*

1. The Salem Witchcraft Trials
2. The Assassination of John F. Kennedy
3. The Signing of the Declaration of Independence
4. John Brown's Capture of Harpers Ferry
5. The Presidential Election

6. Brook Farm
7. The Haymarket Riot in Chicago
8. Lindbergh's Flight Across the Atlantic
9. The American Naval Disaster at Pearl Harbor
10. The Cuban Missile Crisis

**Exercise D**   *Write a narrative of a typical day's cycle of events in a dormitory, fraternity, or rooming house. Make your focus of interest some special quality of the daily living.*

**Exercise E**   *Select some individual who has had a strong influence on you. Write an account of your first meeting with him.*

## SPECIAL TYPES OF NARRATIVE

### Anecdote and Incident

Autobiographies, biographies, and histories sometimes contain smaller units of narrative called anecdotes and incidents. An anecdote is a short narrative usually told for the purpose of bringing out some interesting or odd characteristic of a person or place. It does not contribute to the main movement of a story, though the point which it makes may add something to the background or the atmosphere of the whole. Its interest does not depend upon a dramatic unfolding, but upon the feature or idea it is meant to disclose, which usually appears near the end.

The incident has the same self-contained character, but its interest depends upon the unusual, vivid, or illuminating character of the action itself. What it narrates is exciting or appealing for its own sake rather than for a dramatic structure or a point of interpretation. A small but intense bit of action from a hunt, a rescue at sea, a police raid, or something like these might constitute matter for an incident.

Occasionally anecdotes and incidents are written as independent narratives, to stand alone. They can do this because of their limited function. But in the majority of cases they appear as short narratives within much longer ones, which they help to fill out with character and detail. Below is a brief anecdote appearing in a longer work.

There are croakers in every country, always boding its ruin. Such a one then lived in Philadelphia; a person of note, an elderly man, with a wise look and a very grave manner of speaking; his name was Samuel Mickle. This gentleman, a stranger to me, stopped one day at my door, and asked me if I was the young man who had lately opened a new printing-house. Being answered in the affirmative, he said he was sorry for me, because it was an expensive undertaking, and the expense would be lost; for Philadelphia was a sinking place, the people already half-bankrupts, or near being so; all appearances to the contrary, such as new buildings and the rise of rents, being to his certain knowledge fallacious;

for they were, in fact, among the things that would soon ruin us. And he gave me such a detail of misfortunes now existing, or that were soon to exist that he left me half melancholy. Had I known him before I engaged in this business, probably I should never have done it. This man continued to live in this decaying place, and to declaim in the same strain, refusing for many years to buy a house there, because all was going to destruction; and at last I had the pleasure of seeing him give five times as much for one as he might have bought it for when he first began his croaking.

—Benjamin Franklin, *Autobiography*

Probably the most famous anecdote in American history is that of Washington and the cherry tree. Although the truth of it has been questioned many times, there can be no doubt that as far as composition goes, it is a good anecdote. In its original form, it is filled with interesting circumstantial detail, and it makes a definite point.

The following anecdote is a case in point. It is too valuable to be lost, and too true to be doubted; for it was communicated to me by the same excellent lady to whom I was indebted for the last.

"When George," said she, "was about six years old, he was made the wealthy master of a *hatchet!* of which, like most little boys, he was immoderately fond; and was constantly going about chopping everything that came in his way. One day, in the garden, where he often amused himself by hacking his mother's pea-sticks, he unluckily tried the edge of his hatchet on the body of a beautiful young English cherry-tree, which he barked so terribly that I don't believe the tree ever got the better of it. The next morning the old gentleman, finding out what had befallen his tree, which by the way was a great favorite, came into the house; and with much warmth asked for the mischievous author, declaring at the same time, that he would not have taken five guineas for his tree. Nobody could tell him anything about it. Presently George and his hatchet made their appearance. 'George,' said his father, 'do you know who killed that beautiful little cherry-tree yonder in the garden?' This was a *tough question;* and George staggered under it for a moment; but quickly recovered himself: and looking at his father, with the sweet face of youth brightened by the inexpressible charm of all-conquering truth, he bravely cried out, 'I can't tell a lie, Pa; you know I can't tell a lie! I did cut it with my hatchet.' 'Run to my arms, you dearest boy,' cried his father in transports, 'run to my arms; glad am I, George, that you killed my tree; for you have paid me for it a thousand fold. Such an act of heroism in my son is worth more than a thousand trees, though blossomed of silver and their fruits of purest gold.' "

—M. L. Weems, *The Life of George Washington: with Curious Anecdotes, Equally Honorable to Himself, and Exemplary to his Young Countrymen*

## Sketch

The sketch is usually included in narrative writing despite the fact that it gives little space to action. It is developed through highly selective detail, and it may use a narrative framework of action, or make some use of action in passing from one part of the subject to another. But its aim is to present, somewhat more rapidly and selectively than the full description, the significant features of something. Like the anecdote and the incident, the sketch may be used to furnish background or atmosphere for a larger piece.

The example below, presenting a Wall Street law clerk, "Mr. Canthus," is a good specimen of the type.

> The real brains of the office was the chief clerk, Mr. Canthus, a harassed little man with a bright red nose, who looked like Charles Dana Gibson's historic "Mr. Pipp." He lived in Flushing with a wife, five female offspring and a mother-in-law, neither smoked nor swore, acted as a lay reader in the Presbyterian Church, and received ten thousand dollars a year in return for his ability to maintain a perpetual and beatific calm. He had been with Hotchkiss, Levy, and Hogan for nineteen years, and in a sense he *was* Hotchkiss, Levy, & Hogan. "Ask Mr. Canthus." He was familiar with every point of pleading raised since 1735 and he knew the Civil and Criminal Procedure Reports by heart. He took nobody's word for anything and judges were no more to him than chattering monkeys. He smiled rarely, he never hurried. He spoke only to say "You've left out a comma there," or "You've forgotten the 'and' after 'damages,'" or "The clerk said that, did he? Well, tell him from me that he's a bonehead." He had made but one mistake in his career—in 1891, when in a moment of aphasia he had overlooked the "petition for further relief" in an equity order. He would sit unruffled at his desk amid a hurricane of questions, directions and objurgations, half snowed under with papers awaiting his signature, placidly studying some complaint, answer or judgment which must be filed at the County Court House in exactly nine minutes. In his heart he regarded the title members of the firm as ignorant and debased commercialists and his soul vomited at them and all their works.
>
> —Arthur Train, *Yankee Lawyer*

## Profile

A modern form which combines narration, description, and exposition in various proportions is the profile. Primarily a character sketch, it is presented in such a way as to develop the greatest amount of interest in its subject. As the word itself suggests, the profile shows the chief features of the person being described. It does not pretend to be exhaustive—it may require anything from a few paragraphs to twenty or thirty pages—though it may treat key facts about the life and character in considerable detail. In this way profiles often try to leave a dominant impression of their subject. When we finish reading a good profile, we have the feeling that we have met an individual personally.

The profile owes its form largely to modern journalism. It takes the quick, perceptive look, brings out some striking details of the man's career, discusses his habits and characteristic ways of thought, perhaps shows him in action, and finally estimates him or summarizes the general opinion of him. In most instances it mingles praise and criticism in such a way as to give a detached and balanced view. It is realistic, but it usually depends for interest upon playing up the extraordinary, exciting, or unconventional facts in the life of its subject.

## EXERCISES

**Exercise A**    *Write an anecdote whose point supports one of the following statements.*

1. Old people tend to forget that they were once young themselves.
2. It always pays to tell the truth.
3. Facing an audience for the first time is a frightening experience.
4. The family car is sometimes a source of discord.
5. Two wrongs do not make a right.

**Exercise B**    *Write a sketch of one of the following.*

1. A truck driver
2. The policeman on the beat
3. A college dean
4. A newly arrived foreigner
5. An athletic instructor
6. A restful place in the country
7. A corner of a museum
8. A backyard
9. A new suburban development
10. The busiest corner in town

**Exercise C**    *Choose as your subject some figure currently in the news and write a profile. In gathering facts and background material you may need to consult* Who's Who in America, *a biographical dictionary, magazines, and newspapers. See the suggestions under "Use of the Library."*

# Chapter Five

# Argumentation

A large part of the world's oral and written expression takes the form of argumentation. Although many of us are accustomed to think of an argument as a dispute between two individuals, with more or less heated assertion and denial of some point, the truth is that argumentation is a science in itself, and a good argument is a product of careful thinking. To appreciate this fact we need only recognize the kinds of things that constitute argument. Nearly all of the world's famous speeches have been arguments; most sermons are arguments; the editorials and columns in newspapers, and even a considerable amount of advertising, fall likewise into the category of argument. Consequently, whether we are reading the morning paper, or listening to radio or television, or driving along a highway lined with billboards, or participating in a family discussion about where to spend the Fourth of July, we are being exposed to argument. At no other time in the world's history has it been so necessary to understand how argumentation works—both for the purpose of making our honestly conceived views prevail and for the purpose of protecting ourselves against imposition. The very fact that our age is prolific in means of communication insures that wherever we turn we shall be assailed by argument, and the only way to answer an argument is with another argument.

Argumentation aims to convince and persuade. In other words, argumentation seeks to make people accept a judgment and, sometimes, to act upon it. This desire to bring others around to one's opinion is universal, and indeed the world would be worse off if it were not so. If we have studied some problem intensively, or if we have been through some particularly instructive experience, or if we have come to feel very strongly about the value of a certain thing or a certain course of action, we naturally want to make others agree with us. It is not often that we are able to do this by mere assertion, which would take the form of saying, "Everybody ought to vote for candidate Jenkins," or "The American standard of living is due mainly to the protective tariff system." The simple assertion tells what we believe to be true or feel to be advisable, but it does not tell why we feel as we do. And the world is generally too hardheaded to be convinced until it knows, in addition to our opinion, the grounds for opinion or action. It is the opinion, together with the grounds, which constitutes an argument. Perhaps we feel that something ought to be done to check the increase of divorce, or that atomic energy should be placed under international control, or that intercollegiate athletics should be conducted on a different basis. As has just been pointed out, it is not enough to say, "The increasing divorce rate should be checked," etc. These are assertions which may be the conclusions of arguments, but they are not arguments in themselves. Indeed, we do not have a right to make these statements until we have done the careful spadework of argumentation.

The first step of argumentation in every instance is a clear statement of what the argument is about. Although this might appear too obvious to mention, the fact remains that a large number of the arguments between individuals, as well as a sizable number of public controversies, get nowhere because the issue is not well defined. Sometimes neither participant is aware of what he is arguing for or against, and when this happens, argumentation, instead of being one of the most fruitful kinds of communication, may become only a source of further confusion. For this reason it is essential to say first of all what the argument is to prove or disprove, and this requires casting the subject of the argument into the form of a proposition.

## PROPOSITIONS

### Recognizing Propositions

A proposition may be defined simply as any statement which can be affirmed or denied. "All men are created equal"; "Some Americans are Indians"; "No metals are compounds" are such statements; and one can take an affirmative position and argue for them, or a negative position and argue against them.

These examples will indicate that all propositions are sentences, but it is important to see that not all sentences are propositions. Only those sentences which we classify in grammar as declarative are propositions because declarative sentences alone affirm or deny that something is so. Consequently sentences which we have learned to recognize as interrogative, imperative, or volitive never express propositions. One does not state a proposition in saying "Let us rally to the defense of our liberties," or "Are men more intelligent than women?" or "Mind your own business." One could make each of these into a proposition by changing its grammatical type to the declarative, as in "All of us should rally to the defense of our liberties," "Men are more intelligent than women," and "You should mind your own business." In these revised versions, each sentence makes a definite assertion which, according to the rule just given for propositions, we can either affirm or deny. Only such sentences are arguable.

Exercise:   *In the list below, encircle the number before each sentence which constitutes a proposition. In deciding, you must ask yourself whether or not the sentence makes an assertion. Remember that such sentences are distinguished from those which ask a question, express a wish, or give an order.*

1. The horse is the noblest of animals.
2. Heaven help the old man!
3. How many ounces are in a pound?
4. The Himalayas are the highest mountains on earth.
5. Avoid even the appearance of evil.
6. No one under twenty one is eligible to vote.
7. The centaur is a mythological creature.
8. Would that I had a million dollars!
9. The motor car changed the habits of the American family.
10. Which is the nearest way to the post office?
11. The earth is a sphere 7,918 miles in diameter.
12. Some men have profited by adversity.
13. *Hamlet* is a tragedy written by Shakespeare.
14. No planets are stars.
15. Let well enough alone.
16. All liars are cowards.
17. Am I my brother's keeper?
18. May the best man win!
19. Take the first road on the right.
20. All men are fallible.

## The Structure of Propositions

When we have learned to distinguish the proposition from other types of sentences, we are ready to analyze its structure. We see from the examples before us that the proposition consists of three parts, which are comparable to those of the sentence. In parsing the sentence "Men are rational beings," for example, we distinguish "men" as the subject, "are" as the verb, and "rational beings" as the predicate nominative. In analyzing the same sentence as a logical proposition, we distinguish "men" as the *subject term*, "are" as the linking verb, and "rational beings" as the *predicate term*. We shall later have to recognize other types of propositions, but the pattern of all propositions of the type with which we are beginning is as follows:

subject term        linking verb or "copula"        predicate term

The reason for this structure appears when we review our definition of the proposition as any statement which affirms or denies something. As the above formula helps to explain, the subject term is the part about which the assertion or denial is made, and the predicate term is the part which, with the aid of the copula, makes the assertion or denial. In actual discourse there are many sentences of the declarative type which consist only of a subject and a verb, such as "The sun shines," "Birds fly," etc. For the purpose of logical analysis, however, it is desirable to make these conform with the structure explained above, and this change can be effected by substituting for the verb some form of the copulative verb "to be" and a noun or noun-equivalent. With this kind of substitution, the sentences before us would read "The sun is an object which shines," and "Birds are creatures which fly." A sentence thus expanded may seem somewhat artificial, but since in logic accuracy and explicitness are matters of the highest importance, we must be prepared for changes of this kind. In dealing with the sentence "The sun is an object which shines" we should have no difficulty in distinguishing "sun" as the subject term, "an object which shines" as the predicate term, and "is" as the copula. Tests for logical validity depend upon a clear discrimination of these parts, which is greatly simplified by this fuller and more analytical statement of the meaning of the original sentence.

There is a further advantage in seeing to it that the predicate term is always some noun or noun-equivalent. In ordinary expression we are content to say "All men are rational"; "The rich are proud," and so on. But in logic we are engaged in stating the relationship of things as exactly as possible, and consequently it is essential to have the classes of things named explicitly in our propositions. Thus all of the terms ought to signify classes, but since the predicate terms here, "rational" and "proud," are adjectives, they designate, by the convention of grammar, qualities rather than things, and a class must be made up of things or objects. Accordingly we make the slight change of supplying a noun for each: "All men are rational beings," and "All rich people are proud people." This serves to keep before us the fact that we are referring in our predicate terms to the classes "rational beings" and "proud people."

## Types of Propositions

We have just said that in logic exact and explicit statement of the relationship between subject and predicate classes is of the greatest importance, and we are now going to find that there are yet further demands of explicitness. It is necessary to know also whether the statement made by the proposition is to be taken as applying to the whole of the classes named by the terms or only to parts of the classes. In many statements in ordinary speech we cannot be sure which application is intended. If we are confronted with the statement "Men are rational beings," we cannot be sure whether the predicate "rational beings" applies to the whole class of men or only to part of it. In the case of unqualified statements of this sort we generally assume that the predicate does apply to all of the class named by the subject; yet there are instances in which this is not the intention of the statement, and therefore in argumentation we must insist that the statement of every proposition be definite with regard to quantity. Quantity is that property of the proposition which tells us whether the predicate applies to all of the subject or to less than all. If it applies to all, in this instance to the entire class of men, then the proposition must say, "All men are rational beings"; if it applies to less than all, it must say, "Some men are rational beings." Thus, "all" and "some" are signs by which the quantity of the proposition is denoted. In analyzing the meaning of propositions, "some" is taken as referring to any portion less than the whole.

Propositions which assert something about the whole of a class are said to be *universal;* propositions which assert something about a portion of a class are said to be *particular.*

In addition to quantity, propositions are said to have quality, the property telling us whether they are affirming or denying something. Quality is distinguished as *affirmative* or *negative.* We thus note that the propositions "All men are rational beings" and "Some men are rational beings" are both affirmative in that they affirm something of the subject. If now we retain these propositions but change their quality to negative, we shall have "No men are rational beings" and "Some men are not rational beings." Both of these propositions deny something of the subject, and that is the reason they are said to be negative. Furthermore, since their quantity has been indicated by "No" and "Some," we can say that the first is a universal negative and the second a particular negative proposition. Not until the properties of quantity and quality have been made clear in this manner is a proposition in form for use in argumentation. We shall frequently refer to these properties in analyzing the validity of arguments, and there is some profit in looking briefly at the traditional "square of opposition." This is a diagram showing the relationship of propositions such as the four we have just stated. It will prove useful in determining the validity of arguments.

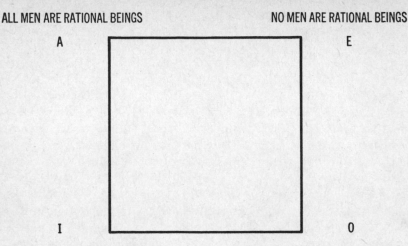

ALL MEN ARE RATIONAL BEINGS

A

NO MEN ARE RATIONAL BEINGS

E

I

SOME MEN ARE RATIONAL BEINGS

0

SOME MEN ARE NOT RATIONAL BEINGS

The propositions at the top of the square are both universal; those at the bottom are both particular. Those on the left-hand side are both affirmative; those on the right-hand side are both negative. Propositions which oppose one another diagonally (as A and O) are said to be contradictories; those which oppose one another at the top of the square (as A and E) are said to be contraries; those at the bottom (as I and O), subcontraries; and propositions which fall under other propositions (as I under A and O under E) are said to be subalterns.

This square has been employed as a ready means of determining what can be inferred from a given proposition. Here we can summarize briefly as follows. If any given proposition is true, its contradictory must be false. (Thus if it is true that all men are rational beings, it is false that some men are not rational beings.) Of two contrary propositions, one must be false if the other is true, but both may be false. (If it is true that all men are rational beings, then it is false that no men are rational beings, but both of these propositions are false if it is true that only some men are rational beings.) If a universal proposition is true, the particular proposition falling under it, which we have called the subaltern, is true also. (Thus if it is true that all men are rational beings, it must be true that some men are rational beings.)

Although the letters A, E, O, and I may seem arbitrary designations, actually they have an explanation. During the Middle Ages, when logic was one of the studies most cultivated in the universities, the affirmative propositions were designated by the first two vowels of the Latin *affirmo* ("I affirm"), and the negative propositions by the two vowels of *nego* ("I deny").

When later we have to distinguish valid and invalid forms of argument, we must be able to recognize immediately the quantity and quality of propositions, and it will be found convenient to refer to the different propositions by these letters.

It is of the utmost importance in logic to be able to cast statements into strict logical form. This form enables us to tell exactly what the proposition is saying and also to see its relationship to other propositions in the argument. To be sure of any conclusion, we have to know the precise import of the propositions backing it up, and this is made explicit by strict propositional form. The requirements of this form may be summarized as follows:

1. The proposition must be a declarative sentence.
2. It must consist of a subject term and a predicate term joined by a copula.
3. The terms must be nouns or noun-equivalents.
4. Both the quantity and the quality of propositions must be definitely indicated.

## Special Problems

Up to this point we have been illustrating with sentences whose meanings are relatively easy to infer, but in practice we find that there are types of sentences which present special difficulties. In some sentences of idiomatic English, we cannot be certain whether the negative *not* applies to the sentence as a whole or to one of the parts which we have to treat as a term. Suppose, for example, we were to encounter the sentence "All of the children are not sick." Probably we would interpret this as meaning "Some of the children are sick" and "Some of the children are not sick"; yet it could be interpreted as meaning "None of the children are sick." To prevent this ambiguity, we should always avoid in our professional statements the form "All . . . are not. . . ." If we intend the modifier *not* to apply to the sense of "All" in a sentence like "All of the children are not sick," we should write "Some of the children are not sick," thus making this a particular negative proposition, the quantity of which is now definitely indicated. If we mean it to apply to the proposition as a whole, then we begin the proposition with "No" or "None," as in "None of the children are sick," thus making it a universal negative proposition.

Difficulties are presented also by statements containing such expressions as "Only," "All . . . but," and "None . . . but." The right method is to treat all such statements as universal affirmative propositions, but close attention is required to tell which terms are subjects and which are predicates. In the sentence "Only the strong survived," we find the meaning to be "All who survived were the strong ones." In all such constructions the term following "Only" must be the predicate when the sentence is thrown into strict propositional form. But if the sentence begins with the expression "The only," then the term following this expression is the subject term.

The only ones rewarded were the party's supporters.
All who were rewarded were the party's supporters.

The only men accepted were volunteers.
All of the men who were accepted were volunteers.

If a sentence begins "All (or none) but. . . ." or "All except. . . .," we negate the term following "but" and make it the subject term. Then "All but minors are eligible" becomes "All non-minors are eligible persons"; "None but the brave deserve the fair" becomes "No non-brave ones deserve the fair ones."

A careful scrutiny of sentences containing "not" and "only" will reveal that these are the trickiest modifiers in the language, and it is therefore necessary, even at the expense of compactness and elegance, to make their application definite in logical propositions.

In listing the four types of propositions, we made no mention of those statements which have singular subjects in the form of proper nouns; that is, such statements as "Socrates was a philosopher," "Washington is the capital of the United States," and the like. These are known as *singular propositions,* and it is the practice to treat them as universal affirmatives, or "A" propositions. Although advanced logic makes some distinctions at this point, it is enough for our purposes to assume that in such cases we are talking about a subject term which stands for a universal class with a membership of one. Obviously, whatever we shall state about Socrates will be about all Socrates and not some Socrates, and so with all other propositions beginning with singular subjects. The convention of treating these singular propositions as universal affirmatives allows us to keep within the rules of formal logic.

There is one further point to be observed with regard to the propositional form of sentences. A proposition beginning with a singular common noun having a generic significance must be recast as a universal affirmative. The reason for this is that English usage frequently employs the singular noun form prefaced by "a" or "the" to stand for the whole of the class of which the thing signified is a member. Thus when we read "The cat is a feline," we understand it to mean "All cats are felines"; when we read "A maple tree is deciduous," we understand it to mean "All maple trees are deciduous," and so forth.

**Exercise:** *Express each of the following statements in strict propositional form. Bear in mind what has been said about the grammatical form of terms and about the indication of quantity and quality. Then label your propositions A, E, O, and I according to their quantity and quality.*

1. Men are not perfect.
2. All gases are compressible.
3. The crocodile is an amphibian.
4. None but the wise are just.

5. Children are imitative.
6. Honesty is the best policy.
7. Not all of the guests arrived on time.
8. Elements are not compounds.
9. Only patriots deserve well of their country.
10. The only crimes punishable by death are felonies.
11. A few men attain the age of 100.
12. Not every one who criticizes the government takes the trouble to vote.
13. Cows are herbivorous.
14. None but the important cases were reviewed by the commission.
15. The only ones who failed were those who were careless.
16. Some professors are not absentminded.
17. Most boys are interested in sports.
18. A great book should be a source of wisdom.
19. The Western hero is a classic American type.
20. Egotists are never popular.

## SUPPORTING THE PROPOSITION

We noted earlier in this chapter that an assertion alone is not an argument, and this principle holds for assertions in strict propositional form as well as it does for ordinary idiomatic sentences. Although we should now be able to take any declarative sentence and put it in a form usable in argument, we still have to learn how arguments are made, or how conclusions are proved. In other words, we need to know what distinguishes proper argument from a simple statement of belief or conviction, however that may be phrased. Naturally this is our real interest in studying the subject of argumentation. If someone announces in our presence, "Excessive speed is the principal cause of automobile accidents," or "All believers in democracy are believers in progress," our impulse is to respond, "How do you know that?" or "What are your grounds for saying so?" The fact is that each of these assertions is a conclusion in propositional form, but neither is accompanied by matter supporting the conclusion. Our next task, therefore, to which everything that we have said thus far is preliminary, is to consider how propositions are proved.

In a general approach to the subject, we find that there are three ways in which propositions are supported, although not every proposition can be supported in all of the three ways.

First of all, there is a class of propositions which are regarded as *intuitive*, or as attainable by immediate apprehension. "Immediate" in this case means without any kind of mediation, or directly. In a sense, these violate what we have been saying about conclusions, since they are never accompanied by proof. For this reason, they constitute a very special group and, strictly speaking, stand outside the province of logic. It is necessary, however, to recognize them because some of the most fundamental propositions involved in our thinking, such as the axioms of mathematics, belong in this group. Sometimes even propositions relating to political and social matters are treated as intuitively true, or as requiring no proof. For example, the Declaration of Independence asserts with reference to a series of propositions: "We hold these truths to be self-evident." It is of course questionable whether propositions about this kind of subject matter have any right to be treated as having the same kind of intuitive certainty as do such propositions as "Things equal to the same thing are equal to each other," but it is well to be aware that even in this area propositions are sometimes put forward as self-proving. At any rate, the number of such propositions which will be received is quite limited, and the student must not suppose that he is free to offer an intuitive or "pre-logical" proposition in order to avoid the labor of adducing proof. The vast majority of conclusions must be supported by reasoning in the form of the modes of inference, which we will now examine.

## Induction

Those propositions which rest upon direct observation of factual evidence are proved by the mode of inference called *induction.* Induction is sometimes called the scientific method because it "goes to the facts." There is a certain historical reason for such characterization, because the birth of science three or four centuries ago was accompanied by an enormous increase in direct observation and experimentation, which contrasted with the practice of earlier periods. Actually, however, we shall find that science makes equal use of another mode of inference called *deduction,* and that without this the fruits of induction would be quite meager. In the scientific method, as in thinking generally, the two are closely related, but here we shall take them one after the other.

In every example of induction we have a general statement resting upon a group of particular instances. The number of instances may vary greatly from example to example, although there must always be at least two. An inductive conclusion, therefore, may be defined simply as a generalization resting upon two or more facts or instances. The method of induction is accordingly easy to state. We examine fact 1, fact 2, fact 3, fact 4 and so on, and whatever we find these facts to agree in we may express as an inductive generalization. Let us suppose that we are interested in finding out the academic year of the members of a college English class. To proceed inductively, we consult the individual instances, in this case the members of the class. We learn that Henry Thompson is a sophomore, that Mary Smith is a sophomore, that Charles Jones is a sophomore, and so on around the room. If we ascertain that every member of the class is a sophomore, we are prepared to make the generalization "All members of this class are sophomores." This is a proposition resting upon direct observation of the evidence, and therefore it constitutes an inductive generalization.

If this example seems somewhat artificial, that is because it is a *perfect induction,* and the number of perfect inductions we may make is comparatively small. An induction is perfect only when we are able to observe every member of the class of things about which our proposition asserts something. "Perfect" here has its derivative meaning of "complete," and it signifies that observation has exhausted the number of instances which exist. With this particular example the process was simple, since all we had to do was check the members of a college class. We might make similar perfect inductions about the months of the year, the presidents of the United States, or the stores in a city block, because the number of these, being relatively small, permits the kind of complete examination upon which a perfect induction rests.

But in most situations it is impossible to observe all the instances included in the class about which we are making an assertion. Let us take the assertion "All Democrats favor the graduated income tax." Now as far as our personal observation goes, this would probably rest upon six to a dozen cases: "Brown is a Democrat and he favors the graduated income tax"; "Johnson is a Democrat and he favors the graduated income tax," and so forth. A dozen cases out of all the registered Democrats is a very small fraction; yet since we have examined more than one case and have found no exception, we have a basis for the generalization "All Democrats are persons who favor the graduated income tax." Many conclusions which rest upon a vastly greater number of observed cases than this are still technically imperfect inductions. That would be true even of the proposition "All men are mortal," for although this has been borne out by the great number of men who have already died, the men living at present constitute instances which cannot be counted. The same must be noted with regard to the law of gravitation. It rests upon a vast amount of observation and experiment, but because these cannot, in the nature of the case, exhaust all the instances of falling bodies, we must classify the law of gravitation too as a generalization resting upon imperfect induction.

It should be emphasized that the word "imperfect" is not to be understood as meaning fallacious or inaccurate. An imperfect induction is a sound inference *as far as the evidence goes.* The term merely tells us that not all of the evidence has been examined. Some logicians, therefore, prefer to treat imperfect induction as establishing only probability, although the degree of probability may be very high. According to this, for example, it is probable that our friend John Smith is mortal, though logically, for the reasons we have been discussing, it is not absolutely certain.

## Analogy

*Analogy* is a subvariety of induction. Analogy may be defined simply as the means of reaching conclusions on the basis of comparison or similarity. Few arguments are more common in ordinary speech than the assertion that such and such a thing must be true because it is much like some other thing which is known to be true. If free trade has proved successful within the United States, it will prove successful within Europe.

If a certain treatment has a known definite effect upon cancer in rats, then it will have a similar effect upon cancer in human beings. As these examples will illustrate, analogy rests upon the theory that a certain degree of resemblance between two things implies a still further degree of resemblance. Thus if A is known to have a certain set of characteristics and B is known to have all the same characteristics save one (but is not known to lack that one), it is probable that B has the one characteristic which has not yet been ascertained. The relationship of the two instances may be set forth as follows:

| Instance A | Instance B |
|:---:|:---:|
| 1 | 1 |
| 2 | 2 |
| 3 | 3 |
| 4 | (4) |

According to our previous explanation, we have two instances, A and B, and we know that A has characteristics 1, 2, 3, and 4. We know that B has characteristics 1, 2, and 3, and we go on to say, on the basis of analogy, that it is probable that B has characteristic 4 also. In other words, a certain amount of resemblance implies still further resemblance, and so we pass from the certainty that A and B have 1, 2, and 3 in common to the probability that they have 4 also in common.

Let us follow this reasoning in a concrete example. One of the most widely used analogies of recent years draws a comparison between the thirteen original colonies of America and the nations of the world today. The analogy proceeds by pointing out that the colonies were a group of independent states with common political objectives and complementary economies, but with antagonisms expressing themselves in boundary disputes, protective tariffs, and various acts of jealousy and suspicion. Then it proceeds to the second instance. It points out that the world today is a group of independent states with more or less common political objectives, with complementary economies, and with antagonisms much like those of the thirteen colonies. We know that it was possible for the thirteen colonies to form a union which produced many benefits for the members. We do not *know* that it is possible for the nations of the present world to do this, but we assume on the basis of these demonstrated resemblances that it is so. In other words, if the possibility of a permanent and beneficial union existed in the case of the colonies, it exists also in the case of the nations of the world today.

| A. | B. |
|---|---|
| The American Colonies | The Nations of the World Today |
| 1. Common political objectives | 1.  Common political objectives |
| 2. Complementary economies | 2.  Complementary economies |
| 3. Acts of hostility and aggression | 3.  Acts of hostility and aggression |
| 4. Possibility of permanent and beneficial union | (4.) Possibility of permanent and beneficial union |

This argument by analogy is intended to establish the probability of success of an organization like the United Nations. Analogy is always used to show that something which cannot be directly observed probably exists or is true. Another familiar example is the analogy supporting the proposition that life exists on the planet Mars. Not even the most powerful telescopes are able to detect life on Mars, and therefore its possible existence must be established in other ways. The "proof" takes the form of a comparison of the planet Earth with Mars. We know that the planet Earth is a spherical body rotating on an axis and moving in an orbit around the sun at a fixed distance. The Earth is composed of certain elements; it has an atmosphere, and it supports life. All of these facts, excepting the last, we know to be true also of the planet Mars. Then it is reasoned that if the Earth and Mars are alike in all these particulars, there is some probability that they are alike in that both support life.

Because analogy is an exceedingly common form of argument, used quite often by those who have never given thought to the principles of argumentation, it is necessary to point out its limitations with some care. The last example we have used affords a good means of doing this.

Many persons after hearing this analogy which purports to establish the probability of life on Mars will have the feeling that after all it is a fairly unconvincing line of argument (and some feel that the analogy involving world union also falls short in the same way). It is necessary, therefore, to emphasize the fact that analogy never gives proof in the strict sense, but only probability, as the terminology we have been using should have suggested. This must not be taken to mean that analogy has no value as argument, because probability is a relative matter. It may range all the way from the negligible to that which falls just short of certainty. And since there is no scientific rule for assessing the force of an argument by analogy, we can only estimate the degree of probability which it establishes. The degree of probability that life exists on the planet Mars, based on the foregoing analogy, will be variously estimated, as we have just remarked. Some persons will feel that it is impressive, whereas others will feel that it is slight. Such difference is always to be expected, but in estimating the value of any argument by analogy, there are certain things we should note. We should give weight not so much to the number of resemblances as to the pertinence of them. The resemblances which carry weight have a direct bearing upon the proposition to be established. The fact that the Earth and Mars both have atmospheres is a pertinent resemblance, closely connected with the possibility of life, whereas some of the other resemblances mentioned have little or no connection with that possibility. The fact that two students, let us say, resemble each other in physical appearance does not imply that they also resemble each other in scholastic ability, although other characteristics in common might be discovered which would serve to establish that probability.

At the same time, if an analogy is to be of value, there must be an absence of pertinent differences. Important differences bearing upon the proposition at issue will nullify superficial resemblances. If the two students who resemble each other in appearance differ in that one has a very high I.Q. and the other a very low one, there would be little ground for inferring their resemblance in scholastic ability. In the same way, the fact that gasoline and water resemble each other in being colorless liquids does not establish a probability that they are equally effective in putting out fires.

We have said that analogy can be regarded as a subvariety of induction, but *analogy never gives the kind of proof that we get by induction proper,* including imperfect induction, for a reason which must be noted. As we saw in our discussion of the inductive process, at least two instances are required to support a generalization arrived at by this mode of inference. After the generalization has been established on the basis of two or more instances, then we apply it to a third or a fifth or a hundredth instance of the same kind, about which it enables us to make a prediction. But analogy differs from this in the important respect that it passes from a single instance to the instance about which the prediction is to be made. In one of the examples used for explanation, we passed from the single instance of the thirteen American colonies to the instance of the nations of the modern world; in another, from the single instance of the planet Earth to the instance of Mars. Accordingly, analogy rests upon fewer than two known instances of any phenomenon. It does not proceed through a general proposition. Only general propositions enable us to say something with certainty about a general class. If we know that all cases of rabies in human beings have thus far proved fatal, we infer from a general law that the next case will prove fatal. But analogy does not establish this kind of generalization, and this is why it is regarded as giving a less positive kind of proof than induction, although both proceed on the basis of direct observation.

## Deduction

*Deduction* is the next mode of inference we must examine. By this method of reasoning propositions are established not by immediate apprehension, and not by direct observation of facts, but by reference to other already established propositions.

It will be evident after a moment's reflection that many of our judgments are reached on the basis of judgments already arrived at, or, to put this in another way, that we accept many conclusions because they are involved in conclusions which we already hold. When we assert any proposition on the ground that it is made necessary by other propositions which have been admitted, we are proving it through the other propositions. Let us exemplify this with an ordinary assertion. We shall suppose that you hear one of your friends remark, "John Jones passed Math I." Now if you should ask him how he knows this, or "What is the proof?" you might be answered as follows, "Well, he is registered for Math II, and the college catalogue says that only those who have passed Math I can register for Math II." If you proceed to analyze this answer, you find that there is nothing to show that your friend has either seen John Jones' official grade card or heard directly from John Jones that he passed the course. Instead, he has arrived at the conclusion through other propositions. These are (1) Only those who have passed Math I can register for Math II, and (2) John Jones is registered for Math II. Now if you press him still further, and if he is able to state his argument in the form of strict logical propositions, you will be given what follows.

> All students·who are registered for Math II are students who have passed Math I.
> John Jones is a student who is registered for Math II.
> Therefore John Jones is a student who has passed Math I.

This is a deductive argument expressed in the form of a *categorical* syllogism, which we must now define.

## The Categorical Syllogism

The *categorical syllogism* is a logical device consisting of three propositions so related that one of them is implied by (or, as we have been saying, is proved by reference to) the other two. To observe this relationship in the preceding argument, we note that the last proposition is proved by the first two, for if it is true that all students registered for Math II are students who have passed Math I, and if it is true that John Jones is registered for Math II, then it must be true that John Jones is a student who has passed Math I. You will notice again that we have received no direct report that John Jones has passed Math I. We reach that conclusion by combining two other statements whose truth has been established. This is the nature of the deductive process. From statements already given or accepted we draw (or deduce) a third statement which is contained in them. The third statement is the proposition which is proved by deduction.

With this relationship in mind, we may proceed to a further examination of the categorical syllogism. In order to achieve correct results with this mode of inference, it is necessary to know a number of things about the formal structure of the syllogism. Let us proceed, therefore, to a careful analysis of its parts.

This type of syllogism consists of three propositions which are called, in the order in which they usually come, the major premise, the minor premise, and the conclusion. These three propositions always contain a total of three terms. In this example the terms are "All students who are registered for Math II," "Students who have passed Math I," and "John Jones." These comprise a major term, a minor term, and a middle term. The middle term can always be identified by the fact that it occurs in both of the premises but does not occur in the conclusion. It is so called because it is the mediating term, the term through which the major term and the minor term are related. Deductive reasoning is sometimes called mediate inference just because it involves this process of mediating, by means of the middle term, between the other two terms, which are called the *extremes*. In a categorical syllogism the major term always appears as the predicate of the conclusion and the minor term as the subject. Thus if we take the syllogism:

> All men are rational beings
> Socrates is a man
> Therefore Socrates is a rational being

we see at once by these rules that "men" is the middle term, "rational beings" is the major term and "Socrates" the minor term. But suppose we were given the argument, "Edison was a genius because he was a great inventor and all great inventors are geniuses." Here, as often happens in actual argument, the conclusion ("Edison was a genius") does not appear in third place, and this illustrates why we cannot say that there is a fixed sequence in which the terms of argument always appear. Consequently, in analyzing any argument, we must identify the conclusion (determine what the argument is proving) before we can proceed further. Once we have ascertained the conclusion, we know that the proposition which contains the conclusion's predicate term is the major premise while the other proposition is the minor premise.

**Exercise:**    *Identify the conclusion in each of the following arguments.*

1. Smith possesses the quality of determination.
   All successful men possess the quality of determination.
   Smith is a successful man.

2. This ring will not rust.
   This ring is made of gold.
   Gold will not rust.

3. No non-alcoholic beverage is intoxicating.
   Grape juice is not intoxicating.
   Grape juice is a non-alcoholic beverage.

4. Every president is commander-in-chief of the armed forces.
   Lincoln was president.
   Lincoln was commander-in-chief of the armed forces.

5. Only laws that have popular support are enforceable.
   This law is enforceable.
   This law has popular support.

In our earlier discussion of terms and propositions, we noted that in this type of syllogism terms stand for things that can be conceived as classes. It follows that categorical propositions make assertions about the inclusion and exclusion of classes, and the categorical syllogism itself may be viewed as a means of stating explicitly the relationship of the three classes signified by the three terms. We may now use one of our examples to explain this relationship. If we say that all great inventors are men of genius, we are taking the two classes "great inventors" and "men of genius" and placing (or including) the first class in the second. The relationship may be diagrammed as follows:

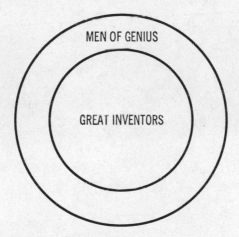

In the same syllogism the minor premise makes a second statement of relationship, asserting that "Edison" is included in the class "great inventors." This relationship would be diagrammed in a similar way.

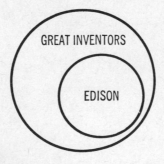

Now if we draw the diagram so that it represents both of the two statements of relationship or inclusion, we have the following:

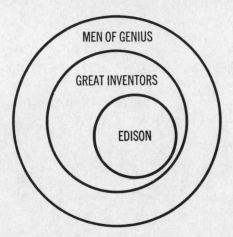

The process is similar with propositions which assert the exclusion of one class from another (although, as we shall see presently, no syllogism can have two such propositions). Thus if we have the proposition "No gold is a metal which rusts," we must diagram it as follows:

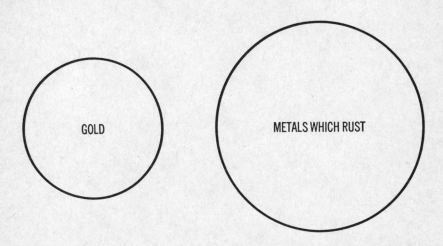

If we now go on to add, "This object is gold," we include "This object" in the circle "Gold" and thereby exclude it from the circle "Metals which rust."

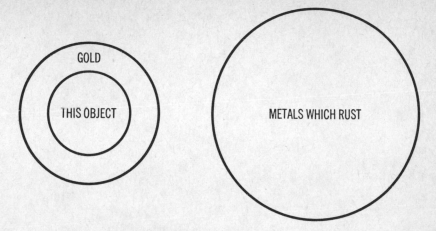

We observed earlier that to arrive at a correct inference by means of the categorical syllogism, it is necessary to know something of its formal structure. We are now prepared to see that there are some forms of the syllogism (or some relationships of inclusion and exclusion) which yield a correct conclusion and some which do not. The rules governing these relationships are known as the formal rules of the syllogism, and the violation of any of them constitutes a formal fallacy. Below are the formal rules with their explanations.

1. *A syllogism has three and only three terms.* The reason for this rule appears in the nature of the middle term. We have seen that the syllogism is an argument by which two terms are related through this middle or "mediating" term. The middle term is the means of indicating this relationship of inclusion or partial inclusion or total exclusion. If an argument has more or fewer than three terms, no such relationship is possible. If we take as an example

> All persons who study are students.
> Henry is a person who attends college.
> Therefore Henry is a student.

we see that we have four terms, "persons who study," "students," "Henry," and "persons who attend college." There is no term relating "Henry" to the class "students." To make this a valid syllogism, we should have to reduce the number of terms to three and state the relationship as follows:

> All persons who attend college are students.
> Henry is a person who attends college.
> Therefore Henry is a student.

Now we have a middle term "persons who attend college" which mediates between the extreme terms "students" and "Henry." The relationship of inclusion will appear thus:

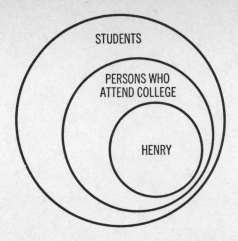

2. *The middle term must be distributed at least once in the premises.*
This rule is the most difficult one for many beginners in logic to grasp
because it makes use of the somewhat technical term "distributed." A
term is said to be distributed when the proposition in which it appears
affirms or denies something about the entire class for which the term
stands. The important point to see is that the *whole* of the term is involved
in the assertion or denial made by the proposition. If we examine the
proposition "All Irishmen are brave men," we perceive at once that we are
affirming something about the entire class of Irishmen, *i.e.*, that they are
brave men. If we examine the proposition "No gold is a metal which rusts,"
we perceive that we are denying something about all gold and also about
all metal which rusts; *i.e.*, we are denying that either of these is included
within the other. But if we examine the proposition "Some men are
rational beings," we see that the proposition does not say anything about
all men or all rational beings and therefore does not contain a distributed
term.

We shall see presently that each of the propositions A, E, O, and I
distributes its terms differently; but we must note carefully here that
unless the middle term is somewhere distributed, there is no way of relating the other two terms. Or, to put this in another way, unless we know
the complete coverage of the mediating term, we have no means of stating
how the other two terms include or exclude one another. This fact is
exemplified by the syllogism which follows.

> Some of my friends are writers.
> Some writers are famous men.
> Some of my friends are famous men.

Now in this syllogism the middle term is "writers," but in neither premise
is the term distributed, or used universally, because neither premise says
anything about *all* writers. It is not affirmed that *all* writers are famous
men, and therefore it is possible that my friends who are writers fall in that

part of the class of writers who are not famous men. The fallacy of the undistributed middle is probably responsible for more faulty reasoning than is any of the other formal fallacies. It is all too easy to arrive at an invalid conclusion through an argument like the following:

> All fascist parties are anti-Marxist parties.
> All conservative parties are anti-Marxist parties.
> Therefore all conservative parties are fascist parties.

An examination of the premises of the argument will show that something is said about all fascist parties and all conservative parties but nothing is said about all anti-Marxist parties. This class may therefore include both fascist parties and conservative parties without any overlapping of these two.

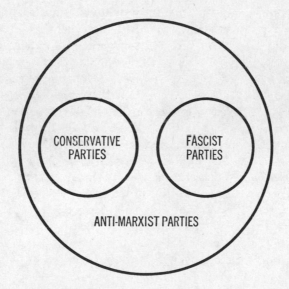

As the diagram shows, we can place both parties in the undistributed anti-Marxist class without either's including any portion of the other.

3. *No term can be distributed in the conclusion which was not distributed at least once in the premises.* This rule reflects the simple principle that a syllogism cannot say anything in the conclusion which was not implied in the premises. Obviously if the conclusion says something not implied in the premises, then it is not coming from the premises (though it might come correctly from other premises). Such terms appearing in a conclusion are called *illicit terms,* the phrase signifying that they are unlawful or contrary to rule.

> All liars are cowards.
> No gentlemen are liars.
> Therefore no gentlemen are cowards.

The fallacy of this argument is that the term "cowards" is distributed in the conclusion but is not distributed in the premise in which it occurs. Some people who are not liars may be cowards. Consequently, the conclusion is sneaked in, through an illicit term. If the term which is thus used is the major term of the syllogism, it is called an *illicit major;* if it is the minor, an *illicit minor.*

There are four more rules which rest upon an equally rigorous analysis of the syllogism, but there is little need for us to go into them in detail. They may be stated with a brief explanation.

4. *From two particular premises, no conclusion is possible.*
5. *From two negative premises, no conclusion is possible.*
6. *If one premise is negative, the conclusion must be negative.*
7. *If one premise is particular, the conclusion must be particular.*

If both premises are particular, it will be found that the syllogism unavoidably violates either rule 2 or rule 3, which have to do with the distribution of terms. The same is true if we try to draw a universal conclusion from a syllogism having one particular premise. No conclusion can be drawn from two negative premises because negative premises tell us merely that the two classes represented by the extremes fall outside the middle term. This leaves us with no means of comparing these classes, and we do not know how they stand in relation to each other. If one premise is negative and one is affirmative, one of the extremes will be excluded from the middle term entirely while the other will be included in it. But if one is excluded and the other is included, this can only mean that these two terms exclude one another, and such a relationship can be stated only in the form of a negative proposition.

In testing for formal correctness, it is necessary to know whether a categorical proposition conforms with the rules we have stated. And in order to do that, we must know how the four types of propositions distribute their terms.

An A proposition distributes its subject term. We readily see that in the proposition "All Chicagoans are Americans" something is affirmed about all Chicagoans. However, nothing is affirmed about all Americans, and hence the predicate term remains undistributed.

An E proposition distributes both subject and predicate terms. In the proposition "No rabbits are indigenous to Australia" we are denying something about the entire class of rabbits (that they are indigenous to Australia), and at the same time we are denying something about the entire class of animals indigenous to Australia (that they are rabbits). In other words we know enough about the two classes to say that each excludes the other entirely, and this is possible only when both classes are distributed.

An I proposition distributes neither term. The proposition "Some voters are Democrats" does not affirm anything about all voters or all Democrats. All that it asserts is that the class voters and the class Democrats overlap to some indefinitely known extent.

An O proposition distributes its predicate term. This generally proves the most difficult proposition to explain; however, it is proved by the principle that if we say "Some voters are not Democrats," we must know at least one thing about the entire class of Democrats in order to be certain that some voters are excluded from that class. As the diagram following illustrates, the entire class of Democrats is known to fall outside the class of some voters.

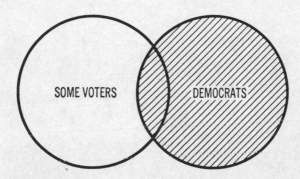

**Exercise:**  *Test the following syllogisms by the rules for formal correctness discussed above. Keep in mind how the four types of propositions distribute their terms. After each of the valid syllogisms place a check mark. After each of the invalid syllogisms write one of the numbers below corresponding to the fallacy.*

1. Four-term argument
2. Undistributed middle term
3. Illicit term
4. Two particular premises
5. Two negative premises

   *Note that in some cases you will have to recast the major premise in order to make clear the meaning of the proposition.*

1. No metals are conductors of electricity.
   Aluminum is a metal.
   Therefore aluminum is not a conductor of electricity.

2. All swallows are birds.
   No thrushes are swallows.
   Therefore some birds are not thrushes.

3. Not all sentences are propositions.
   "Birds fly" is a sentence.
   Therefore "Birds fly" is not a proposition.

4. No men are always in the wrong.
   George III was a man.
   Therefore George III was not always in the wrong.

5. Only voluntary acts are virtuous acts.
   Shoplifting is a voluntary act.
   Therefore shoplifting is a virtuous act.

6. He who spares the rod hates his child.
   Mr. Simms is a parent who spares the rod.
   Therefore Mr. Simms hates his child.

7. No man who was born rich can imagine what it is like to be poor.
   Mr. Adams is not a man who was born rich.
   Therefore Mr. Adams can imagine what it is like to be poor.

8. All that glitters is not gold.
   Mica is a substance that glitters.
   Therefore mica is not gold.

9. Some lazy persons are naturally brilliant.
   Some of my friends are lazy persons.
   Some of my friends are naturally brilliant.

10. All hydrocarbons are combustible.
    Coal is not a hydrocarbon.
    Therefore coal is not combustible.

11. Some rocks are of volcanic origin.
    No granite is of volcanic origin.
    Therefore some rocks are not granites.

12. No illiterates are entitled to vote.
    Some citizens are illiterates.
    Therefore some citizens are not entitled to vote.

13. Some demagogues are poor reasoners.
    Some poor reasoners are successful politicians.
    Therefore some demagogues are successful politicians.

14. No sentimentalists are tough minded.
    Some businessmen are tough minded.
    Therefore some businessmen are not sentimentalists.

15. No gossips are thoughtful persons.
    Some women are not gossips.
    Therefore some women are thoughtful persons.

### The Hypothetical Syllogism

We turn now to a second type of syllogism, called the *hypothetical*. Syllogisms take their name from the nature of their major premise, and the hypothetical syllogism has as its major premise a proposition containing a hypothetical (or conditional) statement. The formula for this kind of proposition is often expressed thus:

If P, then Q.

Both the minor premise and the conclusion are, however, categorical propositions. The structure of the entire syllogism is, therefore, as follows:

If P, then Q.
P.
Then Q.

If it does not rain, the crops will fail.
It does not rain.
Therefore the crops will fail.

It will be noted that the major premise actually consists of two statements, "If it does not rain," and "the crops will fail." These are called respectively the *antecedent* and the *consequent,* and the proposition as a whole asserts a relationship of implication between the two. And this type of syllogism, like the categorical, has certain forms which will give a correct result and others which will give an incorrect one. For a correct result, the minor premise must either affirm the antecedent or must deny the consequent. Then the conclusion will either affirm the consequent or, in the second case, deny the antecedent. We see in the example above one of the two correct conclusions we can reach with the hypothetical syllogism. In the second correct form, as previously noted, the minor premise denies the consequent and the conclusion denies the antecedent.

If it does not rain, the crops will fail.
The crops will not fail.
Therefore it does rain.

The theory of the hypothetical syllogism is that the truth of the antecedent implies the truth of the consequent, and the falsity of the consequent implies the falsity of the antecedent. That means simply that if you affirm the truth of the antecedent, you may affirm the truth of the consequent, and if you deny the truth of the consequent, you may deny the truth of the antecedent. But these relationships do not hold in the opposite direction; and the reversal of them results in fallacies in the use of the hypothetical syllogism. Thus in the argument we are examining, it would be fallacious to say:

The crops will fail.
Therefore it does not rain.
If it does not rain, the crops will fail.

*or*

If it does not rain, the crops will fail.
It does rain.
Therefore the crops will not fail.

This rule is sometimes explained by saying that the relationship of implication is not necessarily symmetrical. Expressed more simply, this means that although a given cause always implies a certain effect, a given effect does not always imply a certain cause, inasmuch as there may be more than one cause of an effect. In the case before us, the cause is drought and the effect is ruin of the crops. Now the occurrence of drought will always imply ruin of the crops, but the ruin of the crops will not always imply drought, since the ruin of the crops can be brought about by other causes, such as blight or pests. This relationship might be illustrated as follows:

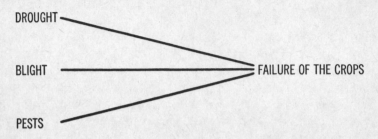

DROUGHT

BLIGHT                                          FAILURE OF THE CROPS

PESTS

Now if we can affirm either drought, blight, or pests, we can affirm failure of the crops; that is, any one of those causes will produce that effect. But if we affirm failure of the crops we cannot necessarily affirm drought, since the cause could be blight or pests. Thus the existence of any one of the causes entails existence of the effect (or "consequent"), and the denial of the effect entails the denial of all the causes. With this we understand why it is possible to move from an affirmation of the antecedent to an affirmation of the consequent, and from a denial of the consequent to a denial of the antecedent, but not possible to move in the opposite directions.

**Exercise:**   *Criticize the following hypothetical syllogisms:*

1. If a person is civic minded, he will vote in local elections.
   Joseph Kelly votes in local elections.
   Therefore Joseph Kelly is civic minded.

2. If two men are friends, they trust each other.
   Edward and William do not trust each other.
   Therefore Edward and William are not friends.

3. If a man becomes angry, he loses his power of judgment.
   William Jones never becomes angry.
   William Jones never loses his power of judgment.

4. If a man is wise, he has known sorrow.
   A young man cannot be wise.
   Therefore a young man cannot have known sorrow.

5. If a person has been victimized, he is doubly suspicious.
   Mr. Martin has been victimized.
   Therefore Mr. Martin is doubly suspicious.

6. If the country is prosperous, the incumbent party will remain in power.
   The incumbent party has not remained in power.
   Therefore the country is not prosperous.

7. If there is no hell, there is no justice.
   There is justice.
   Therefore there is a hell.

## The Alternative Syllogism

The third and last type of syllogism is called the *alternative* or *disjunctive* syllogism, because the major premise is an alternative proposition. This means that it presents alternatives. The minor premise is a categorical proposition which either accepts or rejects one of the alternatives. If the minor premise accepts one alternative, the conclusion must reject the other; if it rejects one, the conclusion must accept the other. The formula of the alternative syllogism can be written thus:

A is either B or C.               A is either B or C.
A is B.                           A is not B.
Therefore A is not C.             Therefore A is C.

Accordingly, if we are given the major premise "George is either in the library or the laboratory," our minor premise may assert "George is in the library," and our conclusion will be "George is not in the laboratory." Or our minor premise may assert "George is not in the library," and our conclusion will be "George is in the laboratory."

In order to arrive at a correct conclusion with the alternative syllogism, we must first be certain that the alternatives offered are mutually exclusive, so that the affirmation of one necessarily involves the denial of the other. Second, we must be certain that all of the possible alternatives have been taken into account. The syllogism of our illustration satisfies the first rule *if* we have enough knowledge to be sure that George is in one of the two places enumerated. Since he could not be in both places at the same time, the two possibilities exclude each other. But if it were possible for George to be in a third place, say the gymnasium, the syllogism would violate the second rule, since not all possibilities were enumerated. Similarly, a syllogism with the major premise "Schultz is either a Democrat or a Republican" could not yield a valid conclusion unless we could be sure that these were the only two possibilities. If it were possible for Schultz to be a Socialist or a Progressive or a Prohibitionist, we would not be limited to these two choices, and the syllogism would not yield a correct conclusion. A syllogism of this type in which the choices do not exclude one another is said to commit the fallacy of *imperfect disjunction;* one in which not all of the possible choices are given is said to commit the fallacy of *incomplete enumeration.*

**Exercise:** *Criticize the following alternative propositions in the light of these two rules.*

1. John is either a fool or a knave.
2. There are two ways of curing the evils of faction: one is to remove its causes; the other is to control its effects.

3. Every person is either a non-smoker or a tobacco addict.
4. Either you are with us or against us.
5. Mr. Barnes is either a farmer or a trader.
6. The witness had either forgotten or he committed perjury.

## The Dilemma

A form of argument related to the last two is the dilemma. The dilemma is a compound hypothetical syllogism partly disjunctive in form. This is because the major premise is made up of two hypothetical propositions, while the minor premise and the conclusion are disjunctive propositions.

If a nation enters into foreign alliances, it gives up part of its freedom; if it does not enter into foreign alliances, it leaves itself unprotected.
It must either enter into foreign alliances or not enter into them.
Therefore it must either give up part of its freedom or leave itself unprotected.

The two hypothetical propositions are spoken of as the "horns" of the dilemma. Both of them entail unpleasant consequences. If it is a true dilemma, the opponent will be gored by one of the horns, because he must accept one of them.

There are two ways of meeting a dilemma: "seizing one of the horns" and "escaping between the horns." If one adopts the first course and seizes a horn, he accepts one of the alternatives but denies the causal reasoning implied. In this case he might accept the alternative of entering into foreign alliances but deny that this is necessarily followed by a loss of freedom. Or, he might accept the alternative of staying out of foreign alliances and attack the idea that this would necessarily leave the nation unprotected. Note that in both instances he attempts to refute the cause-and-effect reasoning implied in the propositions of the major premises.

By the second course, one attempts to show that not all of the possible alternatives have been enumerated. Thus he might show that there is possible a third policy, which would not have the unpleasant consequences of the other two. This is "escaping between the horns"; and it is the same as pointing out the fallacy of incomplete enumeration, which we studied in connection with the disjunctive syllogism.

A dilemma which can be answered in either of these two ways is a false dilemma.

## The Enthymeme

It is natural for the syllogism to appear at first a somewhat cumbersome and artificial mode of expressing our everyday reasoning. We pointed out at the beginning, however, that to make sure of the correctness of arguments, it is necessary to be both full and explicit in statement, and the syllogism is merely a fully expanded form which we use when we undertake to prove one proposition by other propositions. It is true, none the less, that actual arguments do not always appear in this fully expanded form. In perhaps a majority of the instances, they appear with one of the three propositions omitted or suppressed. A deductive argument with one of its propositions thus missing is called an *enthymeme* (from a combination of Greek words signifying "in the mind"). As already intimated, the missing proposition may be the major premise, the minor premise, or the conclusion. In every instance the one to whom the argument is addressed is supposed to supply the missing proposition. Let us suppose that someone presents the argument "X would make an ideal candidate for president because he was born in a log cabin." It is evident after a moment's analysis that we have here the minor premise and the conclusion of a syllogism. The major premise, which is "All who were born in log cabins make ideal candidates for president," has been withheld. "Every American is pledged to do his duty, and you are an American" is another form of the enthymeme. Here it is the conclusion "You are pledged to do your duty" which is withheld. In the enthymeme "All property owners should vote for the bond issue; you should vote for the bond issue" it is the minor premise which must supplied.

Since a great many of the world's arguments appear in the form of enthymemes, it is of great value to acquire some facility in expanding the enthymeme into a complete syllogism. Then, whether or not we shall be persuaded by the argument will depend upon whether or not we accept *both* of the premises. And even if we can accept both of the premises, we must be able to see whether the conclusion emerges in accordance with the formal rules of the syllogism.

**Exercise:** *Supply the missing proposition in each of the following arguments, and identify the major premise, minor premise, and conclusion.*

1. No poet has any business ability.
   Harold is a poet.
2. Smith must be an idealist, for he is in favor of general disarmament.
3. I wouldn't do such a thing.
   No gentleman would.
4. This team cannot be considered the national champion because it didn't meet any first-class competition.
5. Blessed are the meek, for they shall inherit the earth.
6. Bill must be from the West because he has that free and easy air.
7. No paper receiving a mark lower than 70 passes the examination.
   This paper does not pass the examination.

The missing proposition of an enthymeme is sometimes suppressed because the maker of the argument knows that if we look carefully at his premises, we may question or reject one of them. He wishes to sneak his suppressed premise by unnoticed. It is not unfair to say that a large fraction of advertising is presented in the form of enthymemes for just this purpose, and the student of logic will find it a valuable exercise to go through the pages of any popular magazine and determine the suppressed premise in the texts of advertisements. The same may be said of a considerable part of political argumentation, and even of those arguments heard from supposedly non-partisan sources. It is a good rule always to stay on the alert to see on what the maker of an argument is really basing his case.

Still, all enthymemes are not offered with the object of deceiving or imposing upon the unwary. Many enthymemic arguments are perfectly frank and honest, the maker feeling that the unstated premise is too obvious or too generally accepted to require stating. It is "in the mind" of everyone he is addressing.

For this very reason the enthymeme has been called since ancient times the *rhetorical syllogism*. This expression requires a little interpretation, but an understanding of it is essential to the remainder of what we have to say about argumentation.

## RELATION OF LOGIC TO RHETORIC

To understand the full scope of argumentation, we must make a distinction between *convincing* and *persuading*. Although these words are often used interchangeably in ordinary speech, the student of rhetoric recognizes that to convince is not always to persuade. The term *convince* has a narrower meaning; it signifies forcing someone to accept a conclusion through the processes of valid argument. If people were changed in their attitudes and actions by being made to grasp the lines of an argument, the world might be a very different place, and we would no longer doubt whether or not man is a rational animal. But in truth the world is not governed by the syllogism, and everyone has witnessed the wisdom of the lines

> A man convinced against his will
> Is of the same opinion still.

We must not, of course, illogically jump from this to the conclusion that logic is useless. Logic is indispensable, but it will not accomplish everything. It has to be supplemented in most instances by an art to which the name "rhetoric" is sometimes specially applied. This art influences that part of our being not won over by pure reasoning. Although there have been many highly rhetorical discourses which were notable for their bad logic, rhetoric itself is not illogical. As Francis Bacon pointed out, rhetoric no more teaches men to make the worse appear the better cause than logic teaches them to reason fallaciously. Rhetoric is a means of persuasion which takes up where logic ends. After logic has convinced the mind, rhetoric wins the full assent. Therefore in looking at rhetoric, we turn our attention to what one does after making his logical argument.

First, however, we must pursue this distinction further by saying something about the difference between *truth* and *validity*. Most authorities on logic use the terms "valid" and "invalid" to indicate whether or not an argument is correct in form. It is essential to understand that these terms apply to the argument as a whole and not to its single propositions. A single proposition is true or false; an argument is valid or invalid. This is so simply because "valid" and "invalid" have reference to form, and not to some kind of correspondence with reality, as do "true" and "false." It is perfectly possible, therefore, to frame a valid syllogism having one or more false propositions. The only test of validity is correctness of form, as we saw in our study of the rules for deductive arguments. Consider for example the following syllogism:

> All animals are carnivorous.
> The cow is an animal.
> Therefore the cow is carnivorous.

Everyone knows that the major premise of this argument is false; nevertheless, if we accept the premise, the conclusion necessarily follows, and this is all that is required to make a valid syllogism. The purely formal nature of valid deductive argument can be seen strikingly if we make a syllogism with nonsense terms, such as the one below.

> All arps are frimps.
> All frimps are wackles.
> Therefore all arps are wackles.

Or we can take a syllogism which consists of notation in the form of symbols.

> All S is M.
> All M is P.
> All S is P.

Now it will be granted that these three arguments "convince" through their formal validity, but they do not persuade in the sense in which we are employing this term. We assent indifferently to the proposition "All S is P" because it does not refer to anything outside its system of symbolization. But as soon as we substitute for the symbols terms which have referents in the real world, our attitude changes. Suppose our syllogism now reads

> All men are mortal.
> The President is a man.
> Therefore the President is mortal.

This argument not only convinces us; it also persuades us, which is to say, it affects our attitude, or it initiates a course of action. In this case, it might be pointed out, one of the courses of action is to maintain the office of vice president. What has entered the argument to make this difference? The new factor is a statement about the world which we accept or reject according to our conception of what is true. Our interest is shifted here to the material truth of a proposition. We no longer ask merely "Is it in proper form?"; we ask also "Is it instantial?" which is to say, "Is it an instance of something factually true?" The syllogism thus contains not only a valid structure of argument, but also an assertion about the world of reality which has some effect upon our impulse or action. This is where rhetoric appears to supplement logic. Logic addresses itself to the mind; rhetoric addresses itself to the total being, which includes the will. Man is not merely a thinking machine, which is why it is seldom if ever sufficient to give him a conclusion punched out in a machine-like operation. Consequently a complete argument, in addition to obeying the laws of thought, must embody something that we recognize as true about existence. We will be swayed by the argument according to our estimate of the truth of the assertion.

Our next step, therefore, is to discuss where the rhetorical impulse of any argument is to be sought. If our argument is to have more persuasive power than "All arps are wackles," then a true or probably true perception about the world as we know it must be present.

Now as we return to our syllogism which has real terms and read it searchingly for the kind of predication that it makes about the world, we see that the middle term "man" relates the minor term "President" to the major term "mortal beings." Thus the argument runs that if the President belongs in the class "man" and if all men belong in the class "mortal beings," then the President too belongs in the class "mortal beings." In other words, the President has the generic attribute "mortal being." In this way the argument depends for its rhetorical force upon the acceptance of the class "mortal beings" as a class having a certain attribute (in this case the certainty of death) which can be ascribed distributively to every member of the class.

## THE TOPICS

If this approach seems to leave some questions unanswered, let us go back to a more fundamental position and think for a moment about the types of assertions we make. We soon become aware that all our assertions reflect our interpretation of the phenomena of existence, and that this interpretation is expressed through certain ultimate conceptions. The most basic of these are, in the language of philosophy, being, cause, and relationship; but we need to translate these terms into language more suited to our purpose. Accordingly, in our everyday assertions we say that a thing exists as a member of a class, or that it is the known cause of a certain effect or the known effect of a certain cause, or that it has points of resemblance with some other thing. "All Democrats are friends of the people" is an assertion of the first type; "War is a cause of inflation" is one of the second, and "Life is like a voyage" is one of the third. These statements about the nature of things enter into arguments (or, strictly speaking, into propositions) and it is the forcefulness with which they impress us that supplies the rhetorical effectiveness of any argument.

Let us restate this from another point of view. It is never enough to have merely a device of argument. A device is only a form, and though forms may delight the intellect, they are seldom if ever sufficient to move that refractory object which is our total being. The total being is moved, if at all, by the *content* of the argument, and it is content alone with which we are now dealing.

The first writer to give due recognition to content in addition to form was Aristotle, the founder of logic and the author of a treatise on rhetoric. He conceived the content of argument as a group of sources or "topics." It sheds some light upon this terminology to know that "topics" comes from the Greek word *topoi,* which signifies "regions" or "places" (cf. *topography*). The connection becomes clearer when we understand that the "topics" are comprised of those regions of experience from which the propositions of argument can be drawn. We have emphasized the fact that our propositions in argument consist of assertions which reflect our reading of experience. They must say things that we know to be true according to these necessary ways of knowing our world. In proportion as we make the propositions seem truthful, we give an argument power to impel the hearer.

No useful end would be served by going over Aristotle's list of topics minutely, for there is doubt as to whether he arranged them systematically. Moreover, the topics are not a matter which should be settled by appeal to authority, since we ourselves are qualified judges of the kinds of assertions that move people to acceptance. But taking up the list selectively, we find that the following topics or kinds of statements are the ones most widely understood and most effective in persuading.

1. Genus or definition
2. Cause and effect
3. Circumstance
4. Similitude
5. Comparison
6. Contraries
7. Testimony
8. Authority

### Genus or Definition

Our first example, involving "mortal beings," was an instance of the topic *genus,* which consists of all arguments made from the nature of a thing. It depends for its force upon the principle that there are fixed classes, and that what is true of a class may be imputed to every member of that class. In other words, any object will have the generic attributes of the class to which it belongs. Accordingly, if there is a genus "mortal beings," and if "man" is a member of this genus, then man will have the attribute of mortality. The language in which the theory of this source of argument has been presented should not obscure the fact that genus is an exceedingly common source. Every time we hear a proposition such as "All Irishmen are brave" or "No politicians are honest" or "Some novels are romances," we are encountering the topic genus, through which one object or class of objects is given, or denied, the attributes of another class.

For example, a teacher of French says to his class: "In writing French, never omit the accent marks. To a Frenchman accent marks are a part of spelling." This is an argument from definition clearly because accent marks have been defined as a part of spelling. To omit them therefore is the same as to leave something misspelled. This argument also implies a consequence, as do most arguments from definition. But as far as it goes, it says simply that the proper use of accent marks is one with correct spelling. Thus an argument for using French accent marks finds its support in a definition.

It may be helpful to recognize this source of argument in an historical context. Abraham Lincoln in many of his speeches against the spread of slavery put his case in the form of an argument from genus. In a speech made on October 16, 1854, for example, he reasoned as follows:

> But if the Negro is a man, is it not to that extent a total destruction of self-government to say that he shall not govern himself? When the white man governs himself, that is self-government; but when he governs himself and also governs another man, that is more than self-government—that is despotism. If the Negro is a man, why then my ancient faith teaches me that 'all men are created equal,' and that there can be no moral right in connection with one man's making a slave of another.

In this utterance it is clearly seen that Lincoln is employing "man" as a genus; that is to say, he is putting "man" in the same place in the argument in which we found "mortal beings" in the argument of our illustration. Now if it is conceded that the Negro belongs to the genus man, it has to be conceded that he has the attributes of manhood, one of which is the right to self-government. In brief, Lincoln is insisting that the attributes of the genus apply distributively to every member of the genus, and this is the rhetorical force of his argument.

It is necessary to understand that the success of this rhetoric depends upon a common acknowledgement of the genus "man." If there is no common conviction that there is such a fixed genus, about which a definite set of predications can be made, then the argument must fail to exert rhetorical force. This fact will explain why many arguments contain lengthy definitions of their terms. Such definitions are nothing more than attempts to fix the genera which are to be used as terms in syllogistic reasoning. In the examples we have been studying, the genera are well established and accepted, and therefore there is little point in defining them. Obviously in most situations it would be needless or even absurd to define "man" or "mortal being." But there are many genera whose attributes have never been carefully analyzed, and there are others which have been employed so much by pressure groups that the prevailing conception of them is a distorted one. When one is using a genus of this kind, one has no choice but to define or to redefine what he conceives it to be. When John Stuart Mill wrote his classic essay entitled "On Liberty," he wished to establish certain conclusions about the liberty to which every individual is entitled. But realizing that the term itself had been so variously used by philosophers and by political partisans, he felt compelled to give a lengthy definition of it. Only after that definition was fixed could he use "liberty" in his argument with some hope of persuading people to agree with his conclusion.

The necessity of extended definition of a key term may be illustrated from contemporary usage. It would be a usual thing to hear someone observe, "This is the right course because this is the course of liberalism." The argument as it stands is an enthymeme, which could be expanded as follows:

> All courses of liberalism are right courses.
> This is a course of liberalism.
> Therefore this is a right course.

Now this argument will carry persuasive force if we know what liberalism is, and if we are for it. If we do not know what it is, naturally we cannot be for it, and in that case the argument would have no rhetorical impulsion. Therefore a minimum need would be to define liberalism, and since this word has suffered greatly from careless and partisan usage, we should take some pains with the definition. The same is at present true of the word "democracy," despite some supposition that it is a universally understood term. It has been used to describe not only divergent but even contrary political conditions. If one used the word without defining it, one might find it creating an impulse quite different from what was intended.

Arguments from genus and from definition are the same in essence, since both of them are arguments from the nature of a thing, or from an established classification. In the case of the former, the classification is already established, or it is one of the fixed concepts in the mind of the audience to which the argument is addressed. In the case of the second, the work of establishing the classification must be done in the course of the argument, after which the defined term will be used as would any genus.

Arguments based on example belong to this group because an example always implies a general class. A genus must be involved because that is what the example is used to exemplify. It is the first step in an induction which, if carried out, would produce a generalization. When a speaker dwells on the fate of Napoleon at Waterloo, he is saying in effect: here is an instance of the truth that ambitious military conquerors finally overreach themselves and meet disaster. He may play up details of the event to make the instance vivid, but the force of the argument lies in the general proposition about military conquerors, which the example suggests.

## Cause and Effect

The topic which depends on *cause-and-effect* relationship makes use of causal reasoning. It affirms that a given cause implies an effect of proportionate gravity, or that a given effect implies a cause of proportionate gravity. Accordingly, if there is a serious cause, we shall find ourselves in serious plight; if we are now in serious plight, there must exist a serious cause. Let us look at this topic as it might appear in the syllogism.

> Extravagance produces want.
> This is a case of extravagance.
> This is a case which will produce want.

The rhetorical force of the argument depends upon our acceptance of the truth of the cause-and-effect relationship which is affirmed in the major premise. If we grant that extravagance always has, as one of its effects, want, we may be moved to avoid extravagance by our understanding of this relationship. In this way our perception of the causal linkages of phenomena enters into a syllogism as part of its content.

Again let us study the topic in a historical context. When the framers of the Declaration of Independence sat down to produce a persuasive argument for the separation of the American colonies from Great Britain, they relied chiefly upon the argument from effect. The effect was the "facts" which were to be submitted to a candid world. Under seventeen heads the framers listed a large number of particulars in which the colonies had suffered by the policy of the king of Great Britain. Most of us will recall the general tenor if not the content of these. "He has refused his assent to laws, the most wholesome and necessary for the public good. . . . He has dissolved representative Houses repeatedly, for opposing with manly firmness his invasions on the rights of the people. . . ." and so on. Now all of these abuses are pointed out as grave effects which indicate a grave cause, and the cause was seen as a desire to reduce the people of the colonies under an absolute despotism. The colonists were determined that the grave cause should be followed by a different effect, which was to be their separation from the oppressive government of George III. But as far as the rhetorical effect of the argument goes, it is enough to recognize that the proposition asserts a relationship between the suppression of local rights and liberties and despotic rule. Insofar as we are impressed by the truth of that relationship, we will feel a persuasive force in the argument. Enough has been said to show that the argument beginning with cause and moving to effect operates in the same way; if grievous causes exist, grievous effects must follow.

### Circumstance

A kind of subvariety of the topic cause is the topic *circumstance*. The argument from circumstance is well summed up in the expression we sometimes hear, "There is nothing else to do about it." If the situation is such that the facts dictate one course of action, even though that course cannot be vindicated by principle and even though its effect can not be demonstrated, then we are driven back upon the argument from circumstance. We may state its pattern thus: the situation being what it is, there exists no alternative to the action that I recommend. The classic example of the argument from circumstance is Hannibal's address to his troops upon entering Italy.

> You are hemmed in on the right and left by two seas, and you do not have so much as a single ship upon either of them. Then there is the Po before you and the Alps behind. The Po is a deeper, and a more rapid and turbulent river than the Rhone; and as for the Alps, it was with the utmost difficulty that you passed over them when you were in full strength and vigor; they are an insurmountable wall to you now. You are therefore shut in, like our prisoners, on every side, and have no hope of life and liberty but in battle and victory.

In this famous speech, all emphasis is placed upon the coercive nature of the circumstances of the Carthaginian army. This is why we say that it is a simple appeal to circumstances for rhetorical motivation.

But sometimes the argument from circumstances appears in more complex situations. Edmund Burke's famous speech on conciliation with the colonies is filled with appeals to this source. Indeed, the central point of the speech may be called an argument from circumstance, for Burke was saying to Parliament: since the American colonies are so strong now, and have such a mighty potential for the future, and are so far removed from us, what are you going to do except make peace with them through concessions? The statement often quoted from this speech, "I do not know the method of drawing up an indictment against a whole people," is again purely an argument from circumstance, because it maintains that the circumstance of the offenders' being a whole people overshadows the normal course of the law. But the source is seen in its clearest aspect when Burke, after reviewing the fierce spirit of the colonists, declares: "The question is not, whether this spirit deserves praise or blame, but—what, in the name of God, shall we do with it?"

Circumstance belongs to the order of causal relations, but it is the least perceptive, or one might say the least philosophical of the topics. It admits a kind of helplessness in the hands of circumstance—an inability to demonstrate relationships other than the presence of overpowering fact. We recognize this appeal in many advertising and political slogans. The statement that the popular swing is to this kind of cigarette or that kind of automobile, or that 85% of the people buy this kind of breakfast food, or that you should vote for candidate X because he is sure to win, are all slightly disguised arguments from circumstance. Of course these appeals are sometimes supplemented by other arguments, but as far as they themselves go, they utilize only the circumstance of popularity.

## *Similitude*

The argument from *similitude* derives its force from a statement about the likeness of two things. To understand how it persuades, we must recall what was said about analogy in our discussion of the devices of logic. We saw that all analogy depends upon a theory that if two things resemble in a certain number of respects, it is probable that they resemble in still further respects. When we argue from similitude, what the major premise does is assert this principle of similarity or comparability. The minor premise then asserts the fact of the similarity and the conclusion asserts the probability of still further similarity. The process may be best seen in the form of a hypothetical syllogism:

If S resembles P in X particulars, it is probable that S resembles
    P in one or more further particulars.
S does resemble P in X particulars.
Therefore it is probable that S resembles P in one or more further particulars.

As we learned when we examined the theory of analogy, the weight of this probability will depend upon the number and the pertinence of the particulars in which the two instances resemble. Here again we have to observe that the rhetoric of the argument is in direct relation to the soundness of the predication about the world. If the analogy is weak, the argument will have little power to persuade; but if it is strong, the power will be proportionately great.

In speaking against the policy of national armaments, William Jennings Bryan used the following argument based on similitude.

Suppose nearby you have two farmers living side by side, good farmers, well-meaning farmers who wanted to be friends, and suppose they tried to maintain peace on the European plan, how would they go at it? One would go to the nearest town and buy the best gun he could find, and then he would put a notice in the paper saying that he loved his neighbor and that he had no thought of trespassing upon his neighbor's rights; but that he was determined to defend his own rights and protect his honor at any cost, that he had secured the best gun in the market and that if his neighbor interfered with him, he would shoot him. Then suppose the neighbor went to town the next day and got him a better gun and, with the same frankness, consulted the newspaper and put in a similar notice explaining that he loved peace as well as his neighbor did but that he was just as determined to defend his own rights and protect his honor and that he had a better gun than his neighbor and that, if his neighbor crossed his line, he would kill him. And suppose then the first man, when he read that notice, went to town and got two guns and advertised that fact in the paper, and the second man, when he read it, went to town and got three guns, and so on, each alternately buying guns. What would be the result? Every undertaker in that vicinity would go out and become personally acquainted with the two men, because he would know there would be at least one funeral in that neighborhood. That is the European plan. One country gets a battleship and announces that it can blow any other battleship out of the water; then a rival nation gets a dreadnaught that can sink the battleship; then the first nation gets a super-dreadnaught; then they go to the dictionary and look for prefixes for the names of their battleships as they build them larger and larger; and they make guns larger and larger and they equip armies larger and larger, all the time talking about how much they love peace and all the while boasting that they are ready for a fight.

Go back to the time when they commenced to pass laws against the carrying of concealed weapons and you can get all the material you can want for a speech on preparedness, because the arguments made in favor of carrying revolvers can be put into the speeches made today in favor of preparedness, without changing a word. Did you ever hear of a man who wanted to carry a revolver to be aggressive? No, it was just to protect his rights and defend his honor, especially his honor, but they found by experience that the man who carried a revolver generally carried it with a disposition to use it on slight provocation and to provoke its use by others. For the promotion of peace, every state in the union has abolished preparedness on the part of individuals because it did not preserve peace. It provoked trouble, and unless we can convince ourselves that there is a moral philosophy applicable to nations that is just the opposite of the moral philosophy applied to individuals, we must conclude that, as the pistol-toting man is a menace to the peace of a community, so the pistol-toting nation is a menace to the peace of the world.
—The Proposal for a League to Enforce Peace—Negative—

The essence of Bryan's argument is that if the conduct of the two neighbors results in a shooting affray, that of the two nations, which resembles it in all important particulars, will result in war. We are rhetorically moved by the argument to the extent that we are impressed with the strength of the analogy.

## Comparison

Although their names resemble each other, the topic *comparison* differs somewhat from the topic *similitude*. *Comparison* involves a relationship which is sometimes expressed by the Latin phrase *a fortiori* ("all the stronger"). This argument sets up two possibilities, the second of which is more probable than the first, so that if we affirm the first, we can affirm the second with even greater force, or *a fortiori*. Using this source of argument, we might say, "If a man will steal from his friend, he will steal from a stranger." When we look at this assertion analytically, we find we are saying that if a certain man, Richard Roe, belongs to that class of men who will steal from their friends, he is at the same time included, and with greater certainty, in that class of men who will steal from strangers. An excellent example of the argument from comparison is the line from Chaucer: "If gold rusts, what shall iron do?" Here the relationship may be expressed as follows: in a situation where gold will rust, it is much more to be expected that iron will rust. Although the explanation of this source of argument is perhaps not as simple as that of the preceding ones, it will be noted that the source is often employed in actual controversy, *e.g.*, "If even honest men are corrupted by office, what can you expect of crooks?"

### Contraries

The last of the group of sources based on the concept of relationship is that of *contraries*. The argument from contraries implies that if we are benefiting from a certain fact or situation, then the contrary of the fact or situation will injure us; or, if we are being injured by the situation now existing, we can expect to be benefited by a situation contrary to it. In other words, my present failure or dissatisfaction implies the desirability of the contrary of what I now have; *e.g.*, if we are suffering from war, what we need is peace. If Russia is pleased with the result of our policy in Asia, then what we need is a policy contrary to our present one, and so on.

One of the most interesting examples of the argument from contraries may be found in the "back to nature" movement of the eighteenth century. In this period there developed a highly formal culture, and a number of its prominent thinkers believed that it was suffering from too much formalism. In consequence, there appeared many pleas for a return to a more primitive or natural mode of life, together with admiration for people like the American Indians, who were thought to be unspoiled by civilization. Analysis shows that the "back to nature" movement rested on the following argument: if what we are suffering from is too much artificiality, then what we need is a return to the natural; or, if civilization is the source of our distresses, then we can expect to be benefited by its contrary. This produced an idealization of the primitive, and a desire to recapture the simple and unaffected life such as one encounters in the poetry of Wordsworth.

### Testimony and Authority

All of the sources we have analyzed thus far are "internal" in the sense that they involve our own interpretation of experience. But there are two "external" sources, which utilize the interpretation of others.

These are *testimony* and *authority*. The difference is that whereas the internal source, such as genus or cause, is a direct perception by us of an aspect of phenomena, the external source is a report of such perception on the part of someone else. If a police officer declares in court that he saw you drive through a red light at the intersection of 16th and Walnut, the court accepts his statement as testimony. After this is done, the statement goes into a syllogistic argument as a true proposition, constituting one of the premises. The point we must emphasize is that the proposition, as used in the argument, does not rest upon direct interpretation of genus, or cause, or similitude, but upon the credit of someone who is testifying. In the same way, a man who is charged with a crime gets someone to testify that he was otherwise occupied at the time the crime was committed (this is the true meaning of the charged person's *alibi*, which is the Latin word for "elsewhere"). By this means, statements by people presumed to be in a position to know are brought into an argument and take the place of direct or logical interpretation of evidence.

Let us bear in mind that such arguments are external in the sense of being imported from the outside. Instead of affirming a fact or relationship themselves, they affirm that someone else affirms it. Thus the argument would not say that Tony Moreno was seventeen miles away from the scene at the time of a gangland slaying on Chicago's south side. It says rather that his friend Joe Mangione testifies that Moreno was at his place, which is seventeen miles away from the scene, at the time of the slaying. How good this testimony is must be judged with reference to a number of things. The point of interest to us is that, in estimating its rhetorical force, we regard it not as a fact but as testimony.

Closely related to testimony is *authority*. Arguments from authority bring in a great name or some other exalted source whose word on the subject in question is regarded as final. Such arguments reflect a supposition that it would be presumptuous to go beyond the authority. The foreign missionary work carried on by many Christian churches rests upon the conclusion of an argument drawn from authority. According to the book of *Matthew*, Christ said to his disciples (28:19): "Go ye therefore and teach all nations." The argument then proceeds: if Christ commanded his disciples to spread the gospel to all the world, this is what his followers must do. The Biblical text is thus used to supply a middle term, the authority of Christ, which functions in a syllogistic argument.

All of us have encountered, and perhaps some of us have used, arguments based on the authority of the Bible. If St. Paul said that the greatest of gifts is charity, we must accept this as so. Solomon declared that where there is no vision, the people perish, and we use this as a premise in argument. Arguments from authority are sometimes employed in the political arena. When Washington's statement that we should avoid entangling alliances with foreign countries is cited in debate over foreign policy, it is the authority of Washington as father and first president of our nation which furnishes the rhetorical force. Sometimes even the subject matter of science is expressed in the form of arguments from authority, since it is obviously impossible to re-investigate every one of the established laws of science every time we wish to make a predication in this field. What we do, therefore, is accept a law on the authority of some competent scientist. When, for example, H. H. Newman, Professor of Zoology at the University of Chicago, declares: "Evolution has been tried and tested in every conceivable way for considerably over half a century. Vast numbers of biological facts have been examined in the light of this principle and without a single exception they have been found entirely compatible with it," the average layman is disposed to regard this as true. Again we note that it is the authority of the source rather than any direct investigation of the content which gives propositions of this sort a standing in argument.

We repeat that it is the nature of arguments based on testimony and authority to have no intrinsic force; whatever persuasive power they carry is derived from the credit of the testifier or the weight of the authority. People who have been taught to venerate the Bible will be moved by a Biblical proposition; a proposition from the Koran would have little if any power to move them, though it would carry weight with a Moslem. In using such arguments it is accordingly essential to keep in mind the credit of the source of testimony and the status of the authority. Testimony is usually well regarded if the one offering it is in a position to know the facts and if he is disinterested with reference to the outcome of the argument.

In studying any extended piece of argumentation for its effect, you will find it invaluable to identify the rhetorical sources being employed. In no other way can you determine how much content an argument really has and how much weight it is probably going to carry with a specific audience. You will find below some exercises in the detection of topics. It hardly needs mentioning that few speeches of any length will confine themselves to one topic alone. The great majority will use several, and a long speech like Edmund Burke's "On Conciliation with the Colonies" will be found drawing upon virtually every topic in the list.

**Exercise:**   *Study carefully the selections below and identify each source of argument (genus, cause, similitude, etc.) used to give the appeal its rhetorical force.*

The hope of abolishing war is largely based upon the fact that men have long since abandoned the appeal to arms in their private disputes and submitted themselves to the jurisdiction of courts. Starting from this fact, it is contended that disputes between nations should be settled in the same manner, and that the adoption of the reform would greatly promote the happiness of the world.

Unluckily, there are three flaws in the argument. The first, which is obvious, lies in the circumstances that a system of legal remedies is of no value if it is not backed by sufficient force to impose its decisions upon even the most powerful litigants—a sheer impossibility in international affairs, for even if one powerful litigant might be coerced, it would be plainly impossible to coerce a combination, and it is precisely a combination of the powerful that is most to be feared. The second lies in the fact that any legal system, to be worthy of credit, must be administered by judges who have no personal interest in the litigation before them—another impossibility, for all the judges in the international court, in the case of disputes between first-class powers, would either be appointees of those powers, or appointees of inferior powers that were under their direct influence, or obliged to consider the effects of their enmity. The third objection lies in the fact, frequently forgotten, that the courts of justice which now exist do not actually dispense justice, but only law, and that this law is frequently in direct conflict, not only with what one litigant honestly believes to be his rights, but also with what he believes to be his honor. Practically every litigation, in truth, ends with either one litigant or the other nursing what appears to him as an outrage upon him. For both litigants to go away satisfied that justice has been done is almost unheard of.

In disputes between man and man this dissatisfaction is not of serious consequence. The aggrieved party has no feasible remedy; if he doesn't like it, he must lump it. In particular, he has no feasible remedy against a judge or a juryman who, in his view, has treated him ill; if he essayed vengeance, the whole strength of the unbiased masses of men would be exerted to destroy him, and that strength is so enormous, compared to his own puny might, that it would swiftly and certainly overwhelm him. But in the case of first-class nations there would be no such overwhelming force in restraint. In a few cases the general opinion of the world might be so largely against them that it would force them to acquiesce in the judgment rendered, but in perhaps a majority of important cases there would be sharply divided sympathies, and it would constantly encourage resistance. Against that resistance there would be nothing save the counter-resistance of the opposition—*i.e.*, the judge against the aggrieved litigant, the twelve jurymen against the aggrieved litigant's friends, with no vast and impersonal force of neutral public opinion behind the former.

—H. L. Mencken, Minority Report

I agree with you that there is a natural aristocracy among men. The grounds of this are virtue and talents. Formerly, bodily powers gave place among the *aristoi*. But since the invention of gunpowder has armed the weak as well as the strong with missile death, bodily strength, like beauty, good humor, politeness and other accomplishments, has become but an auxiliary ground for distinction. There is also an artificial aristocracy, founded on wealth and birth without either virtue or talents; for with these it would belong to the first class. The natural aristocracy I consider as the most precious gift of nature, for the instruction, the trusts, and government of society. And indeed, it would have been inconsistent in creation to have formed man for the social state, and not to have provided virtue and wisdom enough to manage the concerns of the society.

May we not even say, that that form of government is the best, which provides the most effectually for a pure selection of these natural *aristoi* into the offices of government? The artificial aristocracy is a mischievous ingredient in government, and provision should be made to prevent its ascendency. On the question, what is the best provision, you and I differ; but we differ as rational friends, using the free exercise of our own reason, and mutually indulging its errors. You think it best to put the *pseudo-aristoi* into a separate chamber of legislation, where they may be hindered from doing mischief by their co-ordinate branches, and where, also, they may be a protection to wealth against the agrarian and plundering enterprises of the majority of the people. I think that to give them power in order to prevent them from doing mischief, is arming them for it, and increasing instead of remedying the evil. For if the co-ordinate branches can arrest their action, so may they that of the co-ordinates. Mischief may be done negatively as well as positively. Of this, a cabal in the Senate of the United States has furnished many proofs. Nor do I believe them necessary to protect the wealthy; because enough of these will find their way into every branch of the legislature, to protect themselves. From fifteen to twenty legislatures of our own, in action for thirty years past, have proved that no fears of an equalization of property are to be apprehended from them. I think the best remedy is exactly that provided by all our constitutions, to leave to the citizens the free election and separation of the *aristoi* from the *pseudo-aristoi*, of the wheat from the chaff. In general they will elect the really good and wise. In some instances, wealth may corrupt, and birth blind them; but not in sufficient degree to endanger the society.

It is probable that our difference of opinion may, in some measure, be produced by a difference of character in those among whom we live. From what I have seen of Massachusetts and Connecticut myself, and still more from what I have heard, and the character given of the former by yourself, who know them so much better, there seems to be in those two States a traditionary reverence for certain families, which has rendered the offices of the government nearly hereditary in those families. I presume that from an early period of your history, members of those families happening to possess virtue and talents, have honestly exercised them for the good of the people, and by their services have endeared their names to them. In coupling Connecticut with you, I mean it politically only, not morally. For having made the Bible the common law of their land, they seem to have modeled their morality on the story of Jacob and Laban. But although this hereditary succession to office with you, may, in some degree, be founded in real family merit, yet in a much higher degree, it has proceeded from your strict alliance of Church and State. These families are canonised in the eyes of the people on common principles, "you tickle me, and I will tickle you." In Virginia we have nothing of this. Our clergy, before the Revolution, having been secured against rivalship by fixed salaries, did not give themselves the trouble of acquiring influence over the people. Of wealth, there were great accumulations in particular families, handed down from generation to generation under the English law of entails. But the only object of ambition for the wealthy was a seat in the King's Council. All their court then was paid to the crown and its creatures; and they Philipised in all collisions between the King and the people. Hence they were unpopular; and that unpopularity continues attached to their names. A Randolph, a Carter, or a Burwell must have great personal superiority over a common competitor to be elected by the people even at this day. At the first session of our legislature after the Declaration of Independence, we passed a law abolishing entails. And this was followed by one abolishing the privilege of primogeniture, and dividing the lands of intestates equally among all their children, or other representatives. These laws, drawn by myself, laid the ax to the foot of pseudo-aristocracy. And had another which I prepared been adopted by the legislature, our work would have been complete. It was a bill for the more general diffusion of learning. This proposed to divide every county into wards of five or six miles square, like your townships; to establish in each ward a free school for reading, writing, and common arithmetic; to provide for the annual selection of the best subjects from these schools, who might receive, at the public expense, a higher degree of education at a district school; and from these district schools to select a certain number of the most promising subjects, to be completed at an University, where all the useful sciences should be taught. Worth and genius would thus have been sought out from every condition of life, and completely prepared by education for defeating the competition of wealth and birth for public trusts. My proposition had, for a further object, to impart to these wards those portions of self-government for which they are best qualified, by confiding to them the care of their poor, their roads, police, elections, the nomination of jurors, administration of justice in small cases, elementary exercises of militia; in short, to have made them little republics, with a warden at the head of each, for all those concerns which, being under their eye, they would better manage than the larger republics of the county or State. A general call of ward meetings by their wardens on the same day through the State, would at any time produce the genuine sense of the people on any required point, and would enable the State to act in mass, as your people have so often done, and with so much effect by their town meeting. The law for religious freedom, which made a part of this system, having put down the aristocracy of the clergy, and restored to the citizen the freedom of the mind, and those of entails and descents nurturing an equality of conditions among them, this on education would have raised the mass of the people to the high ground of moral respectability necessary to their own safety, and to orderly government; and would have completed the great object of qualifying them to select the veritable *aristoi*, for the trusts of government, to the exclusion of the pseudalists; and the same Theognis who has furnished the epigraphs of your two letters, assures us that "Not yet, Kurmus, have good men destroyed a state."

Although this law has not yet been acted on but in a small and inefficient degree, it is still considered as before the legislature, with other bills of the revised code, not yet taken up, and I have great hope that some patriotic spirit will, at a favorable moment, call it up, and make it the keystone of the arch of our government.

With respect to aristocracy, we should further consider, that before the establishment of the American States, nothing was known to history but the man of the old world, crowded within limits either small or over-charged, and steeped in the vices which that situation generates. A government adapted to such men would be one thing; but a very different one, that for the man of these States. Here every one may have land to labor for himself, if he chooses; or, preferring the exercise of any other industry, may exact for it such compensation as not only to afford a comfortable subsistence, but wherewith to provide for a cessation from labor in old age. Every one, by his property, or by his satisfactory situation, is interested in the support of law and order. And such men may safely and advantageously reserve to themselves a wholesome control over their public affairs, and a degree of freedom, which, in the hands of the *Canaille* of the cities of Europe, would be instantly perverted to the demolition and destruction of everything public and private. The history of the last twenty-five years of France, and of the last forty years in America, nay of its last two-hundred years, proves the truth of both parts of this observation.

But even in Europe a change has sensibly taken place in the mind of man. Science had liberated the ideas of those who read and reflect, and the American example had kindled feelings of right in the people. An insurrection has consequently begun, of science, talents, and courage, against rank and birth, which have fallen into contempt. It has failed in its first effort, because the mobs of the cities, the instrument used for its accomplishment, debased by ignorance, poverty, and vice, could not be restrained to rational action. But the world will recover from the panic of this first catastrophe. Science is progressive, and talents and enterprise on the alert. Resort may be had to the people of the country, a more governable power from their principles and subordination; and rank, and birth, and tinsel-aristocracy will finally shrink into insignificance, even there. This, however, we have no right to meddle with. It suffices for us, if the moral and physical condition of our own citizens qualifies them to select the able and good for the direction of their government, with a recurrence of elections at such short periods as will enable them to displace an unfaithful servant, before the mischief he meditates may be irremediable.

—Thomas Jefferson, Letter to John Adams, October 28, 1813

SIR,

It is with reluctance that I rise to express a disapprobation of any one article of the plan, for which we are so much obliged to the honorable gentleman who laid it before us. From its first reading, I have borne a good will to it, and, in general, wished it success. In this particular of salaries to the executive branch, I happen to differ; and, as my opinion may appear new and chimerical, it is only from a persuasion that it is right, and from a sense of duty, that I hazard it. The Committee will judge of my reasons when they have heard them, and their judgment may possibly change mine. I think I see inconveniences in the appointment of salaries; I see none in refusing them, but on the contrary great advantages.

Sir, there are two passions which have a powerful influence in the affairs of men. These are *ambition* and *avarice;* the love of power and the love of money. Separately, each of these has great force in prompting men of action; but when united in view of the same object, they have in many minds the most violent effects. Place before the eyes of such men a post of *honor,* that shall at the same time be a place of *profit,* and they will move heaven and earth to obtain it. The vast number of such places it is that renders the British government so tempestuous. The struggles for them are the true source of all those factions which are perpetually dividing the nation, distracting its councils, hurrying it sometimes into fruitless and mischievous wars, and often compelling a submission to dishonorable terms of peace.

And of what kind are the men that will strive for this profitable preeminence, through all the bustle of cabal, the heat of contention, the infinite mutual abuse of parties, tearing to pieces the best of characters? It will not be the wise and moderate, the lovers of peace and good order, the men fittest for the trust. It will be the bold and the violent, the men of strong passions and indefatigable activity in their selfish pursuits. These will thrust themselves into your government, and be your rulers. And these, too, will be mistaken in the expected happiness of their situation; for their vanquished competitors, of the same spirit, and from the same motives, will perpetually be endeavoring to distress their administration, thwart their measures, and render them odious to the people.

Besides these evils, sir, though we may set out in the beginning with moderate salaries, we shall find that such will not be of long continuance. Reasons will never be wanting for proposed augmentations, and there will always be a party for giving more to the rulers, that the rulers may be able in return to give more to them. Hence, as all history informs us, there has been in every state and kingdom a constant kind of warfare between the governing and the governed; the one striving to obtain more for its support, and the other to pay less. And this has alone occasioned great convulsions, actual civil wars, ending either in dethroning of the princes or enslaving of the people. Generally, indeed, the ruling power carries its point, and we see the revenues of princes constantly increasing, and we see that they are never satisfied, but always in want of more. The more the people are discontented with the oppression of taxes, the greater need the prince has of money to distribute among his partisans, and pay the troops that are to suppress all resistance and enable him to plunder at pleasure. There is scarce a king in a hundred, who would not, if he could, follow the example of Pharaoh,—get first all the people's money, then all their lands, and then make them and their children servants for ever. It will be said that we do not propose to establish kings. I know it. But there is a natural inclination in mankind to kingly government. It sometimes relieves them from aristocratic domination. They had rather have one tyrant than 500. It gives more of the appearance of equality among citizens; and that they like. I am apprehensive, therefore—perhaps too apprehensive—that the government of these states may in future times end in a monarchy. But this catastrophe, I think, may be long delayed, if in our proposed system we do not sow the seeds of contention, faction, and tumult, by making our posts of honor places of profit. If we do, I fear, that, though we employ at first a number and not a single person, the number will in time be set aside; it will only nourish the foetus of a king (as the honorable gentleman from Virginia very aptly expressed it), and a king will the sooner be set over us.

It may be imagined by some, that this is an utopian idea, and that we can never find men to serve us in the executive department, without paying them well for their services. I conceive this to be a mistake. Some existing facts present themselves to me, which incline me to a contrary opinion. The High Sheriff of a county in England is an honorable office, but it is not a profitable one. It is rather expensive, and therefore not sought for. But yet it is executed, and well executed, and usually by some of the principal gentlemen of the county. In France, the office of Counsellor, or member of their judiciary parliaments, is more honorable. It is therefore purchased at a high price; there are indeed fees on the law proceedings, which are divided among them, but these fees do not amount to more than three per cent on the sum paid for the place. Therefore, as legal interest is there at five per cent, they in fact pay two per cent for being allowed to do the judiciary business of the nation, which is at the same time entirely exempt from the burden of paying them any salaries for their services. I do not, however, mean to recommend this as an eligible mode for our judiciary department. I only bring the instance to show, that the pleasure of doing good and serving their country, and the respect such conduct entitles them to, are sufficient motives with some minds, to give up a great portion of their time to the public, without the mean inducement of pecuniary satisfaction.

Another instance is that of a respectable society, who have made the experiment, and practised it with success, now more than a hundred years. I mean the Quakers. It is an established rule with them that they are not to go to law, but in their controversies they must apply to their monthly, quarterly, and yearly meetings. Committees of these sit with patience to hear the parties, and spend much time in composing their differences. In doing this, they are supported by a sense of duty, and the respect paid to usefulness. It is honorable to be so employed, but it was never made profitable by salaries, fees, or perquisites. And indeed, in all cases of public service, the less the profit the greater the honor.

To bring the matter nearer home, have we not seen the greatest and most important of our offices, that of General of our Armies, executed for eight years together, without the smallest salary, by a patriot whom I will not now offend by any other praise; and this, through fatigues and distresses, in common with the other brave men, his military friends and companions, and the constant anxieties peculiar to his station? And shall we doubt finding three or four men in all the United States, with public spirit enough to bear sitting in peaceful council, for perhaps an equal term, merely to preside over our civil concerns, and see that our laws are duly executed? Sir, I have a better opinion of our country. I think we shall never be without a sufficient number of wise and good men to undertake, and execute well and faithfully, the office in question.

Sir, the saving of the salaries, that may at first be proposed, is not an object with me. The subsequent mischiefs of proposing them are what I apprehend. And therefore it is that I move the amendment. If it is not seconded or accepted, I must be contented with the satisfaction of having delivered my opinion frankly, and done my duty.

—Benjamin Franklin, *Speech in the Constitutional
Convention on the Subject of Salaries,*
June 2, 1789

## RIGHT AND WRONG

Every one has heard people quarrelling. Sometimes it sounds funny and sometimes it sounds merely unpleasant; but however it sounds, I believe we can learn something very important from listening to the kind of things they say. They say things like this: "That's my seat, I was there first"—"Leave him alone, he isn't doing you any harm"—"Why should you shove in first?"—"Give me a bit of your orange, I gave you a bit of mine"—"How'd you like it if anyone did the same to you?"—"Come on, you promised." People say things like that every day, educated people as well as uneducated, and children as well as grown-ups.

Now what interests me about all these remarks is that the man who makes them isn't just saying that the other man's behaviour doesn't happen to please him. He is appealing to some kind of standard of behaviour which he expects the other man to know about. And the other man very seldom replies, "To hell with your standard." Nearly always he tries to make out that what he has been doing doesn't really go against the standard, or that if it does, there is some special excuse. He pretends there is some special reason in this particular case why the person who took the seat first should not keep it, or that things were quite different when he was given the bit of orange, or that something has turned up which lets him off keeping his promise. It looks, in fact, very much as if both parties had in mind some kind of Law or Rule of fair play or decent behaviour or morality or whatever you like to call it, about which they really agreed. And they have. If they hadn't, they might, of course, fight like animals, but they couldn't *quarrel* in the human sense of the word. Quarrelling means trying to show that the other man's in the wrong. And there'd be no sense in trying to do that unless you and he had some sort of agreement as to what Right and Wrong are; just as there'd be no sense in saying that a footballer had committed a foul unless there was some agreement about the rules of football.

Now this Law or Rule about Right and Wrong used to be called the Law of Nature. Nowadays when we talk of the "laws of nature" we usually mean things like gravitation, or heredity, or the laws of chemistry. But when the older thinkers called the Law of Right and Wrong the Law of Nature, they really meant the Law of *Human* Nature. The idea was that, just as falling stones are governed by the law of gravitation and chemicals by chemical laws, so the creature called man also had *his* law—with this great difference, that the stone couldn't choose whether it obeyed the law of gravitation or not, but a man could choose either to obey the Law of Human Nature or to disobey it. They called it Law of Nature because they thought that every one knew it by nature and didn't need to be taught it. They didn't mean, of course, that you mightn't find an odd individual here and there who didn't know it, just as you find a few people here and there who are colour-blind or have no ear for a tune. But taking the race as a whole, they thought that the human idea of Decent Behaviour was obvious to every one. And I believe they were right. If they weren't, then all the things we say about war are nonsense. What is the sense in saying the enemy are in the wrong unless Right is a real thing which they at bottom know as well as we do and ought to practise? If they had no notion of what we mean by right, then, though we might still have to fight them, we could no more blame them for that than for the colour of their hair.

I know that some people say the idea of a Law of Nature or decent behaviour known to all men is unsound, because different civilisations and different ages have had quite different moralities. But they haven't. They have only had *slightly* different moralities. Just think what a *quite* different morality would mean. Think of a country where people were *admired* for running away in battle, or where a man felt *proud* for double-crossing all the people who had been kindest to him. You might just as well try to imagine a country where two and two make five. Men have differed as regards what people you ought to be unselfish to—whether it was only your own family, or your fellow countrymen, or every one. But they have always agreed that you oughtn't to put yourself first. Selfishness has never been admired. Men have differed as to whether you should have one wife or four. But they have always agreed that you mustn't simply have any woman you liked.

But the most remarkable thing is this. Whenever you find a man who says he doesn't believe in a real Right and Wrong, you will find the same man going back on his statement a moment later. He may break his promise to you, but if you try breaking one to him he'll be complaining, "It's not fair" before you can say Jack Robinson. A nation may say treaties don't matter; but then, next minute, they spoil their case by saying that the particular treaty they want to break was an unfair one. But if treaties don't matter, and if there's no such thing as Right and Wrong—in other words, if there is no Law of Nature—what is the difference between a fair treaty and an unfair one? Haven't they given away the fact that, whatever they say, they really know the Law of Nature just like anyone else?

It seems then, that we are forced to believe in a real Right and Wrong. People may be sometimes mistaken about them, just as people sometimes get their sums wrong; but they are not a matter of mere taste and opinion any more than the multiplication table. Now if we're agreed about that, I go on to my next point, which is this: none of us are really keeping the Law of Nature. If there are any exceptions among you, I apologise to them. They'd better switch on to another station, for nothing I'm going to say concerns them. And now, turning to the ordinary human beings who are left:

I hope you won't misunderstand what I'm going to say. I'm not preaching, and Heaven knows I'm not pretending that I'm better than anyone else. I'm only trying to call attention to a fact: the fact that this year, or this month, or, more likely, this very day, we have failed to practise ourselves the kind of behaviour we expect from other people. There may be all sorts of excuses for us. That time you were so unfair to the children was when you were very tired. That slightly shady business about the money—the one you'd almost forgotten—came when you were very hard up. And what you promised to do for old So-and-so and have never done—well, you never would have promised if you'd known how frightfully busy you were going to be. And as for your behaviour to your wife (or husband), if I knew how irritating they could be, I wouldn't wonder at it—and who the dickens am I, anyway? I am just the same. That is to say, I don't succeed in keeping the Law of Nature very well, and the moment anyone tells me I'm not keeping it, there starts up in my mind a string of excuses as long as your arm. The question at the moment is not whether they are good excuses. The point is that they are one more proof of how deeply, whether we like it or not, we believe in the Law of Nature. If we didn't believe in decent behaviour, why should we be so anxious to make excuses for not having behaved decently? The truth is, we believe in decency so much—we feel the Rule or Law pressing on us so—that we can't bear to face the fact that we're breaking it, and consequently we try to shift the responsibility. For you notice that it's only for our bad behaviour that we find all these explanations. We put our *bad* temper down to being tired or worried or hungry; we put our good temper down to ourselves.

Well, those are the two points I wanted to make. First, that human beings, all over the earth, have this curious idea that they *ought* to behave in a certain way, and can't really get rid of it. Secondly, that they don't in fact behave in that way. They know the Law of Nature; they break it. These two facts are the foundation of all clear thinking about ourselves and the universe we live in.

—C. S. Lewis, "Right and Wrong," *The Case for Christianity*

## COMMON MATERIAL FALLACIES

*Formal fallacies* are those that appear in the form or structure of an argument. An example is the undistributed middle term, which we have studied. (Review pages 123–128 for other formal fallacies.) But there is another group of fallacies which are distinguished as *material,* because with them the error lies not in the structure but in the matter of the argument. These *material fallacies* fall broadly into two classes: the first comprises instances of unwarranted assumption; the second, instances of irrelevant conclusion. In dealing with the first group, we must criticize the implication of a premise. In dealing with the second, we must call attention to the lack of connection between the premises and the conclusion.

### Begging the Question

One of the most common material fallacies is *begging the question.* This consists of assuming in one of the premises what is supposed to be proved by the argument. If a disputant is allowed to do this, obviously he avoids the necessity of argument, for he is assuming as true what he would otherwise have to prove true. He is "begging the question" because he is getting the conclusion he wants without having earned it through the normal process of reasoning.

If one asserted, "All useless subjects like mathematics should be dropped from the curriculum," one would be begging the question. It will be granted that all useless subjects should be dropped from the curriculum. But the question is whether mathematics is a useless subject. This is what the arguer is responsible for proving. If the proposition stands as stated, he reaches the conclusion without having passed through a process of argument. In this sense the conclusion has been "begged."

This fallacy often appears in the form of a "question-begging epithet," like the word "useless" in the illustration above.

Here are a few more examples of question-begging propositions.

Unwholesome works like the *Confessions* of Rousseau should be banned from the public library.

Blows to our prosperity like low tariffs should be opposed by the people.

The candidate's unfair methods ought to be condemned by every citizen.

## Complex Question

This is another fallacy of unwarranted assumption. The question itself is founded upon a presumption, so that one cannot answer it simply without admitting something which may be untrue. The classic example of the complex question is, "Have you stopped beating your wife?" Whether the respondent answers "yes" or "no," he admits that he has been beating his wife, which fact has not been established. Other examples would be "Have you given up your bad habits?" and "Do people in your part of the country still go barefooted?" The "leading question" with which lawyers sometimes try to entrap witnesses is often of this kind.

The way to expose the fallacy is to demand that the question be divided into its parts so that they can be answered separately.

## Post Hoc, Ergo Propter Hoc
## ("after this, therefore because of this")

The post hoc fallacy is simply the assumption that an event which comes after another event is necessarily a result of it. Nearly all superstitions rest on this fallacious reasoning. Homer Smith saw a black cat run across the driveway as he was leaving home this morning. Before he reached town he was involved in an automobile accident. Therefore seeing the black cat caused the accident.

The proving of cause-and-effect relationship is a far more complex undertaking than this. It requires a careful use of the rules of inductive inquiry. The establishment of a time sequence is not enough; there must be also some demonstrable causal linkage. Mrs. Brown began taking a certain patent medicine. At the end of six months she was feeling better. She maintains that the patent medicine was the cause of her improvement. But no physician (or any trained reasoner) would accept this as proving that the medicine has value. Mrs. Brown's improvement after six months could have been caused by a number of things, and it might have occurred in spite of the patent medicine. All that is proved is that it came after the medicine was taken.

## Hypostatization

This term refers to a very common form of fallacious statement. The fallacy consists of taking something which has only a conceptual or imaginary existence and treating it as if it were a simple concrete reality. In different words, it is a process of assuming a reality where none exists. Such a fallacy is encountered in nearly every statement beginning "History teaches. . . .", "Science knows. . . .", and "Medicine has found. . . ." The assumption in each case is that history or science or medicine is a single entity speaking with one voice. A little reflection shows us that there is no history in this sense, but rather many different historians; no science, but many practicing scientists and research workers; no medicine, but many physicians and medical researchers. They almost never all agree on any one thing; they hold different theories and different opinions. It is unwarranted, therefore, to assume that all history teaches any one lesson, that all science supports some one hypothesis, and so on. When made to square with the facts, these statements will read "Some historians teach. . . .", "Some (or many) scientists believe. . . ." and the like.

You are justified in being critical of anyone who presumes to speak in such large and lofty abstractions as these.

## Argumentum ad Hominem
### ("argument directed to the man")

This is one of several forms of evading the issue of an argument. If a person feels that he cannot refute the proposition of his opponent, he may try to divert attention from this by attacking the opponent's character. In this way he sidesteps the real question and tries to substitute in its place a different one.

If a member of a city council offers a proposal, and the opposition tries to discredit it by dwelling on the fact, say, that this councilman is foreign-born, it is committing the fallacy of *argumentum ad hominem*. The proposal ought to be argued on its own merits. As far as logic is concerned, the source of the proposal is irrelevant.

All attempts to combat arguments by proving that the one making them is foreign-born, or is a professor, or a farmer, or a millionaire are instances of the *argumentum ad hominem*. They may succeed in turning the audience against an individual, but they do nothing to answer the real argument. From the standpoint of strict logic, they have no value.

### Argumentum ad Populum
### ("argument directed to the multitude")

This fallacy is seen when a speaker or writer deserts the question at issue and brings in some other topic about which he knows the mass to be excitable. He then plays upon their emotions in regard to this to obscure the original question or turn them against the proposal he is attacking. Thus if a man were charged with some breach of law and his defender talked of little except the man's patriotism as shown in a brilliant war record, he would be resorting to the *argumentum ad populum*. Crowds, and even juries, are prone to become emotional over ideas such as patriotism and loyalty, and exploitation of these can lead them to ignore the real question to be settled.

### Non Sequitur
### ("it does not follow")

This expression was originally applied to the formal fallacy of affirming the consequent. As we saw in the discussion of the syllogism, the affirmation of a consequent leaves the conclusion indeterminate because there may be some other antecedent producing this consequent.

Today, however, it is a designation applied to any loose argument whose conclusion does not follow from the premises. For example, one might say that because Professor Thomas knows his subject thoroughly, he will be a brilliant lecturer. Unfortunately we know that thorough knowledge of a subject is not always accompanied by gifts of eloquence and clarity, and hence this is not a necessary conclusion. *Post hoc* fallacies also may be called *non sequiturs*. The expression thus does not refer to a specific misstep in logic but is a convenient label for any faulty logical process in which the conclusion does not proceed from the premises given.

### EXERCISES

**Exercise A**   *Write an argument in which you establish a generalization by induction. First, give a preliminary statement of your generalization. Next enumerate the instances or examples which constitute your proof, describing them to the extent which seems appropriate. In the conclusion state your generalization clearly and firmly.*

**Exercise B**   *A syllogism is among other things sometimes a very useful device for structuring an essay. Choose a subject in which* *you are interested and write an argument following the normal order of the categorical syllogism. The first step will state and develop a major premise. The second step will state and develop the minor premise. The third step will draw and elaborate the conclusion.*

**Exercise C** *Choose one of the following topics and write two propositions related to it which constitute an enthymeme. Then write a paper expanding the enthymeme into a full argument.*

1. Early entrance to college
2. Orientation week
3. Summer employment
4. Religion on the campus
5. Specialization in medicine
6. Good manners
7. Studying a foreign language
8. Minimum wage laws
9. Television
10. Human nature
11. The United Nations
12. The exploration of space
13. Political leadership
14. Meeting a celebrity

**Exercise D** *Write an editorial in favor of some current proposal which you would like to see adopted.*

**Exercise E** *Review Benjamin Franklin's argument against the appointment of salaries for members of the executive branch of the government (pages 150–153). Write an argument for or against such a proposal in the light of modern conditions.*

**Exercise F** *Find an argument which impresses you as valid because one of the terms is vaguely or improperly defined or is used in an equivocal sense. Write an argument in which you stipulate the definition clearly and draw your own conclusions.*

**Exercise G** *Find an article in some magazine which argues a proposition of policy.*

A proposition of policy is one which asserts that something should be done. An article of this kind might argue that the voting privilege should be broadened or further restricted, that the government should allow more freedom to private enterprise, that public school education should prepare one for a vocation, or that this nation should continue aid to foreign countries.

State the argument contained in the article as clearly as you can. If the argument can be formulated as a syllogism, you may wish to attack one or both of the supporting premises. For example, if the article says that the schools should train for citizenship and that the best way to be a good citizen is to make a good living, you might object to one or both of these suppositions.

Bear in mind that a refutation is essentially a counter-argument, in which you try to establish an opposite of the conclusion you are attacking.

**Exercise H**   *Think of at least three different "sources" of argument (defi-nition, cause, etc.) on which you might draw in arguing the following propositions. Choose the proposition which appeals to you most and write the argument.*

1. Colleges should abolish the elective system.
2. Men and women should be equally liable to military service.
3. The constitution should be amended so as to prohibit an income tax rate higher than 25%.
4. Federal aid to education will result in regimentation.
5. No man should be forced to join a union in order to hold a job.
6. States' rights are essential to encourage the feeling of local responsibility.
7. National sovereignty has been outmoded by the atomic age.
8. An individual should have complete liberty in those actions which con-cern only himself.

**Exercise I**   *Read the work of a newspaper columnist for a period of time. Study his arguments and determine which are induc-tive, deductive, and analogical. Which of these forms of ar-gument does he seem to prefer?*

**Exercise J**   *Study the full-page advertisements in some magazine of large circulation. Determine the source of their rhetorical appeal to the reader.*

For example, if an advertisement tells you to buy something because "millions of people are buying it," the source is circumstance—the familiar "bandwagon" appeal. If another advises you to purchase a certain product because a noted racing driver says that it is the best of its kind, the source is testimony. All of the sources we have been studying in the section on persuasion can be found in advertisements.

# Part Three

## Special Problems of Composition

# Chapter Six

# The Sentence

The sentence is our most important building block. Although it is true that we learn words before we begin to put together sentences, the sentence is the unit which makes a predication, or effects the linking of a subject and verb. We use words to name things—objects, qualities, and so on—but it is the sentence which *says something*. We use the sentence form as *the* means of developing our thought systematically. That is why a composition, or any other ordered form of communication, will be made up of sentences. Further the clearness and force of any piece of writing depend largely upon the individual sentences making it up. If the piece as a whole is to have these qualities, the sentences must have them too.

## THE SENTENCE DEFINED

It is commonly said that a sentence is a group of words expressing a complete thought. This definition undoubtedly gives a certain insight into the nature of the sentence, even though the meaning of "a complete thought" is hard to pin down. Probably nobody can say finally what the difference between "a complete thought" and "an incomplete thought" is. For this reason, in the *Handbook* we approach the definition of the sentence through its form, and call it a group of words consisting of subject and predicate which does not depend on any larger grammatical construction. In a way this definition points to the idea of complete meaning, since a group which is not part of a larger grammatical construction is presumed to be able to stand alone. As an independent group, it will have a kind of completeness, though in fact it may express several thoughts.

The advantage of this definition is that it focuses attention upon the requirement of subject and predicate for the full sentence. When we began by pointing out that the sentence *says something,* we were affirming that it asserts something in relation to a subject. Thus the sentence may be recognized by the fact that it predicates, or states the occurrence or existence of something.

> The sun shines.
> Men hope.
> The trees are green.

In these simple sentences it is predicated of the sun that it shines, of men that they hope, of the trees that they are green. Note that the predication takes the form of a finite verb; that is to say, of a verb which has number, person, and voice. If we had written instead "The sun shining," "Men hoping," or "The trees being green," we would not have composed full sentences. These are only participial phrases, because the verb form necessary to express occurrence or existence is missing from both. Some form of the finite verb is essential to any sentence. Without it the group would not have one of the two elements required by the definition—the element which does the asserting. The surest way to tell whether a group can constitute a sentence is to look for the verb. Sometimes groups are mistaken for sentences when they contain a verbal instead of a verb. Remember that participles, gerunds, and infinitives by themselves can never play the role of verbs. They have certain properties of the verb, but they are all *infinite* or indeterminate as opposed to *finite.* A finite verb is needed to express a definite, limited action or state of being. Test your ability to distinguish finite from non-finite forms by pointing out which of the groups below are sentences.

1. To have a lot of fun.
2. Russell arrived on time.
3. Reading the newspaper at the table every morning.
4. The door opened quietly.
5. The phone ringing and everybody talking at the same time.
6. Tall building gleaming in the morning sunlight.
7. Smoking a pipe, he settled into a chair.
8. A week having passed and no letter having arrived.
9. To get up early and to be at work before nine.
10. The wheat crop was below the estimate of the Department of Agriculture.
11. Walking unexpectedly into the midst of things.
12. Inviting his friends to the party.
13. The floor covered with rich carpets and the walls hung with pictures.
14. Finding a trunk full of old letters while rummaging around in the attic.
15. The engine started with a roar.

16. Hoping to avoid detection in the darkness.
17. Each evening after supper he worked in the garden.
18. Entering into all civic activities and becoming one of the town's leading citizens.
19. The land sloping gently.
20. Expecting to acquire enough wealth to retire for the rest of his life.

The groups which do not contain a finite verb arc incomplete or fragmentary sentences. In the first group, for example, "To have a lot of fun" is not a complete statement. It could become part of an assertion by being made a subject ("To have a lot of fun was the main purpose"), or an object ("They wished to have a lot of fun"). In both of these instances we have completed the sentence by adding a verb in the finite form, *was* in the first example, and *wished* in the second.

Another type of incomplete sentence is the group which does contain a finite verb, but which does not meet the requirement of being independent of other grammatical constructions. It is incomplete because it cannot be set off by itself without leaving some pertinent question unanswered. The answer is supplied by the larger group in which this group properly belongs. This kind of fragment is the *dependent clause,* whose very name suggests a necessary relationship to something else. Suppose you encounter the words "If it docs not rain." Clearly this is a group whose introductory word "If" indicates that it is to be attached to another group for the completing of any idea. As a mere conditional clause, this expression is meaningless unless it is followed by a clause of result. The combination of the two will make a full sentence. Thus, by adding any clause which will express a result following from the condition, we can make the group a complete sentence: "If it does not rain, we can have the picnic"; "If it does not rain, the washing will dry"; "If it does not rain, the ball game will be played"; "If it does not rain, the flowers must be watered," and so on. The point is that this dependent group must function as part of a larger group in order to have significance.

Identify the groups below which are complete sentences.

1. While everybody slept.
2. If Albert completes the work today.
3. When he came to the intersection, he sounded his horn.
4. If honors came easily, they would not be valued.
5. Unless the terms of the contract are fulfilled.
6. When he considered the difficulty, when he thought of the expense, when he estimated the time likely to be lost.
7. As they prospered through trading with the Indians.
8. The boy whistled a lively tune as he turned the corner.
9. Milling and jostling, the crowd moved toward the gate.
10. Because grammar was the one subject she had disliked in high school.
11. Reclining lazily as the current bore them down stream.

12. With which he grew disgusted.
13. Which is believed to be the largest specimen ever grown in this country.
14. As the earth revolves on its axis.
15. She returned to the store where she had made the purchase.

We emphasize the difference between complete and incomplete groups because composition employs, with very few exceptions, the complete sentence. We write in terms of linked subjects and predicates which exist as independent groups. This is a form which the reader is accustomed to expect, moreover, and departures from it must be handled with care.

There are, nevertheless, two types of incomplete groups which are occasionally used in standard written English. These may be called *minor sentences,* because they function as sentences without meeting our definition of the full sentence. In some instances a minor sentence is a clause; in others only a phrase or a word.

Most minor sentences are elliptical in the sense that the part lacking is clearly indicated by what has gone before or by something in the general speech or writing situation. The meaning has already been implied; completing the sentence is merely giving linguistic expression to the implication which is present. Nothing is added beyond what the context already suggests.

> "How many did you count?"
> "Nine."

In this exchange, the word "Nine" is a minor sentence. The response in this instance would probably be

> "I counted nine."

This group is a full sentence made by expanding the elliptical expression "nine."

> "Will Rebecca be at the party?"
> "Probably."

Here the completion probably would be "Rebecca will probably be at the party." The principle is the same for elliptical elements consisting of dependent clauses.

> "What did he say?"
> [He said] "That he is satisfied."

> "Where will the meeting be held?"
> [It will be held] "Wherever they can find a hall."

> "Will Thompson get into the game Saturday?"
> [He will get into the game] "If his knee is better."

The non-elliptical minor sentence differs from the elliptical in that it can be understood or "translated" in a number of ways. Such expressions often appear as exclamations or ejaculations. Thus the expression "In trouble again!" might be understood as "What a shame that John is in trouble again!" or "I knew you would be in trouble again!" or "He's not in trouble again!"

The expressions below can be expanded with similar freedom and variety.

> No sign of water!
> In the very middle of the night.
> Alone among all those people.
> The very crown of his effort.
> Bewitched by one of the local sirens.
> All in one throw.

It will be obvious that minor sentences are most frequently used in dialogue. There the speech situation and the trend of the discourse indicate how we are to expand them or interpret them. In reality they are found not to be isolated fragments. Occasionally, however, a minor sentence of the elliptical kind will be found in expository prose of the more serious kind. Each of the groups below contains such a sentence.

> To learn the secrets of any science, we go to specialists, even though they may be eccentric persons, and not to commonplace pupils. We combine what they tell us with the rest of our wisdom, and form our final judgment independently. Even so with religion.
> —William James, *The Varieties of Religious Experience*

> The first in time and the first in importance of the influences upon the mind is that of nature. Every day, the sun; and, after sunset, night and her stars.
> —Ralph Waldo Emerson, "The American Scholar"

> The subject of this essay is not the so-called Liberty of the Will, so unfortunately opposed to the misnamed doctrine of Philosophical Necessity; but Civil, or Social Liberty: the nature and limits of the power which can be legitimately exercised by society over the individual. A question seldom stated and hardly ever discussed, in general terms, but which profoundly influences the practical controversies of the age by its latent presence, and is likely soon to make itself recognized as the vital question of the future.
> —John Stuart Mill, "On Liberty"

Here the connection of the incomplete groups with what goes before is quite clear. There is no fragmentation of the kind that results in incoherence. The continuity is preserved, and this is a point to be borne in mind carefully by anyone who wishes to risk the less than full sentence form.

This is all that needs to be said about the incomplete sentence. Although it is not entirely avoided, its use is restricted. Expository writing sprinkled with minor sentences is likely to be a sign of illiteracy.

Sentences are the building blocks of composition, but not all of the blocks are of the same size and shape. If they were, we could put together only a rudimentary kind of structure, such as a child might build with his blocks. Differences in size and design, however, enable us to build much more elaborate and serviceable structures than this. For that purpose, we need to have a critical understanding of these differences.

Every sentence has both a grammatical aspect and a rhetorical aspect. In reality, these are closely related, for grammatical elements have their rhetorical qualities, and the rhetorical qualities of any unit of expression are to some extent arranged and brought out by the grammar. Still, the distinction between the two is useful for purposes of analysis. We frequently need to know when we are talking about a problem which is mainly grammatical and when about one which is mainly rhetorical, even though the two kinds of problems may not be finally separable. In deciding the merits of a sentence, we have to determine why an intended meaning is not getting through, or why an emphasis is falling in some unwanted place, or why the sentence fails to have persuasive force despite clarity and fullness of detail. Here grammatical and rhetorical analysis are essential means to criticism and improvement. They can give us, sometimes separately and sometimes in combination, the answer to these and similar questions.

## GRAMMATICAL PATTERNS OF SENTENCES

### The Simple Sentence

It is explained in the *Handbook* that sentences fall into simple and composite types. The simple type has only one clause; the composite has two or more. In its barest form, a simple sentence consists of a subject and a predicate.

> Iron rusts.
> A soldier must be brave.

But a group may be elaborated far beyond this without losing its simple-sentence structure. For one thing, both subjects and predicates can be compounded:

> Wheat and corn are produced in abundance.

This is a simple sentence with a compound subject. The next is a simple sentence with a compound predicate:

> The campers fished and swam in the nearby lake.

Elaboration of a sentence of simple structure also may be carried further than this by the use of modifying words and phrases, so that the simple sentence need not be a short sentence. Generally, however, it tends to be short, and its easily grasped structure allows it to focus attention rather well upon the subject and the predicate. It is rhetorically effective when two things are to be grouped simply—a couple of substantives, or a substantive and an action.

> The animal was a bear.
> The men were mowing a field.

The simplicity of this structure suggests an elementary level of perception. Indeed, this is the level upon which a child perceives things. When a child reports an adventure he is likely to do it in a string of simple sentences, because this simple conjoining of two things is the way we first begin to take in the world. It is the way we see things before we have grown sophisticated about causes and values. For this reason, a style made up predominantly of simple sentences is sometimes called a "primer" style. It is common in simple reporting where it is apt to consist of flat assertions and direct characterizations. In the hands of a master, though, the simple-sentence style can be used to accomplish something more. Ernest Hemingway often employs the very terseness and restrained development of such sentences to give to his stories an implicativeness and a suppressed emotion. Study for example, the following passage from his *The Sun Also Rises.*

> In the morning it was raining. A fog had come over the mountains from the sea. You could not see the tops of the mountains. The plateau was dull and gloomy, and the shapes of the trees and the houses were changed. I walked out beyond the town to look at the weather. The bad weather was coming over the mountains from the sea.

Here as often with Hemingway the simple sentence represents the severity of a method. In his hands it becomes a carefully used art form with definite powers. But for most of us, who have less special objectives, the simple sentence is most useful for reporting, for the occasional synoptic statement which comes fittingly near the beginning or end of a piece of writing, and for an important, often dramatic statement to which we wish to call attention. Statements such as "These are the facts"; "Now we turn to another part of the question," and "Today the world is interested in peace" derive part of their effect from the fact that the simple sentence emphasizes a subject and a predicate and does little else. To know this and to use the simple sentence where such emphasis is needed is to help grammar forward one's design in writing. Many beginners in writing fail badly because the grammar of their sentences works at cross purposes with their meaning and rhetorical intention. It is when we get all of these working in cooperation that we achieve the best result.

## The Compound Sentence

With the compound sentence, we enter the group of composite structures. The compound sentence is a more developed kind of sentence; it has not one predication but two or more. Its characteristic form is a series of similar grammatical structures (usually a series of simple sentences) separated by internal punctuation. The effect of such a sentence is that we have to extend our attention to the point of taking in more than one subject-predicate relationship. Consider the following examples.

The wind blew, and the rain came in sheets.

The world admires success, and few people have the patience to listen to excuses for failure.

The language and traditions common to England and America are like the other family bonds: they draw kindred together at the great crises of life, but they also occasion at times a little friction and fault-finding.
—George Santayana, "Materialism and Idealism in American Life"

## The Balanced Sentence

In these examples, the compound sentence develops by joining clauses and there are certain effects that may result from this kind of construction. One of these is the feeling of "balance" given by the compound sentence when its clauses are about equally long and when they produce a sort of equilibrium. In two-clause sentences, each clause is a counterpoise to the other. Frequent use of sentences of this kind results in what has been called the "balanced" style. In the eighteenth century, this style was brought to a high degree of order and elegance. Today an occasional balanced sentence can give a reflective turn to one's composition, although too much striving for balance usually leaves an impression of artificiality. Below are three specimens from the great period of this style. Note, in addition to the clarity and precision, the general philosophic tone of these sentences.

The religion of Constantine achieved, in less than a century, the final conquest of the Roman empire: but the victors themselves were insensibly subdued by the arts of their vanquished rivals.
—Edward Gibbon, *Decline and Fall of the Roman Empire*

A crowd of princes and prelates disputed the ruins of the empire: the lords of innumerable castles were less prone to obey than to imitate their superiors; and, according to the measure of their strength, their incessant hostilities received the names of conquest or robbery.
—Edward Gibbon, *Ibid*.

He had read with critical eyes the important volume of human life, and he knew the heart of man, from the depths of strategem to the surface of affectation.
—Samuel Johnson, *Life of Addison*

The balanced sentence is often found in reflective writing, but it may be used effectively in any situation in which the writer wishes to show a particularly close relationship between points that could stand alone in simple sentences. For example, the second point may be a statement of the cause for the first point; the second may repeat the first with a change of focus; or it may place an important qualification on what the first has said. The balanced sentence often gives us a complete statement by offering two views of a subject, or a view with an explanation, or a qualifying view which seems to finish off the assertion. This kind of sentence sounds definitive or final. Probably this is the reason it has been favored for uses where it is necessary to present a judgment of things. The poetical books of the King James Bible have many balanced compound sentences, and their frequent use there may have influenced our feeling that it is suited to a rather grave style.

> He cometh forth like a flower and is cut down: he fleeth also as a shadow, and continueth not.
>
> —Job 14:2

> The foolish woman is clamorous; she is simple, and knoweth nothing.
> —Proverbs 9:13

> Day unto day uttereth speech, and night unto night showeth knowledge.
> —Psalms 19:2

A style which uses too many balanced sentences, however, appears very formal and suggests a lack of spontaneity, of directness, of simplicity. The balanced sentence can be a useful resource but it must not be overused. The balanced sentence is only one form of the compound sentence. Other compound sentences have something of the same effect, with two or more independent clauses giving relatively heavy emphasis to two or more predications. Obviously the clauses in a compound sentence must be fairly closely related—even when their purpose is to express contrast or concession—to justify their being placed in one sentence unit.

## The Complex Sentence

The complex sentence contains, in addition to its independent clause, one or more dependent clauses. Since there is no limit, theoretically, to the number of dependent clauses which may be added, a complex sentence can be very long. In the seventeenth century it was the custom to write very long ones, adding clause after clause. There is some profit in comparing the sentence below from *Areopagitica,* Milton's famous defense of freedom of the press, with modern style. Here Milton writes a complex sentence of more than one hundred words. Its object is to set forth an ideal of fairness in the public discussion of truth, unhampered by censorship or licensing.

> When a man hath been laboring the hardest labor in the deep mines of knowledge, hath furnished out his findings in all their equipage, drawn forth his reasons as it were a battle arranged, scattered and defeated all objections in his way, calls out his adversary into the plain, offers him the

advantage of wind and sun, if he please, only that he may try the matter by dint of argument; for his opponents then to skulk, to lay ambushments, to keep a narrow bridge of licensing where the challenger should pass, though it be valor enough in soldiership, is but weakness and cowardice in the wars of truth.

Today we seldom encounter a sentence of this complexity and length. Most complex sentences in contemporary prose are modest affairs compared with this, with from one to three dependent clauses.

There was never a time when mankind was without some kind of philosophy, or a set of beliefs about the world we live in.
—William E. Hocking, *Some Types of Philosophy*

And who will deny that a world in which the wealthy are powerful is still a better world than one in which only the already powerful can become wealthy?
—F. A. Hayek, *The Road to Serfdom*

The danger in specialization is that a man will fail to recognize that there are cogent ways of thinking markedly different from those he customarily employs.
—Arthur Bestor, *Educational Wastelands*

Inspection will show that the complex sentence is usually a vehicle for ordering our thoughts. The independent clause presents one important point; the dependent clause or clauses related points. The complex sentence is therefore generally a good device for expressing those ideas which we have considered in such a way that we wish to give them an ordering. When we think systematically about any subject, we choose one idea as the focus of a sentence. The other ideas cluster about it in various relationships, some expressing a cause, some a condition, some a qualification, some a description. Such a complex of relationships is generally best expressed through a grammatical structure which has different levels and which is a system of meaningful subordination. We can see how this operates in a simple instance.

There is the man whom I met yesterday.

In this sentence the idea which is given a central position by the writer or speaker is "there is the man." The clause "whom I met yesterday" is a full predication, but it is given less importance in the communication than the idea of the other clause. It is put there to describe or limit. We find the same in the sentence

There were few people on the streets because it was early.

The dependent clause "because it was early" is used to explain the fact stated by the main clause. Its function can be considered a subordinate one.

The special advantage of the complex sentence is that it allows us to order points like the ones above. We can indicate by the very structure of our sentence which point the reader is to take as primary. Faced with a sentence like "George Washington was the first president of the United States and he was born in Virginia," the reader would not know which of the two ideas expressed the writer wishes to emphasize, except by the order in which they occur, and this is not a dependable sign. But by making the sentence complex and putting one of the ideas in a dependent clause, we may say either "George Washington, who was born in Virginia, was the first president of the United States" or "George Washington, who was the first president of the United States, was born in Virginia." In both of these revised sentences there is a chief point, not two equal points in a sort of rivalry for attention. Of course, successful use of the complex sentence demands careful attention to which of the two or more ideas is to receive the emphasis, and we shall deal with this more fully under "Proper Subordination." We now see that as a sentence form it is useful for making those discriminations among ideas which are characteristic of all mature thinking. One of the sure signs of progress in writing is increased skill in handling the complex sentence. It is a flexible unit which can be used to accommodate groups of thoughts without confusion if one is careful about the construction.

Since the compound-complex sentence is distinguished from the complex only by having two or more independent clauses, nothing special needs to be said about it. What is said of the other types of composite sentences will be true in its case, with the difference that it makes possible a still more elaborate grouping of ideas. However, in writing the compound-complex sentence, it is necessary to avoid over-extending the sentence unit. A practiced writer may fit a large number of ideas into a sentence while maintaining good integration, but the inexperienced writer is in danger of allowing his sentence to continue until it sprawls. If your compound-complex sentences seem less close-knit than they should, it is probably advisable to break them up into two or more sentences. Like other sentences, the compound-complex is justified only so long as it expresses a reasonably unified group of thoughts. Below are a few illustrations of successful constructions of the compound-complex type.

> He had no curiosity about what men had thought; but about what they had felt and lived, he had a great deal.
>
> —Willa Cather, *Lost Lady*

> There may be too many publishers; there are certainly too many books published; and the journals ever incite the reader to "keep up" with what is being published.
>
> —T. S. Eliot, "Religion and Literature"

> Men are much more unwilling to have their weaknesses and their imperfections known than their crimes; and if you hint to a man that you think him silly, ignorant, or even ill bred or awkward, he will hate you more and longer than if you tell him plainly that you think him a rogue.
>
> —Lord Chesterfield, *Letters to His Son*

These are some ways in which sentence pattern can contribute to effectiveness and style in writing. Well constructed sentences are the surest sign that the writer is moving from the level of mere competence and mediocrity to that of excellence. They show he is attaining that degree of control at which he can choose his effect. Meaning and emphasis are no longer matters of hit and miss. The very form of his sentences helps him to say what he has in mind and to stress what he regards as important.

## The Position of Modifiers

Even after the clause structure of a sentence has been settled, problems often arise in regard to the placing of modifiers. This is primarily a question for grammar, but the solution frequently has important bearing on the rhetorical success of the sentence.

### Placing Modifying Words

In English, single adjectives nearly always precede the substantive they modify. We write "the blue sky," "the fast horse," "the great book," and so on. There are, however, a few instances in which the adjective is placed after the noun to preserve a traditional phrase, as in expressions like "the castle perilous," "the bar sinister," "the heir apparent," and a few others. Poets sometimes place the adjective after the noun, for their purposes, but on the whole there is little need for experimenting with the order of the single adjective and its substantive.

The problem is different with the adverb, which is the most mobile part of speech. It can be placed almost anywhere in the sentence, as long as we realize that different positions sometimes result in different meanings.

> *Warmly* he took the side of his friend.
> He *warmly* took the side of his friend.
> He took the side of his friend *warmly*.

The shift of position of *warmly* in this sentence does not alter the meaning of the group. Nevertheless there are situations in which the shift of an adverbial modifier does effect a perceptible change of meaning. Study the two sentences below and notice the difference made by a shift in position of *truly*.

> *Truly* it was an occasion which everyone enjoyed.
> It was an occasion which everyone *truly* enjoyed.

The first "truly" expresses the attitude of the writer toward the assertion which the sentence makes. But the "truly" of the second sentence applies to "enjoyed" and serves to qualify this verb.

In careful writing, caution should be used in placing the modifier "not." It is more accurate to write "Not all who came were welcome" than "All who came were not welcome," since the modifier is intended to apply to "all."

Special care must be observed with the modifiers *only* and *even*. Both can be interpreted as restricting the word or phrase before which they stand; and consequently there is a difference between writing "I only dropped the book" and "I dropped only the book"; between writing "He was even reproached by his friends" and "He was reproached even by his friends."

In the same way,

I only heard about the robbery. (I did not see it.)
I heard only about the robbery. (I did not hear about anything else.)

For the same general reason it is important to avoid "squinting modifiers," or modifiers which can apply equally well to more than one element in the sentence. Many adverbs can be construed as modifying either an element which precedes them in the sentence or an element which follows them. When an adverbial modifier appears in this position, the sentence should be recast to prevent the ambiguity.

AMBIGUOUS: To change the oil often is a good practice.

In this sentence *often* can be interpreted as modifying either *to change the oil* or *is*.

CLEAR: It is good practice to change the oil often.
AMBIGUOUS: The money he had saved slowly disappeared.
CLEAR: The money he had slowly saved disappeared.
CLEAR: The money he had saved disappeared slowly.
AMBIGUOUS: The kind of work he was doing promptly caused him to lose his job.
CLEAR: The kind of work he was doing caused him to lose his job promptly.
AMBIGUOUS: After he had worked out a plan with the help of his parents he continued in school.
CLEAR: After he had worked out a plan, he continued in school with the help of his parents.
CLEAR: After he had worked out a plan with the help of his parents, he continued in school.

**Exercise:** *All of the sentences below contain modifiers which are misplaced or which "squint." Revise the sentences by changing the position of the modifier or by recasting the sentence so that the meaning cannot be mistaken.*

1. All of the children were not sleepy when nine o'clock arrived.
2. The prisoner only confessed when confronted with the victim.
3. Everybody practically needed some help with the lesson.
4. To speak the truth always is the best rule.
5. The Spanish-American War only lasted a few months.
6. Everyone does not vote in national elections.
7. A prize is awarded to the one who makes the highest grades annually.
8. Football is a rough sport, and even some players get killed.
9. All who wished to hear the speech could not get into the hall.

10. Everyone nearly suffers when a business depression occurs.
11. Children were even admitted.
12. All that tastes good is not safe to eat.
13. The coat that Joe was wearing happily was his own.
14. People who go to church usually are good citizens.
15. The letter which Mark had addressed supposedly never reached its destination.

## Placing Modifying Clauses

The adverbial clause often can be placed in a number of positions without altering the meaning of the sentence. For example:

Because the results exceeded his expectations, Homer was jubilant.
Homer, because the results exceeded his expectations, was jubilant.
Homer was jubilant because the results exceeded his expectations.

The placing of adjective clauses, however, is a different matter; and one of the main problems of grouping within the sentence is the proper position of adjective clauses with respect to the substantives which they modify. It would be improper to write:

He dropped the book at the sound of the fire alarm which he had taken from the library.

The clause "which he had taken from the library" is obviously intended to modify "book" and not "fire alarm." Therefore the sentence should read:

At the sound of the fire alarm he dropped the book which he had taken from the library.

Such faulty groupings are especially likely to occur when the relative pronoun is "that," since this pronoun can refer both to persons and to objects.

The man in the city that I visited was my uncle.

In this sentence "that" could refer either to "man" or "city." A relocation of the relative clause removes the difficulty.

The man that I visited in the city was my uncle.

Similarly ambiguous reference in the following sentence has been removed by placing the relative clause immediately after the noun which is being modified.

AMBIGUOUS:    Merchandise was sold by the company that had been damaged by fire.
CLEAR:    Merchandise that had been damaged by fire was sold by the company.

## Placing Modifying Phrases

Phrase modifiers as well usually need to be placed after the element which they modify in the sentence.

CONFUSING: The teacher handed the paper to the student covered with red marks.

CLEAR: The teacher handed to the student the paper covered with red marks.

CONFUSING: He stopped his car before the house in the street with green shutters.

CLEAR: He stopped his car in the street before the house with green shutters.

CONFUSING: A small boy was found lost in a cowboy suit in the West End section.

CLEAR: A small boy in a cowboy suit was found lost in the West End section.

CONFUSING: Tom recognized the girl he had met at the dance with the beautiful eyes.

CLEAR: Tom recognized the girl with the beautiful eyes he had met at the dance.

CONFUSING: For sale: 1952 Ford by owner with low mileage.

CLEAR: For sale by owner: 1952 Ford with low mileage.

### Dangling Modifiers

In a well-written sentence every modifier usually has something to modify. Sometimes a sentence is confusing because a modifier has been used in the absence of anything to which it can correctly apply. Such modifiers, because there is nothing to which they can be tied, are said to "dangle." Often they result in an absurd meaning.

Sometimes a clause is left elliptical by the omission of subject and verb. If the group is then taken as a modifier, it may have nothing to modify. This leaves it dangling, or without function in the sentence.

When twelve years old, his father failed in business.
Although in the country, the temptations of city life proved strong.

One method of correction is to supply a substantive which the group can properly modify.

When twelve years old, Oscar learned that his father had failed in business.
Although in the country, Frank found the temptations of city life strong.

A dangling elliptical clause may also be corrected by expanding the clause to its full form.

When Oscar was twelve years old, his father failed in business.
Although Frank was in the country, he found the temptations of city life strong.

More common than the dangling elliptical clause is the dangling participial phrase. Grammar classifies the participle as an adjective—a word that describes or limits a substantive. In the absence of a substantive to which it can meaningfully apply, the participial phrase dangles in the same way as the dangling elliptical clause. Below are sentences faulty because they contain dangling participial phrases.

> Being lonesome, the time passed slowly.
> Rattling along in our old car, the picnic ground soon came into view.
> Entering the library, a bust of Cicero is seen.

Each of these sentences though common in conversation is considered confusing in prose. This is so because in reading the sentence we first pick up the participial phrase and then look for something to attach it to—something which it can modify in its function as an adjective. In a carefully constructed sentence, the participial phrase usually modifies the subject of the following clause.

> Looking studious, Katherine opened the book.

But in the sentences above, this kind of modification produces nonsense. The time is not being lonesome, the picnic ground is not rattling along in an old car, and the bust of Cicero is not entering the library.

The dangling participial phrase is corrected in the same ways as the dangling elliptical clause. We can supply a substantive which it can modify.

> Being lonesome, Ted found that the time passed slowly.
> Rattling along in our old car, we soon reached the picnic ground.
> Entering the library, one sees a bust of Cicero.

Or we can convert the phrase into a clause and thus do away with the participial construction.

> Because Ted was lonesome, the time passed slowly.
> As we rattled along in our old car, the picnic ground soon came into view.
> As one enters the library, one sees a bust of Cicero.

Avoid also the dangling infinitive phrase. An infinitive phrase coming at the beginning of the sentence is usually attached by the reader to the subject of the following clause. If such attachment makes nonsense, the infinitive phrase is said to dangle.

> To lift heavy weights, the back should be kept rigid.
> To live comfortably in the tropics, light clothing should be worn.

The problem is such sentences is to decide whether the infinitive phrase applies to the subject of the clause following. We shall probably decide that it is not the back which is lifting heavy weights (at least in the intended sense of the sentence) and that it is not light clothing which is going to live comfortably in the tropics. To prevent even initial misreadings of this sort, it is best to cast the sentences in some such form as the following.

> To lift heavy weights, one should keep the back rigid.
> To live comfortably in the tropics, people should wear light clothing.

The same problem arises with those gerund phrases which are made up of a preposition followed by a gerund. The tendency of such phrases to attach themselves to the subject of the following clause must be taken into account.

Upon opening the door, a tall stranger appeared.

It is hardly the true meaning of the sentence that the tall stranger was opening the door. Therefore we should write:

Upon opening the door, James saw a tall stranger.

And likewise,

After leaving home, a period of anxiety was felt.

Since it is not the period of anxiety which has left home, we should write:

After leaving home, Priscilla felt a period of anxiety.

If there is any likelihood that an infinitive phrase or a gerund phrase in this position may result in confusion, the sentence should be revised. The importance of a clear train of thought is such that even momentary hesitations over meaning should be prevented.

**Exercise:** *Rewrite the following sentences, removing all dangling elements.*

1. Having prepared the night before, the test was not difficult.
2. By planting early, the garden will produce a crop of beans by mid-summer.
3. Visiting New York for the first time, the skyscrapers were truly impressive.
4. While still in high school, his ambition was to be a physician.
5. Fearing to arouse opposition, a conciliatory tone was adopted.
6. When sufficiently cooked, the next step is to add pepper and salt.
7. On being interviewed, the applicant's experience is carefully considered.
8. Once initiated, fraternity life proved quite exciting.
9. Upon inspecting the damage, a large dent in the fender was found.
10. Looking out the window, a novel sight met William's gaze.
11. To succeed in a competitive society, education must be thorough.
12. While marching in the ranks, his big feet were usually out of step.
13. By reading history, one's appreciation of the past increases.
14. Finding no one at home, a note was left under the door.
15. Crossing the field, an Indian arrowhead was discovered.
16. After arising in the morning, the day began with a good breakfast.
17. Driving at a faster rate, home was reached in time for dinner.
18. When angry, the pulse rate quickens.
19. To see in the dark, a flashlight was brought along.
20. Being a foreigner, his ignorance of local customs made him feel helpless.

## RHETORICAL PATTERNS OF SENTENCES

The grammatical and the rhetorical qualities of sentences interact constantly. Indeed, it is scarcely possible to disengage the one quality entirely from the other. We have seen earlier in this chapter how the types of sentence organization which are usually discussed under the heading "grammar" have their rhetorical properties and tendencies. They affect the meaning, the force, and the tone of the particular utterance. Their very structure has expressive power. In pointing out how one kind of group expresses one kind of thought, we have been talking, in reality, about the rhetoric of grammar. Now we shall turn to a more systematic examination of the subject.

The primary question is, as before, how to write good sentences. But answers must now be given relative to the effect that one wishes to produce, taking into account the aim and the particular audience. Within the bounds allowed by grammar there are many kinds of "good" sentences. In looking at sentences for their rhetorical qualities, however, we shall be asking, good for what? We were forced to consider this matter somewhat when we studied sentences for their clause structure; now we must attend to it in regard to such matters as order, loose and periodic structure, and length. These are features of the sentence which have a definite bearing on its effectiveness.

### Sentence Order

Most sentences in English have a normal order, which consists of the subject, the verb, the indirect object (if any), and the object or complement (if any).

The man (subject) killed (verb) the bear (object).

In English, order is frequently part of the total expression of the meaning. The English language has comparatively few inflectional forms, and it has no accusative (objective) form for the noun. This means that we cannot tell by means of a case ending what noun in a sentence is the object of the action of the verb. Consider the difference between these two sentences:

The man killed the bear.
The bear killed the man.

The difference results from the order of the words. The significance of this fact about English may be seen by looking at a comparable sentence in another language. Students of Latin will recognize that there is no possibility of mistaking the object in the sentence:

Caesarem interfecit Brutus.

Here the accusative form "Caesarem" tells us that Caesar is the object of the action expressed by the verb. But if the words stood in this order in English, we would interpret it as saying:

Caesar killed Brutus.

Here "Caesar" stands in the normal position of subject and "Brutus" follows the verb.

Because readers of English are accustomed to a normal order the writer should follow a normal order in most of his sentences. Such advice is especially valuable to those who find themselves writing awkward or confusing sentences, for the very regularity of the normal sentence order will assist the reader in his interpretation. And even departures from a fixed order, when they seem advisable, derive their effect partly from the fact that there is something fixed or normal to depart from.

There are two alterations of normal order which are sometimes used for rhetorical purpose. One of these is the inverted order, and the other is the interrupted order.

The inverted order is most often used when it is desirable to place special emphasis upon an object or a predicate noun or adjective. In these cases the element to be emphasized is placed at the beginning of the sentence, where the subject regularly goes. The subject and verb then follow in their normal order.

This job he held four years.

Plainly the intent of this sentence is to emphasize that he held *this job*, as contrasted with other jobs, for four years.

That part we could well believe.
His dog, however, he would not give up.
Adventures and narrow escapes they had in plenty.

When a predicate noun or adjective is placed first for this kind of emphasis, it is customary for the verb to follow and the subject to come last.

Interesting is the story of his career.
A strong leader John seemed at the time.
Peaceful was last night.

Sometimes a phrase which modifies the verb or object and which would normally follow these is placed at the beginning of the sentence for emphasis.

In such a country almost anything might happen.

With methods like these what did he expect to accomplish?

From this passage the schoolboy will learn about literature precisely nothing.

—C. S. Lewis, *The Abolition of Man*

Inversions are also a useful means of adding variety to one's sentence pattern. However valuable for clearness and directness the normal order may be, it can become monotonous. It is well to change this order occasionally. A little variation gives the style a flexibility, a kind of athletic quality.

The progress of a sentence through its normal order is sometimes halted by an interrupting phrase or clause. Such elements may appear between a subject and its verb or between a verb and its object. Such a placement of modifiers tends to slow down the movement of the sentence, and their value in a given sentence must be gauged accordingly.

> Norma, thanks to her mother's insistence that she dress warmly, had come well prepared.

> The candidate saw, on the strength of an excellent showing in the primary, that he had a good chance to win.

> He felt in Scotland, with its romantic castles, its clans, and its memories of the House of Stuart, the stirring of the past.

> It has been the lot of the unfortunate aborigines of America, in the early periods of colonization, to be doubly wronged by the white men.
> —Washington Irving, "Traits of Indian Character"

Sentence interrupters must be justified by their effect. Do not use them if they serve only to give the sentence a halting movement when it needs to move smoothly forward. And take care that the sentence is well constructed so that it will hold up despite the added weight which interrupters impose. But if these requirements are met, interrupters can be of advantage in placing emphasis, in accommodating details, in breaking up monotony, and in giving the sentence the kind of pace that induces a thoughtful reading.

## Loose and Periodic Structure

A useful rhetorical classification divides sentences into those which make a major point near or at the beginning of the sentence and then add to that point—the *loose* sentences—and those which delay, by interruptions and qualifications, the major point till the end of the sentence—the *periodic* sentences. The basis for this division is essentially grammatical. The loose sentence will usually begin with a complete simple sentence and add phrases, clauses or more sentences. For example,

> *Harvey missed the train,* although he had started packing early and had looked at his watch every half hour.

On the other hand, the periodic sentence will usually not complete the central grammatical structure until the end of the sentence. Thus,

*Harvey*, although he had started packing early and had looked at his watch every half hour, *missed the train.*

The loose sentence is so-called because it seems to deliver one important point first before proceeding with matters of less importance. It seems to "go on," adding detail after detail. Further it is a characteristic structure of spoken English. For these reasons it is a structure with informal connotations, though it is certainly not confined either to speech or informal writing. The following examples will show some of the contexts in which a loose sentence can be a particularly effective rhetorical device.

What we commonly have in mind when we speak of religion is a set of doctrines, of a more or less metaphysical character, formulated in a creed and supported by an organization distinct from the state.
—G. Lowes Dickinson, *The Greek View of Life*

I had come over the hills and on foot in serene summer days, plucking raspberries by the wayside, and occasionally buying a loaf of bread at a farmer's house, with a knapsack on my back, which held a few traveler's books and a change of clothing, and a staff in my hand.
—Henry David Thoreau,
*A Week on the Concord and Merrimac Rivers*

Ibsen had now written three immense dramas, all dealing with the effect of idealism on individual egotists of exceptional imaginative excitability.
—G. B. Shaw, *The Quintessence of Ibsenism*

The inside of the hut, as it now presented itself, was cosy and alluring, and the scarlet handful of fire in addition to the candle, reflecting its own genial color upon whatever it could reach, flung associations of enjoyment over utensils and tools.
—Thomas Hardy, *Far from the Madding Crowd*

I have suggested elsewhere that a growing weakness of our culture has been the increasing isolation of élites from each other, so that the political, the philosophical, the artistic, the scientific, are separated to the great loss of each of them, not merely through the arrest of any general circulation of ideas, but through the lack of those contacts and mutual influences at a less conscious level, which are perhaps even more important than ideas.
—T. S. Eliot, *Notes Toward the Definition of Culture*

As we have seen, loose sentences tend to unfold somewhat as the sentences in conversation do. They do not give the impression of being highly contrived. They express their main point first and other points follow to complete or enlarge the meaning.

The periodic sentence is, by contrast, a contrived type of sentence, whose structure seems designed to sustain the interest of the reader until the end. It uses the effective means of suspense to retain and even increase attention. Unless a sentence is unduly extended, the longer we have to wait for its principal idea, the more curious we are as to what that idea is. Usually the periodic sentence will commence with a series of dependent clauses or phrases. If these are skillfully chosen and arranged, the important point coming at the end will be felt with much more force than if it had been casually delivered at the beginning. The periodic sentence may be thought of as the orator's sentence. The orator normally wishes to work his audience up to a pitch of interest and feeling. Therefore he finds useful for his purpose sentences which have a climactic order and which deliver a "punch" at the end. Because it has this special effect, the periodic sentence is hardly the form in which we wish to express every thought. Yet it cannot be spared from writing in which an appeal to the emotions is an important consideration. It is a dramatic type of sentence when compared to the loose type, and it can be used to give vitality to a style which suffers from lifelessness. Study the quality of the periodic sentences below.

> If, in adopting the Constitution, nothing were done but acceding to a compact, nothing would seem necessary in order to break it up, but to secede from the same compact.
> —Daniel Webster, "Constitution not a Compact"

> If I thought mottoes and slogans did any good, I would replace the "God bless our happy home" of a generation or two ago, and the "Say it quick" of our offices today, with old Emerson's "Be Yourself."
> —James Truslow Adams, *Our Business Civilization*

> A major theme in American history, evidenced by armed risings of the back country against the tidewater in the South and by the assault upon Eastern bastions of privilege by the Populists of the East and West, has been the recurring sense of regional deprivation as a deliberate infliction by favored regions upon the rest of the country.
> —Donald R. Fleming, "The Big Money and High
> Politics of Science"

In reading each of these you must continue to the end before you learn what the sentence is about. This withholding of the meaning, if it is not too prolonged or tedious, has the natural effect of whetting interest. We become eager to see for what so much subordination of detail is preparing. The satisfaction of this interest then completes a normal rhythm of attention.

One does not make either loose or periodic sentences an object of writing. Ordinary attention to the requirements of a subject will tell one when a thought is best presented in a loose structure and when in a periodic or suspended one. We discover, as a matter of practice, that the loose sentence tends to be more common and that the periodic sentence is better for those less frequent occasions when we wish to arouse the reader's attention by suspension of meaning. When we are revising manuscript for the purpose of improving the general effectiveness of our style, however, it can be quite helpful to identify the two types. If the writing strikes us as dull and inert, it may be that we have adhered monotonously to the loose sentence and missed opportunities to make our sentence pattern bring out the natural interest of the subject. But if, on the other hand, the writing appears artificial and overdone in its striving for effect, we may have fallen into a habit of writing periodic sentences. In such case we will need more loose sentences to make the style relaxed.

It may be further noted that the loose and periodic sentence make a natural kind of sequence, since the sort of detail which constitutes the ending of the former constitutes the beginning of the latter; or, the main idea which appears at the close of the periodic sentence appears at the beginning of a following loose sentence. Thus the one type of sentence flows into the other. It would be harmful to make a sequence of this kind the dominant feature of a style, but used occasionally it will both improve continuity and add variety. Observe how these two sentences from James Bryce fit together.

> Those who have observed the uniformity I have been attempting to describe have commonly set it down, as Europeans do most American phenomena, to what they call democracy. Democratic government has not in reality much to do with it except insofar as such government helps to induce that deference of individuals to the mass which strengthens a dominant type, whether of ideas, of institutions, or of manners.
> —James Bryce, *American Commonwealth*

## Expletive Construction

There is a minor type of suspended construction which is very commonly used to throw emphasis upon the subject of a sentence. This construction is known as the *expletive*. The expletive is in reality an anticipatory subject consisting of *there* or *it*. As a device, it has the effect of suspending the sentence momentarily until the true subject arrives. Remember that *there* and *it* when used as expletives are never true subjects. They are merely forms which delay the sentence until our attention is ready for the true subject. Note the difference between the two sentences below.

> Five pages are missing from this book.
> There are five pages missing from this book.

In the first, the subject "five pages" appears without any particular emphasis. But in the second sentence, which begins with the expletive "there," a degree of emphasis is thrown upon "five pages." This emphasis is the result of a temporary suspension provided by the expletive. The same change of emphasis will be seen in the two sentences below.

> His intention was not to injure his friend.
> It was not his intention to injure his friend.

Observe the following expletive beginnings.

> There is only one right answer.
>
> It was disclosed in Washington yesterday that Congress may be called in special session.
>
> There are thirty-one days in January.
>
> It is the policy of our government to maintain friendly relations with all countries.

**Exercise:** *Most students need more practice in writing periodic sentences than in writing loose ones. Rewrite each of the sentences below in periodic form (using expletives where necessary) and note the difference in emphasis that results.*

1. I will call you if you insist.
2. The boat neared the finish line, the rowers bending rhythmically and the oars flashing in the sun.
3. The United States has many fine museums even though most Americans regard art as something foreign and believe that a man should concern himself with success in business.
4. Indian allies were in Burgoyne's army at Saratoga.
5. Her literary tastes were old-fashioned, being founded on a belief that the novel had ended with Jane Austen.
6. They stood the cold for an hour, stamping their feet and blowing on their fingers.
7. Examinations finally came around, although Nancy in the rush of parties and dances had managed to forget them.
8. Herman found that he still had not arrived at the correct total, although he checked his figures and added again.
9. They gave the house a thorough inspection, poking in the cellar, tramping up and down stairs, and even visiting the attic.
10. Three miles of rough water lay between the ship and the shore.

## Passive Voice

Still another way to give emphasis to parts of the sentence which normal order does not emphasize is to change the leading verb from active to passive voice. When the verb is in the active voice, the subject of the sentence is the initiator or agent of the action expressed. But when the verb is changed to the passive, the receiver or object of the action expressed becomes the subject. By means of this change, direct and indirect objects can be emphasized through being converted into subjects of the sentence. The result of such change may be seen in the following.

> A foul ball struck one of the players.
> One of the players was struck by a foul ball.

In the second sentence, the former object "one of the players" is placed in the important position of subject, and the attention of the reader is centered upon this phrase. Similarly, in the sentences below, observe how the subject of a passive verb receives the emphasis of the sentence.

Jackson was elected president by the class.
A commotion was heard in the street about midnight.
A few dollars had been saved for emergencies.

An indirect object can be emphasized in like manner. Instead of writing, "He gave us his word that he would be on time," we can write, "We were given his word that he would be on time." And so with the following:

The company sent James a bill.
James was sent a bill by the company.

His aunt always gave him a Christmas present.
He was always given a Christmas present by his aunt.

Despite the usefulness of the passive construction in varying emphasis, there are certain dangers in using it thoughtlessly. The passive voice tends to be less forceful than the active, and a series of passive constructions is likely to produce an effect of limpness and lack of energy. The very word "passive" means suffering or enduring an action rather than instigating or causing it. A too frequent use of the passive voice, consequently, deprives the style of that forward movement which occurs when a subject acts directly on an object through the verb.

Another danger of the passive lies in the temptation that it offers to the lazy or irresponsible writer to leave the expression of his thought incomplete. Some passive constructions are a means of avoiding mention of the agent of the action expressed by the verb. For example, the sentence "It is said that a new cure for cancer has been found" does not tell us who said it. It is possible that the writer of the sentence does not know; in this case he probably should do more research. If he does know, he should tell us in the interest of full communication. Otherwise he may be only spreading a rumor. Using the passive voice to evade a full statement of the thought is too often an easy way out.

It is believed that Shakespeare was really Francis Bacon.

The School of Engineering of Midland University is rated the best in the nation.

Who believes that Shakespeare was really Francis Bacon; and what agency rated the Engineering School at Midland University the best in the nation? If these facts are known, they ought to be given, inasmuch as they will be important in any discussion of these statements. It is only a matter of common honesty to provide full relevant information when one possesses it. The writer should check himself whenever he feels that he is yielding to the temptation to conceal ignorance or to withhold information by resorting to the passive construction.

Admittedly there are times when the passive construction is an appropriate vehicle for what there is to say. A newspaper reporter who writes, "It is rumored in Washington that the President may appoint Senator Blank Associate Justice of the Supreme Court" may be doing well to use the passive if the real source of the news is not known to him. In such case the author is actually ignorant of the agent of the action expressed by the verb. He is telling all that he knows. Occasionally too, considerations of confidence and privacy will dictate such use of the passive construction. Newspapermen sometimes enter into tacit agreements not to reveal the source of news which may have political repercussions. In general, however, it is best to avoid the "irresponsible passive." Apart from the matter of intellectual integrity, which should be of prime concern to every writer, it devitalizes style and it contributes to jargon. Do not allow it to become your sentence pattern out of laziness.

## Parallelism

Parallelism is a helpful device for showing a reader the function of groups within a sentence. Expressed as a rule, it prescribes that elements which are alike in function should be alike in form, or structure. The fact that they are alike in form is taken as a signal that they are fulfilling the same role in the expression. Let us suppose that we have a sentence containing a series of predicate nominatives. As all the members of this series are to function as this kind of grammatical element, they should be alike, or parallel, in form. The sentence might read:

> Ben's job was to work in the garden, to feed the chickens, and to keep the grass cut.

This sentence obeys the rule of parallelism because these predicate nominatives are all infinitive phrases. But suppose the sentence were to read:

> Ben's job was to work in the garden, feed the chickens, and keeping the grass cut.

The reader might hesitate over this sentence because the third member of the series, "keeping the grass cut," marks a shift from infinitive phrase to gerund phrase. The shift might cause him to wonder whether there is a shift of intended meaning also. There is no such shift of meaning, because the sentence is still stating the things that constitute Ben's job. Therefore the parallel order should be preserved.

> He hoped to specialize in biology and that he might become a research scientist.
> PARALLEL: He hoped to specialize in biology and to become a research scientist.

> A good education should teach one to read critically, to speak and write effectively, and getting along with one's fellow men.

PARALLEL: A good education should teach one to read critically, to speak and write effectively, and to get along with one's fellow men.

PARALLEL: But seeing how great and manifold are the inevitable sufferings of men; how profoundly important it is that all should give their best will and devote their best intelligence to the alleviation of those sufferings which can be diminished, by seeking out, and, as far as lies within human power, removing their causes; it is surely lamentable that they should be drawn away by speculative chimaeras from the attempt to find that narrow path which for nations, as for individual men, is the sole road to permanent well being.

—T. H. Huxley, "On the Natural Inequality of Men"

In this striking sentence the parallel elements may be seen as follows:

| | |
|---|---|
| how great and manifold are | how profoundly important it is |
| give their best will | devote their best intelligence |
| by seeking out | [by] removing |
| for nations | for individual men |

Here is a somewhat less elaborate example by a contemporary writer.

From the submission of our desires springs the virtue of resignation; from the freedom of our thoughts springs the whole world of art and philosophy, and the vision of beauty by which, at last, we half reconquer the reluctant world.

—Bertrand Russell, "A Free Man's Worship," from *Mysticism and Logic*

In Russell's sentence the parallel elements are:

| | |
|---|---|
| from the submission of our desires | from the freedom of our thoughts |
| the whole world of art and philosophy | the vision of beauty |

Parallelism must be recognized also as an important means of coordination. It puts equivalent elements in structures which call attention to their equivalence. Sometimes it enables us to play off such elements against one another, when a contrast is desired, as the first parallelism in Russell exemplifies. At the minimum, it is a device for keeping the reader on the track, and it can serve as an organizing principle for rather extensive or complex thought groups.

## Sentence Length

There is no way of determining by fixed rule the best length for a sentence. Length may be influenced by the kind of subject matter we are dealing with, by the audience to which the piece is addressed, and by the general nature of the occasion for which it is written. It may also be influenced, and importantly, by the length of the sentences which accompany it, including those coming before and those following.

It is a fair generalization to say that our age prefers the short sentence. The reasons for this are interesting in themselves, although they cannot be discussed at length here. The hurried pace at which one is forced to catch buses and subways, the necessity of meeting business schedules, the timed precision of many forms of entertainment, the limitations which newspaper make-up imposes on style, the general tendency to estimate things by the degree of thrill they provide—all of these factors discourage the kind of leisurely and sustained attention that our forebears gave to the written or printed page. Such conditions of living virtually compel people to favor the sentence whose meaning can be picked up quickly. In consequence, our age, as compared to an age like the eighteenth or nineteenth century, employs the relatively short sentence unit.

It scarcely needs pointing out that "short" is itself a relative term. Most sentences found today in news stories, business letters, and the popular magazines average 10-20 words. Those in the learned journals and in works of serious exposition are somewhat longer. Occasionally you will find sentences of 40-50 words, but a style made up of sentences of this length would be considered involved and too slow.

Sometimes a set of conspicuously short sentences can be used for good effect. The effect may be to keep details separate, to emphasize a point by giving it full-sentence expression, or to concentrate our attention when a climax of feeling is approaching. In the hands of an experienced writer, the short sentence is usually purposely short and so has a planned function. In the passage below William G. Carleton uses a series of short sentences to stress Lincoln's awareness of long-term objectives in the midst of practical politics.

> Lincoln, of course, was no opportunist. Certainly during the national phase of his career he never confused ends and means. His resiliency did not indicate a surrender of values. He knew well his general direction. He kept constantly in mind large, ultimate goals.
> —William G. Carleton, "What Lincoln Means Today"

In the next passage, Daniel Webster is picturing for a jury the scene of a murder. He wishes to fix the minds of his hearers upon the cold-blooded nature of the crime. The important thing for him to stress is the deliberate quality of the act. Observe the way in which Webster shortens his sentences when he wishes the impression to be most vivid.

> The deed was executed with a degree of steadiness and self-possession equal to the wickedness with which it was planned. The circumstances now clearly in evidence spread out the scene before us. Deep sleep had fallen upon the destined victim, and all beneath his roof. A healthful old man, to whom sleep was sweet, the first sound slumbers of the night held him in their soft but strong embrace. The assassin enters, through a window already prepared, into an unoccupied apartment. With noiseless foot he paces the lonely hall, half-lighted by the moon; he winds up the ascent of the stairs, and reaches the door of the chamber. Of this, he moves the

lock by soft and continued pressure, till it turns on its hinges without noise; and he enters, and beholds his victim before him. The room is uncommonly open to the admission of light. The face of the innocent sleeper is turned from the murderer, and the beams of the moon, resting on the gray locks of his aged temple, show him where to strike. The fatal blow is given! and the victim passes, without a struggle or a motion, from the repose of sleep to the repose of death! It is the assassin's purpose to make sure work; and he plies the dagger, though it is obvious that life has been destroyed by the blow of the bludgeon. He even raises the aged arm, that he may not fail in his aim at the heart, and replaces it again over the wounds of the poniard! To finish the picture, he explores the wrist for the pulse! He feels for it, and ascertains that it beats no longer! It is accomplished. The deed is done. He retreats, retraces his steps to the window, passes out through it as he came in, and escapes. He has done the murder. No eye has seen him, no ear has heard him. The secret is his own, and it is safe!

—Daniel Webster, "Argument in the
Trial of John Francis Knapp"

One of the natural ways to make sentence length an element of style is to alternate long and short sentences so that they will contrast with one another. A short sentence coming after a group of long ones or a long one coming after a group of short ones will naturally stand out. A thoughtful, as distinguished from a mechanical, alternation of this kind will produce a variety pleasing in itself. It also gives prominence to the idea in the contrasting sentence. A style with this shift from short to long and long to short seems to change pace. It is consequently more fresh and agreeable than one which appears unimaginatively tied to a single sentence length. You will notice this effect from an alternation of longer and shorter sentences in this passage by Walter Lippmann.

For nations, as for families, the level may vary at which a solvent balance is struck. If its expenditures are safely within its assured means, a family is solvent when it is poor, or is well-to-do, or is rich. The same principle holds true of nations. The statesman of a strong country may balance its commitments at a high level or at a low. But whether he is conducting the affairs of Germany, which has dynamic ambitions, or the affairs of Switzerland, which seeks only to hold what it already has, or of the United States, he must still bring his ends and means into balance. If he does not, he will follow a course that leads to disaster.

—Walter Lippmann, *U. S. Foreign Policy*

Finally, practical writers will often employ a short sentence to close a paragraph or even a longer unit of writing. There its very brevity is a sign of summation. It shows that the writer is rounding off what he has to say. Observe how this effect is produced by the sentence "It is this temperament which makes the Western nations 'progressive' " at the close of the paragraph from Bertrand Russell below.

We in the West make a fetish of "progress," which is the ethical camouflage of the desire to be the cause of changes. If we are asked, for instance, whether machinery has really improved the world, the question strikes us as foolish: it has brought great changes and therefore great "progress." What we believe to be a love of progress is really, in nine cases out of ten, a love of power, an enjoyment of the feeling that by our fiat we can make things different. For the sake of this pleasure, a young American will work so hard that, by the time he has acquired his millions, he has become a victim of dyspepsia, compelled to live on toast and water, and to be a mere spectator at the feasts that he offers to his guests. But he consoles himself with the thought that he can control politics and provoke or prevent wars, as may suit his investments. It is this temperament which makes Western nations "progressive."

—Bertrand Russell, "The Chinese Character," *Selected Papers*

Clearly there is no such thing as an ideal sentence length. However, a beginning writer who feels that he has not acquired a highly developed "sentence sense" will do well to write sentences of a moderate length. It is easier to combine short sentences into long ones if the need seems to arise than to straighten out the grouping of a long sentence which has gotten out of hand and become disorganized. The goal is a considerable range of sentence length and is best approached by most of us through the sentence of easily manageable size.

## RHETORICAL ANALYSIS OF SENTENCES

We have seen that the good sentence has a grammar supporting a rhetoric and a rhetoric deriving its force in part from an intelligent use of the possibilities of grammar. Grammar brings the sentence up to the level of acceptability. At this point, rhetoric takes over and makes the sentence more clear or graceful or forceful or dramatic. What has been said about grammatical and rhetorical aspects prepares us for the more complete kind of analysis we are going to make next.

It is now time to study all the factors of a good sentence in combination. We shall take into account everything that seems to contribute to its effect. The object is simply to see what enters into the complete and accomplished sentence. Later we should be able to improve our own sentences by including or partly imitating some of these features. The examples we shall deal with are all peculiarly successful in one way or another.

Let us begin by looking at a sentence which is likely to impress us at first as somewhat simple and lacking in effect. In the midst of some observations about the condition of man, Henry David Thoreau wrote in *Walden:*

The mass of men lead lives of quiet desperation.

This sentence perhaps strikes us first of all with its brevity. As we have seen earlier, short sentences tend to be emphatic, and the emphasis will be increased if the sentence turns out to be heavily charged with meaning.

Our example seems to be of that kind, and we sense at once the quality of an aphorism. We note that its order is normal and that it is grammatically a simple sentence, with neither subject nor predicate compounded. As far as these basic features go, it is virtually a "primer" sentence. The order, the structure, and the predominance of monosyllabic words enable us to read it rapidly. The sentence seems at this stage to present no problems at all.

It is when we begin to ponder the diction, or the choice of the words and phrases, that we begin to see the craftsmanship of Thoreau. Why did he use the phrase "mass of men" instead of "most men" or "many men"? A less perceptive writer probably would have been satisfied to write, "Most men lead lives of quiet desperation." Such phrasing, however, would leave out one of the most important meanings of the sentence. It is essential to the purpose here that we see men as a mass, not as a group made up of many distinct individuals. It is in fact their "massness" that Thoreau wishes to point out in connection with their "quiet desperation." It is a sign of their helplessness, of their inability to meet the circumstances of their lives with the sort of positive action that we expect of the hero. To be a member of a mass is to be featureless and undifferentiated, to be beaten down. And that is precisely the kind of plight that Thoreau is talking about. His phrase expresses it, and probably no other phrase would express it as well.

The same kind of discrimination appears when we come to the next phrase, "lead lives." Does it carry out the motive of the sentence better than, say, "live lives"? It seems that here again the word which Thoreau has chosen expresses better the condition of this kind of man. The verb "live" suggests something more free and more effortless than "lead"; and "lead," moreover, has connotations of strain and of contending against resistance which the other does not have. We might even picture the man of Thoreau's mass as leading his life in the way that one leads a balky animal. The object of the sentence is to convey the thought that for a large portion of mankind life is something of a burden and a struggle.

The most effective use of diction, however, undoubtedly appears in the last phrase, "quiet desperation." Our interest is immediately aroused by this because it expresses a paradox; that is, it says something which seems to embody a contradiction. Desperation and quietness are not usually associated. We normally think of a desperate man as being noisy and demonstrative, as giving many signs of his unhappy situation. Yet we realize upon reflection that desperation may be subdued and undemonstrative; and we may feel that this kind of desperation, because it is without vents, is the gravest kind of all. The paradox contains meaning, and the sentence therefore embodies a perception which is fresh and which has some depth. Following the meaning thus, we are likely to arrive at the feeling that Thoreau really "said something" and said it well.

While we have been concentrating upon these features, the qualities of sound have been playing upon us. Sound patterns in this sentence are a considerable factor in its effect. We first become aware of the prominent alliteration in the phrases "mass of men" and "lead lives." Alliteration is the use of two or more words beginning with the same consonant sound. It is quite common in poetry, but it appears also in prose, with similar effect. That effect is to join and to emphasize the words which are alliterative and to produce a certain feeling of inevitable movement or occurrence. Given the conditions that he has described, Thoreau would say that this is an inevitable result; the stylizing of it through an alliterative pattern is therefore in keeping with the aim of the sentence. We observe finally that in the last word, "desperation," there occur the phonetically hard *d* and *p* sounds, which may well be suggestive of the internal struggle and obstruction which Thoreau is affirming. And at the very close the sentence trails off with a diminuendo ending in the last syllable. This expresses a note of finality, and perhaps of resignation as far as men in the mass are concerned.

This short sentence, like many of Thoreau's, is thus a work of real artistry. If you feel that we have gone beyond the point of profit in talking about small particulars, remember that good effects rest upon an accumulation of small details. Almost nothing is too small to be talked about if we wish to develop a knowledge of what words and constructions can do.

Let us try this method of analysis next upon a sentence from Patrick Henry's famous address to the Virginia Convention in 1775.

> The next gale that sweeps from the north will bring to our ears the clash of resounding arms.

Those familiar with the address will remember the tenseness of the part in which this expression appears. Undoubtedly the sentence derives some of its quality from the general style of Henry's appeal near the close of the speech. But even apart from those qualities which it draws from its context, the sentence has qualities of its own which make it exciting and dramatic. What are these qualities?

The first thing we notice is that the sentence is in normal order, with the sequence subject-verb-object. Few will question that this is a suitable order for the meaning to be conveyed, since the sentence is supposed to express a rapid, onrushing movement, meeting no impediments which can withstand it and hurrying on to its inevitable end. The order therefore comports with and reinforces the meaning. It cooperates as part of the total expression.

Nevertheless, when we examine the grammatical structure of the sentence we might at first decide to qualify our observation regarding its rapid forward movement. It is a complex sentence with one dependent clause; and the dependent clause, "that sweeps from the north," comes between the subject phrase and the verb phrase and therefore may be felt as a kind of interrupter. The clause is a restrictive modifier, however, and in speech there is normally no pause between a subject and a restrictive modifier. Study of the total effect will probably convince us that this element has a function in delaying the important idea, and that whatever interruption is created is more than compensated for by the periodic structure of the sentence as a whole. For it is not until we reach "the clash of resounding arms" that we learn what the sentence is about. The fact that its meaning is suspended until the very end produces the rising excitement found in all periodic sentences. Thus the order of the sentence and the periodic structure make it an utterance of strong impact—the kind of sentence calculated to arouse emotion and even bring cheers.

Note further that this movement is accentuated by a swelling rhythm. The rhythm is produced by a gradual lengthening of the phrasal groups.

> The next gale / that sweeps from the north / will bring to our ears / the clash of resounding arms.

Observe that these progress from three syllables in the subject phrase at the beginning to seven in the object phrase at the end. Such increase in volume may be especially effective in a sentence which is to be spoken.

Finally we turn our attention to the qualities of sound, which, as we have already intimated, must never be overlooked in a rhetorical analysis. Even when a sentence is not written to be spoken, we tend to hear the sounds of the words as we read it, and these can have a strong subconscious influence upon our response to the utterance. Poor combinations of sound distract us from the intended effect, and good ones can greatly enhance it. In the sentence we are now considering, the sound effects are unusually fine. The verb "sweeps" is a successful employment of onomatopoeia, or the use of a word whose sound suggests the thing that is being symbolized. When we read "the next gale that sweeps from the north," we therefore both see and hear the occurrence which the speaker wishes to make vivid. But an even more successful use of onomatopoeia comes with the phrase "the clash of resounding arms," which suggests noise of battle. It is this which Henry wishes to bring "to our ears," or so close to those who were hearing it that they would be startled out of their complacency and seized with a determination to do something.

Even now we have not noted all the resources of this sentence. But we have examined the chief features of structure, diction, and sound, in which most sentence qualities will be found.

> It is safe to say that, without Hamilton's cast of mind, building the past into the future with a deep passion for order and old wisdom, our national life would have miscarried at the very first.
> —Woodrow Wilson, "A Calendar of Great Americans"

It seems evident that this sentence owes its force chiefly to a finely suspended structure. The expletive beginning serves to delay the appearance of the subject, "that our national life would have miscarried at the very first." Then, just as the subject is being introduced by the subordinating conjunction "that," we encounter a long interrupter in the expression "without Hamilton's cast of mind, building the past into the future with a deep love for order and old wisdom." This effects a rather extraordinary displacement, which has the result of emphasizing the thought of the interrupting element, highly important to the sentence, and of further delaying the appearance of the subject. As it is, the subject does not arrive until we are at the end, and therefore this sentence too is of the periodic type. Through two means of suspension, the expletive and the interrupter, it keeps our interest waiting for satisfaction. To appreciate the effect of such arrangements, consider a version of the sentence without suspensions.

> That our national life would have miscarried at the very first without Hamilton's cast of mind, building the past into the future with a deep passion for order and old wisdom, is safe to say.

This form seems in comparison limp, lacking in emphasis at the right points, and even anti-climactic. Arrangement clearly had a great deal to do with giving the original sentence its distinctive force.

Although this sentence does not seem outstanding for sound effects, most readers will find pleasing the assonance, or similarity of vowel sounds, in "order and old wisdom." And there is value in the way that "first" brings the sentence to a firm, emphatic stop.

> It is a contradiction in terms, it is a blasphemy in religion, it is wickedness in politics, to say that any man can have arbitrary power.
> —Edmund Burke, "Impeachment of Warren Hastings"

This sentence also depends for its effectiveness especially on features of structure, although in this instance we must take note of some different kinds. The most obvious is the device known by the technical name *anaphora*. Anaphora is the use of similar beginnings, particularly with clauses. Here we observe a series of three clauses, each starting with "it is." This constitutes a figure of repetition which, like all repetition, creates in the reader or hearer a compulsion to continue. A second prominent feature of this structure is the *isocolon,* which is a series of elements, usually clauses, of approximately equal length. Here we see it in the three clauses, "It is a contradiction in terms, it is a blasphemy in religion, it is wickedness in politics." A chief function of the isocolon is to permit a strong rhythm to develop, as is apparent in this case.

The diction too has some significant features. Each of the clauses in the series contains a substantive of heavy and arresting connotation, "contradiction," "blasphemy," and "wickedness," and the same may be affirmed of the closing phrase, "arbitrary power." The words themselves suggest that something of superlative evil is being described, and this obviously was the intention of the author. The diction is thereby successful in bringing to our minds ideas of the dire and the harmful. Furthermore the series of phrases, passing from "contradiction in terms," or logic, to "religion," and then to "politics," exhibits a progression toward the more concrete, and the concrete is most likely to affect men's attitudes. These features, together with the expletive beginning and the periodic structure of the whole, make this unit a very forceful sentence.

Let us examine another particularly effective sentence.

About the middle of the nineteenth century, in the quiet sunshine of a provincial prosperity, New England had an Indian summer of the mind; and an agreeable reflective literature showed how brilliant that russet and yellow season could be.

—George Santayana, *Character and Opinion in the United States*

This sentence by Santayana balances two long phrases and a short simple sentence in the first half against a complex sentence in the second half. The pleasing rhythm of this sentence can be attributed, in part, to the variety and order of the grammatical structures. In the first half we find an initial balancing, in suspension, of two similar grammatical phrases followed by a short, emphatic simple sentence. Then in a tight complex sentence, whose point is a particularly apt development and expansion of the point in the preceding simple sentence, and whose structure suggests that it be read without pause, the author smoothly reveals the main theme of the whole sentence.

The two introductory phrases mention conditions in the light of which the assertion is to be made. You will find that experienced writers very often put circumstantial material of this kind at the beginning. In so doing, they give the reader the background he needs in order to appreciate the significance of the sentence and at the same time they get the details out of the way and keep them from interfering with the main movement of the sentence. If we should place one of these details at a later position in the group, we would find that the smooth progression of the thought had been interrupted without the gain of any rhetorical advantage.

The sentence owes its effectiveness chiefly, however, to the extended use of a metaphor. The author is employing "Indian summer" to stand for that period of intellectual and artistic activity which distinguished the New England states in the forties and fifties of the last century. Notice carefully how the metaphor is carried out; the subject is presented as an Indian summer, which, like all Indian summers, has its "sunshine" and turns brilliant with "russet and yellow." The image of Indian summer thus constitutes a frame for the sentence, in which the author can place a number of descriptive details serving to fill out the picture.

A close look at the language shows how successful Santayana has been in his choice of modifiers. Our attention is struck first by the phrase "quiet sunshine." How can sunshine be described as "quiet"? "Quiet" is a modifier which is normally applied to things that are reported by the ear, and sunshine is something we see. Here the writer had used what is called a *transmodal modifier*. A transmodal modifier is a modifier taken out of the sphere in which it is normally used and applied to something from a different sphere. Poets often use it for the sake of the richness and freshness that it gives.

> So evenings die, in their green going
> A wave, interminably flowing.
> > —Wallace Stevens, "Peter Quince at the Clavier,"
> > from *Harmonium*

And prose writers can avail themselves of it, as Santayana does, to express a fresh or unusual perception of things. So, the sunshine in this passage, instead of being described as "bright" or "golden," is described as being "quiet." The word brings in another kind of sensory experience and thus adds another dimension to what is presented. The effect of the transmodality is to increase the depth and suggestibility of the picture. In somewhat the same manner we find "prosperity" described as "provincial" and "literature" as "agreeable." These are hardly to be regarded as transmodal modifiers, but they are original in the sense of being seldom applied to these particular nouns. By this means Santayana has avoided the cliché modifier, which is dulling and wearying to our perception. We have the feeling that the author has seen the picture with his own eyes and is reporting it, not through stereotypes, but in its individuality, with the particular qualities he felt it possessed.

These features of diction, together with the touches of color provided by "brilliant," "russet," and "yellow," give the sentence an imaginative and finely discriminating quality.

## EXERCISES

**Exercise A**   *Improve the rhetorical effectiveness of the following sentences by regrouping. Take into account all that you have learned about order, subordination, suspension, balance, and parallelism. Revise each sentence as if you wished it to stand out or to bear the emphasis of some passage.*

1. Propaganda is the attempt to influence the attitudes of other persons for a selfish purpose, and oftentimes it works through means that are veiled.
2. The train plunged into the darkness of the tunnel under the Hudson as Carter felt a mounting excitement over his arrival in New York.
3. After a year in college Ray had learned poise and especially how to meet people naturally.
4. You can be a fool without a book as easily as a fool with one, although many people distrust book learning and think that reading fills the mind with impractical notions.
5. Retirement at the age of sixty-five held no terrors for him, for he had developed a set of hobbies.
6. He took part in all civic activities, becoming before long a respected citizen.

7. To write themes on dull topics, to solve problems in algebra, and learning the declension of Latin nouns—these seemed an intolerable bore to Sylvia, whose secret ambition was to be a ballet dancer.

8. Mr. Edwards had no practical experience in politics; and he was surprised to find how difficult it is to get people to agree, even on small matters.

9. Greek culture was distinguished by an idealization of reason and a worship of beauty, and it has influenced posterity for two thousand years.

10. Economics has been called the dismal science; and it is equated by many with graphs and statistics; actually, however, it deserves to rank as a liberal study.

**Exercise B** *Something can be learned by imitating a sentence pattern, even though you never expect to compose in the style of another writer. You begin to sense new possibilities of grouping and of rhythm, and you see how skillful writers extend a sentence without allowing it to sprawl or collapse. Study the examples below and try writing sentences of your own with approximately the same structure.*

1. To think very differently from his hearers, may often be a sign of the orator's wisdom and worth; but *they* are not likely to consider it so.
   —Richard Whately, *Elements of Rhetoric*

2. The enthusiasm of the first crusade is a natural and simple event, while hope was fresh, danger untried, and enterprise congenial to the spirit of the times.
   —Edward Gibbon, *Decline and Fall of the Roman Empire*

3. There was nothing new about Lily Bart, yet he could never see her without a faint movement of interest: it was characteristic of her that she always aroused speculation, that her simplest acts seemed the result of far-reaching intentions.
   —Edith Wharton, *The House of Mirth*

4. The same nominal humanitarianism, inwardly contradicted by a militant hatred towards almost all human institutions and affections, has descended from the wealth-loving liberals to the poverty-hating communists.
   —George Santayana, *Dominations and Powers*

5. A dull, plain girl she was called by rigorous critics—a quiet, lady-like girl by those of the more imaginative sort; but by neither class was she very elaborately discussed.
   —Henry James, *Washington Square*

6. Of course, government in general, any government anywhere, is a thing of exquisite comicality to the discerning mind; but really we Spanish-Americans do overstep the bounds.
   —Joseph Conrad, *Nostromo*

7. Do not hire a man who does your work for money, but him who does it for love, and pay him well.

—Henry David Thoreau, *Journal*

8. As fashionable conversation is a sacrifice to politeness, so the conversation of low life is nothing but rudeness. They contradict you without giving a reason, or if they do, it is a very bad one—swear, talk loud, repeat the same thing fifty times over, get to calling names, and from words proceed to blows.

—William Hazlitt, "On the Conversation of Authors"

9. Yet it is folly to argue against determined hardness; eloquence may strike the ear, and the language of sorrow draw forth the tear of compassion, but nothing can reach the heart that is steeled with prejudice.

—Thomas Paine, "The Crisis"

10. The existence of man in political society is historical existence; and a theory of politics, if it penetrates to principles, must at the same time be a theory of history.

—Eric Voegelin, *The New Science of Politics*

11. The birth of language is the dawn of humanity.

—Susanne K. Langer, "The Lord of Creation"

12. A great mind cannot, without injurious restraint, shrink itself to the grasp of common passive readers.

—W. E. Channing, "Writings of Milton"

13. Human happiness has always its abatements; the brightest sunshine of success is not without a cloud.

—Samuel Johnson, *Life of Addison*

14. Our political system is placed in a just correspondence and symmetry with the order of the world, and with the mode of existence decreed to a permanent body composed of transitory parts—wherein, by the disposition of a stupendous wisdom, moulding together the great mysterious incorporation of the human race, the whole, at one time, is never old or middle-aged or young, but, in a condition of unchangeable constancy, moves on through the varied tenor of perpetual decay, fall, renovation, and progression.

—Edmund Burke, *Reflections on the Revolution in France*

# Chapter Seven

# The Paragraph

## THE FUNCTION OF PARAGRAPHS

The mind naturally looks for lines of division in anything it is considering. By these it is enabled to take in, or understand, because understanding is largely a matter of perceiving parts and their relationships. The paragraph is a kind of division, and paragraphing is a way of separating out the parts of a composition. Standing between the sentence as a unit at one end of the scale and the section or chapter at the other, the paragraph has the useful role of organizing our thoughts into groups of intermediate size.

The usefulness of a visual aid to division was recognized long before paragraphs were set off as they are today. In medieval manuscripts, which do not have the sort of indentation that we employ now, a symbol was written in the margin to mark a turn in the thought; and the word "paragraph" means "something written beside." Where the medieval scribe used a symbol, we use indentation. But the purpose served is the same, and that is to advise the reader that a new set of thoughts is beginning.

A paragraph may therefore be understood as a visible division of the subject matter. The division is initially a convenience to the reader, as it prepares him to turn his attention to something new. But beyond this, most paragraphs have an internal unity, and they can be analyzed as compositions in miniature.

Occasionally one finds paragraphs which are compositions in the sense that they are not parts of a larger piece of writing. These occur in the form of single-paragraph statements, themes, and even stories, which are complete and which are not related to anything outside themselves. They will naturally reflect the rules of good composition if they are successful writing. They will have unity, coherence, and emphasis. They will be about something; they will make a progression, and they will have a major point.

Substantially the same may be said about paragraphs which are parts of a composition. They will have a relative self-containment, or basic unity and coherence, and they will emphasize some point or idea. Therefore what we have said about the composition in its entirety may be said with almost equal application of single paragraphs within the larger piece. Especially is it true that the subject must be reasonably definite and that the development must follow some plan, although the possible plans of development are various.

The point is that the relative independence of the paragraph rests upon something. The paragraph is not a device marked off at mechanical intervals simply because it is felt that the reader needs a change. He does need a change, but the place of the change must be related to the course of the thought. Where that changes significantly, a new paragraph begins. It is a signal that something else is starting. This may be a different phase of the subject, an illustration, a qualification, a change of scale, or any one of a large number of things which can mark the course of systematic thinking about a subject.

## PARAGRAPH UNITY

Within the paragraph there will be a basically unified subject matter, laid out according to some plan. Poor paragraphs are planless or ill-planned. This is our reason for studying the structural unity of the paragraph.

The most common means for achieving unity in the paragraph is the *topic sentence*. The topic sentence is a program sentence; it announces what the paragraph is to be about, and sometimes it gives, in generalized form, the content. It is fairly easy to imagine, for example, what would follow in paragraphs opening with sentences like those below.

> Although Robert's behavior made him a nuisance, almost everyone could see that he was suffering from an inferiority complex.

> There are three practical methods of drilling for oil.

> Political parties may differ on issues and candidates, but they all seem to agree that the voter likes to be flattered.

These sentences are beginnings. They introduce subject matter which we expect to see expanded through the bringing in of details, through explanation of causes, through illustrations, or in other ways. They mark out the scope of the paragraph, and the writer who stays within the scope will maintain unity.

The topic sentence often is the opening sentence of the paragraph just because it has this task of stating the program. A long series of paragraphs all beginning in this way would, however, produce an effect of woodenness. There is no rule governing the position of the topic sentence; it may, in fact, be found anywhere in the paragraph. It may appear at the end, where it sums up or generalizes what has been presented in detail. Again, it may appear in the middle, with the detailed development of the topic coming both before and after. Such latitude permits a great deal of variety in paragraph style; and occasionally one will find in good writing a paragraph which has no definite topic sentence. A paragraph of this kind depends upon a kind of felt unity, emerging from an accumulation of like details, or from some quality of mood or tone. The principle remains, of course, that the paragraph is a unit of expression, even when no single sentence can be found to give the summation.

Here is an example of a paragraph which opens with a topic sentence.

> The Southern planter often lived in feudal splendor. The "big house" or the plantation mansion generally stood on an elevation near the main road, flanked by slave cabins, kitchen, office, stables, smokehouse, and other outbuildings. It was usually a wooden structure of not more than fifteen rooms, but it was made imposing by a row of white columns as tall as the house itself and by a lavish garden. There was a screen of spreading trees, borders of the odorous boxwood, and a tangled mass of flowering and sweet-smelling shrubs. Ample use was made of such semi-tropical plants as Cherokee rose, live oak, crepe myrtle, magnolia, and the pride of India. The interior of the house was dominated by huge halls with impressive stairways. On the first floor were the parlors, dining room, and library; on the second floor were bedrooms for family and guests. High ceilings, heavily shaded porches, and drafty passageways gave comfort in summer, but no protection in the sharp Southern winters, although fireplaces were large and wood was plentiful. Floors were rather sparsely covered with thin carpets, and the furniture was of a plain but massive elegance. A tall clock in the hall was the family's pride, even though its warnings concerning the passing of time failed to disturb the lazy tempo of plantation life. On the walls were family portraits or steel engravings of battle scenes or of George Washington. Sometimes the dining room was separated from the main body of the house by a porch, and usually the kitchen was well apart so that its odors, heat, and clatter might not contaminate the main house.
>
> —Francis Butler Simkins, *The South Old and New*

Notice that the opening sentence asserts one general fact. Everything that follows must be regarded as an itemization of this fact. The "feudal splendor" of the Southern planter is thus presented through a series of particular details which derive their meaning from the opening assertion. The topic sentence tells what the paragraph is to be about, and the sentences of detail provide the substance. In this example we can see with unusual distinctness the relationship between the "program" sentence and the matter of the paragraph.

**Exercise:**   *In each of the paragraphs below, locate the topic sentence. If no topic sentence appears, try to explain the unity of the paragraph by reference to its content, style, tone, etc.*

The first half of the eighteenth century was an age of convention, in both good and bad senses, convention in politics, in manners, in thought, in art, in morals. There is nothing like convention to breed rebels, and the last half of the eighteenth century, with the first years of the nineteenth, is a fruitful time for studying the type. The rebel hates control, restraint, limit, demands and delights in the free, abundant exercise of his own will, his own ardent sense of initiative and personality. He likes to assert himself, to make others feel that there is something there to assert; it affords him a concrete assurance of the fact, which is comforting; and it appears that nothing gives us more evidence of our own stability and reality than to destroy something else. The rebel has a splendid, joyous confidence in his own convictions, believes that this bright, glittering reason was given to hew and cut and thrust through all that seems to him sham and pretense, and old, worm-eaten, time-consecrated falsity. He pursues his triumphant, disastrous way, untroubled by the criticism and abuse of spite and malice, indeed rather stimulated by them; and his royal self-assurance is rarely disturbed by the subtle intrusion of sceptical humor: if he has humor, it turns him from a rebel into something else. Finally, the rebel, at his best, is saved by a passionate enthusiasm for humanity. He wants to make the world over. Of course the way to do this is to begin by turning it upside down. The great ideal rebels are Satan and Prometheus, though perhaps the human enthusiasm was a little more evident in the latter.
      —Gamaliel Bradford, "Thomas Paine," *Damaged Souls*

Every observer of our Western civilization is aware of the fact that something has happened to religion. It especially strikes the observer of the American scene. Everywhere he finds symptoms of what one has called religious revival or, more modestly, the revival of interest in religion. He finds them in the churches with their rapidly increasing membership. He finds them in the mushroom growth of sects. He finds them on college campuses and in the theological faculties of universities. Most conspicuously, he finds them in the tremendous success of men like Billy Graham and Norman Vincent Peale, who attract masses of people Sunday after Sunday, meeting after meeting. The facts cannot be denied, but how should they be interpreted? It is my intention to show that these facts must be seen as expressions of the predicament of Western man in the second half of the twentieth century. But I would even go a step further. I believe that the predicament of man in our period gives us also an important insight into the predicament of man generally—at all times and in all parts of the earth.
      —Paul Tillich, "The Lost Dimension in Religion"

Why are writers the active enemies of social science? When one looks at the slow transformation of cultural forms the enmity is not surprising. It is natural. As a culture develops in complexity and richness, it develops also in the division of labor, and social science would have to take away from the writers part of what the writers think is their job. The attainment of scientific thinking about ourselves, as persons, is one of the last stages in the development of the division of labor. It is not yet achieved in any real degree, but we can see it coming. It will come in spite of the fact that the writers resent encroachment unconsciously and resent with explicit scorn the use of any other methods than their own in dealing with what they think are their own peculiar questions. When it does come, this division of labor, writers in the forms of literature will not have lost anything but their claims to know the only valid kinds of description of human behavior.

—Lyman Bryson, "Writers: Enemies of Social Science"

Beyond two or three Greek plays, the student got nothing from the ancient languages. Beyond some incoherent theories of free-trade and protection, he got little from Political Economy. He could not afterwards remember to have heard the name of Karl Marx mentioned, or the title of "Capital." He was equally ignorant of Auguste Comte. These were the two writers of the time who most influenced its thought. The bit of practical teaching he afterwards reviewed with most curiosity was the course in Chemistry, which taught him a number of theories which befogged his mind for a lifetime. The only teaching that appealed to his imagination was a course of lectures by Louis Agassiz on the Glacial Period and Paleontology, which had more influence on his curiosity than the rest of the college instruction altogether. The entire work of the four years could have been easily put into the work of any four months in after life.

—Henry Adams, *The Education of Henry Adams*

Habit is thus the enormous fly-wheel of society, its most precious conservative agent. It alone is what keeps us all within the bounds of ordinance, and saves the children of fortune from the envious uprisings of the poor. It alone prevents the hardest and most repulsive walks of life from being deserted by those brought up to tread therein. It keeps the fisherman and deck-hand at sea through the winter; it holds the miner in his darkness, and nails the countryman to his log cabin and his lonely farm through all the months of snow; it protects us from invasion by natives of the desert and the frozen zone. It dooms us all to fight out the battle of life upon the lines of our nurture or our early choice, and to make the best of a pursuit that disagrees because there is no other for which we are fitted, and it is too late to begin again. It keeps different social strata from mixing. Already at the age of twenty-five you see the professional mannerism settling down on the young commercial traveler, on the young minister, or on the young counsellor-at-law. You see the little lines of cleavage running through the character, the tricks of thought, the prejudices, the ways of the "shop," in a word, from which the man can by-and-by no more escape than his coat sleeve can suddenly fall into a new set of folds. On the whole, it is best that he should not escape. It is well for the world that in most of us, by the age of thirty, the character has set like plaster, and will never soften again.

—William James, *Principles of Psychology*

Our current ethic is a curious mixture of superstition and rationalism. Murder is an ancient crime, and we view it through a mist of age-long horror. Forgery is a modern crime, and we view it rationally. We punish forgers, but we do not feel them strange beings set apart, as we do murderers. And we still think in social practice, whatever we may hold in theory, that virtue consists in not doing rather than in doing. The man who abstains from certain acts labeled "sin" is a good man, even though he never does anything to further the welfare of others. This, of course, is not the attitude inculcated in the Gospels: "Love thy neighbor as thyself" is a positive precept. But in all Christian communities the man who obeys this precept is persecuted, suffering at least poverty, usually imprisonment, and sometimes death. The world is full of injustice, and those who profit by injustice are in a position to administer rewards and punishments. The rewards go to those who invent ingenious justifications for inequality, the punishments to those who try to remedy it. I do not know of any country where a man who has a genuine love for his neighbor can long avoid obloquy. In Paris, just before the outbreak of the war, Jean Jaurès, the best citizen of France, was murdered; the murderer was acquitted, on the ground that he had performed a public service. This case was peculiarly dramatic, but the same sort of thing happens everywhere.

—Bertrand Russell, "The Harm that Good Men Do"

## PARAGRAPH COHERENCE

Although unity is essential in the paragraph, this alone does not suffice. We have seen earlier, in our discussion of the theme as a whole, that unity may exist without order. Every detail in a group of sentences may be about the same thing more or less directly, but unless these details are arranged in some kind of sequence, the result may be unexpressive or confusing. That is why coherence is a basic requirement. Coherence is nothing more than the orderly progression of thought. Whenever we think about any subject systematically, we are compelled to realize that certain things come first, others second, and so on. The thoughts must be strung one after another on some thread of meaning. When this has been accomplished, the composition has not only unity but also a plan or order. A discernible plan enables the mind to take in material much more quickly and easily. We are naturally gratified whenever we discover organization and structure.

In the great majority of instances we find that paragraphs are organized according to those principles found in the longer and more complete pieces of writing. Some paragraphs reflect the natural order of what they are describing or narrating; some are developed by enumeration of particulars falling under a general statement; some follow a cause-and-effect connection. These are only a few of the methods, and indeed the means of paragraph development are so varied that it seems unwise to attempt a complete listing. It is enough to keep in mind the general need of coherence and to look at a number of successful paragraphs to see what plan they reveal. From such inspection certain usable patterns will emerge, and the student must decide upon their applicability to the different kinds of subject matter with which he has to deal. The following paragraphs are models, in the sense in which we use the term "model"; that is to say, they are recommended forms, but they are not to be followed slavishly. They are to be adapted or improved upon to meet the need of the specific writing task.

## PARAGRAPH PATTERNS

### Spatial

An elementary form of organization is *spatial pattern*. Note how well a plan of this kind has succeeded in the paragraph below.

> The broad stretch of desert which extends from the shores of the Atlantic Ocean across Africa and Western Asia, almost to the foot of the Zagros mountain range, is pierced in one place only by a thin thread of verdure. A single stream, issuing from the equatorial regions, has the strength to penetrate the "frightful desert of interminable scorching sand," and to bring its waters safely through two thousand miles of arid, thirsty plain, in order to mingle them with the blue waves of the Mediterranean. It is this fact which has produced Egypt. The life-giving fluid, on its way through the desert, spreads verdure and fertility along its course on either bank; and a strip of most productive territory is thus created, suited to attract the attention of such a being as man, and to become the home of a powerful nation. Egypt proper is the land to which the river gave birth, and from which it took its name, or, at any rate, that land to a certain distance from the Mediterranean; but, as the race settled in this home naturally and almost necessarily exercises domination beyond the narrow bounds of the valley, it is usual and it is right to include under the name of "Egypt" a certain quantity of the arid territory on either side of the Nile, and thus to give to the country an expansion considerably beyond that which it would have if we confined the name strictly to the fluvial and alluvial region.
>
> —George Rawlinson, *History of Ancient Egypt*

The purpose of this group of sentences is to describe Egypt. Observe that Rawlinson approaches it from a distance, first locating it with reference to the world's greatest tract of desert land. This approach is helpful because it permits us to see the region he is describing in the broadest perspective. With such a view given first, we are able to follow with ease the more detailed exposition. Then the description begins at the southern end of the region already marked off and follows the course of the Nile northward to the Mediterranean. By this simple expedient the author gives us both the longitude and the latitude, while working in a good bit of incidental description. Having fixed on the Nile River as the geographical fact which gave rise to Egypt, he briefly alludes to the civilization which grew up along its banks. Finally he expands the picture somewhat beyond the valley itself to take in all of what has been known historically as Egypt. The pattern is thus one of spatial progression, from west to east, from south to north, and then outward from either bank of the Nile. With a few simple strokes, carried out in a natural order, the author places before us the scene of his history. This paragraph is a model of lucidity achieved through natural order.

## Temporal

We have seen earlier that the *temporal pattern* of organization is simply the order of time. Events are given substantially as they occurred, although there may occasionally be a look backward for the purpose of filling in necessary detail. Such is the organization of the paragraph below, in which E. S. Creasy narrates the advance of General Burgoyne's army toward Saratoga preliminary to the famous battle of that name.

> Burgoyne assembled his troops and confederates near the River Bonquet, on the west side of Lake Champlain. He then, on the 21st of June, 1777, gave his red allies a war feast, and harangued them on the necessity of abstaining from their usual cruel practices against unarmed people and prisoners. At the same time, he published a pompous manifesto to the Americans, in which he threatened the refractory with all the horrors of war, Indian as well as European. The army proceeded by water to Crown Point, a fortification which the Americans held at the northern extremity of the inlet, by which the water from Lake George is conveyed to Lake Champlain. He landed here without opposition; but the reduction of Ticonderoga, a fortification about twelve miles from Crown Point, was a more serious matter, and was supposed to be the most critical part of the expedition. Ticonderoga commanded the passage along the lakes, and was considered to be the key to the route which Burgoyne wished to follow. The English had been repulsed in an attack on it in the war with the French in 1758 with severe loss. But Burgoyne now invested it with great skill; and the American general, St. Clair, who had only an ill-equipped army of 3,000 men, evacuated it on the 5th of July. It seems evident that a different course would have caused the destruction or capture of his whole army, which, weak as it was, was the chief force then in the field for the protection of the New England States. When censured by some of his countrymen for abandoning Ticonderoga St. Clair truly replied "that he had lost a post but saved a province." Burgoyne's troops pursued the retiring Americans, gained several advantages over them, and took a large part of their artillery and military stores.
>
> —E. S. Creasy, *The Fifteen Decisive Battles of the World from Marathon to Waterloo*

## Example and Illustration

Among the elementary methods of development are example and illustration. They are alike in that they have the function of making clear by presenting cases. Though there is not much point in entering into their difference here, it may be mentioned that examples are sometimes generalized or even hypothetical, whereas illustrations usually take the form of concrete cases. In the paragraph below Dr. Morris Fishbein gives examples of medical quackery as it flourished in the eighteenth century.

> If scientific medicine is today withstanding nonchalantly the assaults of a myriad of systems, cults, and quackeries, it is merely repeating the history of other periods. The Eighteenth Century, for example, was predominantly a time of revolutionary systems and theories of medicine. There was the dynamico-organic system of Stahl, who believed that the soul was the supreme principle of disease. There was the mechanico-dynamic system of Hoffmann, teaching that life expresses itself in motion, and that all manifestations in the body are controlled by nervous spirit. The school of Montpelier taught that various organs possess individual life. Mesmer, prince of impostors, claimed that magnetic fluid poured from the hand, and the Brunonian system claimed that it was only necessary for a cure to determine the grade of disease in accordance with the strength or weakness of the active irritation, and to adjust the right proportion of strengthening or weakening medicines to the case. Further, there remained from previous centuries phlogistic and antiphlogistic theories, the view that all disease was caused by the impaction of debris and obstruction of the intestines, and half a dozen other assorted hypotheses.
>
> —Morris Fishbein, M.D., *The Medical Follies*

The paragraph presents no problem of organization. A topic sentence, appearing at the beginning, tells us that medicine has always had to combat quackeries and fake systems. The second sentence supports this observation by its allusion to systems and theories of the eighteenth century. The following sentences present some of the specific forms that quackery and imposture took during that period. The fact that these are in no particular order contributes to the effect of the paragraph, since a random listing suggests a sort of chaos of theory and practice, and this was evidently the impression the author wished to give.

Paragraphs of example and illustration are essentially paragraphs developed by details. Sometimes the details are not easy to classify under either of the two heads. They may be merely particulars enumerated in the presentation of a thought. As their number increases, the thought becomes more clear, until finally it emerges distinctly. It may be puzzling to state the exact relationship of any one of them to the main idea, yet the accumulation of them adds up to a unit. The next two paragraphs seem to depend for their unity and coherence upon this kind of incremental detail.

> What could you do with a man like this [William Lloyd] Garrison? He had no social position to lose. He was in debt to nobody. No one had any hold upon him with which to padlock his utterances. He had no sacrifices to make. Furthermore, he insisted upon living an absolutely blameless private life, which was a great vexation to his enemies. You threw him into jail, and he liked it immensely, and utilized the opportunity to strike off his best bit of verse. You put a price on his head and he glorified in it. You threatened him with death and dragged him through the streets with a

rope around his waist, and he showed his courage by failing even to be excited, and went home to utilize your outbreak against him in a most effective sermon against the thing that you were seeking to uphold. You tried to reach him through his bank account, or his social affiliations, or his desire for power, and you found that he had none of these.

—Oswald Garrison Villard, *Fighting Years*

Adjustment is exactly what a man gains when he comes to himself. Some men gain it late, some early; some get it all at once, as if by one act of deliberate accommodation; others get it by degrees and quite imperceptibly. No doubt to most men it comes by the slow process of experience —at each stage of life a little. A college man feels the shock of it at graduation, when the boy's life has been lived out and the man's life suddenly begins. He has measured himself with boys; he knows their code and feels the spur of their ideals of achievement. But what the world expects of him he has yet to find out, and it works, when he has discovered it, a veritable revolution in his ways both of thought and action. He finds a new sort of fitness demanded of him, executive, thorough-going, careful of details, full of drudgery and obedience to orders. Everybody is ahead of him. Just now he was a senior, at the top of the world he knew and reigned in, a finished product and pattern of good form. Of a sudden he is a novice again, as green as in his first school year, studying a thing that seems to have no rules—at sea amid crosswinds, and a bit seasick withal. Presently, if he be made of stuff that will shake into shape and fitness, he settles to his task and is comfortable. He has come to himself: he understands what his capacity is, and what it is meant for; sees that his training was not for ornament or personal gratification, but to teach him how to use himself and develop faculties worth using. Henceforth there is zest in action, and he loves to see his strokes tell.

—Woodrow Wilson, "When a Man Comes to Himself"

**Exercise:**   *Make your own analysis of the following two paragraphs.*

Cooper's gift in the way of invention was not a rich endowment; but such as it was he liked to work it, he was pleased with the effects, and indeed he did some quite sweet things with it. In his little box of stage-properties he kept six or eight cunning devices, tricks, artifices for his savages and woodsmen to deceive and circumvent each other with, and he was never so happy as when he was working these innocent things and seeing them go. A favorite one was to make a moccasined person tread in the tracks of the moccasined enemy, and thus hide his own trail. Cooper wore out barrels and barrels of moccasins in working that trick. Another stage-property that he pulled out of his box pretty frequently was his broken twig. He prized his broken twig above all the rest of his effects, and worked it the hardest. It is a restful chapter in any book of his when somebody doesn't step on a dry twig and alarm all the reds and whites for two hundred yards around. Every time a Cooper person is in peril, and absolute silence is worth four dollars a minute, he is sure to step on a dry twig. There may be a hundred handier things to step on, but that wouldn't satisfy Cooper. Cooper requires him to turn out and find a dry twig; and if he can't do it, go and borrow one. In fact, the Leatherstocking Series ought to have been called the Broken Twig Series.

—Mark Twain, "Fenimore Cooper's Literary Offenses"

Anyone who has ever ridden on a railroad train knows how rapidly another train flashes by when it is traveling in the opposite direction, and conversely how it may look almost motionless when it is moving in the same direction. A variation of this effect can be very deceptive in an enclosed station like Grand Central Terminal in New York. Once in a while a train gets under way so gently that passengers feel no recoil whatever. Then if they happen to look out the window and see another train slide past on the next track, they have no way of knowing which train is in motion and which is at rest; nor can they tell how fast either one is moving or in what direction. The only way they can judge their situation is by looking out the other side of the car for some fixed body of reference like the station platform or a signal light. Sir Isaac Newton was aware of these tricks of motions, only he thought in terms of ships. He knew that on a calm day at sea a sailor can shave himself or drink soup as comfortably as when his ship is lying motionless in harbor. The water in his basin, the soup in his bowl, will remain unruffled whether the ship is making five knots, 15 knots, or 25 knots. So unless he peers out at the sea it will be impossible for him to know how fast his ship is moving or indeed if it is moving at all. Of course if the sea should get rough or the ship change course abruptly, then he will sense his state of motion. But granted the idealized conditions of a glass-calm sea and a silent ship, nothing that happens below decks—no amount of observation or mechanical experiment performed *inside* the ship—will disclose its velocity through the sea. The physical principle suggested by these considerations was formulated by Newton in 1687. "The motions of bodies included in a given space," he wrote, "are the same among themselves, whether that space is at rest or moves uniformly forward in a straight line." This is known as the Newtonian or Galilean Relativity Principle. It can also be phrased in more general terms: mechanical laws which are valid in one place are equally valid in any other place which moves uniformly relative to the first.

—Lincoln Barnett, *The Universe and Dr. Einstein*

## Comparison and Contrast

Somewhat more complex but at times indispensable is the paragraph developed by comparison and contrast. Obviously much of our thinking is done by comparison. If we wish to understand something for the purpose of arriving at a definition, we often begin by looking for points of resemblance with and points of difference from other things. If we wish to describe something, we may start by remarking its resemblance or contrast with something familiar. Even in reasoning from cause to effect, we may start with a comparison and find that things which are alike in a number of particulars are further alike in that they have the same effect. This is the process of analogy, which we have already treated in the section on argumentation.

When we undertake this kind of paragraph development, we soon realize that all comparison involves contrast and all contrast involves comparison. This is true simply because we would not bother either to compare things which are exactly alike or to contrast things which are completely different. If you undertake to compare fresh-water fishing with deep-sea fishing, you do so because the two are partly similar and partly dissimilar. Or, if you undertake to contrast the novel with the epic poem, you do so because there exists some likeness along with the difference.

The paragraph organized by comparison and contrast presents one particular problem: if you place all the likenesses in the first half and all the differences in the second, the reader may not retain all the details of the former when he is reading the latter. If you are comparing two cities as to size, inhabitants, climate, industry, and culture, it may lead to confusion to give all these facts for city A and then repeat them for city B. The alternative is to discuss the size of both A and B, then the inhabitants, and so on. The relative brevity of the paragraph unit makes it unlikely that the reader will often be called upon to remember too much; nevertheless, in long paragraphs having many details, the point-by-point comparison may be an advantage.

Here, in a paragraph from Herbert Croly's *The Promise of American Life*, Abraham Lincoln is compared and contrasted with the typical American of his day. Notice how the paragraph is organized to present the similarities, and then, in somewhat greater detail and with emphasis, the dissimilarities which made Lincoln outstanding among his countrymen.

> Lincoln's humility, no less than his liberal intelligence and his magnanimous disposition, is more democratic than it is American; but in this, as in so many other cases, his personal moral dignity and his peculiar moral insight did not separate him from his associates. Like them, he wanted professional success, public office, and the ordinary rewards of public life; and like them, he bears no trace of political or moral purism. But unlike them, he was not the intellectual and moral victim of his own purposes and ambitions; and unlike them, his life is a tribute to the sincerity and depth of his moral insight. He could never have become a national leader by the ordinary road of insistent and clamorous self-assertion. Had he not been restored to public life by the crisis, he would have remained in all probability a comparatively obscure and wholly under-valued man. But the political ferment of 1856 and the threat of ruin overhanging the American Union pushed him again on to the political highway; and once there, his years of intellectual discipline enabled him to play a leading and a decisive part. His personality obtained momentum, direction, and increasing dignity from its identification with great issues and events. He became the individual instrument whereby an essential and salutary purpose was fulfilled; and the instrument was admirably effective, precisely because it

had been silently and unconsciously tempered and formed for high achievement. Issue as he was of a society in which the cheap tool, whether mechanical or personal, was the immediately successful tool, he had none the
less labored long in the making of a consummate individual instrument.
—Herbert Croly, *The Promise of American Life*

The next paragraph shows the point-by-point method of comparison.

There is a character of a gentleman; so there is a character of a scholar,
which is no less easily recognized. The one has an air of books about him,
as the other has of good breeding. The one wears his thoughts as the other
does his clothes, gracefully; and even if they are a little old-fashioned, they
are not ridiculous: they have had their day. The gentleman shows, by his
manner, that he has been used to respect from others: the scholar that he
lays claim to self-respect and to a certain independence of opinion. The one
has been accustomed to the best company; the other has passed his time
in cultivating an intimacy with the best authors. There is nothing forward
or vulgar in the behavior of the one; nothing shrewd or petulant in the
observations of the other, as if he should astonish the bystanders, or was
astonished himself at his own discoveries. Good taste and good sense, like
common politeness, are, or are supposed to be, matters of course. One is
distinguished by an appearance of marked attention to every one present;
the other manifests an habitual air of abstraction and absence of mind.
The one is not an upstart, with all the self-important airs of the founder of
his own fortune; nor the other a self-taught man, with the repulsive self-
sufficiency which arises from an ignorance of what hundreds have known
before him. We must excuse perhaps a little conscious family pride in the
one, and a little harmless pedantry in the other. As there is a class of the
first character which sinks into the mere gentleman, that is, which has
nothing but this sense of respectability and propriety to support it—so the
character of a scholar not unfrequently dwindles down into the shadow
of a shade, till nothing is left of it but the mere bookworm. There is often
something amiable as well as enviable in this last character. I know one
such instance, at least. The person I mean has an admiration for learning,
if he is only dazzled by its light. He lives among old authors, if he does not
enter much into their spirit. He handles the covers, and turns over the
page, and is familiar with the names and dates. He is busy and self-
involved. He hangs like a film and cobweb upon letters, or is like the dust
upon the outside of knowledge, which should not be rudely brushed aside.
He follows learning as its shadow; but as such, he is respectable. He
browses on the husks and leaves of books, as the young fawn browses on
the bark and leaves of trees. Such a one lives all his life in a dream of
learning, and has never once had his sleep broken by a real sense of
things. He believes implicitly in genius, truth, virtue, liberty, because he
finds the names of these things in books. He thinks that love and friendship are the finest things imaginable, both in practice and theory. The
legend of good women is to him no fiction. When he steals from the twi-
light of his cell, the scene breaks upon him like an illuminated missal, and
all the people that he sees are but so many figures in a *camera obscura*.
He reads the world, like a favorite volume, only to find beauties in it, or

like an edition of some old work which he is preparing for the press, only to make emendations in it, and correct the errors that have inadvertently slipped in. He and his dog Tray are much the same honest, simple-hearted, faithful, affectionate creatures—if Tray could but read! His mind cannot take the impression of vice: but the gentleness of his nature turns gall to milk. He would not hurt a fly. He draws the picture of mankind from the guileless simplicity of his own heart: and when he dies, his spirit will take its smiling leave, without having ever had an ill thought of others, or the consciousness of one in itself!

—William Hazlitt, "On the Conversation of Authors"

In the earlier part, the gentleman and the scholar are compared and contrasted in one point after another as the paragraph develops. We do not pass from all the likenesses to all the differences, but take the two concurrently. In the latter part, with the sentence beginning "As there is a class of the first character," the theme shifts to a comparison of the scholar with the mere bookworm. This too begins as a point-by-point comparison of the bookworm with the more perceptive and realistic scholar, before becoming at the end a general description of the former.

Paragraphs of comparison and contrast are capable of more complex development. Follow the structure of the one given next, in which Everett Dean Martin compares "learning from life" with "learning from books." As the paragraph proceeds, it turns into a comparison of "true methods of learning" with "false methods of learning," in which both books and life are regarded as the objects of knowledge.

> I am of the opinion, however, that anyone who can learn from life can also learn from books without spoiling his mind. There is a difference between learning from books and merely learning to repeat passages from them. I had thought that in really learning from books one was learning from life. Whether one can get more information from books than from things depends somewhat on the books, and also what it is one wishes to learn, as well as one's capacity to learn. Manipulation of objects—doing— has no more educational value than repeating words. Either may become a mere routine exercise. Education is the organization of knowledge into human excellence. It is not the mere possession of knowledge, but the ability to reflect upon it and grow in wisdom. It would seem that as few people acquire wisdom from practical experience as from books.

—Everett Dean Martin, *The Meaning of a Liberal Education*

**Exercise:** *Make your own analysis of the following paragraph.*

> You will, therefore, not listen to those who tell you that these matters are above you, and ought to be left entirely to those into whose hands the King has put them. The public interest is more your business than theirs; and it is from want of spirit, and not from want of ability, that you can become wholly unfit to argue or to judge upon it. For in this very thing lies the difference between freemen and those that are not free. In a free country every man thinks he has a concern in all public matters; that he

has a right to form and a right to deliver an opinion upon them. They sift, examine, and discuss them. They are curious, eager, attentive, and jealous; and by making such matters the daily subjects of their thoughts and discoveries, vast numbers contract a very tolerable knowledge of them, and some a very considerable one. And this it is that fills free countries with men of ability in all stations. Whereas in other countries none but men whose office calls them to it having much care or thought about public affairs, and not daring to try the force of the opinions with one another, ability of this sort is extremely rare in any station of life. In free countries, there is often found more real public wisdom and sagacity in shops and manufactories than in the cabinets of princes in countries where none dares to have an opinion until he comes into them. Your whole importance, therefore, depends upon a constant, discreet use of your own reason; otherwise you and your country sink to nothing. If upon any particular occasion you should be roused, you will not know what to do. Your fire will be a fire in straw, fitter to waste and consume yourselves than to warm or enliven anything else. You will be only a giddy mob, upon whom no sort of reliance is to be had. You may disturb your country, but you never can reform your government. . . .

—Edmund Burke, *Correspondence*

## Cause and Effect

Paragraphs which are developed by cause and effect follow a logical pattern. Their progression is from a cause or set of causes to an effect or set of effects, or *vice versa*. Usually some reference is made to the causal reasoning that underlies this connection, but normally a single paragraph is too brief for a complete investigation of a causal relationship. The paragraph will be judged successful as writing if the cause (or causes) and the effect (or effects) are made distinct and if the language is clear enough to make their connection apparent. Transitional expressions are important in helping the reader to pass from cause to effect or effect to cause. The cross reference between these needs to be fairly frequent and explicit so that the reader will see the relationship of all the facts that are introduced. A paragraph with a clear thread of cause and effect can exhibit a nice coherence, as we may observe in the one given below.

The essential weakness of such a democracy is rather the importance it assigns to the average man with his petty opinions, which are sometimes right and sometimes wrong, his total lack of comprehension of all that is great and exceptional, his self-satisfied dilettantism and his complacency before the accredited and trite in thought. This is far less true of a republic like the French, with its genius for scepticism, a republic nourished in aesthetic traditions and founded on the ruins of an empire. The intellectual conditions are there quite different. But in an ethical democracy, where self-direction is a serious issue, domination by the average intelligence is inevitable; and those who are truly great find no scope for their powers. Those who appear great are merely men who are exploiting to the utmost the tendencies of the day. There are no great distinctions or premiums for truly high achievements which do not immediately concern the average man, and therefore the best energies of the nation are not spurred on to their keenest activity. All ambition is directed necessarily toward such achievements as the average man can understand and compete for—athletic virtuosity and wealth. Therefore the spirit of sport and of money-getting concerns the people more nearly than art or science, and even in politics the domination of the majority easily crowds from the arena those whose qualifications do not appeal to its mediocre taste. And by as much as mature and capable minds withdraw from political life, by so much are the well-intentioned masses more easily led astray by sharp and self-interested politicians and politics made to cater to mean instincts. In short, the danger is not from any wild lawlessness, but from a crass philistinism. The seditious demagogue who appeals to passion is less dangerous than the sly political wire-puller who exploits the indolence and indifference of the people; and evil intent is less to be feared than dilettantism and the intellectual limitations of the general public.

　　　　　　　　　　　—Hugo Munsterberg, *The Americans*

In this paragraph, which was written as a criticism of American democracy, the author sums up the cause which he is discussing in the phrase "domination by the average intelligence." What follows is concerned with the effects which flow from this. Therefore he talks about the emphasis upon sport and money-getting, the tendency of the better minds to withdraw from public affairs, the predominance of philistinism, and a general intellectual indolence and indifference on the part of the ruling majority. These details have their place in the scheme of the paragraph just because they stand in the relationship of effects to the concept with which he started. They are presented as specific results flowing from that general cause. Be sure to notice how certain phrases in the early part of the paragraph look forward to certain others at the end, and how, conversely, certain ones at the end look back toward certain others at the beginning. For example, "the average man with his petty opinions" seems to anticipate "politics made to cater to mean instincts"; and "intellectual limitations of the general public" refers to, or echoes "total lack of comprehension of all that is great and exceptional," and so on. Paragraphs organized by cause and effect are often held together by this kind of reference back and forth.

In the paragraph below F. A. Hayek is interested in tracing the connection between the planned type of society and certain effects which he thinks will come from it.

　　　Once a government has embarked on planning for the sake of justice, it cannot refuse responsibility for anybody's fate or position. In a planned society we shall all know that we are better or worse off than others, not because of circumstances which nobody controls, and which it is impossible to foresee with certainty, but because some authority wills it. And all our efforts directed toward improving our position will have to aim, not at foreseeing and preparing as well as we can for the circumstances over which we have no control, but at influencing in our favor the authority which has the power. The nightmare of English nineteenth-century political thinkers, the state in which "no avenue to wealth and honor would exist save through the government," would be realized in a completeness they never imagined—though familiar enough in some countries which have since passed to totalitarianism.

—F. A. Hayek, *The Road to Serfdom*

There is here, as in the preceding paragraph, a certain amount of looking back and forth between the cause at the beginning and the effect at the end. The reason for this is that anything which can be explained by cause and effect is by that very fact a conceptual whole and "cause" and "effect" are terms which we use in analyzing it. Consequently, when one mentions a cause, one is implying an effect; and when one mentions an effect, one is implying a cause. In a clearly organized paragraph, the citing of a cause must be followed at not too great a distance by the citing of the effect and, conversely, on the principle we have described. Let us observe this kind of coherence in the following paragraph.

Lenin is said to have declared that the best way to destroy the Capitalist System was to debauch the currency. By a continuing process of inflation governments can confiscate, secretly and unobserved, an important part of the wealth of their citizens. By this method they not only confiscate, but they confiscate *arbitrarily;* and, while the process impoverishes many, it actually enriches some. The sight of this arbitrary rearrangement of riches strikes not only at security, but at confidence in the equity of the existing distribution of wealth. Those to whom the system brings windfalls, beyond their deserts and even beyond their expectations or desires, become "profiteers," who are the object of the hatred of the bourgeoisie, whom the inflation has impoverished, not less than the proletariat. As the inflation proceeds and the real value of the currency fluctuates wildly from month to month, all permanent relations between debtors and creditors, which form the ultimate foundations of capitalism, become so utterly disordered as to be almost meaningless; and the process of wealth-getting degenerates into gamble and lottery.

—John Maynard Keynes, *The Economic Consequences*

The chief cause named in this paragraph of cause and effect is "continuing process of inflation." Notice that it is immediately followed by verbs expressive of its results, "confiscate," "impoverishes," and "enriches," and by the noun group "arbitrary rearrangement of riches." This exemplifies what is meant by a close relation or togetherness of cause and effect. It is this opportunity to pass readily from one to another that insures the coherence of the paragraph.

**Exercise:** *Make your own analysis of the cause-and-effect structure of the following short paragraph by Pearl Buck.*

And speaking of cruelty, this is perhaps the place to mention the cruelty to animals which shocks so many foreigners when they visit China. There is indeed a vast difference between the way in which animals are treated in China and the way in which they are treated in the West. Animals are not petted and fondled and made much of by the Chinese. On the contrary, Chinese visitors in the United States are usually shocked and disgusted by the affection with which animals are treated, an emotion which the Chinese feel should be reserved for human beings. I believe in kindness toward animals and human beings and I used to wonder why my Chinese friends, whom I knew to be merciful and considerate toward people, could be quite indifferent to suffering animals. The cause, I discovered as I grew older, lay in the permeation of Chinese thought by Buddhist theory. Though most Chinese were not religious and therefore not Buddhist, yet the doctrine of the reincarnation of the human soul influenced their thinking, and the essence of that theory is that an evil human being after death becomes an animal in his next incarnation. Therefore every animal was once a wicked human being. While the average Chinese might deny direct belief in this theory, yet the pervading belief led him to feel contempt for animals.

—Pearl Buck, *My Several Worlds*

## Definition and Analysis

Other types of paragraphs are developed primarily by the processes of definition or analysis, or the combination of these two. Sometimes you will find a single paragraph employed to set up a definition which is to be used throughout a long discussion. The paragraph below presents such a definition of rhetoric. We find that the definition is developed through contrast of the subject with other things, through mention of purpose, and through pointing out the relation of the subject to other subjects—the very means that we employ, on a large scale, in writing extended definitions.

Rhetoric may be defined as the faculty of observing in any given case the available means of persuasion. This is not a function of any other art. Every other art can instruct or persuade about its own subject-matter; for instance, medicine about what is healthy and unhealthy, geometry about the properties of magnitudes, and the same is true of the other arts and sciences. But rhetoric we look upon as the power of observing the means of persuasion on almost any subject presented to us; and that is why we say that, in its technical character, it is not concerned with any special or definite class of subjects.

—Aristotle, *Rhetoric,* translated by W. Rhys Roberts

The same is true of paragraphs developed by analysis. In the next paragraph, Lafcadio Hearn is analyzing the institution of Japanese ancestor worship. He shows how its growth falls into three stages, which are presented in their relationship to the whole institution and in their relationship to one another. This is a small-scale use of the principle that underlies all partition and classification as we saw in the section on "Exposition." It organizes the paragraph by making a division of the subject which is being analyzed.

Three stages of ancestor-worship are to be distinguished in the general course of religious and social evolution; and each of these finds illustration in the history of Japanese society. The first stage is that which exists before the establishment of a settled civilization, when there is yet no national ruler, and when the unit of society is the great patriarchal family, with its elders or war-chiefs for lords. Under these conditions, the spirits of the family-ancestors only are worshipped—each family propitiating its own dead, and recognizing no other form of worship. As the patriarchal families, later on, become grouped into tribal clans, there grows up the custom of tribal sacrifice to the spirits of the clan-rulers—this cult being superadded to the family cult, and marking the second stage of ancestor-worship. Finally, with the union of all the clans or tribes under one supreme head, there is developed the custom of propitiating the spirits of national rulers. This third form of the cult becomes the obligatory religion of the country; but it does not replace either of the preceding cults: the three continue to exist together.

—Lafcadio Hearn, *Japan: An Attempt at Interpretation*

**Exercise:** *Make your own analysis of the method of development in the following paragraph.*

Again, let it be considered in what frame of mind, from one cause or another, most of those are who seek these interviews. Suitors and claimants are the most numerous class. It may be supposed that the interests which they have, or conceive themselves to have, at stake—the importance to themselves of the objects which they have in view—would infallibly induce such parties as these at least to take the utmost pains beforehand to make the interviews which they seek available to them. Yet most men who have been in office will have observed with how little preparation of their own minds even this class of persons do commonly present themselves to profit by the audience which they have solicited. One man is humble and ignorant of the world, has never set eyes on a minister before, and acts as if the mere admission to the presence of such a personage was all that was needful, which being accomplished he must naturally flourish ever after. Another is romantic and sanguine, his imagination is excited, and he has thought that he can do everything by some happy phrase or lively appeal, which, in the embarrassment of the critical moment, escapes his memory, or finds no place, or the wrong place, in the conversation. A third brings a letter of introduction from some person who is great in *his* eyes but possibly inconsiderable in those of the minister; he puts his trust in the recommendation and appears to expect that the minister should suggest to him, rather than he to the minister, what is the particular object to be accomplished for him; he "lacks advancement," and that, he thinks, is enough said. A fourth has not made up his mind how high he shall pitch his demands; he is afraid on the one hand to offend by presumption, on the other to lose by diffidence; he proposes, therefore, to feel his way and be governed by what the minister shall say to him; but the minister naturally has nothing to say to him—never having considered the matter and takir.g no interest in it. Thus it is that, through various misconceptions, the instances will be found in practice to be a minority, in which a claimant or suitor who obtains an interview has distinctly made up his mind as to the specific thing which he will ask, propose, or state. Still less does he forecast the several means and resources, objections and difficulties, conditions and stipulations, which may happen to be topics essential to a full development and consideration of his case.

—Henry Taylor, *The Statesman*

## Combined Patterns

A good percentage of the paragraphs to be found in actual writing employ more than one method of development. Here again the comparison with the composition as a whole has some point: just as the composition may employ a number of devices for the adequate treatment of its subject, so the paragraph may draw upon more than one means of treating its unit of thought. Naturally the comparative brevity of the paragraph has some influence and usually prevents the use of more than two or three methods of development. But one may expect to find such a combination as a paragraph developing by spatial pattern and at the same time following the temporal pattern of an event or a process. Paragraphs whose main object is definition will rather frequently make use of comparison and contrast to limit the meaning of the term defined, as does Aristotle's definition of rhetoric given earlier. But the same kind of paragraph might make an analysis or give an enumeration of parts to show what goes to make up the thing defined. Paragraphs developed by cause and effect sometimes bring in example and illustration to make clear causal relationships. The number of possible combinations is virtually unlimited, but these are suggested as a few of the more common ones.

It would be a mistake then to suppose that paragraphs must exemplify this or that structure in pure form. It would also be wrong to suppose that most writers work consciously at paragraph structure. The successful writer keeps his mind on his meaning and works until he has made his paragraph unit intelligible. Such knowledge as he has of formal paragraph structure should be at his side as a resource rather than as a set of commands. He draws upon it as needed, and he may find it of most value when he makes his revision. He can then use the various plans of paragraph development to test and to improve the coherence of what he has written.

## PARAGRAPHS WITH SPECIAL FUNCTION

In this connection we note that certain paragraphs have a specialized function with reference to the whole composition. These are introductory, transitional, and concluding paragraphs.

## Introductory Paragraphs

The *introductory* paragraph, as the name suggests, presents the subject matter in general and sometimes indicates the plan of the piece. For this reason, it tends to be comprehensive and systematic. It is a "topic" paragraph just as the general introductory sentence is a topic sentence. But there are so many ways of making introductions that beyond this its structure can scarcely be specified. Below is a paragraph which introduces a discussion of the defects of American education.

> Education has one thing in common with religion. One must come to it with clean hands and a pure heart or one can never know the secret power of it. This is as true of a nation as of the individual. As a people we have certain traits which may be praiseworthy in themselves, but are distinctly hostile to the work of education. I will enumerate them and then briefly indicate their element of hostility. They are, first, our genius for organization; second, our well-known utilitarianism; and third, our cleverness in finding shortcuts to the ends we seek; fourth, our tendency to make propaganda.
> —Everett Dean Martin, *The Meaning of a Liberal Education*

Here is a short but serviceable paragraph which precedes Bertrand Russell's analysis of an aspect of Einstein's theory.

> The reasons for accepting Einstein's law of gravitation are partly empirical, partly logical. We will begin with the former.
> —Bertrand Russell, *ABC of Relativity*

## Transitional Paragraphs

Beginning writers are often unaware that an entire paragraph may be used for transitional purposes alone. The readability of many papers, especially those dealing with abstract subjects, can be greatly increased by a paragraph inserted here and there purely to effect a transition. Such units can serve quite successfully to pull the larger groupings of the thought together. Sometimes they are needed to sum up one set of ideas in preparation for turning to another set. Sometimes they are useful to give a specific idea as to what the writer intends to do next. Sometimes, as in the following paragraph, they signal a turn from analysis to illustration.

> The principle on which I have been insisting is so obvious, and instances in point are so ready, that I should think it tiresome to proceed with the subject, except that one or two illustrations may serve to explain my own language about it, which may not have done justice to the doctrine which it has been intended to enforce.
> —John Henry Newman, "What is a University?"

### Concluding Paragraphs

There are cases where an article comes to an end naturally, without need of restatement or summation. At other times, however, the article needs to be concluded or rounded off by what is termed a concluding paragraph. There is no set pattern for this paragraph, its purpose being simply to give the piece a satisfactory ending. Sometimes it takes the form of a resumé of the matter which appears in detail in the body of the composition. Sometimes it returns to the chief point of the composition and gives it an expression which awakens the reader to the timeliness of the subject. Sometimes it merely calls attention to the limits which the writer has observed in his treatment. These and other purposes may be served by a final paragraph. But whatever the purpose, the paragraph should not look like an afterthought, and it should be something more than a mere flourish. It should have a sufficiently clear relationship with the whole piece to justify its concluding role. In the paragraph below E. B. White concludes an essay discussing peculiarities of speech heard in Maine with a few sentences which point up the significance of the subject.

> Country talk is alive and accurate and contains more pictures and images than city talk. It usually has an unmistakable sincerity which gives it distinction. I think there is less talking merely for the sound which it makes. At any rate, I seldom tire of listening to even the most common- place stuff, directly and sincerely spoken; and I still recall with dread the feeling that occasionally used to come over me at parties in town when the air was crowded with intellectual formations—the feeling that there wasn't a remark in the room that couldn't be brought down with a common pin.
>
> —E. B. White, "Main Speech" from
> *One Man's Meat*

Here is a good specimen concluding paragraph:

> There is much more which might be said, and which ought to be said, of Shelley; but our limits are reached. We have not attempted a complete criticism; we have only aimed at showing how some of the peculiarities of his works and life may be traced to the peculiarity of his nature.
>
> —Walter Bagehot, "Percy Bysshe Shelley"

### Paragraphs in Dialogue

A word remains to be said about the paragraph as a unit of conveni- ence in the writing of dialogue. Naturally the reader must be made aware of each change of speaker; and the rule of beginning each person's speech with a fresh paragraph is a practical means of calling attention to this shift. Long speeches by one person are often divided into several para- graphs, and in these cases the second pair of quotation marks will signalize the close of the complete speech. The paragraphing within a single speech of course follows the ordinary principle of division according to units of thought. But regardless of what they are saying, the writer keeps the different speakers distinct by starting a new paragraph with each change of speaker.

"I don't see why he doesn't want to marry Cousin Amanda. It would be so suitable."

"That's probably the reason. The suitable is the last thing we ever want."

"Anyhow, I'm going to ask her."

"Well, run on. It will be improper, but thank the Lord you live in an age when you can be improper without having to go abroad. . . ."

—Ellen Glasgow, *The Romantic Comedians*

## PARAGRAPH LENGTH

A paragraph should be long enough to do its job. Some paragraphs have a combined job to accomplish and make use of more than one plan of development, as we have seen; therefore this generalization provides much leeway. For whatever the norm of the average may be worth, it can be mentioned that most paragraphs in present-day writing run between 100 and 350 words. This does not mean that you are prohibited from writing a paragraph of 10 words or a paragraph of 500 words. At either of the two extremes of brevity and length, however, certain practical considerations come into play. Since our attention seeks resting places at intervals, a long paragraph, especially if it contains much detail, may overtax. In such case, it is best to break it up into shorter units at the most natural dividing places. On the other hand, a series of paragraphs which are very short may only annoy the reader. He may feel that they are an unfair means of bidding for his attention, because the separate paragraphs may not represent stages in the development important enough to be so set off. A piece written in this style of paragraphing may at first seem snappy and alive, but it is unlikely to wear well as the reading progresses. We may sense that the writer is using indention to get an interest which he could not get otherwise, and interest aroused in this manner does not last.

The best plan is to make your paragraphs conform reasonably with the units of your thought. If it seems that you are paragraphing too often, or too seldom, reconsider your thinking on the topic and adapt your paragraphs accordingly.

## TRANSITIONS WITHIN THE PARAGRAPH

The problem of achieving coherence within the paragraph is only partly solved by working out a plan of development. The plan takes care of the underlying organization and so makes the order of thought easy to follow. But this order needs to be made clear at the linguistic level, too. That is to say, words must be included which will show explicitly the progression of the thought. A paragraph may have a high degree of both unity and coherence and yet be difficult to read if the verbal transitions are not clear. The verbal transitions are those expressions whose primary job it is to keep the thread of discourse in sight—to *say* in what direction the thought is moving. Pronouns, conjunctions and conjunctive adverbs, and repeated key words are the expressions most useful for this purpose.

A *pronoun* by its reference to an antecedent establishes a connection. We are quite familiar with transitions like this in such simple forms as "When Fred was twelve years old, *he* joined the Boy Scouts," and "Mr. Thompson trusted *his* secretary." But a series of pronouns may serve to link together a whole paragraph or even several paragraphs. It is most necessary that the antecedent of the pronoun be near enough to be easily found, and of course there must be no ambiguous reference. And sometimes an alternating use of the pronoun and the antecedent is needed to prevent monotonous repetition. When these conditions are met, the pronoun can serve well to knit matter together.

*Conjunctions,* of course, have the specific job of making connections. It is easy to see this in the case of simple conjunctions like *and, but,* and *for.* But it is equally true of the conjunctive adverbs such as *however, moreover,* and *thus.* We need to give special attention to the latter group because they have explicit meanings which play a part in the transition; they indicate the kind of thought that is coming next, or they characterize the connection rather more fully than do the simple conjunctions. For example, *however* tells us that a reservation or qualification is going to be made; *therefore* means that a conclusion or a consequence is going to be presented; *thus* means that something of like manner or kind is going to be mentioned. You will be able to improve your writing by having at your finger tips a list of adverbial conjunctions to signalize the steps in your thought. But at the same time you may need to learn their exact meanings. Do not be satisfied with what you have picked up by hearing careless everyday use. Make sure that the adverbial connective you choose is the most accurate one to introduce your thought. Do not write *thus* when you mean *therefore;* do not write *therefore* when you mean *accordingly.* A precise use of adverbial connectives can do much toward spelling out for the reader the logic of your thought.

Below is a list of words commonly used as *conjunctive adverbs* which you should have as a ready resource.

| | |
|---|---|
| accordingly | finally |
| again | furthermore |
| also | hence |
| anyhow | however |
| besides | indeed |
| consequently | likewise |

| | |
|---|---|
| moreover | so |
| otherwise | still |
| nevertheless | then |
| nonetheless | therefore |
| similarly | yet |

NOTE: Sometimes simple adverbs, too, like *now, soon,* and *here,* will establish a clear transition, as in "Soon the fun would begin"; "Here was the reason for his success"; "Now we turn to a further point."

The *repetition of a key word* often helps to make the transition clear. This is especially true when the key word is the real subject of the paragraph, as may frequently be the case. As this word reappears, sometimes in noun form and sometimes in adjective or adverbial form as part of a phrase, it keeps before us the essential subject while developments and fresh applications are being made. In a paragraph dealing with science, for example, we must expect to encounter, in addition to the word "science" itself, such phrases as "scientific investigation," "scientifically established laws" and the like. All such expressions keep the thematic word "science" before us but vary it and combine it according to the needs of the development.

In the paragraph below note the constant use of transitional expressions, and observe how they keep the thread of thought clear.

> The style that lasts, the good *style* that has resources behind *it,* almost never resorts to the loud pedal. *It* unconsciously avoids the clever phrase, unless the *phrase* is more than *clever,* together with every sort of emphasis, and is *therefore* never tiresome. Most of the characteristic modern *styles,* in music and painting as well as writing, take for granted the "law of acceleration" that Henry Adams described. *But* to take *such laws* of the outer world for granted, in the sense of adjusting one's rhythm to them, is to be a goose by definition. *As* the great composers prevail in the end, over the *composers* of the moment, in the midst of an *accelerated world, so* it is with writers. The type of American *writers who* have *prevailed,* over and through the "jazz age," are *those* for *whom* the *age* has existed but not the *jazz* in the *age. Those who* have accepted the *"law of acceleration"* have perished by *this law. They* obeyed the rule of the subway, "Step lively." *They who* were so afraid to see the door slammed in their faces *have seen the door slammed* on their backs.
> —Van Wyck Brooks, *The Opinions of Oliver Allston*

The same sets of expressions which are used to mark transitions within paragraphs are used to link paragraphs together. Pronouns, conjunctions and conjunctive adverbs, and repeated key words serve to show the continuity here just as well as within the single paragraph. The only difference is that the units which are being linked by these visible aids are in this case longer. In the selection below a variety of transitional expressions performs the function of linking.

Accompanying the formal training afforded by courses of study is *another informal kind of training*, particularly during the high school years. *The high school*, with *its* athletics, clubs, sororities and fraternities, dances and parties, and other "extracurricular activities," is a fairly complete social cosmos in itself, and about this city within a city the *social* life of the intermediate generation centers. *Here* the *social* sifting devices of *their* elders—money, clothes, personal attractiveness, male physical prowess, exclusive clubs, election to positions of leadership—are all for the first time set going with a population as yet largely undifferentiated save as regards *their* business class and working class parents. *This informal training* is not a preparation for a vague future that must be taken on trust, as is the case with so much of the academic work; to many of the boys and girls in *high school this* is "the life," the thing *they* personally like best about going to *school*.

The *school* is taking over more and more of the child's life. Both *high school* and grades have departed from the attitude of fifty years ago, when the Board directed:

> 'Pupils shall not be permitted to remain on the school grounds after dismissal. The teachers shall often remind the pupils that the first duty when dismissed is to proceed quietly and directly home to render all needed assistance to their parents.'

*Today the school* is becoming not a place to which the children go from *their* homes for a few hours daily but a place from which *they* go *home* to eat and sleep.

An index to *this* widening of the *school's* function appears in a comparison of the 1924 *high school* with the first annual, published thirty years before, though even *this comparison* does not reflect the full extent of the shift since 1890, *for* innovations had been so numerous in the years just preceding 1894 as to dwarf the extent of the 1894–1924 contrast. *Next* in importance to the pictures of the senior class and other *class* data in the earlier book, as measured by the percentage of space occupied, were the pages devoted to the faculty and the courses taught by *them*, *while* in the current *book* athletics shares the position of honor with the *class data*, and a *faculty* twelve times as large occupies relatively only half as much space. Interest in small selective group "activities" has increased at the expense of the earlier total class *activities*. *But such* a numerical *comparison* can only faintly suggest the difference in tone of the two *books*. The description of academic work in the early *annual* beginning, "Among the various changes that have been effected in grade work are . . ." and ending "regular monthly teachers' meetings have been inaugurated," seems as foreign to the present *high school* as does the early class motto "Deo Duce"; equally far from 1890 is the *present* dedication, "To the Bearcats."

—Robert S. and Helen Merrell Lynd, *Middletown*

## SUMMARY

In writing the paragraph, as in writing the composition as a whole, you are faced with the basic requirements of unity and coherence. The topic sentence is a common means of achieving paragraph unity, although not all paragraphs have topic sentences. A few paragraphs derive their unity from the likeness of their details, the consistency of their tone or some other factor. Unity must be aided by coherence, since the paragraph is expected to develop a thought or to "get somewhere." A number of structural principles can be used to give a paragraph orderly development. Spatial and temporal patterns, definition and analysis, and development by causal reasoning will serve here just as they serve in the full composition. Not infrequently a paragraph will use more than one plan of development.

The plan of development usually needs to be brought to the surface, or to be indicated by visible markers. This requirement is best met through the use of certain expressions which are recognized as connecting links or direction givers. These are pronouns, conjunctions and conjunctive adverbs, and repeated key words. Most beginning writers will profit by a more liberal use of these connectives, especially conjunctive adverbs and repeated key words. These expressions keep before the reader the development of the thought both within paragraphs and between paragraphs in a series.

## EXERCISES

**Exercise A**  *Suggest possible topic sentences for a paragraph on each of the following topics.*

1. The advantage of budgeting one's time.
2. The distinction between wit and humor.
3. Superhighways.
4. A famous book that bored me.
5. Modern house architecture.
6. How college students really feel about religion.
7. The theory that every voter has a duty to vote.
8. The role of mathematics in science.
9. The separation of powers in the United States government.
10. The problem of choosing a career.
11. The social significance of styles in dress.
12. The most important rule for safe driving.
13. Killing animals for sport.
14. Money and prestige in my community.
15. The career woman.

**Exercise B**  *Make a sentence outline of the first twelve paragraphs of Chapter 2, "Exposition," by copying the topic sentence of each paragraph.*

**Exercise C**  *Study the paragraphs in the selection from Hayakawa's "Popular Songs vs. the Facts of Life" (pages 64–65). Underline all the transitional words and phrases within and between the paragraphs.*

**Exercise D**   *Take any one of the topics in Exercise A and write down, in phrases, the ideas it suggests just as they come to you. Then rearrange them according to some plan and express them in sentence form. The result should be an organized paragraph produced by a method that some writers actually use.*

# Chapter Eight

## Diction

Diction may be defined as the choice of words, and good diction enables us to express our meaning and feeling in the way best suited to our purpose. The study of diction is therefore a vital part of composition. The organization and proportioning of material, good paragraphing, and skillful sentence structure can do much for us, but all of them combined cannot save a piece of writing filled with fumbling and faulty selection of words. There is ample ground for saying that the *life* of any piece of writing is in its diction. All of the techniques we have been studying are supporting devices; but the words are the substance itself. Failures made in the choice of words are quickly detected by almost any reader, even though he may not be able to supply better words himself. Improvement in diction, consequently, may play a large role in improvement of expression.

## STANDARDS OF DICTION

### Accuracy

Since the student will have many matters of diction called to his attention, it is well at the beginning to distinguish between those faults which are outright mistakes and those which are merely inferior choices. Some mistakes with words are made through simple ignorance, or through a misunderstanding of what the word signifies. If, for example, we write "affect" when we mean "effect" or "respectfully" when we mean "respectively," we are using a word with a dictionary meaning different from that we wish to convey. Such choices are definite errors, which must be corrected by consulting a dictionary. But there are other faults in diction which are really matters of degree; that is to say, the writer has used a certain word when another word more appropriate is available. His choice is not entirely wrong, but he is not using the most effective language for his purpose. A leading student of language has likened searching for the right word to shooting at the bull's eye in archery. It is likely that the first two or three shots will hit in the outer circles. They do not miss the target completely, but neither do they find the exact spot at which they were aimed. So the archer keeps on trying until he finally reaches the bull's eye, or the exact center of meaning which he has been seeking. For illustration, let us suppose that the writer wishes to express the idea of communicating something in an indirect way. He may try "hint," "imply," "suggest," and "intimate." But he finally decides that "insinuate" is the most accurate shot at the target he has in mind. This is the bull's-eye word. Or he may hesitate between "ran," "hastened," "scrambled," "flew," "hurried," and "dashed." A close study of differences shows which one of the six is the most exact for his purpose. The other words may say the same thing "in a general way," but in our best writing we do not wish to be general; we wish to be precise. The successful writer always seeks the accurate word, the word that will come closest to the bull's eye, the idea which he wishes to express.

## Levels of Usage

As a general thing we do not use the same language in the college classroom that we use on a fishing trip or the same language at the card table that we would use in a serious business interview. Many of the words will of course be the same, but we all sense that different situations call for some difference in choice of language. Certain words and constructions that sound right in one place just do not seem to fit in another. To a certain extent we change our speech as we change our clothing for the occasion. Adapting our diction to special situations and for specific purposes can be extremely important. It can mean on occasions the difference between success and disaster in writing and speaking. Most of us have a practical knowledge of the kinds of vocabulary expected in different places, but knowledge of the broader levels of usage may make some choices easier.

The varieties of language have been described in a number of ways, and the fact that the basic vocabulary and structure of a language is much the same at all levels and among all speakers makes it difficult to draw hard and fast lines. It is perhaps most useful to distinguish between major *functional varieties* of language, on the one hand, and between *standard and substandard* language on the other hand. The two major functional levels of language are usually described as the *formal* and the *informal*.

## Formal Level

The highest level of language, from the standpoint of complexity, is the formal level. Formal English is characterized by a relatively learned and Latinate vocabulary as well as by a complexity in sentence structure. Many of its words will impress the average reader as "big," many will be highly specialized, and many will suggest scholarly or literary activity. Although the writer of formal English will use a very large number of words, locutions, and structures that appear regularly in informal English and sometimes in vulgate English, he will tend to be more serious, more precise, and more consciously dignified than the writer of informal English. Formal diction is the language of the prepared address, the legal brief, the scientific paper, the business report, and many college textbooks. It speaks accurately and with authority, maintains a clear standard of propriety, but avoids primness and artificial elegance. It often reflects the rhythms and patterns of conversation, but it is less relaxed than ordinary spoken English. Except in rare instances, such as the formal lecture, it is a written English. The passage below will serve to illustrate its characteristics.

> The place of science in a program of liberal education is not a new problem; it has been at the focus of reflection on educational philosophy and practice since Plato. Nevertheless, although the basic issues may not have undergone radical transformation with the passage of centuries, the problem has acquired new dimensions and fresh complexities in contemporary American society.
>
> Until comparatively recent times, the theoretical sciences were regarded as branches of philosophical inquiry, having for their ultimate objective knowledge of man's supreme good in the light of his place in the universe; education designed for developing enlightened and cultivated minds was reserved for small minorities in relatively small populations; and the organization of human life did not require large groups of highly trained scientific personnel. Under the circumstances, it was easy enough for Plato and his successors to argue persuasively for a conception of liberal education in which the study of science occupied a prominent place. But these circumstances are no longer present. It is in consequence more difficult today to win effective general agreement that a solid grounding in natural and social science is an indispensable part of a humanistically oriented education, and that such grounding is no less essential for the formation of a liberal intelligence than is thorough exposure to the materials traditionally classified as belonging to the humanities.
>
> —Ernest Nagel, "Science and the Humanities"

## Informal Level

Informal English might be described as formal English somewhat relaxed. It is broadly the level of conversation of cultivated people and the level of writing which reflects the general tone and rhythm of such speech. Almost none of us, of course, speak just as we write; when we are speaking in ordinary situations, we use an informal sentence structure, often leaving some words unexpressed, and we make use of many colloquial expressions. The writer of informal English bases his diction and structure on spoken English, but he is always aware that he is *writing, not speaking*. Like the more formal writer, he strives for clarity and precision, and observes the fundamental rules of unity, coherence, and emphasis, but he works in a more relaxed atmosphere and with a more conversational tone and vocabulary. If he is less consciously dignified than the writer of formal English, he is still conscious of his task as a writer, and he works just as hard. He will prefer the familiar or colloquial word to the unfamiliar, and the loose sentence to the periodic; but he will not hesitate to use the polysyllabic word and an elaborate sentence structure when precision and clarity require. In short, his level of usage is appropriate to his subject matter and right for his audience. The passage below will serve to illustrate the characteristics of written informal English.

> I am a fan for Science. My education is scientific and I have, in one field, contributed a monograph to a scientific journal. Science, to my mind, is applied honesty, the one reliable means we have to find out truth. That is why, when error is committed in the name of Science, I feel the way a man would if his favorite uncle had taken to drink.
>
> Over the years, I have come to feel that way about what science has done to food. I agree that America can set as good a table as any nation in the world. I agree that our food is nutritious and that the diet of most of us is well-balanced. What America eats is handsomely packaged; it is usually clean and pure; it is excellently preserved. The only trouble with it is this: year by year it grows less good to eat. It appeals increasingly to the eye. But who eats with his eyes? Almost everything used to taste better when I was a kid. For quite a long time I thought that observation was merely another index of advancing age. But some years ago I married a girl whose mother is an expert cook of the kind called "old-fashioned." This gifted woman's daughter (my wife) was taught her mother's venerable skills. The mother lives in the country and still plants an old-fashioned garden. She still buys dairy products from the neighbors and, in so far as possible, she uses the same materials her mother and grandmother did— to prepare meals that are superior. They are just as good, in this Year of Grace, as I recall them from my courtship. After eating for a while at the table of my mother-in-law, it is sad to go back to eating with my friends —even the alleged "good cooks" among them. And it is a gruesome experience to have meals at the best big-city restaurants.
>
> —Philip Wylie, "Science Has Spoiled My Supper"

### Standard and Substandard English

The distinction between *standard* and *substandard* English is not a difference in the function to which speakers or writers are putting language, but a difference between the education and social status of the speakers. Standard English *is* the English of educated and cultivated speakers and writers, of those who are the lawyers, doctors, judges, teachers, journalists, business leaders, and officers of the government. Substandard English *is* the language of those who have had little formal education and whose work normally requires little or no writing, or even much dependence on the spoken language. It is characterized by grammatical forms generally avoided by educated speakers, such as "ain't," "them boys," "he done it," and the like. It tends to be more limited in vocabulary, considerably less varied in grammatical constructions, and much less precise than Standard English, although it is often marked by a considerable vividness in its descriptions of everyday life and events. Substandard English does not occur in writing, except in fiction and other literary forms which attempt to reproduce the speech of uneducated people—and of course in such writing as they may occasionally have to do.

## Vocabulary Range

In order to achieve the range and accuracy which are desirable, the great majority of students need to increase their vocabulary both through adding new words to it and through sharpening their sense of the meaning of words they now use. But there is no easy or specific method for doing this. Some people make lists of new words and attempt to learn them by memorizing. Such effort is not wholly wasted, yet words acquired in this manner are not likely to become part of one's functioning vocabulary. One is prone to forget words merely copied down, or to feel unsure about bringing words so acquired into conversation or writing. The most effective vocabulary building takes place gradually and insensibly through contact with the writing and speech of people who have a better knowledge of language than we have. This occurs through reading good literature and through listening to effective speakers—such as teachers, lecturers, and eminent public figures. The advantage of this type of learning is that we see or hear the word in use, and we are helped in our understanding of it by the context in which it appears—by the surrounding words with which it must function in order to make sense in a sentence. Many times an intelligent reader can infer with fair accuracy from a sentence what a word *must* mean, and probably more words are added to the vocabulary by this method than by any other. But even after one has added a word in this manner, it is usually advisable to look the word up in a good dictionary, because words often have special histories which must be taken into account. Furthermore they need to be distinguished from words of similar meaning. In summary, the best policy is to read and listen attentively and to make use of a good dictionary before regarding yourself as master of a new word.

Students formerly had a resource of vocabulary building in their study of foreign languages, especially Greek and Latin. It is estimated that about three quarters of the words in modern English derive from Latin or Greek, and a knowledge of these languages helps one greatly in recognizing the component parts out of which many English words are made. By understanding such component parts, one can usually arrive at a more or less accurate understanding of a term. This holds true especially of technical terms and terms used in the sciences. A student who has learned even a smattering of Greek, for example, can gather instantly the meaning of "epidermis," or "psychosomatic," or "geocentric." Similarly, a student who has learned even a small amount of Latin will not have to pause long over the meaning of "intramural" or "regicide" or "expatriate."

The lack of familiarity with the classical languages can be offset to some extent if one learns the more common Greek and Latin prefixes, stems, and suffixes which are components of modern English words. This amounts to acquiring a vocabulary of terms which have become Anglicized in the sense of entering unchanged, or little changed, into innumerable English words. Learning then requires some memory work, but no other form of vocabulary study provides so ready an insight into meanings. A knowledge of these components gives the key to understanding thousands of words which it would prove highly tedious to learn one at a time. Various books devoted particularly to vocabulary study provide lists of Latin and Greek stems and affixes for the interested student.

## The Dictionary

Dictionaries are storehouses of what we know about the history and meanings of words, and everyone should make himself acquainted with their resources. A first step in dictionary study is to realize that there is no work which can properly be spoken of as "*the* dictionary." That is to say, there is no dictionary which is an absolutely complete and final record of words, although there exist three or four which approximate that ideal. The *New English Dictionary* (sometimes referred to as the "Oxford Dictionary"), and *Webster's Third New International Dictionary*,[1] are the most complete. These are unabridged dictionaries, and you will usually have to find them in libraries. Among the smaller or "desk" dictionaries which are adequate for general purposes are *Webster's Seventh New Collegiate Dictionary*, *The American College Dictionary*, *Funk and Wagnalls Standard Dictionary*, and *Webster's New World Dictionary*, published by the World Publishing Company. It is advisable for every student to keep one of these dictionaries on his desk, and to learn where to find the larger dictionaries when need for full study of a word arises.

[1] The third edition of *Webster's New International Dictionary* differs in significant ways from the second in its lexicographical principles. While more complete than the second in much of the information it provides, it largely eschews attaching usage labels to individual words, a policy which has been considerably criticized by those who look upon the dictionary as a guide rather than as exclusively a record. The heated debate following publication of the third edition sometimes distracted attention from the major contribution to lexicography which the dictionary represents and which will doubtless be increasingly recognized.

Essentially what a good dictionary provides is the natural history of a word. It presents, accordingly, a survey of a word's various forms and meanings, including both the past and the present, the general and the specialized. A full entry discloses all a term has meant and does mean. Words often shift their meanings in the course of time; and it is sometimes necessary to make certain that a particular meaning is current and accepted. Disputes over what a word means cannot be settled without due appreciation of this liability to change, and no dictionary pretends to settle for all time what a word can mean. The method of a dictionary is basically descriptive, and its aim is to record the meanings of actual past and present usage. Since all communication has to take into account the meanings established by usage, dictionaries are indispensable sources of reference. Although they do not freeze language, they do serve as a kind of stabilizer by preserving these records of usage.

The principal information which a good dictionary supplies about a word is as follows:

1. Correct spelling and syllabication
2. Pronunciation
3. Derivation of the word with cognates (*i.e.*, words related to it)
4. Part of speech to which the term as defined belongs
5. General definitions, usually given in a chronological order
6. Technical and other special definitions
7. Synonyms and antonyms

> **¹mind** \'mīnd\ *n* [ME, fr. OE *gemynd*; akin to OHG *gimunt* memory; both fr. a prehistoric EGmc-WGmc compound whose first constituent is represented by OE *ge-* (perfective prefix) and whose second constituent is akin to L *ment-, mens* mind, *monēre* to remind, warn, Gk *menos* spirit, *mnasthai, mimnēskesthai* to remember — more at CO-] **1 :** RECOLLECTION, MEMORY **2 a :** the element or complex of elements in an individual that feels, perceives, thinks, wills, and esp. reasons **b :** the conscious events and capabilities in an organism **c :** the organized conscious and unconscious adaptive activity of an organism **3 :** INTENTION, DESIRE **4 :** the normal or healthy condition of the mental faculties **5 :** OPINION, VIEW **6 :** DISPOSITION, MOOD **7 a :** a person or group embodying mental qualities ⟨the public ∼⟩ **b :** intellectual ability **8** *cap*, *Christian Science :* ²GOD **b** : a conscious substratum or factor in the universe
> **²mind** *vt* **1** *chiefly dial :* REMIND **2** *chiefly dial :* REMEMBER **3 :** to attend to closely **4 a :** to become aware of **:** NOTICE **b** *chiefly*

By permission. From *Webster's Seventh New Collegiate Dictionary*, copyright 1965 by G. & C. Merriam Company, Publishers of the Merriam-Webster Dictionaries.

In the example shown you notice that a correct pronunciation is given in parentheses by a diacritical mark over the letter *i,* which shows how this vowel is to be sounded. Different dictionaries list these symbols of pronunciation in different places; in *Webster's Collegiate Dictionary* they will be found inside the front and back covers. The pronunciation of words having consonants whose sounds must be indicated, and of words having silent vowels is shown by phonetic respelling, as, for example, in *rice* (ris). Following the pronunciation entry there is the abbreviation *n.*, which tells us that *mind* is being defined as a noun.

Next there appears in brackets the etymology or origin of the word. The information for *mind* indicates that the word appeared in Middle English (ME), that it was derived from Old English (OE) *gemynd*, and that it is related ultimately to a word in Old High German (OHG) and to words in Latin (L) and Greek (Gk). The series of definitions follows the bracketed etymological information. Notice that the older and more general meanings are entered first, followed by the more recent and more specialized meanings. The last given definitions indicate that the word, capitalized, has a specialized sense in Christian Science.

The second entry of the word is followed by the abbreviation *vt*, indicating that the word is being redefined, this time as a transitive verb. Notice that most meanings in this series are labeled "chiefly dial(ect)." This label indicates that though these meanings were probably once general, they are now limited, for the most part, to a particular geographical area. Notice also that meaning number 8 in this series is followed by a second series of definitions which are preceded by the abbreviation *vi*, indicating that these are meanings in which the verb is intransitive.

The *American College Dictionary* uses a different form of entry.

**ac·a·dem·ic** (ăk/ə dĕm/ĭk), *adj.* **1.** pertaining to an advanced institution of learning, as a college, university, or academy; relating to higher education. **2.** *U.S.* pertaining to the classical, mathematical, and general literary departments of a college or university, as distinguished from the professional and scientific departments. **3.** theoretical; not practical. **4.** conforming to set rules and traditions; conventional. **—n. 5.** a member of a college or university. **—Syn. 4.** See **formal.**
**ac·a·dem·i·cal** (ăk/ə dĕm/ə kəl), *adj.* **1.** academic. **—n. 2.** (*pl.*) cap and gown. **—ac/a·dem/i·cal·ly,** *adv.*
**academic freedom,** freedom of a teacher to discuss social, economic, or political problems without interference from school or public officials.
**a·cad·e·mi·cian** (ə kăd/ə mĭsh/ən, ăk/ə də-), *n.* a member of a society for promoting literature, art, or science.
**ac·a·dem·i·cism** (ăk/ə dĕm/ə sĭz/əm), *n.* traditionalism or conventionalism in art, literature, etc.
**a·cad·e·mism** (ə kăd/ə mĭz/əm), *n.* **1.** academicism. **2.** *Philos.* the doctrines of the school founded by Plato.
**a·cad·e·my** (ə kăd/ə mĭ), *n., pl.* **-mies. 1.** a secondary school, esp. a private one. **2.** a school for instruction in a particular art or science: *a military academy.* **3.** an association or institution for the promotion of literature, science, or art: *the Academy of Arts and Letters.* **4. the Academy, a.** the French Academy. **b.** (in England) the Royal Academy. **c.** the public grove in Athens, in which Plato taught. **d.** the Platonic school of philosophy. [t. L: m.s. *academīa*, t. Gk.: m. *Akadēmeia* (der. *Akádēmos,* an Attic hero)]

Reprinted from *The American College Dictionary,* copyright 1947, copyright © 1966, by permission of Random House, Inc.

Here you will find that the definitions are listed according to "semantic count," which means that those most frequently occurring are listed first. Thus the most common meaning of the adjective "academic" is "pertaining to an advanced institution of learning, or a college, university, or academy; relating to higher education."

Notice that the expression "academic freedom" is listed as a main entry and defined as a phrase. Notice also that the etymology is given in brackets at the end of the principal noun form "academy," rather than immediately after the indication of pronunciation as in *Webster's New Collegiate*. In addition, the *American College Dictionary* provides an etymology key inside the front cover.

It is usually worth while to look closely at the etymological entry. Many words tend to be affected, sometimes only vaguely, but at other times definitely, by their original meanings. A knowledge of a word's derivation, therefore, often proves helpful in following its various senses, and occasionally it may prevent outright misuse. Since the goal of a writer is to develop an ever sharper sense of a word's possibilities, the knowledge provided by etymology cannot be neglected.

**Exercise:** *Study the etymology of each of the words below in an unabridged dictionary. Suggest ways in which a knowledge of the etymology may clarify meaning or lead to a more precise use.*

| | | |
|---|---|---|
| 1. desperate | 11. martyr | 21. technique |
| 2. infant | 12. literally | 22. inculcate |
| 3. ostracism | 13. venereal | 23. anesthetic |
| 4. orthodox | 14. petition | 24. optimism |
| 5. preposterous | 15. holocaust | 25. epicurean |
| 6. precocious | 16. vocation | 26. antediluvian |
| 7. advent | 17. inspire | 27. orientation |
| 8. doctor | 18. expatriate | 28. confidence |
| 9. independence | 19. legislative | 29. petroleum |
| 10. pandemonium | 20. contortion | 30. belligerent |

A dictionary is a ready reference work for many questions of grammar. A number of nouns in English have two plural forms, one of which is in some cases a retained foreign plural. Should one write "stadiums" or "stadia," "criterions" or "criteria"? *Webster's New Collegiate* says that "stadiums" is the correct plural form when the word is used for the modern structures in which athletic contests are held; and that whereas "criteria" is the more common plural form, "criterions" is permissible.

In cases where the past tense of a verb is formed irregularly (that is, when the past tense is *not* formed by the *addition* of -*t*, -*d*, or -*ed*) a dictionary will supply the correct form of the tense. What is the past tense form of "swing"? of "dive"? of "broadcast"? Is there any preference between the forms "got" and "gotten"; between "proved" and "proven"?

In some instances the part of speech label is important in telling how a word may function in sentences. Does standard diction recognize the use of "clean" as an adverb? Does it sanction the use of "military" as a noun, in expressions such as "The military announced a new policy"? What about the possibility of using certain words which are normally prepositions as adjectives, as in "the above sentence" or "the in group"? The information recorded in a dictionary is not a final and binding authority on these matters, but it is a guide to the practices of general usage.

Another resource of a dictionary which is valuable to students is the definition of foreign words and phrases. One seldom reads far in college assignments without encountering an expression from the Latin, French, German, or Italian which is left untranslated because it has become a more or less stock phrase. What is the meaning of *status quo?* Of *habeas corpus?* What is signified by *belles-lettres?* By *fin de siècle?* What is the meaning of *Zeitgeist?* What is a *prima donna?* Some dictionaries have special lists of common foreign words and phrases, but the modern tendency is to select the most important ones and place them with the regular entries.

Remember that a dictionary is a work to be consulted when the need for information arises rather than a work to be studied systematically in the way that one studies a textbook or a treatise. Spending long periods of study over a dictionary is not the best way to increase your vocabulary. What is acquired in this way does not usually last, and sometimes it leads to affectation, as in showing off with new words. A word is not yours until it is part of your working vocabulary, and you do not add words to your working vocabulary in long lists. Words are added one or two at a time when some special occasion creates the need to learn them. You should look upon a dictionary as a record of forms and usages, rather than as a book to be taken in large bites.

## DENOTATION AND CONNOTATION

The philosopher and logician John Stuart Mill was the first to express the two kinds of meaning that most content words have as *denotation* and *connotation*. Denotation is the central meaning which the word must possess; it is the literal core of its reference. When we are using a word denotatively, we are using it in its extensive meaning, which includes abstractly all the members of the class it stands for. Denotation is thus the irreducible meaning of the word's logical definition. Denotatively the word "home" means "any house, apartment, or other shelter which is the fixed residence of a person"—that and nothing more.

Connotation, on the other hand, expresses the intensive meaning of the word; it gives the meaning in depth rather than range. It presents the special attributes or qualities of the idea or object for which the word stands. It may also include the suggested, incidental, or casually acquired meanings. As a consequence of usage, words pick up meanings from their associations, and some of these may be emotional or evaluative. The connotations that a word has acquired may be described as habitual rather than necessary; nonetheless they can be of prime importance for the word's effect.

To continue with our example: the word "home," defined so barely above, is rich in connotations. It suggests security, comfort, a place where we belong and where we can be ourselves. To many it will suggest domestic affections. More concretely, it may bring to mind a favorite armchair, our kind of cooking, and the customs of our household. Anyone seeking to affect our feelings or imagination through the word "home" would certainly be relying upon these connotations.

For a second illustration, let us compare the denotative and connotative meanings of "money." In its purely denotative sense, money is "a medium of exchange and a measure of value." In its connotative sense it means all those things which we associate with the possession of wealth. Upon hearing the phrase "people of money," we are likely to think of fine homes and fine cars, leisure, the opportunity to travel, and the social prestige which in most communities goes with the possession of money. Extensively money may signify only a medium of exchange, but intensively it means the things that money can buy. Here again the associative meanings of a term have much more power to impress us than the strictly logical class reference.

From these contrasts it will be clear that denotative and connotative meanings are adapted to two different functions. Denotative language is often described as the language of science, and properly so, since science is concerned altogether with meanings which can be logically abstracted and defined. Science is interested in what terms *have* to mean because it is only that which a term has to mean—the meaning that is inseparable from it—which can be used in an equation or in the description of a process. It is the aim of science to rid itself of the indefinite, the incidental, and the subjective in its study of the external world; and this fact explains why the ideal language of science is mathematics, which is the purest form of denotation. Scientists sometimes speak of communicating through pure notation, by which they mean communicating through expressions which symbolize the most strictly defined entities and relationships, like the formulas of physics. That the scientist can only be impeded in his work by indefiniteness and distracted by the intrusion of feeling is easily seen. A scientist preparing to use a dog in an experiment is not interested in such peripheral ideas as whether the dog is man's best friend or whether this particular dog has been the faithful guardian of some home; indeed, he will almost certainly work better in the absence of such disturbing considerations. It is enough for him if the dog falls within the logical class of small domesticated quadrupeds, of carnivorous habits, belonging to the genus *canis*. In the same way we might think of situations in which the connotative meanings of "home" and of "money" would be irrelevant and even distracting.

Denotation and connotation therefore represent two vocabularies using the same sets of words. The denotative usage presents the thing in its essential and objective meaning. The connotative usage presents it enriched by associations and feelings which, though not susceptible of being pinned down, are none the less real. To say, furthermore, that we all have use for both denotative and connotative meanings is but to say that we are all both scientists and artists, or that sometimes we work as scientists and sometimes as artists. When we are working as scientists we need a strictly utilitarian language, for we want words to point out, define, and limit precisely. Everyone has some need for this kind of communication. But whenever we wish to make something exciting or vivid, we call upon the resources of connotation and use words as an artist. We are now seeking some kind of effect, and to achieve an effect, we find that we have to draw upon the shadings, the special histories, and even the resonances of words.

Clearly then we have been using denotation and connotation as long as we have been using language; but we are now making an effort to analyze these two different powers of words. As we have seen previously, denotative meaning has a hard nucleus; it is something determined and fixed, and we always know where it is. But connotative meaning has an irregular shape and even an indefinite boundary. It is because connotative meanings cannot be set down in the same way as denotative meanings that we must represent them as something comparatively formless. We can see that the connotations are there, but we cannot be very precise about their extent, and—what is most important—we observe that they have a habit of shifting. We know that words slough off old connotations and acquire new ones, and sometimes this happens in a relatively short period. It has not been long since the word "pious" had connotations of much that is praiseworthy in human character; today in many contexts it has acquired associations of narrowness, unintelligence, and the notion of being out of step with the times. "Honor" at one time had a forceful connotation which had much bearing upon a man's position in society; today in many contexts it seems to have lost most of this connotation.

The number and the changefulness of connotations are probably the principal factors in making real mastery of language a long and difficult achievement. But we must come to sense connotations if we expect to derive the most from language; no one can write with color, force, and persuasiveness without control over connotation. We should remain alert in both listening and reading to see what qualities words are picking up, and where they are tending in meaning and emphasis. Diction learned in this way has a richness and a current applicability that contribute a great deal to writing.

**Exercise:**   *Test your ability to sense connotation by discriminating between the words listed in each group below. Define the different areas of meaning covered and point out emotional loadings or overtones.*

1. teacher, pedagogue, professor, schoolmaster, instructor
2. battle, fight, contest, fracas, scrap
3. profession, business, calling, vocation, job, field of service
4. lazy, slothful, torpid, sluggish, otiose, indolent, idle
5. quick, hasty, sudden, instantaneous, rapid, immediate, prompt
6. strange, odd, unusual, queer, weird, extraordinary
7. respectable, creditable, praiseworthy, meritorious, laudable
8. wisdom, prudence, knowledge, cleverness, astuteness, sagacity
9. astonish, amaze, dumbfound, surprise, flabbergast
10. entertain, divert, amuse, regale, titillate

The study of connotation sharpens our realization that no two words in the English language mean exactly the same thing. At least, no two words are exactly synonymous when we come to the point of actually using them. Sometimes two words will seem so nearly alike in meaning that we think they are interchangeable. We might find it hard to state their difference in meaning; nevertheless we find that they will not serve equally well in every context. Nuances, or shades of meaning which have gathered about them as a result of their special history or their associations, will inevitably give them different capabilities. Such nuances, we now recognize, constitute their connotation. It is these different connotations of synonymous words which prevent them from being completely interchangeable. There is, accordingly, a theoretically best word for every situation, and the skill of the writer is shown by how close he comes to this best one in his search for the suitable word. We may test this principle by looking at a group of synonyms below:

brave, courageous, bold, fearless, intrepid

Perhaps it will seem at first that "brave" and "courageous" are too close in meaning to permit any important distinction. But we find on reflection that "brave" tends to attach itself to the physical type of thing or to the action of the moment, whereas "courageous" is applied freely to non-physical actions and to states of character which are continuing. Thus we do not ordinarily speak of "moral bravery," though we do speak of "moral courage," and although we might characterize a bandit as "brave" we would feel some hesitation over describing him as "courageous," because courage seems to involve some idea of doing the right thing and not mere physical dash. Furthermore, bravery connotes something outward and spectacular, whereas courage has an inward aspect and seems more controlled by thought. These are but a few of the differences we should encounter if we were to try the two words in a variety of contexts.

On the same principle "bold" could not be freely substituted for the others because, although it denotes bravery, it also connotes a kind of forward or pushing quality, or a determination to bring on the issue regardless. A man of evil purpose would hardly be described as "courageous," though he certainly could be described as bold, as in the phrase "the bold robber."

The word "fearless," as its suffix indicates, connotes a kind of negative quality, a state of being without fear, whether for good or bad objects we do not know. Thus "fearless" would seem to apply to an animal, as in "the fearless tiger" better than would either "brave" or "courageous." Fearless means the lack of fear; it does not carry any overtone of moral or intellectual qualifications, except insofar as freedom from fear might imply a moral soundness.

In one dictionary "fearless" appears as meaning "without fear" and intrepid as "without quaking." Since quaking is usually a sign of fear, does this mean that the words are interchangeable? To a degree, yes, but the sensitive user of diction may feel that a choice between the two must consider the fact that the first word comes from the Anglo-Saxon and the second from the Latin (*intrepidus*). This might appear at first a very slight distinction, yet if the level of usage is an important consideration, "intrepid" might better suit the formal level because of this Latinate derivation, and at the very minimum its tone might harmonize better with the literary or learned style. "Fearless" would then be regarded as a more everyday word, but at the same time perhaps as a word of more forceful assertion.

Good writing requires a constant sorting out of these possibilities, and some occasional experimentation with words in a given context, since few of us always think of the best word the first time we try. We sift through our vocabulary until we find the one whose denotation and connotation seem to combine for the right effect.

Exercise:   *In the series below, choose the word or expression in parentheses which is most closely synonymous with the word underlined in the sentence preceding.*

1. The speaker's remark was entirely apposite. (foolish, fitting, irrelevant, unintelligible, to the point)

2. Prizes will be awarded annually for proficiency. (skill, efficiency, industry, initiative, competence, success)

3. The date for the ceremony was left tentative. (indefinite, undecided, provisional, uncertain, contingent)

4. The well dressed guest seemed strangely diffident. (indifferent, shy, fearful, evasive, embarrassed)

5. The world often seems to set a higher value on prudence than on wisdom. (knowledge, cleverness, expertness, sharpness, practicality, sagacity)

6. Many causes have been suggested to explain the deterioration of moral standards in Roman society. (degeneration, decadence, lowering, decline, decay)

7. The letter was ill written, but it was sincere. (candid, simple, honest, guileless, frank, plain)

8. The furnishings of the stateroom were <u>lavish.</u> (expensive, extravagant, sumptuous, profuse, luxurious, plentiful)

9. In combat an army is no better than its <u>morale.</u> (devotion, spirit, enthusiasm, morality, loyalty, patriotism)

10. The affairs of the nation had now reached a <u>crucial</u> point. (dangerous, decisive, critical, ticklish, difficult, delicate)

# ABSTRACT AND CONCRETE DICTION

For general effectiveness in writing and for stylistic appeal, probably no matter of diction is more important than the difference between the abstract and the concrete word. This difference may be characterized, in a rough way, as the difference between the general and the specific; and it will be seen that just as we require both the denotative and the connotative powers of language, so we require both abstract and concrete words. But everything depends upon an understanding of where each is most useful.

The abstract word is general in the sense that it is broad in coverage, devoid of specific detail, and seldom if ever connected with the memory of sensory experience. The word "justice" is such a term. If we suddenly see or hear the word "justice," it is most unlikely that we will form a picture in mind. We have to think out the content of such a word through a reasoning process. It expresses an *idea* rather than a *perception*.

The concrete word is of opposite quality; it is narrow in the sense of focusing upon some definite thing. It thereby permits detail, and it will usually be found rather closely connected with the memory of some sensory event. The word "blood" may serve as an example of this kind of word. Hearing it, we almost certainly think of something we have seen, or felt, or tasted. "Blood" thus appears sensory and image-bearing. It re-creates in our minds part of the world of experience.

In summary, the tendency of the abstract word is to be conceptual; the tendency of the concrete word is to be sensory. In this difference we can discover our guide to the proper use of them.

To the extent that we are all reasoning beings, we need to communicate through concepts, and for this purpose the abstract term, which is a kind of "portmanteau" word, is indispensable. It has the capacity to enclose a lot of things which we need to handle as a unit and to permit us to speak of them without specific or individual mention. Thus we may all need to talk about "fruit" or "furniture" or "business" or "the nation's affairs" without breaking these down into the specific items which actually compose them.

This necessity, however, is only half of the story. If it is true that we are compelled logically to employ these concept-bearing words, it is equally true that we are psychologically compelled to use the specific or image-bearing word, which might be in these instances "tangerine" or "red leather armchair" or "retail advertising," or "soil conservation." We say this is psychologically necessary because it is the nature of the human mind to crave the specific, the actual detail. It is probably true that education trains us to be more at home with the abstract and the conceptual and to handle such concepts with greater ease and preciseness, but this fact never overcomes entirely our native liking for the concrete and the particular. Even those minds which are most accustomed to abstraction will eventually grow weary of purely abstract discourse, and will look for the oasis of an image or a concrete circumstance. It is probably this which causes the general, if unfortunate, preference for the tabloid newspaper and the comic strip. Whether or not this natural appetite for the concrete is a weakness is hardly a question for us to settle here: our concern is that it confronts the student of rhetoric with an important fact and calls attention to ways in which he can achieve his ends.

Before carrying the discussion further, however, we must forestall any impression that the total vocabulary of English is divided into abstract terms and concrete terms and that any word can be placed absolutely in one or the other category. The truth is that abstractness and concreteness are relative concepts, and that many groups of terms can be arranged on a scale running from the highly abstract to the highly concrete. A useful way to picture this range is to think of a ladder, each step of which represents a word. Then suppose that the steps near the ground are relatively concrete words and those near the top are relatively abstract ones. We can move freely up and down this ladder, but we need to realize that the higher we move up, the more abstract our vocabulary is, and the more we descend, the more concrete it is. Let us try descending from a very abstract expression to a very concrete one. The abstract expression will include the concrete one in its meaning or coverage, but it will not suggest any of its concreteness or particularity. We might then have an order like the following:

1. a thing
2. an instrument
3. a weapon
4. a firearm
5. a pistol
6. a .32 caliber revolver

In like manner we can begin with the most concrete term in a series and ascend to the most abstract one.

1. a 1960 Chevrolet sedan
2. a passenger automobile
3. a motorcar
4. a vehicle
5. a conveyance

A "thing" may be anything; the class "instrument" has a large number of members, many of which are harmless. "Weapon" narrows it down by introducing the idea of what the "instrument" is for. "Firearm" is a particular kind of weapon; a pistol is a particular kind of firearm; and a .32 caliber revolver is a particular type of pistol. We could narrow it down even further and particularize it as "a Smith and Wesson .32 caliber revolver."

The question of from which end of the ladder we wish to draw our terms can be answered only through reference to our purpose. If we wish to produce writing which is vivid, animated, and moving, we shall certainly have to draw liberally from the concrete end. Nearly all good descriptive and narrative discourse makes extensive use of concrete diction, and the reason is easy to find. If we read, "The escaped 22-year-old prisoner was carrying a .32 caliber revolver," we can furnish in our minds an approximate picture of what the terms signify, whereas such a sentence as "The man had a weapon" conveys comparatively little. The terms in the first sentence are definite, and the chances are that they will recall something that we have seen either in our own experience or in pictures.

These advantages of concrete diction do not mean that it is appropriate to every purpose or that it is always the most effective kind of diction. We sometimes need to write on a level of abstraction, as when we are classifying, generalizing, or narrating something on a large scale. There are contexts in which the sentence "People arrived at the fair in every sort of conveyance" would be the best form of expression just because "conveyance" includes a wide variety of means of travel, which the sentence is undoubtedly intended to suggest. Similarly the sentence "The troops laid down their weapons" needs the generic term "weapons" rather than the more specific term "rifles" because the soldiers are, presumably, equipped with a number of kinds of weapons. In the paragraph below James Burnham is presenting a generalized description of capitalism with reference to its production of commodities. Notice that no specific commodity is named and no individual transaction is described. The aim is not to particularize or to visualize. Abstract words describing generalized actions fulfill the need of this broad description.

All societies, except the most primitive, have produced *some* of their goods as commodities. But in every society except the capitalist, and very notably in the feudal society which preceded the capitalist, commodities have made up a very small segment of the total production. In the first place, in other societies by far the greater proportion of goods was produced for use by the immediate producers, did not enter into exchange at all, and therefore had no occasion for functioning as commodities. You cannot eat or wear exchange value or money; not the price of goods but the qualities that enable them to satisfy specific needs are all that enters into subsistence production. But even where goods entered into exchange in other societies, again notably in the feudal society, they ordinarily did not do so as commodities. Exchange for the most part in the Middle Ages was not for money or through the intermediary of money but *in kind;* and there, too, what interested the buying or selling peasant was not the price he could get or would have to pay but whether he had a surplus of one kind of goods capable of satisfying one kind of need that he could trade for something else satisfying some other need.

—James Burnham, *The Managerial Revolution*

We may follow this with a passage whose purpose calls for a far more concrete level of diction. In the paragraph below John Gould Fletcher is writing about the Ozark mountaineers of his native Arkansas. His purpose is to visualize them, their way of life and their character. The specific details and even the proper names contribute to this end. His opening assertion that the region is unique tells us that we are going to get something specific—a description of a particular type in a concrete setting.

This region is unique in yet another way. Circumstances made of the inhabitant of the Ozarks—and the inhabitant of the Ouachitas differed from him in no way except that he lived in still greater isolation—not alone a mountaineer, but still more, a frontiersman facing the semi-civilized Indian Territory. Up to about fifty years ago, well within the lifetime of persons now living, the Ozarker was self-contained and self-dependent. He ground his own corn. His women spun their own thread, made their own clothes. He distilled his own whiskey. Crude furniture was made by whittling, and chairs were seated with twisted withes of willow or un-tanned ox hides. Houses were built by unskilled labor; and I have seen and spent hours in a four-room log cabin—with two massive stone chimneys—built by unskilled mountaineers as late as 1932. Bedspread coverlets there were elaborately made out of patchwork pieces, or woven; and many days in the year were spent in the woods near by, recruiting the scanty larder with squirrels, rabbits, deer, or possums. The life of the Ozarks was wild and primitive, but it was not without its savor. The proximity of the In-dian Territory—it must be remembered that the Cherokee Strip was not opened to settlers before 1889—and the scarcity of all settlements served not only to preserve old mountaineer traditions brought from Tennessee or the Carolinas, but to intensify the frontier type. It is not too much to say that the Ozarker was, if not himself an outlaw, at least in sympathy with the outlaw breed. His favorite heroes had all a strong touch of Jesse James about them and were good men with a gun.

—John Gould Fletcher, *Arkansas*

As these selections illustrate, the writer's true aim is to find the right level of specificity for the writing task he has in hand. If he is dealing with concepts, his level will be relatively abstract. If he is dealing with people in the flesh, with actual events, or with specific things, it must be relatively concrete.

**Exercise:**   *Arrange each of the sequences below in an order from the most abstract to the most concrete.*

1. a) animal   b) organism   c) Pekingese   d) dog
2. a) action   b) crime   c) homicide   d) murder
3. a) book   b) publication   c) literature   d) novel   e) *The Scarlet Letter*
4. a) money   b) funds   c) possessions   d) twenty dollars
5. a) musician   b) pianist   c) artist
6. a) traffic officer   b) officer of the law   c) policeman   d) official
7. a) food   b) pie   c) nutriment   d) pastry   e) apple tart
8. a) clothes   b) suit   c) garb   d) tuxedo
9. a) cooking vessel   b) stew pan   c) kitchenware   d) utensil
10. a) spinach   b) greens   c) produce   d) vegetable

Not all writing which is effective for its purpose is abstract or concrete, for there are some types of writing which demand a balance of the two qualities. It is entirely possible to develop an idea by giving at the same time its abstract aspect and one or more of its concrete aspects. A look at Shakespeare's method, for example, will show that he often pairs abstract and concrete expressions of the same thing—the one giving the ideological character of the object or deed, and the other its appearance, or the way it is observable by the senses.

> *Queen:* O, what a rash and *bloody* deed is this!
> > —*Hamlet*, III, iv, 27
>
> *Othello.* Farewell to the *plumed troop,* and the big wars,
>   That makes ambition virtue,
> > —*Othello*, III, iii, 349–50
>
> *Lear:* Of all these bounds, even from this line to this,
>   With *shadowy forests* and with *champains rich'd,*
>   With *plenteous rivers* and *wide-skirted meads,*
>   We make thee lady.
> > —*King Lear*, I, i, 64–67

In these passages the concrete expressions have been italicized. They are accompanied by abstract expressions which give a more conceptual idea of the same thing. Almost needless to say, an expression using both of these levels at once is usually rich.

It is arguable that in poetry there is a special need for concreteness, and that the use of the concrete modifier or substantive in this medium offers no lesson to the writer of prose. Yet the principle involved is the same, and the prose writer can profit by a balancing of the two qualities. The happy effect of such balance may be particularly seen in passages of difficult exposition, where the concrete word or metaphor is needed to compensate for a "dry" but necessary analysis of ideas. In the passage below, note the skillful employment of the two types of diction to make ideas both clear and vivid.

> Democracy is often mentioned in the same breath with liberty, as if they meant the same thing; and both are sometimes identified with the sort of elective government which prevails in Great Britain and the United States. But just as English liberty seems servitude to some people because

it requires them to cooperate, to submit to the majority, and to grow like them, so English democracy seems tyranny to the wayward masses, because it is constitutional, historical, and sacred, narrowing down the power of any group of people at any time to voting for one or two or three candidates for office, or to saying yes or no to some specific proposal—both the proposals and the candidates being set before them by an invisible agency; and fate was never more inexorable or blinder than is the grinding of this ponderous political mill, where routine, nepotism, pique, and swagger, with the love of office and money, turn all the wheels. And the worst of it is that the revolutionary parties that oppose this historical machine repeat all its abuses, or even aggravate them. It would be well if the people in England and America woke up to the fact that it is in the name of natural liberty and direct democracy that enemies both within and without are already rising up against both their democracy and their liberty. Just as the Papacy once threatened English liberties, because it would maintain one inflexible international religion over all men, so now an international democracy of the disinherited many, led by the disinherited few, threatens English liberties again, since it would abolish those private interests which are the factors in any cooperation, and would reduce everybody to forced membership and forced labor in one universal flock, without property, family, country, or religion. That life under such a system might have its comforts, its arts, and its atomic liberties, is certain, just as under the Catholic system it had its virtues and consolations; but both systems presuppose the universality of a type of human nature which is not English, and perhaps not human.

> —George Santayana, "English Liberty in America," from
> *Character and Opinion in the United States*

It is a general rule that all writing which is reflective has a fair proportion of the conceptual, and that all writing which impresses us as eloquent has much of the concrete. Since there may be occasions on which we will wish to be both reflective and eloquent, a combination of the two elements, as in the passage considered above, is the aim to be sought. Santayana, a philosopher, can write movingly about ideas because he is ever ready with a concrete word or a fresh metaphor. Likewise T. H. Huxley, a scientist, can write about concrete objects in a way to impress us with the implications of science because he is willing to touch upon the large ideas which they involve.

# FIGURATIVE LANGUAGE

## Importance of Figurative Language

Figures of speech, which may be described as non-literal ways of rendering meaning, are a peculiarly important part of diction. Some students of language go so far as to say that there is no completely literal speech because all language is basically metaphorical. They maintain that all language was born through some process of comparing one thing with another. Without arguing for the correctness of this theory, we can see by looking at everyday utterances that many expressions depend for their meaning upon something other than the thing being symbolized. All metaphor is a kind of transference, by which the meaning or appearance of one thing is imaginatively ascribed to some other thing. If one speaks of "a leg of the table," or "an arm of the sea," or "a shoulder of the mountain," one is evidently describing one object through reference to another, and these illustrate the process of all metaphor. There are other expressions in which the metaphor, or use of transferred meaning, is none the less real though not so immediately apparent. Thus if one refers to "the depth of winter" or says that he has been "in touch with a friend," he expresses an idea which might have been literal in its origin, but which is bodied forth in an image as soon as one gets around to expressing it.

In nearly all situations where we need to communicate vividly, we do not look for the literal means of expression; we look in the opposite direction, as the work of sports writers, orators, and poets will prove. The fact that the ordinary man who is trying to be effective in prose makes extensive use of figures of speech is good proof that they are a prime source of expressiveness. Nor is this true only of writing; the discourse of the ordinary citizen in his moments of business and pleasure makes the freest use of them. He may not know that he is using metaphors, but if all metaphors were removed from his speech, he would see a very great difference.

No one has better expressed the indispensability of metaphor to the average person than Louis Untermeyer.

> Even while he scorns poetry, the ordinary man helps himself to its properties and symbols; his daily life is unthinkable without metaphor. Having "slept like a log," he gets up in the morning "fresh as a daisy" or "fit as a fiddle"; he "wolfs down" breakfast, "hungry as a bear," with his wife, who has "a tongue like vinegar," but "a heart of gold." He gets into his car, which "eats up the miles," "steps on the gas," and, as it "purrs" along through the "hum" of traffic, he reaches his office where he is "as busy as a one-armed paper hanger with the hives." Life, for the average man, is not "a bed of roses," his competitor is "sly as a fox" and his own clerks are "slow as molasses in January." But "the day's grind" is finally done and, though it is "raining cats and dogs," he arrives home "happy as a lark."
>
> —Louis Untermeyer, "Play in Poetry"

## Faulty Metaphor

This passage is not an example of very good and certainly not of very fresh metaphor, but it does serve to show that the ordinary citizen is helplessly dependent upon figures of speech when he wants to describe something vividly or give vent to his feelings. The fault of this particular set of metaphors is that they are all badly worn. When trite metaphors are used, the very purpose of figurative language is defeated. We employ metaphors because we want our expression to be fresh, original, and vivid. These effects can be secured only by figures that retain their power to excite the imagination. We must, consequently, avoid those figures which have become dull through overuse. A stale figure of speech fails to sharpen our perception of a thing or its relationships. Metaphors tend to pass into a kind of thoughtless, uncritical currency with which it is impossible to achieve forceful expression. No one who hopes to write as an alert person with some power of original expression will use such recognizably outworn figures as those in the following list:

| | |
|---|---|
| pretty as a picture | heavy as lead |
| sober as a judge | light as a feather |
| innocent as a baby | blind as a bat |
| fast as lightning | hard as a rock |
| hot as Hades | sweet as sugar |
| tight as a drum | like water off a duck's back |

On balance, it probably would be better to avoid the use of metaphor, in spite of all that metaphorical language has to contribute, than to use metaphors that have a deadening effect upon expression. The metaphors listed above might on occasion be restored to freshness by special treatment that would renew some of their vitality. There is probably no such thing as a completely dead metaphor. The man who said "hot as the hinges of hell" instead of "hot as hell" was refurbishing the metaphor by making us think why the hinges of hell should be especially hot. Opportunities for this kind of revision, however, are limited. The best plan is to avoid the dead metaphor. Anyone using metaphors as worn as those in the list above would certainly be regarded as a bore. He would miss the successful writer's effect, which is a live and continuing response in his reader. The best plan is to seek out the fresh comparison, even at the cost of giving up easier and cheaper ways of expressing yourself. One of the things that makes Shakespeare an enduring classic is that he never falls into routine metaphors. He always finds the new, the original, or even the unexpected combination. And though you are not writing in imitation of Shakespeare, the same source of strength is there for your use.

The next important rule is to avoid the mixed metaphor. Metaphors are said to be mixed when one comparison is dropped before its completion and another is substituted. The writer does not really conclude what he had to say with the first. In the worst cases of mixed metaphor, three or four will be run together in a figure that collapses from the weight of incongruity. Of course, no metaphor consists of a complete point-by-point comparison between things; metaphor depends for its very existence upon a certain amount of contrast or dissimilarity between the two things involved. But the reader needs to see that the objects do have a significant amount of similarity. The mixed metaphor does not allow us to see this. Generally speaking, a metaphor is forceful in proportion as it can be prolonged and made to show a series of resemblances between the two things brought together.

The newspaper editor who wrote, "Communism is the snake in the grass which is gnawing at the foundations of our ship of state" was unaware of the perils of mixed metaphor. He began with one figure which is quite possible, the comparison of communism to a snake in the grass. As far as the requirements of rhetoric go, this is well enough; but once having likened communism to a snake in the grass, the writer was under obligation to make it behave as a snake. Instead of this, however, he has the snake gnawing at foundations, and snakes do not act in this way. Unthinkingly, he was bringing in a different concept, perhaps that of termites or rats, which do gnaw at certain kinds of foundations. This concept, however, begins another figure. Moreover, he refers to the "foundations" of our ship of state; and ships do not, in ordinary language, have foundations; they have keels or bottoms. In this part the writer was evidently not thinking about a ship at all but about a building, which does have a foundation and which might be threatened by termites. The worst incongruity comes, however, when we realize that the ship is being attacked by a snake which is in the grass. A ship which can be attacked by a snake in the grass is presumably already wrecked or beached, and we think of our ship of state as steering a bold course on the high seas. The ludicrous result of the metaphor comes from the writer's failure to follow boldly and imaginatively the implications of his original figure of the snake in the grass. Instead of using this for whatever it might prove, he ran in three other images, all of which clash with the first. The metaphor therefore instead of contributing force to the writing provokes amusement and leaves the net effect worse than if no metaphor at all had been used. The consequence of any mixed metaphor is that people usually laugh at you rather than with you. They are not gripped by your image but find it funny. Although there has been discussion among scholars as to whether Shakespeare does not use mixed metaphors in some of the great speeches of his characters, it is safe to say that he never mixes them in the loose and disconcerting fashion we have been analyzing.

**Exercise:** *From the point of view of consistency, criticize the figures of speech appearing in the passages below.*

1. "The American people as a whole must now realize that they are the ones who make the climate of opinion and that they must come to the defense of our public schools and of our institutions of higher learning," declared Mrs. Meyer. "For the independence of our whole educational system will be jeopardized if Velde, Jenner, and McCarthy are not stopped in their tracks before they get under full sail."
   —From a dispatch to The New York *Times*

2. Although the Irish began at the bottom of the social ladder, they have now achieved a niche in the backbone of the nation.
3. By rising above all his contemporaries, he left footprints in the sands of time.
4. Ronald often hatched new ideas and used them to open doors of opportunity.
5. The President rode into office on the laurels of his success as a soldier.
6. Taking the new angle Mr. Brown had furnished, he used it as the thread of his story.
7. He had much experience, and he was able to meet the slings and arrows of outrageous fortune with a broad viewpoint.

## Functions of Metaphor

We now turn to the specific things that metaphors can do, or the various ways in which you can use metaphor to advantage. All metaphor is comparison, but comparisons are made for different purposes and with different degrees of insight and grasp of the subject matter. Some uses of metaphor have only a limited contribution to make; others do more than you may realize. There are four main opportunities in the use of the broad resources of figurative language.

### Giving Concreteness

One can readily discover that much metaphor is used in the interests of concreteness. We touched upon this earlier when we pointed out that figures of speech often bring prose to life. Metaphor by its very nature conveys to the mind an image, and an image is of something concrete. In most cases, indeed, we would not think of using a metaphor unless we felt that the idea or object introduced for the comparison had at least a superior vividness. Some subjects are by their nature dry and colorless; some writing deals with relationships which have to be intellectually conceived. A touch of metaphor now and then, if it does nothing else, will add that element of color which the mind's eye craves. General, concept-bearing words need to be atoned for by words that bring us back to earth. When at the close of his forceful argument on the relationship of virtue and knowledge John Henry Newman says: "Quarry the granite rock with razors or moor the vessel with a thread of silk; then may you hope with such keen and delicate instruments as human knowledge and human reason to contend against those giants the passion and the pride of man," we feel that his eloquence has reached a new height through the use of these pictures. What was ideational only, for a moment takes on shape and color, and our response is one of gratification that the author has highlighted his idea for us.

As the ancient teachers of the subject pointed out, one of the objects of rhetoric is actualization. A good figure of speech is among the best means to actualize an idea, scene, or action.

### Clarifying the Unknown

A second function of metaphor is to make clear, not in the sense of simply rendering something more vivid but in that of aiding our understanding. A basic value of all analogy is that we can communicate meaning by comparing something that is less well known to something that is known. This allows the reader to see, to a helpful extent, the one in terms of the other. This kind of metaphor is most useful when we face the necessity of visualizing something with which we have no previous acquaintance, or a very slight one. The metaphor fills out the picture. Historical accounts of the Battle of Gettysburg have compared the series of ridges held by the Federal army to a question mark turned upside down, to convey an idea of the shape of this position. To explain the structure of the atom, writers on physics have drawn comparisons with our solar system, with the sun at the center and the planets revolving around it. Sometimes metaphors which have the function of elucidating are quite prolonged, so that they constitute in effect extended analogies. When Plato undertakes to set forth in *The Republic* the true nature of education, he employs a figure of human beings in a cave, perceiving dimly at first, but as they are led out of the cave growing able to see by the light of the noonday sun. Thoreau, in a now famous passage, compared Cape Cod and Massachusetts to parts of the human figure.

> Cape Cod is the bared and bended arm of Massachusetts: the shoulder is at Buzzard's Bay; the elbow, or crazy-bone at Cape Mallebarre; the wrist at Truro; and the sandy fist at Provincetown—behind which the State stands on her guard, with her back to the Green Mountains, and her feet planted on the floor of the ocean, like an athlete protecting her Bay— boxing with the northeast storms, and, ever and anon, heaving up her Atlantic adversary from the lap of the earth—ready to thrust forward her other fist, which keeps guard the while upon her breast at Cape Ann.
>
> —Henry David Thoreau, *Cape Cod*

Sidney Lanier gave an insight into the war spirit by comparing it with a powerful wind.

> An afflatus of war was breathed upon us. Like a great wind, it drew on and blew upon men, women, and children. Its sound mingled with the solemnity of the church organs and arose with the earnest words of preachers praying for divine guidance in the matter. It sighed in the half-breathed words of sweethearts conditioning impatient lovers with war services. It thundered splendidly in the impassioned appeals of orators to the people. It whistled through the streets, it stole into the firesides, it clinked glasses in bar-rooms, it lifted the gray hair of our wise men in conventions, it thrilled through the lectures in college halls, it rustled the thumbed book-leaves of the school-rooms.

This wind blew upon all the vanes of all the churches in the country, and turned them one way—toward war.

—Sidney Lanier, *Tiger-lilies*

These metaphors are primarily expository in that their purpose is to make us see something in greater detail. They take what is known in a general way, or half known, and make it fuller or more explicit. They communicate something more to the understanding than did the original expression.

### Expressing the Subjective

The third function of metaphor goes beyond making a subject concrete or clarifying its details; in this third use the metaphor is an indispensable means of statement. To emphasize the importance of such use, we can say that there are certain subjects which, without metaphor, would never get expressed at all, or at least would never get expressed in language. An obvious class of such things is our subjective feelings. The subjective realm forms a very large part of our existence, and much of our expression is devoted to telling others how we feel about matters. Yet most feelings defy direct or literal rendering. Because they are subjective, they have to be described through other things, or through the process of transference which is metaphor. Metaphor is particularly a vehicle for giving expression to our feelings of delight, surprise, elation, frustration, and so forth. A few simple illustrations will show the indispensability of a figure of speech when what we want to convey is a sentiment. A person who finds that he is in a situation where he does not belong will say that he feels "like a fish out of water," and no better way occurs to him of expressing the subjective reality which is his sense of not belonging. A man after a good night's rest may exclaim that he feels "like a million dollars." Another man says that he is "on top of the world" when he gets the girl or the job that he wanted. Although none of these figures have the quality of freshness because of their long use, they do show how natural it is for us to call upon metaphor to express what exists in the form of feeling. And when a poet or anyone gifted in metaphorical speech uses a figure for this end, we may get something very brilliant. For example, Vachel Lindsay wrote:

> My heart is a kicking horse
> Shod with Kentucky steel.

This describes a feeling of excitement and tumult; the heart is likened to a high-spirited Kentucky race horse, rearing and kicking, and the suggestion of the steel-shod hoofs connotes the sharp pain of such an experience. Few of us will be able to approach this level of felicity, nor do we need to on ordinary occasions. It is enough for us to bear in mind that generally feelings have to be expressed through an objective correlative—through something from the outer world that will bear an illuminating comparison with them, whether that be a race horse, a skyrocket, the moon, a flower, a gem, or whatever has the right suggestibility.

**Exercise:** *Each of the following metaphors is concerned primarily with a feeling about something. Try to state in other language what that feeling is.*

1. A jungle of innumerable trees and dangling creepers—it was in this form that parties always presented themselves to Walter Bidlake's imagination. A jungle of noise, and he was lost in the jungle, he was trying to clear a path for himself through its tangled luxuriance. The people were the roots of the trees and their voices were the stems and waving branches and festooned lianas—yes, and the parrots and the chattering monkeys as well.

   —Aldous Huxley, *Point Counter Point*

2. The aspect of the venerable mansion has always affected me like a human countenance, bearing the traces not merely of outward storm and sunshine, but expressive, also, of the long lapse of mortal life, and accompanying vicissitudes that have passed within.

   —Nathaniel Hawthorne, *The House of Seven Gables*

3. New York is a resplendent city. Its high white towers are arrows of will: its streets are the plowings of passionate desire. A lofty, arrogant, lustful city, beaten through by an iron rhythm. But the men and women who have made this city and whose place it is, are lowly, are driven, are drab. Their feet shuffle, their voices are shrill, their eyes do not shine. They are different indeed from their superb creation. Life that should electrify their bodies, quicken them with high movement and high desire is gone from them. And if you seek that life, look to the flashing steel and stone that stands above them, look to the fierce beat of their material affairs. America is the extraverted land. New York is its climax. Here the outside world has taken to itself a soul—a towering, childish soul: and the millions of human sources are sucked void.

   —Waldo Frank, *Our America*

4. The immense accretion of flesh which had descended on her in middle life like a flood of lava on a doomed city had changed her from a plump active little woman with a neatly turned foot and ankle into something as vast and august as a natural phenomenon. She had accepted this submergence as philosophically as all her other trials, and now, in extreme old age, was rewarded by presenting to her mirror an almost unwrinkled expanse of firm and pink white flesh, in the center of which the traces of a small face survived as if awaiting excavation.

   —Edith Wharton, *The Age of Innocence*

5. Perhaps I had a little fever too. One can't live with one's finger everlastingly on one's pulse. I had often 'a little fever,' or a touch of other things—the playful paw-strokes of the wilderness, the preliminary trifling before the more serious onslaught which came in due course.

   —Joseph Conrad, *Heart of Darkness*

## Assisting Thought

A final and a most interesting function of metaphor is its heuristic (from the Greek *heuriskein,* "to find, discover") use. Some metaphors do not merely express their subjects, but shed additional light upon them or explore them further. Used in this way, a metaphor can actually be a bridge to discovery. The comparison, by calling attention to certain resemblances, points the way to finding still other resemblances. This function of metaphor has had an important role even in science, for science has increasingly recognized that some facts of the physical universe can be dealt with only in accordance with other things which they resemble. This amounts to saying that if we *picture* the thing somehow, the picture is about as close as we can get to understanding what it is. Furthermore, the picture will enable us to find out more about it and perhaps in some measure to control it. Thus metaphor becomes intimately bound up with the process of knowing and of further inquiry. The idea that the universe is permeated by an "ether," although no longer regarded as literally true, was a metaphor which gave some known facts a coherency, or allowed their interrelationship to be understood. Certain scientists have been willing to speak of the wave theory of light or the corpuscular theory of light. Light may really be made up neither of waves nor of corpuscles, yet picturing it in one of these fashions enables the scientist to work with it and perform experiments with it in ways that would be impossible without the concept lent by the metaphor. Much of the progress of modern physics seems to depend on finding metaphors or analogies like these, which enable us to conceive of the world in new ways. In many cases they become necessary after some work of observation and experimentation has been done.

Heuristic metaphor has been equally fruitful in social and political thinking. Even in such areas, where the metaphor does not exactly "prove" anything or establish any great degree of likelihood, it may yield one or more genuine insights into the subject. Here general conclusions are bound to be much more controversial; yet the comparison of the state to the fabled beast leviathan, and the attempt to get at the secret of civilizations by comparing their life courses to that of an organism, while they may not yield results that are precisely "so," can nonetheless give illuminating sidelights.

Descending to a more everyday level, we should realize that those innocent-looking metaphors which we use in daily discourse (and which we scarcely distinguish from literal language) may have the potentiality of opening up their subjects, so that we can learn something from them by following them out. We speak of "the fire of ambition," of "the voyage of life," of "the integration of the personality." It is worthwhile to take the metaphor comprising each of these and see whether we can find additional resemblances which increase our understanding of what is signified by the figure. After we have given it some thought, does "ambition" resemble a fire in more ways than we were first aware? A reflective study of such metaphors may be the means to a fuller appreciation of the moral, political, and social world in which we live.

Metaphor lies very close to the creative power of speech, and this creative power is the cause of our peculiarly human dominion of the world. Whether you think about metaphors with the passive object of understanding, or use them with the active object of giving life and meaning to your expression, you will find them to be a most rewarding resource of language.

**Exercise:** *Do the following metaphors open up their subjects by saying more about them than a literal statement possibly could? Are they productive of new ideas of the nature and relationships of their subjects? Decide whether what they say amounts in any sense to a discovery.*

1. In crepeth age alwey, as stille as stoon.

      —Chaucer, *Clerk's Tale*

2. We make an idol of truth itself, whereas truth without charity is not God but his image and an idol.

      —Montaigne

3. The war had divided the people of Kentucky as the false mother would have served the child.

      —James Lane Allen, *Flute and Violin
      and Other Kentucky Tales*

4. Writing a novel is as solemn a business to him as trimming a beard is to a German barber.

      —H. L. Mencken, "Theodore Dreiser"

5. Certainly it is true that the stairway of history "is forever echoing with the wooden shoe going up, the polished boot descending."

      —Peter Viereck, *Conservatism Revisited*

6. Newport was a summer capital. A seaside resort could be more strictly controlled than a great city like New York. And here society's high command laid out the winter campaigns, sitting in open conclave on the Casino terrace, white gloves to the elbow, with parasols and enormous flopping feather hats, lace at the wrists and throats. Laces dragged behind them when they rose. Battles were prepared that would not be actively fought for months. In the evening, intent on strategy, down the great staircases the petticoats trailed, circled with cupids strumming lyres of pure gold, embroidered in true-love knots and seed-pearl doves. It was still August, but the snobbish massacres of December had already been decided.

      —John Peale Bishop, "Newport and the Robber Baronesses"

7. When he tried to think of the future he was like some blundering insect that tries, again and again, to climb up the smooth wall of a dish into which it has fallen.

—Robert Penn Warren, *Night Rider*

8. But Kennerly had gone astray somewhere: he had overdone it; he wore the harried air of a man on the edge of bankruptcy, keeping up an expensive establishment because he dared not retrench. His nerves were bundles of dried twigs, they jabbed his insides every time a thought stirred in his head, they kept his blank blue eyes fixed in a white stare.

—Katherine Anne Porter, "Hacienda," from *Flowering Judas*

## JARGON

The great danger for many writers today is a tendency to succumb to jargon. Jargon has been described by one authority as a "degenerative disease" which is attacking wide areas of modern expression. This metaphor is illuminating, because jargon has the effect of impairing communication and sapping vitality.

Literally it may be defined as a vague, abstract, and usually wordy kind of writing which looks on the surface as though it were saying a great deal whereas in actuality it is saying little or nothing. It uses a vocabulary which suggests learning and authority, and its often complicated sentence structure may make one feel that here is a really resourceful writer. But when one begins to examine the matter for precise content, one discovers that its impressiveness is largely façade. Let us inspect the specimen given below.

> The word poverty is commonly used so indefinitely that any analysis of it necessarily compels a preliminary statement of what is meant thereby. It would seem that it is nothing more nor less than a comparative social condition depending upon relative control over economic goods, the standard of comparison being a social group possessing a maximum of such control, called the rich or wealthy. All who are not so distinguished constitute the poor and to their social condition the noun poverty may be applied. This class, however, comprises a hierarchy of sub-classes each possessing a lesser degree of control over the wealth of its age than the one immediately preceding. Both of the primary as well as the subgroups comprehended in the poor are characterized, also, by distinctive social attitudes and a close similarity to the corporation in that they are continuous associations of men whose personnel is continually changing through members of lower groups being elevated into the higher and vice versa.

This is offered as a definition of poverty by a social scientist. Even after we grant that the concept is not easy to define, there seems to be little excuse for the obfuscation in this paragraph. At the very beginning, the language used by the writer leaves us confused as to whether he is going to analyze poverty as a word or as a concept. The defining of a word as a word is obviously a task for the lexicographer; this writer is going to talk about the specific meaning which the concept has or should have for social science. He ought to have foreseen this ambiguity and stated his purpose clearly. The phrase "necessarily compels" is redundant, for what is compulsive is already necessary. This is mere multiplication of words. "What is meant thereby" is an awkward and wordy passive construction; furthermore, it is superfluous. The writer would have said all that is needful had he written his sentence: "The word poverty is often used so indefinitely that any analysis of its meaning for social science compels a preliminary statement."

In the second sentence "It would seem" and "neither more nor less" are needless qualifiers. They do nothing but encumber, since the reader understands that the writer is going to frame his definition according to his best knowledge and judgment. The qualifiers that are needed should appear in the terms of the definition itself. The remainder of this sentence may be passed over as fairly clear, if still capable of condensation.

The third sentence, however, raises serious doubts as to whether the writer has said what he intended. Does he really mean to say that all who are not rich are poor? This statement may represent a failure in his original analysis. But if this is what he means, there is need for explanation. Moreover, what is his reason for saying that the term "poverty" refers to a social rather than an economic condition? It is usually understood as having economic meaning. There is a real possibility that this sentence contains a concealed assumption that economic classes *are* social classes. Because this assumption is at least controversial, the author should make his position clear. One of the most serious limitations of jargon is its tendency to obscure debatable points in a cloud of wordiness.

The fourth sentence is acceptable, although it might have been clearer if the author had written at the end "than the class above," since he is talking about ranks in a hierarchy, and this phrase keeps the structure of the hierarchy in view.

The final sentence loses its meaning in a jungle of unclear references and obscure diction. What are "the primary as well as the subgroups"? What does "corporation" mean here? What is the sense of referring to "poor people" as "personnel"? Would it not have been better to refer to them simply as "the poor"? What is the purpose in saying that the members of the lower groups "are elevated" into the higher? Does this passive construction really describe the process? Would it not be at once simpler and more accurate to say "they pass"?

We may be in better position to guard against this pretentious kind of language when we recognize some of its causes. It is true that certain factors in modern life tend to encourage the use of jargon. One of these undoubtedly is an unfounded fear of simplicity. A kind of fashionable intellectualism has produced the feeling that to be simple is somehow to be inadequate. In most cases, however, this is a ridiculous assumption. To use overgeneralized, imprecise language is to show that you are confused or timid or impressed with false objectives. To use simple, direct language is to show that you have a definite knowledge of the subject and that you feel no need to show off when talking about it. There is some value for writers in the maxim of conduct, "Be yourself." When we are ourselves, we are likely to be simple, unpretending, and clear. When we are afraid to be ourselves, or are under a mistaken impression that it is wrong for us to be ourselves, we are likely to be inflated, pompous, and unclear.

The difference may be illustrated as follows. Some persons would shrink from writing, "This animal is a cat." They are prone to produce something like "This animal is probably a member of the feline genus." Notice the telltale changes in the diction. First of all, the sentence is longer and the words are larger. To those who take in surfaces only it may, consequently, be more impressive. One notices also that "member of the feline genus" is safe because it has a wide coverage and gives less opportunity for being wrong. The specific commitment is avoided. And this protection is increased by "probably." The timid person always feels safer with a sentence which is hedged with "probably." Lastly, "member of the feline genus" has connotations of science and learning, and it can be depended on to dignify the user. But unless there is some good reason for all the qualifying that is done, these virtues are false compared with the brevity and clarity of "This animal is a cat."

People who are the victims of this fashion feel that in order to be accepted they must use an inflated language which has certain echoes of learning. Their speech and writing, therefore, instead of being simple, direct, and natural is encumbered with needless polysyllables, with circumlocutionary phrases, and other products of artificiality. Sometimes such language is overly explicit when judged by the occasion. It mentions things which need not be mentioned and draws out phrases which are well understood in simple form. There is a kind of labored explicitness which may be less clear than simple, direct expression.

Another factor behind the use of jargon is our tendency to develop bureaucracies of all kinds, political, educational, military, scientific, and other. A peculiar weakness of bureaucracy is that it breeds in its lesser officials a timidity toward those holding higher positions and a consequent fear of taking on responsibility. If they cannot be held responsible for many decisions, they cannot be blamed for many failures. This desire to remain protected leads to a great deal of official jargon, which is often so composed that one cannot be sure what is said or who said it or who authorized the saying of it. It is this kind of language that Congressman Maury Maverick described as "gobbledygook." According to the authors of *Federal Prose,* a government bureaucrat faced with the necessity of asserting "Too many cooks spoil the broth" would couch the old saying as follows:

Undue multiplicity of personnel assigned either concurrently or consecutively to a single function involves deterioration of quality in the
resultant product as compared with the product of the labor of an exact
sufficiency of personnel.

—James R. Masterson and Wendell Brooks
Phillips, *Federal Prose: How to Write
in and/or for Washington*

This caricature brings out most of the characteristic vices of official
jargon: inflated diction, wordiness, the use of euphemisms, the failure to
name anything precisely, and especially the avoidance of definite commitment, as seen here in the highly relativistic phrasing at the end.

The following rules will be found effective in combating a tendency
toward jargon.

1. *Prefer the concrete to the abstract term.* Although some writing
requires abstract terms, as we have seen elsewhere, the truth remains that
an abstract term does not give a sharp image. The sharp image is presented by the term which specifically names the object under discussion.
To recur to an earlier example, a scientific treatise might require the use
of "feline," but for most contexts "alley cat," if this is the subject of the
discussion, would be better. The referent of "plumbers" will be instantly
supplied, but that of "service personnel" will not. We note that concrete
naming always represents a step in the direction of the earthly and the
real. In doing so, it encourages a feeling that the writer knows what he is
talking about.

2. *Avoid unwarranted euphemisms.* The widespread use of these is
part of the false cant of our time. Some sources will say, "The prisoner was
in an alcoholic condition" to avoid saying "The prisoner was drunk." They
will say, "He was separated from the organization" to avoid saying "He
was discharged from his job." In some cases a legitimate concern for
feeling or considerations of policy will excuse such uses, but a language
made up of such euphemisms offends our sense of the fact of things. It
only caters to vanity to call barbers "tonsorial artists" or trash collectors
"sanitary engineers." People who are doing the work of the world can
enjoy ample esteem without the aid of these grandiloquent euphemisms
which indicate, if anything, some anxiety about their real status. Euphemisms try to substitute subjective evaluation for objective description,
and one always needs to be cautious about this type of substitution.

3. *Avoid use of the passive voice when this use has the effect of
concealing the agent of the action expressed by the verb.* There exists a
kind of "irresponsible passive," the real purpose of which is to avoid
mention of the source which bears responsibility for the action, expression,
or opinion which is involved. In simple form, this can be seen in the
difference between "Johnnie broke the window with a baseball" and "The
window was broken with a baseball." Such constructions can have a

serious result when one is writing about matters of importance. Newspapers of the less objective kind frequently use such constructions to "slant" headlines, as in "New Tariff Law Held Unfair" and "President Criticized for Appointment to Labor Department." We also find similar constructions in scholarly writings, where the temptation to avoid committing oneself has produced much jargon. "It is believed that school enrollments will continue at high levels for the next few years" is an example from such a source. If it is known by whom it is believed, or on what basis it is believed, that information probably should be given as a relevant point. Changing the voice to active and thereby naming the agent will usually make a sentence both more meaningful and more convincing.

4. *Avoid as far as possible clichés and other stereotyped expressions.* Because language itself is, in one sense, a stereotype, this rule cannot be followed absolutely. But all of us can, with a little effort, make our language less stereotyped. The stereotype can be a hindrance to communication because the very "typing" prevents the sharp, individualizing effect that is essential to both preciseness and freshness. The stereotype is the expression easy to think of. Because it is so readily available, we tend to use it to avoid doing mental work and make it do jobs that really require more attention. For example, it does not require much thinking to turn up expressions such as "a hair-raising escape," "a rank outsider," "the crack of dawn," and the like. These expressions have acquired a kind of rubber-stamp quality; and though they name the object in a way, they do so without presenting the peculiar quality that belongs to it as a unique thing, and that makes it appear to us real and of the world. Even though these expressions were possibly born in situations where they possessed such power, long-continued and indiscriminate use has deprived them of it. Now they do no more than signify in a vague and approximate way. All prefabricated phrasing has the same effect.

The search for fresh language which will give the reader a feeling of real perception is the perennial quest of the writer, and there are no simple rules for finding it. Probably the soundest advice is to be suspicious of anything that is very easy, because in many cases such expressions will be hand-me-downs which will not fit the specific subject. Usually it is only after we have studied carefully the nature of that subject and have sorted through our vocabulary that we can furnish an expression which will do the real work of naming or describing. The maxim that "easy reading makes hard writing" is nowhere more apparent than in diction, for extra care on the part of the writer greatly increases the ease with which a reader can grasp the ideas. And the reverse of this, "easy writing makes hard reading," is painfully obvious, because the writer who takes the first solution to his problem of diction usually leaves serious difficulties for the reader to face. The simple fact is that if the writer does not do the hard work of saying the thing right, the reader will have to do it—that is, if the reader consents to read on.

# EXERCISES

**Exercise A**   *Study the diction in the following passages. Try to find substitutes for the more important words, and observe the changes made by your substitutions.*

[1] If a foolish consistency is the hobgoblin of little minds, a fatuous optimism is frequently the damnation of expansive minds. As a social optimist ignoring the fact of sin, Emerson was a radical thinker, perhaps the most influential of all American radicals. Believing, like Rousseau, in the supremacy of benevolent instincts, he was hot for discarding all the old ways of society so that ground might be cleared for the new edifices of emotion. Among the warning voices that answered him, those of Hawthorne and Orestes Brownson were the most eloquent.
—Russell Kirk, The Conservative Mind

[2] I had read descriptions of tropical forests by evolutionary scientists and they had all impressed me that I should receive a gloomy and murderous impression from the terrible and ruthless "struggle for life" of the vegetation. With entire docility I prepared, I braced myself beforehand. And what did I find? An extraordinary uprush of happiness at the sight of such exuberant life. Certainly, the closed-in, the sunlessness would affect one's spirits, but then we are savannah creatures—came off the arboreal perch long ago—though that doesn't alter the fact that my impression of a tropical forest is not murder but life. Did I look at the strangling parasites? I did, and I observed that the larger and stronger the tree the more exuberant the parasites. And was I not depressed to think of their life-juices being drained away by these lazy, good-for-nothing, flower-producing, rootless vermin? I did not. I thought they made the trees even more beautiful, and that it was nice of the trees to cooperate with them. How do I know that a tree isn't pleased to be suddenly covered with a glorious colored cloud of alien flowers? And as to the juice-sucking —I observed near the settlements that one of the most exuberant of these "parasites" had fixed itself in great quantities on the telegraph wires. When you tell me how it sucks the life-juice out of the telegraph wires, I'll begin to feel a utiltarian sorrow for the tree.
—Richard Aldington, Artifex (By permission of the author)

[3] Considering the noisiness of the American magazines of today, it is rather instructive to glance back at the timorous and bloodless quality of their progenitors. All of the early ones, when they were not simply monthly newspapers or almanacs, were depressingly "literary" in tone, and dealt chiefly in stupid poetry, silly essays and artificial fiction. The one great fear of their editors seems to have been that of offending some one; all of the pioneer prospectuses were full of assurances that nothing would be printed which even "the most fastidious" could object to. Literature, in those days—say from 1830 to 1860—was almost completely cut off from

contemporary life. It mirrored, not the struggle for existence, so fierce and dramatic in the new nation, but the pallid reflections of poetasters, self-advertising clergymen, sissified "gentlemen of taste," and other such donkeys. Poe waded into these *literati* and shook them up a bit, but even after the Civil War the majority of them continued to spin pretty cobwebs. Edmund Clarence Stedman and Donald G. Mitchell were excellent specimens of the clan; its last survivor was the lachrymose William Winter. The "literature" manufactured by these tear-squeezers, though often enough produced in beer cellars, was frankly aimed at the Young Person. Its main purpose was to avoid giving offense; it breathed a heavy oleaginous piety, a snug niceness, a sickening sweetness. It is as dead today as Baalam's ass.

> —H. L. Mencken, "The American Magazine," from
> *Prejudices: First Series*

**Exercise B**  *What expressions in the following paragraphs from* Huckleberry Finn *determine the quality of the diction? How would you characterize the quality?*

Sometimes we'd have that whole river all to ourselves for the longest time. Yonder was the banks and the islands, across the water; and maybe a spark—which was a candle in a cabin window; and sometimes on the water you could see a spark or two—on a raft or scow, you know; and maybe you could hear a fiddle or a song coming over from one of them crafts. It's lovely to live on a raft. We had the sky up there, all speckled with stars, and we used to lay on our backs and look up at them, and discuss about whether they was made or just happened. Jim he allowed they was made, but I allowed they happened; I judged it would have took too long to *make* so many. Jim said the moon could 'a' laid them; well, that looked kind of reasonable, so I didn't say nothing against it, because I've seen a frog lay most as many, so of course it could be done. We used to watch the stars that fell, too, and see them streak down. Jim allowed they'd got spoiled and was hove out of the nest.

Once or twice of a night we would see a steamboat slipping along in the dark, and now and then she would belch a whole world of sparks up out of her chimbleys, and they would rain down in the river and look awful pretty; then she would turn a corner and her lights would wink out and her powwow shut off and leave the river still again, and by and by her waves would get to us, a long time after she was gone, and joggle the raft a bit, and after that you wouldn't hear nothing for you couldn't tell how long, except maybe frogs or something.

After midnight the people on shore went to bed, and then for two or three hours the shores was black—no more sparks in the cabin windows. These sparks was our clock—the first one that showed again meant morning was coming, so we hunted a place to hide and tie up right away.

> —Samuel L. Clemens, *Adventures of Huckleberry Finn*

**Exercise C**  *If you follow some sports writer regularly, analyze his style for its sources of vividness. Could some of his methods profitably be used with more serious subjects to create or sustain interest?*

**Exercise D**  *The style of* Time Magazine *has been an object of criticism and of uncritical admiration. Select one of the longer articles from* Time, *or two or three shorter articles, and study the specific effects of the diction on the style.*

**Exercise E**  *Good figures of speech usually come to us unexpectedly. The next time you think of an apt one, try developing it beyond the usual single use. A good figure will sometimes provide a framework for a fairly long expository or argumentative essay, appearing first in one application or phase of comparison and later in others.*

**Exercise F**  *Find a passage of jargon or "gobbledygook" and try rewriting it. Bear in mind the guidelines given on pages 261–262, and make your sense of clear communication in English the ultimate standard for your changes.*

## DICTION AND TONE

All writing possesses a quality which is usually defined as tone. So apparent is this quality that often it is the first thing we notice. We perceive even subconsciously whether a tone is sober or gay or careful or flippant; we sense a special quality that seems to emerge from the writing as a whole.

The tonal quality of written language has been compared with vocal tone. The voice in which we express anything can make a tremendous difference in the meaning of what is said and the way in which it is received. Consider the ways in which "Get out" could be spoken. It could be uttered in such a way as to express deep antagonism and hostility. It could express exasperation, or polite and respectful coaxing, or disdain, or boredom. And these do not exhaust the meanings which the tone of the speaker's voice could give to the expression.

In writing we do not have the various qualities of voice which can control and modulate. Nevertheless, the writer has a number of means at his disposal, and the difference they can make in the total expression is almost as great as that produced by changes in the voice.

First of all, however, we must recognize that tone is a manifestation of attitude. How we are going to say something depends on how we feel about several things, and these things make up the rhetorical situation. We are faced with a subject matter, with an audience, and with a more or less specific task of communication. Our feelings toward any one of these may predominate, but in combination they determine the tone of our writing.

Let us examine the possibilities severally. Obviously there is a great range in the seriousness with which a writer may look upon his subject.

He may be deeply impressed by it or even overwhelmed by it. He may be intensely preoccupied with conveying the substance of his subject, so that order, care, and precision will characterize his expression. At the other end of the scale he may regard his subject as a trifle, hardly worth serious attention—as something to be dealt with in a light and detached way. In this case he might give more attention to interesting or novel means of expression. About the same range of attitude can occur with respect to audiences. One may be deeply impressed by an audience or even some-what intimidated by it, or one may take a half serious, playful, or ironical attitude toward it. Such an attitude is often adopted by writers of informal or humorous essays. Sometimes an audience has been led to prefer and expect a certain kind of attitude. On different occasions a writer may have different attitudes toward his own act of writing. He may feel a passionate necessity to get the thing said now and in this form; he takes a com-pletely serious view of this particular job. On other occasions he may be writing because of a deadline, because he has promised something, or even because he has settled into a routine of writing. These different moods of the writer will impart detectable qualities to the tone.

Such are the conditioning factors that influence tone in a general way. When we turn to the specific means through which they operate, we find that diction is the most important. The predominant level of vocabulary, the proportion of familiar or unfamiliar words, the choice of transitional devices, the degree of concreteness, the employment of meta-phor, the use of colloquialisms or quotations or literary allusions—all of these contribute to that feature of style called tone.

If you have worked long at a piece of writing and are dissatisfied with it, you may discover that the trouble lies with the tone. Fortunately, tone may often be changed by rather minor adjustments in diction, though some attention may have to be given concurrently to sentence pattern and length. You may find that all you need to do is to "tone up" or "tone down" the vocabulary, suiting it more exactly to the occasion. This will mean either giving it the dignity of greater seriousness and a more measured pace, or relaxing it to show a less demanding mood. Because diction is the substance of expression, it can enter both subtly and powerfully into the attitude of our expression.

In the following passage, Gibbon is writing in middle life, at a time far removed from his early love affair. His audience is a general but culti-vated one, such as would be interested in reading the autobiography of an eminent historian. His object is to relate this episode, with some account of its effect on him, in the sequence of his life's story.

> I hesitate, from the apprehension of ridicule, when I approach the
> delicate subject of my early love. By this word I do not mean the polite
> attention, the gallantry, without hope or design, which has originated in
> the spirit of chivalry, and is interwoven with the texture of French man-
> ners. I understand by this passion the union of desire, friendship, and
> tenderness, which is inflamed by a single female, which prefers her to

the rest of her sex, and which seeks her possession as the supreme or the sole happiness of our being. I need not blush at recollecting the object of my choice; and though my love was disappointed of success, I am rather proud that I was once capable of feeling such a pure and exalted sentiment. The personal attractions of Mademoiselle Susan Curchod were embellished by the virtues and talents of the mind. Her fortune was humble, but her family was respectable. Her mother, a native of France, had preferred her religion to her country. The profession of her father did not extinguish the moderation and philosophy of his temper, and he lived content with a small salary and laborious duty in the obscure lot of a minister of Crassy, in the mountains that separate the Pays de Vaud from the county of Burgundy. In the solitude of a sequestered village he bestowed a liberal, and even learned, education on his only daughter. She surpassed his hopes by her proficiency in the sciences and languages; and in her short visits to some relations at Lausanne, the wit, the beauty, and erudition of Mademoiselle Curchod were the theme of universal applause. The report of such a prodigy awakened my curiosity; I saw and loved. I found her learned without pedantry, lively in conversation, pure in sentiment, and elegant in manners; and the first sudden emotion was fortified by the habits and knowledge of a more familiar acquaintance. She permitted me to make her two or three visits at her father's house. I passed some happy days there, in the mountains of Burgundy, and her parents honorably encouraged the connection. In a calm retirement the gay vanity of youth no longer fluttered in her bosom, she listened to the voice of truth and passion, and I might presume to hope that I had made some impression on a virtuous heart. At Crassy and Lausanne I indulged my dream of felicity: but on my return to England, I soon discovered that my father would not hear of this strange alliance, and that, without his consent, I was myself destitute and helpless. After a painful struggle I yielded to my fate; I sighed as a lover, I obeyed as a son; my wound was insensibly healed by time, absence, and the habits of a new life.

—Edward Gibbon, *Autobiography*

The dominant tone here is one of elegance, achieved through detachment and distance, and affected somewhat by a self-consciousness over what he is describing. We see this in the mild sort of apology which he offers at the beginning. We see it in his attempt to define, by contrast and comparison, the kind of love he felt at that time. This is enforced by his statement that he is proud of having once been capable of "such a pure and exalted sentiment." An early infatuation is usually recalled with poignancy, accompanied by sharp images, but Gibbon renders all details in language that is abstract and general. We hear only that the object of his love had "personal attractions" which were "embellished by the virtues and talents of her mind." She was distinguished by her "proficiency in the sciences and languages"; and her "wit, beauty, and erudition" were universally applauded by her relatives. The language is consistently that of praise; and Gibbon never allows himself to give a real particular; he is preserving too great a "semantic distance" for that.

The declaration that one addressed a girl with the "voice of truth and passion" we would today consider a very poor account of a courtship, but Gibbon thought it was sufficient. When he comes to the painful topic of the separation, his language loses little of its generality. And when he arrives at his last sentence, instead of dwelling upon his anguish, he expresses his feeling in a neat parallelism: "I sighed as a lover, I obeyed as a son." Then he concludes with a series of three items which seem more philosophical than passionate.

Other sentences, especially the first two, show a kind of contrived quality, suggesting that Gibbon is more interested in a formal controlled style than in arousing a reader's feeling by any direct means. Gibbon lived and wrote in a century which exalted form over feeling, and the reader can find much evidence of his conviction that one should write as the best people write, in accordance with a publicly approved style.

**Exercise:**   *Analyze the tone of each of the following selections. Try to determine the attitude of the writer toward his subject matter and his audience. Consider what he is assuming by his level of approach. Study the qualities of his diction, noting the range of vocabulary, degree of abstractness or concreteness, and the use of metaphor. Estimate what factors are chiefly responsible for the tone that predominates.*

1. There is a vague popular belief that lawyers are necessarily dishonest. I say vague, because when we consider to what extent confidence and honors are reposed in and conferred upon lawyers by the people, it appears improbable that their impression of dishonesty is very distinct and vivid. Yet the impression is common, almost universal. Let no young man choosing the law for a calling for a moment yield to the popular belief—resolve to be honest at all events; and if in your own judgment you cannot be an honest lawyer, resolve to be honest without being a lawyer. Choose some other occupation, rather than one in the choosing of which you do, in advance, consent to be a knave.
   —Abraham Lincoln, "Advice to Young Lawyers"

2. For the child's undeveloped mind, loving your neighbor on Sunday and skinning your neighbor on Monday are not consistent attitudes. Since for a mature and wise person they are consistent attitudes, maturity and wisdom are states to be shunned. To grow up and become like his parents appears to be the worst possible fate, and he will try to avoid it at all costs. He will evade it as long as possible, and when he finds he must accept it he becomes a cynic. The youth's cynicism is therefore due to his distaste for the situation of his elders, and if, for instinctive reasons, he continues to respect his parents, he will despise their situation and assume the cynical attitude toward that. His other alternative is to give up his respect for them. Those who have to do with youth say that their attitudes are equally divided between a general cynicism and a distrust of people.
   —Elijah Jordan, *Business Be Damned*

3. But after a while we didn't have so much time over at our banking house of "Drew, Robinson & Co." for discussing breeds of cattle. We had our hands full in handling the business that began to come in. When you are loaning money, buying and selling railroad and steamboat shares, and such like, it keeps you going. If you don't look out, one slip will make an almighty loss. In fact our house made a slip at the start. One of our customers was a fellow we had known for some time. He owed us $30,000. My partners were for extending the loan. I was against it. They begged—talked about old friendship's sake, and such like. They got me to consent. Result—we lost the money. That taught me a lesson. Sentiment is all right up in the part of the city where your home is. But downtown, no. Down there the dog that snaps the quickest gets the bone. Friendship is very nice for a Sunday afternoon when you're sitting around the dinner table with your relations, talking about the sermon that morning. But nine o'clock Monday morning, such notions should be brushed away like cobwebs from a machine. I never took any stock in a man who mixed up business with anything else. He can go into other things outside of business hours. But when he's in his office, he ought not to have a relation in the world—and least of all a poor relation.

—Bouck White, *The Book of Daniel Drew*

4. Through the windows the moonlight fell. From her pillow Ellen could see the yellow rim of the moon above the ledge. It lay on the golden leafage of the wooded lawns like a veil and over the garden mottled here and there with the various flowers. The great blossoms on the magnolia-trees against the dark were like little moons themselves; and the odor of mimosa, so like the linden-trees at home in June, came drifting past. A bird was singing like none of the birds at home, wonderfully rich and wild, first one kind of music and then another, one voice after another, stranger than the mimosa itself. And there was something everywhere, warm, living, abundant, something exotic and mad, that carried away the senses into a sweet, pagan, terrible world. And then the bird again, this time like a flute; the stream of music went falling and rising against the rustling of the leaves. At the end of the garden she could see a clump of heaven trees outlined against the sky like palms in old paintings of the Nile.

—Stark Young, *Heaven Trees*

5. Auschwitz and Hiroshima. We have seen all that; in some of it we have acquiesced or helped. No wonder we are morally guilty. Men like ourselves have done such things—and at the same time men like ourselves, sometimes the same men who have taken a hand in the horrors, have been showing more concern for the unlucky round them than has ever been shown by a large society in human history. That is the moral paradox in which we have to live.

It is wrong to try to domesticate the horrors. The mass slaughter of the concentration camps was both the most awful and the most degrading set of actions that men have done so far. This set of actions was ordered and controlled by abnormally wicked men, if you like, but down the line the orders were carried out by thousands of people like the rest of us, civil servants, soldiers, engineers, all brought up in an advanced Western and Christian society. While it was people not like the rest of us but a great deal better, people who for imagination and morality, not to speak of intellect, stand among the finest of our race, people like Einstein, Niels Bohr and Franck, who got caught up in the tangle of events which led to Hiroshima and Nagasaki. The dropping of those bombs was of a lesser order of wickedness from what was done at Auschwitz. But Western man ought not to forget that he did it; Eastern man certainly won't.

—C. P. Snow, "The Future of Man"

6. I do not hesitate to say, that those who call themselves Abolitionists should at once effectually withdraw their support, both in person and property, from the government of Massachusetts and not wait till they constitute a majority of one, before they suffer the right to prevail through them. I think that it is enough if they have God on their side, without waiting for that other one. Moreover, any man more right than his neighbors constitutes a majority of one already.

I meet this American government, or its representatives, the state government, directly, and face to face, once a year—no more—in the person of its tax-gatherer; this is the only mode in which a man situated as I am necessarily meets it; and it then says distinctly, Recognize me; and the simplest, most effectual, and, in the present posture of affairs, the indispensablest mode of treating with it on this head, of expressing your little satisfaction with and love for it, is to deny it then. My civil neighbor, the tax-gatherer, is the very man I have to deal with,—for it is, after all, with men and not with parchment that I quarrel,—and he has voluntarily chosen to be an agent of the government. How shall he ever know well what he is and does as an officer of the government, or as a man, until he is obliged to consider whether he shall treat me, his neighbor, for whom he has respect, as a neighbor and well-disposed man, or as a maniac and disturber of the peace, and see if he can get over this obstruction to his neighborliness without a ruder and more impetuous thought of speech corresponding with his action. I know this well, and if one thousand, if one hundred, if ten men whom I could name,—if ten *honest* men only,—ay if *one* HONEST man, in this State of Massachusetts, *ceasing to hold slaves*, were actually to withdraw from this copartnership, and be locked up in the county jail therefor, it would be the abolition of slavery in America.

—Henry David Thoreau, "On the Duty of Civil Disobedience"

# Chapter Nine

## Research Paper

In some of your college courses you will be asked to write research papers based upon your investigation and evaluation of sources. Such papers will require you to define some significant topic, to use the resources of the library effectively to collect relevant data, to record the data in an orderly fashion, to evaluate it, and to write an informative paper presenting your evidence and conclusions in an appropriately annotated form.

Such undergraduate papers are intended primarily to give you experience in the techniques of investigation. The graduate or professional research paper is ideally expected to make an original contribution to learning, but this requires a wider knowledge of subject matter and a greater familiarity with research techniques than is usually expected of the undergraduate. Such original contributions, however, depend upon informed, systematic, careful study and investigation, and it is experience in these which you should try to derive from your undergraduate papers. Your aims should be thoroughness in examining all the evidence relevant to your topic, responsibility in testing the reliability of your sources, accuracy in presenting facts and citing sources, and objectivity in discriminating between facts on the one hand and the conclusions you draw from them on the other. Consistent attention to these aims will prepare you for the more ambitious dissertations, reports, monographs, and articles which are an integral part of the requirements of any advanced study, business, or profession.

In facing the problems of the research paper, it is useful to divide the task into two main parts. First, you must gather and evaluate a substantial body of information about your subject, a process which in turn requires an acquaintance with the resources of the library. Second, you must organize and express these facts in a form which clearly acknowledges all your sources so that your reader may also evaluate your findings.

## GATHERING MATERIALS

### The Library

The library is a central part of any college or university because it is the main storehouse of information. Anything of significance in published or manuscript form is here carefully preserved and arranged for use.

You should familiarize yourself with the arrangement of the library as soon as possible. A college library of even moderate size contains a wide variety of material. Here you can find books of facts which will add to your exact knowledge about the world. You can find books containing ideas and systems of thought which shed light on important questions. You can find novels, short stories, and plays, whose purpose is literary enjoyment. You can find current and past issues of the best periodicals, which will bring you up to date on the important subjects the educated world is discussing.

Although libraries may differ from each other in organization and arrangement, there are certain departments which are found in nearly all of them. These are the bibliography room, the loan or circulation desk, the stacks, and the reference room. Many libraries have in addition a periodical room for current magazines and newspapers, and a browsing room filled with books selected for their general interest.

The bibliography room contains the key to the contents of the entire library. In this room you find the *general card catalogue,* a complete index to everything which the library has acquired. Arranging and keeping track of thousands upon thousands of books, magazines, pamphlets, bulletins, and miscellaneous items is obviously a tremendous task, and libraries have met it by using an elaborate system of filing. Every item that the library acquires is carefully examined, and the important data regarding it is recorded. If the book is at all important, three cards will be made out, one listing it by author, another by title, and another by subject matter. These cards are filed in boxes, which make up the general card catalogue.

The author card usually contains the most complete information about the book. Let us suppose that your preliminary investigation has shown you that you may be able to use V. L. Parrington's *Main Currents in American Thought.* Because you know the name of the author, you turn to the boxes in the card file with entries beginning with the letter "P," and locate "Parrington." The entry which you will find indexing this work appears below if your library uses the Library of Congress system.

PS 88
.P3        Parrington, Vernon Louis, 1871-1929

Main currents in American thought; an interpretation of American literature from the beginning to 1920, by Vernon Louis Parrington . . . New York, Harcourt, Brace, and company, 1927

3 v.     22½ cm

Each volume has special t.-p.

Bibliography at end of each volume

1. American literature—Hist. and crit. 2. U. S.—Civilization. 3. Philosophy, American. 4. U. S.—Religion. 5. U. S.—Pol. and gov't.

          1. Title

Library of Congress     PS88   .P3

Copyright

1. The symbol appearing in the upper left-hand corner is the *call number* of the book, which designates the exact location of the book in the library.

2. "Parrington . . . 1929" gives you the name of the author and the dates of his birth and death, respectively.

3. "Main currents . . . 1927" gives you the full title of the book, its place of publication, the name of the publisher, and the date of publication.

4. "3 v. . . . each volume" tells you that there are 3 volumes (3 v.) in the work; that each is 22½ centimeters high; that each volume has a special title page (t.p.); and that there is a bibliography at the end of each volume.

5. "1. American literature . . . and gov't" tells you that the book is also listed in the card catalogue under five subject headings: (1) under American literature, under the subheading History and criticism; (2) under United States, under the subheading Civilization; and so on. Notice that the first heading given is the major one, the second that of a subheading under the major one. The last entry here (I. Title) indicates a title heading.

6. "Library of Congress PS88.P3" indicates that a copy of the book has been placed in, and catalogued by, The Library of Congress under this call number.

Note that the information on the catalogue card can frequently give you some initial clues as to the potential usefulness of the book for your purposes. The full title will frequently, as it does in this case, give some indication of the scope of the book not given by the conventional brief title. The subject headings under which the book is also catalogued will sometimes indicate an area of its possible reference not indicated even by the full title. The subject heading "U. S.—Religion" is an example. If the catalogue card indicates that the book contains bibliographies, as in the case of Parrington's work, these may be worth checking for additional possibilities even if the book itself proves of limited use. Finally, of course, for many topics the date of a book will be very significant. For a subject which is rapidly changing, a reference may be out of date in a few years. For example, a book on rocketry written in 1959 might be seriously out of date for many purposes in 1966. In examining even such a simple reference as a catalogue card, you will do well to cultivate the habit of examining it closely and critically.

Aside from the card catalogue, your major guide to the resources of the library are its *reference books,* usually housed in a separate reference room. The reference room is a special library department containing those works which are most often consulted for factual information. Among its principal contents are indexes, dictionaries, both English and foreign language, encyclopedias, biographical dictionaries, handbooks of facts, atlases, manuals of scientific terms and formulas, directories, and a wide variety of other publications devoted to recording and classifying information. If you wish to find the meaning of the word *syndrome,* the exact date of the birth of Nathaniel Hawthorne, the area of Pakistan, the population of New York in the 1890 census, the chief natural resources of Brazil, or the address of the congressman from your district, any moderately complete reference library can supply the answers. Some of the standard reference works found in most college or university libraries are listed below. The list provides titles only and makes no attempt to be exhaustive. But it is sufficient to give some idea of the breadth of resources open to you. If you will cultivate an acquaintance with these and the other resources of your library's reference room as early as possible in your college work, you will find that the more specialized work expected of you in advanced courses will be much easier. Note that most libraries employ a reference librarian, a trained expert whose job it is to be fully acquainted with available reference works. Make use of his assistance as freely as you need, but try to do so always with a view to increasing your own independence in using such works.

### Standard Reference Works

ENCYCLOPEDIAS: GENERAL

    *Chamber's Encyclopedia*
    *Collier's Encyclopedia*
    *Columbia Encyclopedia*
    *Encyclopedia Americana*
    *Encyclopaedia Britannica*
    *The New International Encyclopedia*

ENCYCLOPEDIAS COVERING SPECIAL FIELDS

*Catholic Encyclopedia*
*Encyclopedia of American History*
*Encyclopedia of the Social Sciences*
*Engineering Encyclopedia*
*Hasting's Encyclopedia of Religion and Ethics*
*Jewish Encyclopedia*
*New Schaff-Herzog Encyclopedia of Religious Knowledge*
*The Concise Encyclopedia of Western Philosophy and Philosophers*
*The Encyclopedia of Sports*

UNABRIDGED DICTIONARIES OF ENGLISH

*A New English Dictionary on Historical Principles*
*Dictionary of American English on Historical Principles*
*Funk and Wagnalls New Standard Dictionary of the English Language*
*The New Century Dictionary and Cyclopedia*
*Webster's New International Dictionary of the English Language*

BIOGRAPHICAL DICTIONARIES

*A Dictionary of Greek and Roman Biography and Mythology*
*American Men of Science*
*Biographical Directory of the American Congress, 1774–1961*
*Congressional Directory*
*Current Biography*
*Dictionary of American Biography*
*Directory of American Scholars*
*International Who's Who*
*Lippincott's Pronouncing Dictionary of Biography and Mythology*
*Webster's Biographical Dictionary*
*Who's Who in America*
*Who's Who (British)*
*World Biography*
*Who's Who in Commerce and Industry*
*Who's Who in Labor*
*Who's Who in United States Politics*

DICTIONARIES COVERING SPECIAL FIELDS

*A Dictionary of Scientific Terms*
*Baldwin's Dictionary of Philosophy and Psychology*
*Bryan's Dictionary of Painters and Engravers*
*Chambers' Technical Dictionary*
*Dictionary of American History*
*Dictionary of Physics*
*Dictionary of Psychology*
*Encyclopedia of Banking and Finance*
*Encyclopedia of the Social Sciences*
*Fowler's Dictionary of Modern English Usage*
*Funk and Wagnalls Standard Dictionary of Folklore, Mythology,
  and Legend*

Grove's Dictionary of Music and Musicians
Harper's Dictionary of Classical Literature and Antiquities
McGraw-Hill Encyclopedia of Science and Technology
Palgrave's Dictionary of Political Economy
Perrins' Writer's Guide and Index to English
Roget's International Thesaurus
The Dictionary of Sports
The Encyclopedia and Dictionary of Education
The Oxford Classical Dictionary

LITERARY HISTORIES AND HANDBOOKS

Bartlett's Familiar Quotations
Cambridge Bibliography of English Literature
Cambridge History of American Literature
Cambridge History of English Literature
Contemporary American Authors
Contemporary British Literature
Garnett and Gosse's English Literature: an Illustrated Record
Literary History of the United States
Oxford Companion to American Literature
Oxford Companion to English Literature
Strong's Exhaustive Concordance of the Bible
The Columbia Dictionary of Modern European Literature

HANDBOOKS OF FACTS AND STATISTICS

Historical Statistics of the United States, Colonial times to 1957
Lincoln Library of Essential Information
New International Year Book
Statistical Abstract of the United States
Statesman's Yearbook
The American Yearbook
The Book of the States
The Economic Almanac
World Almanac
United Nations Yearbook

ATLASES AND GAZETTEERS

Bartholomew's Advanced Atlas of Modern Geography
Commercial Atlas
Encyclopaedia Britannica World Atlas
Rand McNally Commercial Atlas and Marketing Guide
Webster's Geographical Dictionary

IMPORTANT INDEXES

Book Review Digest
Catalog of United States Government Publications
Cumulative Book Index (a complete list of books published in English dur-
    ing the specified period covered by each volume of the Index)
Essay and General Literature Index
Industrial Arts Index (indexes principally technical and trade periodicals)
International Index to Periodicals (indexes the more scholarly types of
    periodical)

*New York Times Index*
*Poole's Index* (indexes British and American periodicals from 1802 to 1907)
*Reader's Guide to Periodical Literature*

The indexes listed above are supplemented by a wide range of special indexes such as the *Agricultural Index,* the *Catholic Periodical Index,* the *Education Index,* the *Industrial Arts Index* and many others; but the more general indexes are likely to be of most value to you at the earlier stages of your college work. Among those listed, three deserve special note, because you are likely to find them especially helpful in the kind of research topic you define for yourself in the composition course. *The Reader's Guide to Periodical Literature* is the most widely used of the general indexes. Published semi-monthly, and cumulated every three months and annually, it indexes articles from a large number of general periodicals from 1900 on, listing them under author, title, and subject headings. You should learn to use it efficiently, if you do not already do so, and to supplement it with two others: the *International Index to Periodicals,* and *Poole's Index to Periodical Literature.* Of these, the first, which extends from 1907 to the present, deals with more scholarly publications than the *Reader's Guide,* and though the periodicals it indexes are principally American, it covers some foreign publications. *Poole's Index* extends from 1802 to 1881, with supplements through January 1, 1907, thus covering material prior to that indexed by the other two.

## Evaluating the Data

Scholarship means above all accuracy. A scholar is known to the world as a man who has the ability to ascertain facts and to report them. Interpretations of facts often differ, but the scholar must know where to find those things that people will agree on as basically true. These constitute the starting point for any discussion or interpretation. All research, therefore, must be carried on in an objective manner. You do not seek to satisfy prepossessions, fancies, or prejudices. These may indeed give certain clues to areas that should be investigated, but they do not provide answers. The answers, in the form of facts, will be provided by authentic sources of information—histories, scientific studies, reports, statistics, and the like. It should be repeated that factual accuracy is the real aim of every research paper. It would be easy by comparison to sit at one's desk and spin out of the imagination a paper on some subject such as crime prevention, or the displacement of men by machinery, or the influence of French culture on American literature. But fancy and fact are often in conflict, and many problems can never be settled without due reference to the facts. The purpose of the research paper is to provide a basis of facts upon which opinions can be formed and, later perhaps, action can be taken.

This is why the teacher, in assigning the paper, will insist that you go to the proper sources for material, and why he will insist also upon a careful listing of those sources. The value of source material on a given subject may vary widely for a number of reasons. Some sources may be of limited value simply because they are old, and new material has been discovered and published since they appeared. Other sources may be of limited value because they are incomplete. They will contain some facts you can use, but they will have to be supplemented by facts from other sources. Other sources have to be used cautiously because they contain facts that are superficial or facts that are not strictly relevant to the immediate problem. Other sources must be treated similarly because they present facts which are dubious or facts which are disputed by other sources. Finally, in evaluating statements that appear in histories, studies, and articles, one usually has to allow for possible bias on the part of the author, or for an expression of personal opinion in the very language in which they are presented. For instance, one authority writing on "Roosevelt and the New Deal," may select one group of facts and dwell on their consequences, whereas another authority may select a different group for emphasis because his political views are different.

Skill in evaluating material of this kind is not something that you can acquire at once. It is developed through experience and the general widening of one's knowledge of books, men, and points of view. But the research paper is a first step in the acquiring of such skill. In collecting your material you begin to sift the true from the false, the central from the peripheral, the up-to-date from the out-of-date, and the objective from the subjective. No college student should believe that everything in print is true. What you find in print varies in veracity and importance about as much as what you hear. Accordingly, in the research paper you must seek first to pin down the facts and then to connect them with the authorities who can vouch for them.

## Primary and Secondary Sources

This last consideration brings us to the distinction between *primary* source material and *secondary* source material. Most large-scale investigations carried on at the professional level concern themselves with primary sources, or, in other words, with the facts or phenomena in their original form. They do not depend on what other people have said about these facts any more than they have to. If geologists are interested in studying the rock strata of a certain area, they will take a field party there and observe the subject directly. If sociologists wish to study the institutional connections of people in a certain town, they will make a canvass of that town or send out questionnaires. If a historian is investigating a certain period of American history, he may consult volumes of the *Congressional Record* and other official publications of the time. Evidence gathered in these ways is primary, or firsthand, because it is not transmitted through someone else. The investigators have gone to the original sources.

A student writing a research paper for an English course will not have much occasion to consult firsthand or primary sources. There will be, naturally, some exceptions. He may need to consult the first edition of a book to verify a reading, or look up tables of original data in a scientific publication, or make first-hand use of some other kind of material. The research paper we are discussing is by no means designed to discourage that kind of thing. But owing to the nature and scope of the assignment, the student has to accept the opinions of a good many authorities. At this stage, it is more important for him to prepare a good formal report than to settle some problem definitely by going only to primary sources. If the student is writing a paper on Lincoln's role as a war-time president, he probably has no time to settle for himself the exact conditions under which the Gettysburg Address was written. Instead, he may accept the statements of Carl Sandburg in *Abraham Lincoln: the War Years*. There is nothing irresponsible in this. The student is acknowledging that his statement is based upon a secondary source, but it is a respectable one, and he has the right to use it if he makes the proper acknowledgement. If he were writing about the habits of sea turtles, he would have to depend in like manner upon the statements of others who have themselves gathered the first-hand data. His task in such a paper is to read what the experts have said, and to assemble and correlate their statements with the object of producing a coherent account. He may even have to point out contradictions in the material he is using, or he may have to draw inferences where the material is sketchy or lacking. But his operations will be performed largely upon secondary material, or material that is supplied by others.

## Locating Material

The next step in the preparation of the paper is to determine where you can find this kind of material. If the subject you have chosen is a comparatively broad one, and it seems likely that books have been written upon it, you first look up the subject in the general card catalogue of the library. Here you may find a number of books indexed, with brief descriptions of the special phases with which they deal. Most books which make claims to scholarship include a bibliography. This is a list of the books that were found useful or noteworthy by the author. Consequently one good book on the subject may direct you through its bibliography to a number of other books you would like to consult.

If your subject is the kind that is treated by encyclopedias, it will pay you to look it up in a standard encyclopedia. Most encyclopedia articles of any length include bibliographies at the end, and from one of these you may select the books that seem most relevant to your research problem; and of course you may use the bibliographies which these books contain.

If your subject is of limited general interest or if it is of too recent date to have been made the subject of a book, you must go to one of the periodical indexes. These important indexes list the articles published in all the leading periodicals by subject, author, and title. You may look up the topic of your research under subject and note carefully the name of the periodical in which the article appeared, the issue of that periodical (month and year, and day of the month if it is a weekly), the number of the bound volume and the pages.

Many subjects, of course, have been dealt with in both books and articles, and you may need to use both kinds of sources of material.

## Preparing the Bibliography

After you have selected the chief areas in which you can find information, you are ready to prepare your own bibliography. This can be done on sheets of notebook paper, but you will save yourself time and trouble if you make your entries on small 3 x 5 index cards. These cards keep the entries separate, and they make the job of alphabetizing your bibliography a simple matter.

Most students have to learn where to find the information needed for a bibliographical entry. The most accurate and complete information about a book is found on the title page. Remember that both titles and authors' names are sometimes abbreviated or foreshortened on the cover of the book.

The bibliography card should begin with the author's name in full as it appears on the title page. Put down the last name first. If the book is a collection edited by someone, put down the name of the editor. Record the title of the book as given on the title page. Next list the place of publication and the date. Although you will not include the name of the publisher in your final bibliography, it is useful to include it on your bibliography card. Finally, note the edition of the work, and the number of volumes if it contains more than one volume. When your bibliography card is completely filled out, it will look like the examples below:

Allen, Hervey. *Israfel: the Life and Times of Edgar Allan Poe*. New York: George H. Doran and Company, 1926. 2 vols.

Mencken, H. L. *The American Language*. 4th ed. New York: Alfred A. Knopf, 1949.

Wiggins, James W. and Helmut Scholck, eds. *Foreign Aid Reexamined*. Washington, D.C.: Public Affairs Press, 1958.

The bibliographical card for an article published in a periodical takes a somewhat different form. The name of the author goes first; then the title of the article, and then the title of the periodical. This is followed by the volume number of the periodical, the date of the issue in which the article appears (placed in parentheses), and the pages it includes. A bibliographical card for this kind of source will accordingly appear as follows:

Woolcock, C. W. "Needs of Gifted and Talented Students." *School and Society*, LXXXVIII (November 5, 1960), 413–415.

If the article is unsigned, the title is placed first and is used in alphabetizing the bibliography.

"Bell Tolls for Hemingway." *Christian Century*, LXXVIII (July 19, 1961), 869.

A card for a newspaper article should bear the title of the article, the name of the newspaper, the date of issue in which it appears, the section, the page, and the column.

"Rhine Sands Yield Prehistoric Tools." New York *Times*, May 16, 1954, sec. 1, p. 13, col. 1.

It pays to take pains the first time to make the bibliographical card both accurate and complete. Remember that these cards will be used both in footnoting and in preparing the bibliography that goes with every research paper. If they are careless or incomplete, you will be running back and forth to the library to correct inaccuracies and to supply omissions. But a properly filled out bibliography card gives you everything you need for the final draft of the paper.

## SELECTING MATERIAL

After you have made up what looks like a reasonably extensive bibliography, the next step is to start reading. It will not be necessary to read through every book and article on your list. In many cases only parts of the book will be of use to you. You can find those parts by looking down the table of contents and especially by consulting the index of the book. A quick scanning of a magazine article will usually tell you whether it has anything for your purpose. In some cases you will find that you cannot use the article at all. It is important to have the outline of your subject well in mind because this will enable you to decide quickly what is pertinent. Do not waste time going over material which falls outside the limits of your subject.

As you begin to read, you take notes. It is the best practice to place these notes on cards, which can eventually be arranged in the order in which you wish to deal with the information you collect. Use a different card for each note. You will simplify procedure if you write only on one side. Bear in mind that the statements you are now preparing to make in the paper must be footnoted. This means that you must have an exact record of their source. Every note should accordingly have the name of the authority you are drawing on (usually the name of an author), the title of the work, and the exact page or pages on which the information is found. On note cards these entries may be abbreviated, but they must be full enough to refer you to the right item in your bibliography. A helpful practice is to write in the upper left-hand corner of the card a phrase or a short sentence telling as concisely as possible what the note is about. This gives you a means of seeing quickly whether a particular note will be of use in a particular part of your paper and thus prevents a tedious rereading of notes.

There are two types of items which you will be chiefly interested in recording. The first is factual data, which may be noted in the form of short statements, phrases, and, depending on the kind of material with which you are dealing, figures. The other type consists of matter copied from your source which you will later use as direct quotation. Nearly all research papers contain a certain amount of directly quoted material. These passages may range in length from brief phrases to several paragraphs. When you copy for direct quotation, make sure that you copy correctly, because every directly quoted passage must be reproduced *exactly* as it appears in the original.

*(A specimen note card)*

Congress. Its work of investigation. Burnham, *Congress and the American Tradition,* p. 234.

Historically Congress has investigated two areas: 1) the activities of private citizens or groups of citizens which were felt to have some impact upon the public interest, and 2) the activities of administrative officials and employees of the government. "Through public investigation Congress informs the citizens about the nation's problems at the same time that it is informing itself."

Observe that this note is essentially about one thing, the kinds of activities that Congress has thought it should investigate. Limiting the note this way helps the writer to find the right place for it in his outline. Moreover, it contains a rather succinct sentence of direct quotation. He may wish to use this to sum up his own more detailed treatment of the subject.

## WRITING THE PAPER

After you have compiled what seems a sufficiency of notes and have arranged them in the general order you propose to follow, you are ready to write. There is no special kind of composition for the research paper. In organizing and expressing your thoughts, you will follow the principles of writing you have already studied. You are, however, presenting a subject which is more or less specialized. This calls for great attention to clarity and completeness. You cannot assume that a person who has not done this research will know as much about the problem as you know. You must provide the facts necessary for understanding. And you must make the connections clear.

Because you are basing the paper largely on borrowed material, there are certain dangers it is most important to avoid. These may be listed under a few headings.

## Direct Quotations

1. *Remember that the paper is to be written in your own words.* A mere string of direct quotations is not a research paper. Direct quotations are often valuable, but they are to be used only when necessary. Resist the tendency to overindulge in quotation. It is a good plan to use a direct quotation only when it expresses the matter better than you could express it *in that place,* when it calls attention to one of the authorities upon whom you are depending, or when it serves as a succinct introduction or conclusion.

2. *Quotations must not be merely tossed in.* Rather, they must be carefully fitted in with what you have to say. This calls for scrutinizing them closely to see whether they express the thought that is needed at this point. If they do not, perhaps an allusion or a paraphrase would be better.

3. *There is need for considerable skill and variety in the introducing of quotations.* Do not fall into the monotonous pattern of writing, "Walter Blair says in *Native American Humor.* . . ." This form becomes wooden and tedious if repeated, and it even casts doubt upon whether you are using the quotation thoughtfully. The many different ways of introducing a quotation will show the kind of use you have for it and also the value you assign to it. Below are a few of the many expressions that are suitable for this purpose.

George F. Whicher in *This Was a Poet* presents the following description of Emily Dickinson:

In his introduction to *The Far Side of Paradise,* Arthur Mizener observes that

As Arthur Bestor points out in his study of American education,

A critic writing in *The Saturday Review of Literature* declared:

In the words of William H. Herndon, who was Lincoln's law partner for a number of years,

The impact of science on society has perhaps never been better expressed than in the following paragraph:

A different view of the problem was held by those who maintained that

The following passage from Emerson's *Journals* is further evidence that he took a strong interest in contemporary problems:

These are examples of the many combinations which can be used to introduce a quotation and to point up its significance. Remember, however, that though it is good to be inventive, it is more important to be exact. Make the introductory phrase or sentence suit the purpose for which you are introducing the passage.

## Footnotes

A system of footnotes is used to give credit for what has been borrowed for the research paper. The writer is under obligation to acknowledge the source of three kinds of material: (1) direct quotations, (2) facts which he has taken from someone else, and (3) expressions of opinion which are not his own. He need not, however, footnote such things as proverbial sayings, passages from literature which have in a sense become common property, or information that has become general knowledge. Ordinarily he does not footnote minute particulars, but he does footnote those borrowings which are substantial contributions to his paper.

Although footnotes require time and attention, they serve two important ends. First, they show that the writer has consulted the recognized authorities on his subject and that he is therefore basing his conclusions on published information. Second, they are a means of telling the reader where he may find additional information. If the reader of a research article is seriously interested in the subject with which the article deals, he may wish to go to a library and gather further information himself. Footnotes, by their specific references, tell him precisely where he can turn for more facts about or fuller discussion of the various aspects of the subject. Scholars often bring important works to one another's attention by footnoted references.

If you look through many books, you will discover a considerable variety of form in footnotes. It is best, however, to learn one form which gives all the information that is necessary and to use this form consistently. Once you have learned it and used it a few times, you will find that you follow it almost automatically. This saves comparing, checking for completeness, and other delays that will occur if one has not settled his footnote form.[1]

Modern practice demands that a complete footnote include the following:

*The name of the author of the work.* If an author is not given, the name of the editor must be cited. Sometimes the names of both author and editor are included in a footnote.

*The title of the work.* If the title is of a book or periodical, it must be underlined. But if the title is of an article in a periodical, a chapter of a book, or a poem or short story in an anthology, the title is placed in

---

[1] For a complete guide to bibliographical form see *The MLA Style Sheet* (Modern Language Association) or Kate L. Turabian, *A Manual for Writers of Term Papers, Theses and Dissertations* (Chicago: University of Chicago Press, 1955). Footnote and bibliography forms here follow *The MLA Style Sheet.*

quotation marks. Titles of long poems (for example, *Paradise Lost*) and titles of plays which are published as books are underlined.

*The edition (if there is more than one) and the place and date of publication.* This information may be necessary to distinguish one edition of a work from other editions, either by the same or different publishers. The pagination of an earlier or later edition may be different from that of the one you are using.

*The volume,* if there is more than one volume, and *the page number (s).*

A footnote numeral must be placed in the text of your paper following the passage for which a reference is being cited. Asterisks and other symbols at one time employed to indicate footnotes are no longer generally used. The footnote numeral should be placed to the right and slightly above the close of the passage to which the footnote refers, whether that passage be a direct quotation, a sentence or paraphrase, or merely an allusion.

At the bottom of the page two blank spaces or a typewritten line should separate the footnotes from the body of the text. A footnote numeral corresponding to the one entered in the text is placed, indented and raised, before the footnote itself. The footnotes are single-spaced and separated by a blank space to allow for the raised footnote numbers.

Sample footnotes for representative kinds of sources may be seen in the following list.

*For a work by a single author*

[1] Perry Miller, *The New England Mind* (New York, 1939), p. 175.

*For a work by two or more authors*

[1] Stephen Kemp Bailey and Howard D. Samuel, *Congress at Work* (New York, 1952), pp. 112–115.

*For a signed article in an edited book containing articles by several authors*

[1] John Dos Passos, "A Question of Elbow Room," *Essays on Individuality,* ed. Felix Morley (Philadelphia, 1958), p. 15.

*For an edited book*

[1] Paul M. Angle, ed. *Created Equal? The Complete Lincoln-Douglas Debates of 1858* (Chicago, 1958), p. 125.

*For a translated work*

[1] Charles Péguy, *Basic Verities,* trans. Ann and Julian Green (New York, 1943), p. 163.

### For a book for which no author or editor is given

[1] *Yearbook of the United Nations 1960* (New York, 1961), p. 124.

### For a magazine article

[1] M. L. Weidenbaum, "Inflationary Effects of Government Programs," *American Journal of Economics*, XIX (January, 1960), 136.

### For an article in an encyclopedia

[1] "Banks and Finance," *Encyclopedia Americana*, I, 152.

### For a government bulletin

[1] *Story of Hoover Dam*. Reclamation Bureau, Conservation Bulletin 9 (Washington, 1961), p. 3.

### For a newspaper article

[1] "The Vatican Guides Activities of a Vast Catholic World," New York *Times*, October 14, 1962, Sec. 4, p. 4.

### For a reference to the Bible

[1] Genesis 4:9–11.

### For a reference to a play

[1] *Hamlet* III: 2:27–30.

A footnote needs to be entered in full only the first time the reference is cited in your paper. Thereafter the reference need consist only of the author's name (or abbreviated title of the book if reference has been made to more than one book by the same author) and the page numbers. *Ibid*. (Latin *ibidem*, "in the same place") and *op. cit*. (Latin *opere citato*, "in the work cited") are much less frequently used. A typical sequence of footnotes would appear as follows:

[1] Perry Miller, *The New England Mind* (New York, 1939), p. 175.
[2] Van Wyck Brooks, *The Flowering of New England* (New York, 1937), p. 277.
[3] Miller, p. 201.

Various other footnote abbreviations and notations may be useful. The abbreviation *loc. cit*. ("in the place cited") may be used if the reference is exactly the same as a reference cited earlier. For example:

[1] Brooks, *loc. cit*.

This refers the reader to the same passage in Brooks as that cited by the full footnote above.

The word *passim* ("here and there, throughout") may be used if you wish to refer the reader to a number of unspecified passages throughout a book or article.

The abbreviation *f.* ("and the following page") is used when a passage cited begins on one page and runs on to the next page. If the passage extends for several pages, the abbreviation *ff.* ("and the following pages") is used.

> [1] Miller, p. 21 f.
> [2] Brooks, p. 130 ff.

The expression *sic* ("thus, in this form") is used following an error in a direct quotation. Frequently it is used after misspellings in a quoted text to call attention to the fact that the misspelling is in the original. It is enclosed in brackets.

> As this writer observes, "The treason of Benidict [*sic*] Arnold is all the more strange in view of his brilliant record in the Revolutionary Army."

## The Bibliography

The bibliography is placed at the end of the paper. It should be arranged alphabetically according to the surnames of the authors and entered according to the form which you have used on your bibliography card. When a large number of sources have been consulted and the bibliography is comparatively long, it may be advisable to divide the items into different groups. Sometimes books and articles are grouped separately. If you have drawn upon a number of general works, such as encyclopedias, handbooks, and dictionaries of special subjects, it may be best to form a group headed "General" and to alphabetize these items by their titles. For some projects of research, it may be advisable to separate those items which are primary sources from those which are secondary. The nature of your material may suggest other divisions which will show the reader the different kinds of sources you have used.

### Form of a Bibliography

Acheson, Dean G. *A Citizen Looks at Congress.* New York, 1957.

Binkley, W. E. "President and Congress," *Journal of Politics,* XI (February, 1949), 65–79.

Burnham, James. *Congress and the American Tradition.* Chicago, 1959.

Carleton, W. G. "Our Congressional Elections: In Defense of the Traditional System," *Political Science Quarterly,* LXX (September, 1955), 341–357.

Flynn, John T. *Meet Your Congress.* Garden City, N.Y., 1944.

Galloway, G. B. "Leadership in the House of Representatives," *Western Political Quarterly*, XII (June, 1959), 417–441.

Griffith, Ernest Stacey. *Congress: Its Contemporary Role*. New York, 1951.

Wilson, Woodrow. *Congressional Government: A Study in American Politics*. Boston and New York, 1913.

Young, Roland Arnold. *The American Congress*. New York, 1958.

Clearly the paraphernalia of footnotes and bibliography, however indispensable to the purpose of a research paper, do not alone make a good one. They are subsidiary to discussing some subject with knowledge, perspective, and thoroughness. Those things which will make the paper effective and worth doing must be considered from the beginning and during the whole process of writing. They will include finding a subject area and defining a true subject within it, constructing a workable plan and proportioning the parts with regard to the central point, and conscientiously excluding irrelevant material, however enticing it may be in itself. It will be clear that these are in fact the prerequisites for any effective essay. We hardly need note that those qualities of style—good sentences, exact diction, consistency of tone—are as necessary in the research paper as elsewhere.

## SUGGESTED TOPICS

For many reasons you may be asked by your instructor, even in a freshman English course, to limit your topic to some specified area, or to choose a particular kind of topic. If you are free to select any topic which you wish to investigate, the range of possibilities is as broad as your interest and the resources of your library. The following list suggests something of the diversity of possibilities; you may find it a useful stimulant to your ideas if you wish to review topics to fix upon one of special interest to you. Note that all of these topics are really subject areas, within which you would have to find a true focus if you were to produce a satisfactory paper.

The New England Town Meeting
The First Transcontinental Railroad
The Shaker Sect
The Poetry of Amy Lowell
Rommel's North African Campaign in World War II
The Bessemer Steel Process
The Mormon Church
John Brown's Raid at Harpers Ferry
The Conquest of Tuberculosis
The Chicago School of Literary Realism

Radar
The Carlsbad Caverns
Esperanto
Anti-trust Legislation
Rabies
The Purchase of Alaska
The Origin of Phi Beta Kappa Society
H. L. Mencken
The Williamsburg Restoration
The Taft-Hartley Labor Act
The Cherokee Indians
Sugar Production in the United States

The Economic Theories of Thorstein Veblen

The Evolution of the Styles of Automobiles

The Scopes Trial at Dayton, Tennessee

Andrew Jackson's Victory at New Orleans

The Influence of the Tabloid on American Journalism

Indiana Humorists

The Yalta Conference of the Allied Leaders

Football in the 1890's

The Function of Chlorophyll

Modern Psychiatric Care

The Development of Toll Highways

The Story of the King James Version of the Bible

The Development of Cotton Growing in California

The Construction of the Erie Canal

Lincoln's Career as a Lawyer

Spectrum Analysis

Boulder Dam

The Value of Reforestation

The Muckraking Movement

Thomas Paine's Role in the American Revolution

Smoke Abatement in Cities

The Novels of Robert Penn Warren

The Novels of E. M. Forster

T. S. Eliot as a Critic

The "Fugitive" Poets

The Off-Broadway Theater

The Sacco-Vanzetti Case

The European Common Market

The Medieval University

The Theory of the Business Cycle

Uranium

The American Civil Liberties Union

The "Bull Moose" Movement

J. D. Salinger

The Chicago Fire of 1871

The Modern Educational and Charitable Foundation

Automation

The Career of Jesse James

Rock Collecting

Contemporary Negro Literature

Magnesium

William Jennings Bryan

The Short Stories of O. Henry

Migratory Birds

Adult Education Programs

Custer's Last Stand

The Plays of Tennessee Williams

# SPECIMEN RESEARCH PAPER

The author of the following article is a professor of English and a specialist in American literature. Very few undergraduates, of course, could produce such a finished piece of writing. Nevertheless, the article can serve as a model, both in its organization and in its documentation, for the research paper you may be assigned.

*The title* accurately reflects the subject matter of the article. Because he has limited himself to consideration of one aspect of one play, the author is able to say something significant and offer substantial evidence in an article of approximately three thousand words. He does not preclude the possibility of discussing other plays by O'Neill or the works of other authors, but he does make clear to the reader that all the material he presents will be clearly relevant to "O'Neill's Universalizing Technique in *The Iceman Cometh.*" The student writer would do well to limit his subject wisely and to establish the limitations he has set in a carefully worded title.

The student will profit by studying the *organization* of the following paper. Whether or not the author did in fact follow a carefully prepared outline is beside the point; what is important is that the reader can, even as he reads, work out his own outline. The paper contains an introduction, a step by step development of the topic, a conclusion, and a summary. The reader can move easily from point *A* to point *B* to point *C*; he knows when discussion of one aspect of the topic has been completed and when the next begins, and he welcomes the precise transitional signals.

*Introduction.*   In the first paragraph the author establishes his critical premise—that works of universal appeal must have particular roots—and he acknowledges his debt to two O'Neill biographers who have provided the necessary particulars for his study. In the second paragraph the author states in general terms what he is attempting to do and how he plans to do it. In a sense he is saying to the reader, "I am doing this in this manner because . . ." The student writer, too, should mention the work of writers to whom he is heavily indebted and establish—if possible, justify—his methodology. In the third paragraph the author provides a rough outline of all that is to follow. Note that he tells the reader what the major portion of the paper will be. The reader can now expect a certain proportioning of material and is ready to follow the development of the central idea.

I. In this brief section the author presents representative adverse criticism of *The Iceman Cometh.* One could argue that this material could just as well have been placed at the beginning of Section VI, where the author responds to the critics he has cited, but the pattern Mr. Wright follows recognizes the value of introducing contrary opinions before developing one's own point of view. The reader is thus in the position to evaluate the writer's statements in the light of opposing viewpoints.

II. In these two paragraphs the author prepares the ground for his major consideration by establishing the particulars ("the base in reality") of which he spoke in his opening paragraph. Note how in footnote 9 the author provides additional supporting information which he does not wish to include in the text.

III, IV, V. Here is the major portion of the paper, the sections in which the author shows how the particulars he has mentioned "achieve universal meaning." The author closely follows the rough outline he has given in the introductory section. Section III deals with the "identification with the spirit of Man," Section IV with "the language of ritual, myth, and symbol," and Section V with "poetic density." Each section is fully developed, thoroughly documented, and connected by precise transitional devices. It is clear that the author has done what he has told us he would do in this introduction. We cannot know what the author's writing process was, but many writers begin to work on their introduction *after* they have completed at least a rough draft of the rest of the paper.

VI. In the final section the author returns to the negative criticism he has cited in Section I and shows that "the qualities that give the play its chance to live forever . . . grow out of the elements of the play most often criticized," and he takes these up point by point. He then provides the reader with an effective summary of the article and concludes with a quotation from O'Neill himself.

*Bibliography.* Because no bibliography was given in the journal in which the article appeared, the *List of Works Cited,* a more accurate heading than *Bibliography,* was prepared by making reference to the footnotes. The items are arranged in alphabetical order and follow the conventions of *The MLA Style Sheet.*

---

# O'Neill's Universalizing
# Technique in
# The Iceman Cometh

## Robert C. Wright

---

One measure of greatness in a work of art is its ability to speak to men in different ages. Yet, paradoxically, to achieve this universal appeal all great works must have their roots in particular individuals who move about in a particular setting at a particular time. The universal characteristics of plays by a Sophocles or a Shakespeare make them meaningful today, even though the particulars upon which those plays were based have long been lost. Of course it is still too early to say whether or not Eugene O'Neill's play, *The Iceman Cometh,* will have the permanence of *Hamlet,* yet it does have some of those elements which make for universal appeal and for permanence. It is especially fortunate, moreover, that the particulars basic to *The Iceman Cometh* are not lost but have been revealed with some detail in recent O'Neill biographies, one by Doris Alexander[1] and another by Arthur and Barbara Gelb.[2]

The purpose of this article will be to examine the process by which O'Neill in *The Iceman Cometh* is able to develop universal significance

Robert C. Wright. Reprinted from *Modern Drama,* VIII (May, 1965), 1–11. By permission of *Modern Drama* and of the author.

[1] Doris Alexander, *The Tempering of Eugene O'Neill* (New York, 1962).
[2] Arthur and Barbara Gelb, *O'Neill* (New York, 1962).

out of the sordid lives he examined firsthand in Greenwich Village saloons. The focus, then, is on methodology and not on interpretation, on the creative process and not on philosophical implications. Yet such an examination is bound to touch philosophy at several points, and an understanding of O'Neill's method will have a bearing upon interpretation. It will, in fact, tend to correct the work of some critics who did not understand the magnitude of O'Neill's vision or the sweep of his canvas.

The first business of the paper will be to summarize briefly the major negative criticisms of the play and then to identify the particulars upon which the drama is founded. The major portion of the paper will show how these particulars achieve universal meaning in at least three ways: through their identification with the spirit of Man; through the language of ritual, myth, and symbol; and through poetic density. Finally, the paper will show how an understanding of O'Neill's universalizing techniques negates much of the criticism directed at the play.

I

The most frequent criticism of *The Iceman Cometh* is that it is too long and repetitious. Eric Bentley would like to cut the play by an hour, making most cuts in the speeches of Larry, because he says Larry's pessimism is easy to understand, or of Hugo, whose talk Bentley says is "pretentious, unimaginative symbolism." [3]

Bonamy Dobree, who reviewed *The Iceman* for the *Sewanee Review* prior to seeing the play performed, wrote that it is "too long for dramatic tension to be maintained," that we are given more than we need to know for drama, that, in fact, the play is more novel than drama.[4] Several of the first-night reviewers of the original Broadway production mentioned length and repetition as weaknesses. John Mason Brown accused O'Neill of saying everything twice; "too long" said Louis Kronenberger; Brooks Atkinson wrote that it was one of his best plays but long.[5]

To the charges of wordiness and repetition, critics added those of sordidness and lack of humor. "It shows complete lack of humor," Brooks Atkinson wrote in *The New York Times*,[6] and Kronenberger of *PM* thought sickness was too easily applauded.[7] Eric Bentley asked: "How could one be ennobled by identifying oneself with any of his characters?" [8] The rest of this article, by detailing the ennobling process, will provide some answers to Bentley's question.

[3] Eric Bentley, "Trying to Like O'Neill," *Kenyon Review*, XIV (Summer 1952), 476–492. (Quoted from *O'Neill and His Plays*, ed. Oscar Cargill, New York, 1961, p. 334.)
[4] Bonamy Dobree, "Mr. O'Neill's Latest Play," *The Sewanee Review*, LVI (Winter 1948), 123.
[5] Gelb, p. 875.
[6] Brooks Atkinson, "The Iceman Cometh," *The New York Times*, October 20, 1946.
[7] Gelb, p. 875.
[8] Bentley, p. 339.

## II

The Gelb biography establishes beyond question the solid and sordid base in reality of *The Iceman Cometh*. Originals of Hope's saloon are described in detail, and comparisons between real people and the fictional characters of O'Neill's play are striking.[9]

The Gelbs show beyond doubt that there is a basis in particular individuals and scenes upon which O'Neill could work to build a play of universal significance. O'Neill himself was conscious of both the depths and heights, the particular and the universal, inherent in this sordid environment. Of his characters he once said, "They were a hard lot, at first glance, every type—sailors on shore leave or stranded; longshoremen, waterfront riffraff, gangsters, down-and-outers, drifters from the ends of the earth." [10] But in the artist's mind the characters were already ennobled, for at another time he said, "Remember, goodness can surmount anything. The people in that saloon were the best friends I've ever known. Their weakness was not an evil. It is a weakness found in all men." [11]

## III

O'Neill obviously had no difficulty in identifying himself with these human derelicts, but to give his play universality he had to lead an audience into a similar identification. This identification is made possible, paradoxically, by the distance set up between the world of Harry Hope and the world of the audience. Quite obviously, as S. K. Winther points out, no point of similarity can be established on the basis of social position, income, houses, or any of the hundred standards by which ordinary men live.[12]

O'Neill has used a universalizing technique common to Shakespeare and Sophocles, but he has put a reverse twist on it. Shakespearean and Greek heroes are raised so high above the audience that unimportant similarities drop away, whereas O'Neill heroes are lowered so far below

---

[9] For example, the Gelbs show that Harry Hope's saloon is a composite of three New York saloons patronized by O'Neill between 1912 and 1915. Harry Hope himself is shown to be a combination of Tom Wallace, proprietor of the Hell Hole, and Jimmy-the-Priest, another bartender. Hickey turns out to be most like a character from the Hell Hole called "Happy," a collector for a laundry chain, but he also has some traits the Gelbs note in Jamie, Eugene's brother. Jamie appears, too, in the character of Willy Oban, who has a resentful emotional dependence on his father. Jimmy Tomorrow is shown to be a character drawn from O'Neill's roommate at Jimmy-the-Priest's, J. Findlater-Byth, who was also James O'Neill's press agent. Hugo Kalmar is a picture of Hippolyte Havel; Cecil Lewis, the captain, is taken from a Major Adams whom O'Neill knew; Parritt is partly drawn from Louis Holliday; Larry Slade is Terry Carlin.

[10] Gelb, p. 171.

[11] Croswell Bowen, *The Curse of the Misbegotten* (New York, 1959), pp. 308–310.

[12] S. K. Winther, *Eugene O'Neill* (New York, 1961), p. 303.

the audience that the same aesthetic distance is achieved. In both cases, the members of the audience are led to identify themselves, not with the hero as individual, but more importantly with the spirit of the hero as Man. Winther says of O'Neill:

> He reduced the outer shell of man almost to ultimate negation. Stripped bare as a forked radish, all that remained is the Pipe Dream, the great *Tomorrow Movement* which is imbedded in the hearts of men. It is this abstract ideal of life that gives universality to the tragic character and not social status. It is what Matthew Arnold called an inward condition of the spirit, not an outward set of circumstances that measures the meaning of life.

Cyrus Day puts it another way in comparing *The Iceman Cometh* with *Death of a Salesman*: "Willie Loman of *Death of a Salesman* is adrift in contemporary American society; Hickey is adrift in the universe. The difference is the difference between O'Neill's aims and the aims of all other modern dramatists." [13]

That O'Neill himself was consciously striving for the universal is clear in a letter he wrote to Arthur Hobson Quinn in which he says that he tries to see the transfiguring nobility of tragedy in seemingly the most ignoble debased lives—here he comes as near tragedy in the Greek sense as one can.

> And just here is where I am a most confirmed mystic too, always trying to interpret Life in terms of lives, never just lives in terms of characters. I'm always acutely conscious of the Force behind (Fate, God, our biological past creating our present, whatever one calls it—mystery certainly) and of the one eternal tragedy of Man in his glorious self-destructive struggle to make the force express him instead of being, as an animal is, an infinitesimal incident in its expression.[14]

## IV

In addition to the technique of encouraging identification with the spirit of Man, O'Neill achieves universality in *The Iceman Cometh* by using the symbolic language of ritual and myth, which Erich Fromm calls "the forgotten language." O'Neill's understanding of that language comes in large part through his study of the Greek plays and through Nietzsche's analysis of the Dionysian and Apollonian elements in them. In *The Birth of Tragedy*, Nietzsche shows how the Greek satyr chorus of the dithyramb was the salvation of Greek art.[15] Dionysian art is characterized by Nietzsche as music; Apollonian as image and concept. The music of the Dionysian chorus, Nietzsche says, "incites us to symbolic

---

[13] Cyrus Day, "The Iceman and the Bridegroom," *Modern Drama*, I (May, 1958), 3.

[14] Bentley, p. 339.

[15] Friedrich Nietzsche, *The Birth of Tragedy* (New York, 1956), p. 52.

intuition of the Dionysiac universality; second, it endows that symbolic image with supreme significance. Music alone allows us to understand the delight felt at the annihilation of the individual."

But music did not function alone in Greek tragedy. It was combined with myth. Nietzsche asks: How can ugliness and disharmony, which are the content of tragic myth, inspire aesthetic delight? In answer, he says that this world can be justified only as an aesthetic phenomenon:

> On this view, tragic myth has convinced us that even the ugly and discordant are merely an aesthetic game which the will, in its utter exuberance, plays with itself. . . . The delight created by tragic myth has the same origin as the delight dissonance in music creates.

Nietzsche says that both music and tragic myth shed light on a region in whose rapt harmony dissonance and the horror of existence fade away in enchantment. "Confident of their superior powers, they both toy with the sting of displeasure, and by their toying they both justify the existence of even the 'worst possible world.' "

O'Neill's most ambitious attempt to get at the universality that music and tragic myth offer is *Lazarus Laughed,* a play for what he called an imaginative theater. He described such a theater as

> a legitimate descendant of the first theater that sprang, by virtue of man's imaginative interpretation of life, out of his worship of Dionysus . . . a theater returned to its highest and sole significant function as Temple where the religion of poetical interpretation and symbolical celebration of life is communicated to human beings, starved in spirit by their soul stifling daily struggle to exist as masks among the masks of the living.[16]

Thus through Nietzsche, O'Neill came to see the theater as a place of religious expression, a temple where rituals were enacted celebrating the mystery of human life. This religious atmosphere is quite readily apparent in *Lazarus Laughed,* but it is not so apparent in *The Iceman Cometh.* Yet, according to Leonard Chabrowe, *The Iceman* in a subtle way is no less Dionysian than *Lazarus.* He sees the play as a transportation of *Lazarus* to an idiom suitable for the New York stage. "It is different from Lazarus in naturalistic setting and pessimistic mood," he writes, "but in action and main characters appears to have been completely derived." The mask scheme, the large crowds, the ecstatic singing and dancing of *Lazarus* are missing, yet celebratory ritual is still achieved by means of a chorus, a repetitive rhythm in the dialogue, and an archetypal pattern in the action. Chabrowe sees a parallel to the theater of Lazarus in *The Iceman's* Hickey. Both stimulate movement of action. The music of *Lazarus* he sees in the rhythmic structure of the dialogue in *The Iceman.* Where *Lazarus Laughed* celebrates an acceptance of life, *The Iceman Cometh* celebrates a despair of life, but in both one who is reborn, who finds a second life on earth, comes to save Man himself.

[16] Leonard Chabrowe, "Dionysus in 'The Iceman Cometh,' " *Modern Drama,* IV (February, 1962), 378.

In *The Iceman Cometh*, the residents of the saloon provide a chorus of sorts. Each resident has an individual identity and distinct pipe dream, but Chabrowe believes all have a more distinct identity as a member of the group. He finds a contrapuntal effect in the way the chorus reacts to the birthday party. O'Neill's directions say, "a chorus of sneering taunts begins, punctuated by nasty jeering laughter." However, in Act IV when Parritt asks Rocky sarcastically why Larry does not take a hop off the fire escape, the chorus is unified. Rocky's reply is echoed by everybody "almost in a chorus of one voice." Chabrowe contends that in this ritual effect O'Neill celebrates life in the flesh. The effect is enhanced by other ritual forms even more disguised—the musical structure of the dialogue, the repetition, the psychological movement which takes the place of physical movement in *Lazarus*. It would take a more ambitious article than this to trace the musical patterns in *The Iceman* or to explain the function of the repetitive phrases, such as Hugo's "Soon you vill eat hot dogs beneath the villow trees and trink free wine." That the ritual structure is there and that an understanding director can interpret it powerfully was demonstrated in the successful José Quintero production of *The Iceman Cometh* in 1957. Quintero wrote of the play as follows:

> It resembles a complex musical form, with themes repeating themselves with slight variations as melodies do in a symphony. It is a valid device, though O'Neill has often been criticized for it by those who do not see the strength and depth of meaning the repetition achieves.

Through an experiencing of ritual, which is a singing and dancing about life, one is led to an aesthetic justification of despair. Life, no matter how sordid, is renewed by a celebratory experience of it.

Tragic myth is perhaps even less obvious in *The Iceman Cometh* than ritual, and it is not so evident here as in other O'Neill plays, but it is used nevertheless. The Dionysus myth as analyzed by Nietzsche provided him with a method, and the Apollonian myth with an understanding of illusion. One might see the Oedipus myth in the relationship between Parritt and his mother. Although Parritt finally admits that he hated her, a reader familiar with O'Neill's thesis that the presence of hate is a sure sign of love would see Parritt's betrayal of his mother as motivated by love and jealousy.

Much more significant than these myths, however, is O'Neill's imitation of the Last Supper of the New Testament in his grouping of the twelve disciples at Hope's birthday party, where Hickey comes in as savior. Cyrus Day has pointed out the striking parallels. The grouping of the party is carefully detailed in O'Neill's stage directions and is reminiscent of Leonardo da Vinci's painting of the Last Supper. Day points out that Hickey leaves the party as Christ does, aware that he is to be executed. The three whores resemble the three Marys. Parritt could be likened to Judas Iscariot: he is twelfth on the list of characters just as Judas was twelfth; he betrays his mother for a small sum just as Judas betrayed Christ for thirty pieces of silver; Hickey reads Parritt's mind and motives just as Christ read those of Judas.

Thus, as Nietzsche says, "Music and tragic myth . . . both shed their transfiguring light on a region in whose rapt harmony dissonance and horror of existence fade away in enchantment."

In addition to the universality achieved through the symbolism of ritual and myth, O'Neill used other symbols to lift his play above the particular. According to Erich Fromm, symbols may be conventional, accidental, or universal. "The universal symbol," Fromm says, "is rooted in the properties of our body, our senses, and our mind, which are common to all men and, therefore, not restricted to individuals or specific groups. Indeed the language of the universal symbol is the one common tongue developed by the human race, a language which it forgot before it succeeded in developing a universal conventional language." [17]

In *The Iceman Cometh,* O'Neill chooses symbols that can be shared by all, using the physical world to give expression to an inner experience. What better visualization could he find for "hopeless hope" than Harry Hope's saloon? "It's the No Chance Saloon," Larry says. "It's Bedrock Bar, The End of the Line Cafe, The Bottom of the Sea Rathskeller." What better way to give physical representation to a pipe dream than through those alcoholic dreams created on nickel whiskey. Under the influence of Hickey's reform, the drunks find their liquor impotent, but when Hickey is believed to be insane the alcohol again can create dreams. "Bejees, fellers, I'm feeling the old kick, or I'm a liar! It's putting life back in me!" Hope shouts jubilantly.

The characters themselves function as symbols, and a paper could be devoted to their roles as representatives of universal truths. As a brief indication of the symbolic gold to be mined, consider Hickey. Cyrus Day points out that he is most obviously representative of death, but that he can be linked to both the secular savior Freud and the Christian Savior Christ. In representing death, not love, Hickey rejects the Christian gospel; in proving that man can't live without illusions, which religions were to Freud, Hickey rejects Freud too. Rosamond Gilder suggests that Hickey, Parritt, and Larry symbolize three aspects of Man—each element loving and loathing the other.[18] Even the two women who never appear on stage assume symbolic meaning. Edwin Engel thinks Hickey's wife and Parritt's mother represent antithetical aspects of love—the former an excess of love and forgiveness, the latter a deficiency. Both generate hate in men.[19] Each character in turn could be examined for his symbolic role, but these examples will serve to illustrate how O'Neill uses character as symbol.

Even the title carries a heavy symbolic load and lends support to the

[17] Erich Fromm, *The Forgotten Language* (New York, 1957), p. 18.

[18] Rosamond Gilder, "Each in His Own Way . . . *The Iceman Cometh,*" *Theatre Arts,* XXX (December, 1946), 687–688.

[19] Edwin A. Engel, *The Haunted Heroes of Eugene O'Neill* (Cambridge, 1953), p. 286.

New Testament parallel. The Biblical "cometh" suggests Matthew 25:5-6: "While the bridegroom tarried, they all slumbered and slept. And at midnight there was a cry made, Behold the bridegroom cometh." Cyrus Day has shown how O'Neill substitutes the iceman for the bridegroom and lets him stand for death, the opposite of Christ, the bridegroom, who stands for man's hope of redemption, victory over death, and salvation in the world to come. Larry says, "Well, be God, it fits, for Death was the Iceman Hickey called to his home!" Union with the bridegroom is parodied in union with the iceman, who is a symbol of adulterous love. Such a union results in surrender to death and acquiescence to personal annihilation. Finally, in addition to the twentieth century association of the iceman with adultery, there is implicit in the title a seventeenth century poetic convention in which "to die" carried often the secondary implication of sexual consummation.

## V

This density of meaning in the title is typical of the poetic density inherent in the whole play—a density that contributes to universality by providing something for everyone. Critics have found at least five serious themes in The Iceman Cometh. They center around the concepts of love, death, illusion, peace, and existence. The following comments indicate the type of thinking the play generates.

Engel says that the unmasking of love is the main intention of the play because the tragedies of individual characters achieved that end— love has been converted into its opposite, death. "Out of the unmasking," he says, "one truth, together with its corollary emerges above all others: Love is an illusion and all women are bitches or whores." Strangely enough, in the same play Bentley finds the admonition not to hate and punish but to love and forgive.

As for the theme of death, Chabrowe says the implied message of The Iceman Cometh is that "if men were capable of a higher form of spiritual life by which they could overcome reality, they would not have to escape it in death. Reality is a choice between psychological and physical death. If the pipe dream is shattered, there is no choice but physical death since life then is unlivable." As stated by Day, the death theme is that "all men are waiting for the iceman, but only those who have shed their ultimate illusions are aware that the final end and unrealized meaning of their lives is death."

The role of illusion in the play is variously interpreted. Doris Falk says the play shows that all self-images are illusions, projected by a self that is worthless, if it exists at all. The self and the ideal are both equal, according to her view of the play, and both also equal to zero. The thesis of the play, according to the Gelbs, is that man cannot live without illusions, that he must cling to his pipe dreams, even knowing they are pipe dreams, in order to survive.

Peace is the central human need *The Iceman* defines, according to Engel, but a peace without love. He points to three ways in which O'Neill's characters find peace: in dreams, in drunkenness, and in death. The play has been seen as an unmasking of existence. Rosamond Gilder sees *The Iceman* as an allegory of man's pitiful state, a parable of his search for redemption. Doris Falk sees Larry struggling with the "existential" dilemma: man's chief struggle, according to this mode of thought, is not with something but with nothing, not with evil but with valuelessness that is neither good nor evil. Man is completely responsible both for the values he creates and for the actions predicated on them. Such utter self-contingency can be paralyzing; it provides freedom, but it is that terrifying freedom from which, as Fromm points out, man feels compelled to escape.

This brief survey of opinion should indicate something of the density the play achieves. It was this quality of density that Dudley Nichols had in mind when he wrote, "The truth about *The Iceman* is that all kinds of things are happening all the time, but you have to listen and watch." And it is this quality that led the Gelbs to anticipate the accumulation of as large a body of criticism for *The Iceman Cometh* as has been gathered on *Hamlet*.

## VI

The deliberate building of density, then, along with the encouragement of audience identification with the spirit of Man and the use of the universal language of ritual, myth, and symbol, are the universalizing techniques O'Neill uses in *The Iceman Cometh*. Ironically enough, these universalizing techniques—the qualities that give the play its chance to live forever—grow out of the elements in the play most often criticized: length, sordid material, and even lack of humor.

With respect to length, the play must be long in order to accommodate the devices of ritual. It is a symbolic play, not a realistic play, and must be judged on how well it achieves its own purposes. It is long, but the long format is necessary, as we have seen, to provide the necessary vehicle for the symbolic language of ritual and myth.

Although Bentley fails to see how one can be ennobled by any of O'Neill's characters, the very sordidness and hopelessness of these derelicts provides the aesthetic distance necessary for us to identify ourselves, not with any one individual, but with the spirit of Man. This identification, too, is in keeping with O'Neill's purpose in emphasizing spiritual values—negative though they may be.

Humor plays its role too, as a universalizing factor, even though Brooks Atkinson finds *The Iceman* completely lacking in that quality. Vivian Hopkins, in comparing *The Iceman* to Gorky's *The Lower Depths*, feels that O'Neill's lines fail to attain the quick bite of Gorky's humor, perhaps as a consequence of the symbolic purpose of the play.[20] The difference is that between the humor of a realistic play and that of a symbolic play. In *The Iceman,* the humor isn't so much in the lines themselves as in the situation. For example, we find humor in Harry Hope's attempt to overcome his pipe dream and cross the street. We smile at his hesitation, his elaborate preparations to accomplish so simple an act, and at his rationalizing of his retreat. We find that the smile links us to Harry in such a way that our own exaggerated attempts to break out of our daydreams seem tragically funny too. We smile at Harry, at ourselves, and at Man. And in the smile we realize a universal truth. Drew Pallette says, "His humor in the last plays functions to intensify the portrayal of man's position. But it is also a very personal affirmation of the value of all human beings." [21]

In its length, then, in its sordidness, and in its humor, as well as in its density, *The Iceman Cometh* achieves universality. These qualities are strengths, not weaknesses. Some indication that *The Iceman* is already on its way to transcending time and place is suggested in Hopkins' comparison of O'Neill's play to *The Lower Depths.* She shows how Gorky uses a similar set of characters to promote a hopeful pre-Revolutionary theory, while O'Neill uses the same basic group to present a post-Revolutionary disillusionment and despair. O'Neill dates the play clearly in postdepression and prewar 1939, but Hopkins sees it reading equally well as a symptom of postwar despair in the Sartre manner.

When the few weaknesses attributed to *The Iceman Cometh* turn out to be strengths, when the play already seems to break the bounds of time and place, is it any wonder that O'Neill could say of the play, "I have a confident hunch that this play, as drama, is one of the best things I've ever done. In some ways, perhaps *the* best."

### List of Works Cited

Alexander, Doris. *The Tempering of Eugene O'Neill.* New York, 1962.

Atkinson, Brooks. "The Iceman Cometh," The New York *Times,* October 20, 1946.

Bentley, Eric. "Trying to Like O'Neill," Kenyon Review, XIV (Summer 1952), 476–492.

Bowen, Croswell. *The Curse of the Misbegotten.* New York, 1959.

Chabrowe, Leonard. "Dionysus in 'The Iceman Cometh,'" *Modern Drama,* IV (February 1962), 378.

Day, Cyrus. "The Iceman and the Bridegroom," *Modern Drama,* I (May 1958), 3.

Dobree, Bonamy. "Mr. O'Neill's Latest Play," *The Sewanee Review,* LVI (Winter 1948), 123.

Engel, Edwin A. *The Haunted Heroes of Eugene O'Neill.* Cambridge, 1953.

[20] Vivian C. Hopkins, " 'The Iceman' Seen through 'The Lower Depths,' " *College English,* II (November, 1949), 87.
[21] Drew B. Pallette, "O'Neill and the Comic Spirit," *Modern Drama,* III (December, 1960), 278.

Fromm, Erich. *The Forgotten Language.* New York, 1957.

Gelb, Arthur, Barbara Gelb. *O'Neill.* New York, 1962.

Gilder, Rosamond. "Each in His Own Way . . . *The Iceman Cometh*," *Theatre Arts,* XXX (December 1946), 687–688.

Hopkins, Vivian C. " 'The Iceman' Seen through 'The Lower Depths,' " *College English,* II (November 1949), 87.

Nietzsche, Friedrich. *The Birth of Tragedy.* New York, 1956.

Pallette, Drew B. "O'Neill and the Comic Spirit," *Modern Drama,* III (December 1960), 278.

Winther, S. K. *Eugene O'Neill.* New York, 1961.

# Part Four

## A Concise Handbook

# Grammar

Grammar may be defined as the science which describes the elements of language and the principles by which they are combined to form units of meaning. In some older studies of language, a distinction was often drawn between grammar and syntax. By this distinction, grammar was limited to the classification of elements and syntax to the rules which explain how they function together. However, since the purpose of the following section is to enable us to analyze the structure of acceptable English sentences we shall use the single term, grammar, for we must deal with both the classification of elements, or parts, and the rules which govern their relationship to one another.

## THE PARTS OF SPEECH

Most languages of the general family to which English belongs classify all words into parts of speech. This classification is made partly on the basis of the word's meaning, partly on the basis of its function, and, in some instances, partly on the basis of its form. It must be emphasized at the beginning that the meaning which a word has does not always determine the part of speech to which it belongs in an utterance. The part of speech to which it belongs can sometimes be determined only by its use in a given construction.

### The Noun

1A   The noun is often defined, on the basis of meaning, as a word which stands for a thing. This definition is not amiss if we understand that "thing" may symbolize an entity which is conceptual as well as one which is tangible. In sentences such as "The *orange* is a fruit," "*Snow* is cold," and "The *book* lies on the table," we have no trouble in perceiving that the italicized words are nouns, since they stand for concrete objects. We must note, however, that things created by our imagination or intellect are equally nouns in terms of this definition. The word "centaur," standing for an imaginary beast, is a noun in the sentence "The centaur is a mythological creature." In the sentences "*Justice* is the aim of every state," "*Nothing* comes from nothing," and "*Faith* is the evidence of things hoped for," the italicized words are equally nouns in that they stand for something which has a conceptual, though not a material, substance.

**1B**   The noun can also be described on the basis of form. In written English the vast majority of nouns form their plural, which is the number signifying more than one, by adding *-s* or *-es* to the singular form: *boy, boys; box, boxes,* etc. Some nouns have a change of consonant in addition to this change: *leaf, leaves; hoof, hooves; scarf, scarves;* or a change of internal vowel: *man, men; mouse, mice; goose, geese.* A few nouns exhibit no change in the plural: *deer, deer; sheep, sheep.* In spoken English the majority of plural nouns end in an *s*, a *z*, or an *iz* sound, depending on what the final sound of the singular is: *cat* (*s*); *dog* (*z*); *church* (*iz*).

**1C**   The noun can further be described on the basis of its function. It functions as the subject of a verb, the object of a verb, the object of a preposition, or in some other capacity.

**1D**   On the basis of their meanings and their grammatical functions, nouns can be divided into subclasses. Some of the common subclasses are collective nouns, common nouns, proper nouns, mass nouns, and count nouns.

**1E**   Nouns are said to be collective when they stand not for a single thing but for a collection or group of things. The words *jury, committee, team,* and *company* are examples. Grammatically these nouns are distinctive because they sometimes occur with plural verbs and in plural pronoun forms.

**1F**   A noun is said to be common when it stands for any one of a class of things. The words *boy, city, holiday* are common nouns.

**1G**   A noun is classified as proper when it stands for a particular individual or a unique thing. Thus *Huckleberry Finn, Chicago, Thomas,* and the *Fourth of July* are proper nouns. Grammatically, proper nouns, unlike common nouns, are not preceded by an article (*a, the*) unless they are modified (*The Chicago of 1965 is different from the Chicago of 1900*).

**1H**   A noun is called a mass noun when it refers to a substance or a property that we normally do not think of as being separable into individual units. *Air, electricity, sugar* are mass nouns. Grammatically mass nouns are not preceded by articles unless they are modified.

1I A count noun refers to things that can be separated into individual units. A *chair*, a *boy*, a *city* are count nouns.

1J The preceding subclasses are not exclusive. *Boy* is a count noun and a common noun. *Team* is a collective noun and a count noun.

1K Because the noun is a word standing for something which has material or conceptual substance, it is sometimes called a **substantive**.

## The Verb

2A The verb is a word which asserts that something occurs or exists. This means that the verb either narrates an action or affirms a state of being.

> Henry *threw* his hat in the ring.
> She *walked* the entire distance.
> The student *wrote* the paper.

> There *are* twenty-four hours in a day.
> The room *seems* warm.
> The man *appeared* honest.

Formally, the verb can be described as a class which takes the following series of suffixes: *-s* (third person singular, present), *-ing* (present progressive), *-ed* (simple past), *-en* (past participle). The last two suffixes vary in form according to the verb.

2B Verbs can occur in a simple form, as in the simple present and in the imperative, for example.

> I *talk* to him every day.
> *Go* home.

2C The simple form can be changed, or added to by a suffix, as in the simple past and in the present progressive, for example.

> He talk*ed* too long.
> He sp*o*ke to his brother. (sp*ea*k to sp*o*ke)
> He is walk*ing* to town.

2D Simple and changed forms of the verb can occur in combination with auxiliary (helping) verbs, as in the future and past perfect, for example.

> I *will go* at eight.
> He *had spoken* before.

The common auxiliaries are: shall, will, can, may, should, would, could, might, must, ought to, have, be, and do.

**2E**   The number of changes, additions, and combinations that can qualify the meaning of the English verb give it a remarkable variety and flexibility; it is estimated that over 120 different grammatical meanings (such as, I *am walking*, I *could have walked*, I *must have been walking*, and so on) can be expressed by the English verbal system. Some of these meanings are suggested below.

**2F**   TENSE. Verbs can be qualified to indicate *time* of occurrence or state of being.

The **simple present** indicates an action which is habitual or customary, not temporary.

He *walks* to school every day.

NOTE: This same simple form can be used together with a word or a phrase to indicate future time.

The concert series *begins* on Sunday.

The **simple past** indicates an action which took place at a time remote from the present, usually in the past.

He *walked* to town yesterday.

The **simple future** indicates an action which will take place in future time.

He *will walk* more quickly tomorrow.

The **present perfect** generally expresses an action which began in past time and either continues up to the present or has some reference to the present.

He *has walked* three miles already.

The **past perfect** indicates an action which was completed at some point in the past before the completion of another action in the past.

He *had walked* four miles before he found a gas station.

The **future perfect** indicates an action which will have been completed at some point in the future.

He *will have walked* ten miles by the time he reaches here.

**2G**   ASPECT. Verbs can be qualified to indicate the nature of the action being described.

Forms of the verb *to be* combine with the simple form *ing* to indicate actions which are not permanent.

He *is playing* tennis now.
I *had been walking* for two hours when the bus passed.

**2H** MOOD. Verbs can be qualified to indicate the attitude of the user toward the action or state of being.

The auxiliaries combine with the verb to indicate possibility, doubt, tentativeness, obligation.

> He *can walk* now.
> He *may be here* by seven.
> He *could do* it, if he wanted to.
> They *should wear* ties and jackets.

The simple form is used to express a command. This is called the imperative.

> *Listen* to this.

In some constructions when (1) the sentence expresses a hypothetical condition, or a condition contrary to fact, or (2) an object clause follows certain verbs, there is a change in the verb form, called the **subjunctive.** Its use, however, is decreasing.

Hypothetical condition:

> If I *were* in his place, I would do something quickly.
> (*was* changed to *were*.)

After certain verbs followed by object clause.

> He urged that John *consult* a doctor.
> They demanded that Harry *be* a candidate.

**2I** VOICE. Verbs can be qualified to indicate whether the subject is acting or being acted upon. If the subject acts, the verb is said to be **active.**

> The student *found* the book.

If the subject and verb are so related that the subject of the verb is the recipient of the action, the verb is said to be **passive.**

> The book *was found* by the student.

When a verb is changed from active to passive voice, the original subject nearly always becomes the object of a preposition.

> The children *raised* a cry.
> A cry *was raised* by the children.

Verbs which can be made into passives, that is, those which can take objects, are sometimes called **transitive verbs.** Those which do not have objects are called **intransitive verbs.**

Notice that the same verb may be transitive or intransitive according to the construction in which it occurs.

> Mr. Brown *farms* a tract of 300 acres.
> Mr. Brown owns a store, and he also *farms*.

**2J** PERSON. Verbs can indicate that the subject is being spoken about by adding an *s* to the simple form in the third person singular of the present.

He talk*s* a lot.

For an indication that the subject is speaking or is being spoken to, English depends on the pronouns.

*I* enjoy *it.*
*You* will enjoy *it.*

**2K** NUMBER. Verbs can indicate whether the subject of the verb is singular or plural in the third person of the simple present, or where *to be* or *have* is used as an auxiliary.

He *comes* to work at eight.
They *come* to work at nine.
She *is talking* to her aunt.
They *are talking* to the principal.

## *The Adjective*

**3A** An adjective is a word which qualifies or limits the meaning of a noun: a *bright* morning; *yellow* flowers; the *next* season; the *seventh* wave.

**3B** Adjectives are accordingly classified as **descriptive** or **limiting.** The **descriptive** adjective expresses a quality of the thing symbolized by the noun: the *tall* soldier, the *wise* man, the *new* building. The **descriptive** adjective usually appears before the noun or after linking verbs.

A *wise* man is not always *wise.*

The **limiting** adjective restricts the noun as to quantity, or shows its relation to other members of its class. It usually appears only before the noun.

| | |
|---|---|
| *much* labor | the *third* chapter |
| *every* day | the *latter* half |
| *several* people | *such* animals |

Often included with the limiting adjectives are the question words: "*Which* desert do you prefer?"; "*What* book did he mention?" and the *articles, a (an)* and *the.* The indefinite article *a (an)* refers to any one of a group: *a* chair, *an* apple; the definite article refers to a particular object or to one which has already been mentioned (*the* chair).

**3C** Nearly all descriptive adjectives and a few limiting adjectives undergo **comparison,** by which different degrees of the quality expressed is indicated.

The **positive degree** is indicated by the simple form: *wise, healthy.*

The **comparative degree,** which is a degree higher than the positive, is indicated by adding *-r* or *-er* to the simple form of adjectives of one or two syllables: *wiser, healthier,* etc., and also through the use of *more: more wise, more healthy,* and so forth.

The **superlative degree,** which is the highest degree of all, is indicated by adding *-st* or *-est* to the simple form: *wise, wisest; healthy, healthiest,* etc., and through the use of *most.* Note that when *most* is used, *est* is not.

Some adjectives of two syllables and nearly all of three syllables or more normally indicate their comparative and superlative degrees by the use of *more* and *most.*

> *more beautiful, most beautiful*
> *more cooperative, most cooperative*
> *more important, most important*

**3D** A few common adjectives have irregular forms in comparison.

> *good, better, best*
> *bad, worse, worst*
> *much, more, most*
> *little, less, least*

## The Adverb

**4A** The adverb is a part of speech used to qualify the meaning of a verb, an adjective, or another adverb.

> The stream flowed *rapidly.*
> The price was *unusually* low.

**4B** The adverb in English has a characteristic ending in *-ly.* Almost any English adjective can be made into an adverb by the addition of this ending: *cold, coldly; beautiful, beautifully.*

However, there are a number of simple adverbs which do not take this ending: *here, now, right, hard, much, fast.*

**4C** Adverbs, like adjectives, undergo comparison. Nearly all adverbs which have the *-ly* ending are compared with *more* and *most: more coldly, most coldly, more beautifully, most beautifully.*

But nearly all adverbs which are identical in form with the positive degree of adjectives are compared by the addition of *-(e)r* and *-(e)st: hard, harder, hardest; fast, faster, fastest.* Simple adverbs like *now, here,* and *where* are not compared.

**4D** When used to qualify the meaning of a verb, an adverb usually specifies the time, place, cause, or manner of action expressed. When it is used to qualify the meaning of an adjective or of another adverb, it usually indicates the degree of the quality expressed by the adjective or adverb.

The report was *fairly* long.
He drove *much* faster.

**4E**   Frequently the adverb is used to modify the meaning of an entire sentence. In these instances it usually expresses the attitude of the speaker toward what is asserted in the sentence.

*Certainly* the program was attractive.

In some few cases words which are regularly used to modify verbs or adjectives and which are therefore traditionally classed as adverbs are found modifying nouns or pronouns.

The man *there* will take your ticket.
The boy *here* will run the errand.
They regard the proposal as *quite* the thing.

It is best to regard these words as adverbs, since they do not have the normal position of an adjective modifying a noun.

**4F**   Adverbs can appear in different positions; for example, *occasionally* and similar adverbs can occur before the verb, after the verb, and in the middle of a verb phrase.

He *occasionally* talks to his sister by phone.
He talks *occasionally* to his sister by phone.
He has *occasionally* spoken to his sister by phone.

However, when a group of adverbs or adverb phrases occurs in the same sentence, the order is usually: adverbs of place, adverbs of time, adverbs of manner.

## The Pronoun

**5A**   The pronoun is a part of speech used primarily to take the place of a noun or a noun equivalent. Since it regularly substitutes for the part of speech which symbolizes a material or conceptual object, the pronoun too is classified as a substantive.

In the great majority of instances, a pronoun is used to avoid the necessity of repeating a noun. In the sentence "Bill dropped the ball and Harry picked it up," the pronoun *it* is used to avoid the necessity of repeating *ball*. When pronouns are used in constructions such as this, the noun for which the pronoun substitutes is said to be its **antecedent**. The pronoun will of course have the same meaning as the antecedent. Thus in the sentence above, *it* means the same as *ball*. In the sentence "John saw Mary and called to her," *Mary* and *her* have the same meaning.

Not all pronouns, however, have antecedents. Sometimes a pronoun is used to stand for something which is being introduced into the discourse for the first time. In sentences such as "What did he say he wanted?" and

"This is the shortest way to Norwich," *what* and *this* cannot be said to replace nouns already used. However, they stand for things which could be symbolized by nouns, and hence by our definition they are pronouns.

Pronouns in English can be classified in a number of ways, but the following classes are probably the most commonly recognized.

**5B** **Personal pronouns** are a class of pronouns used to replace other substantives or to point to persons and things not otherwise symbolized in the discourse. Thus third person pronouns usually have antecedents (the *boy*, *he*; the *people*, *they*); but first and second person pronouns point to persons not otherwise symbolized in the discourse (*I* am here; *you* missed the best part of the show). The personal pronouns are the most highly inflected parts of speech in English, inasmuch as they change form to show person, number, and case, and in the third person singular, to show gender. The inflection of personal pronouns is shown below.

### FIRST PERSON

|  | Singular | Plural |
|---|---|---|
| NOMINATIVE | I | we |
| POSSESSIVE | my | our |
| OBJECTIVE | me | us |

### SECOND PERSON

|  | Singular | Plural |
|---|---|---|
| NOMINATIVE | you | you |
| POSSESSIVE | your | your |
| OBJECTIVE | you | you |

### THIRD PERSON

|  | | Singular | |
|---|---|---|---|
|  | Masculine | Feminine | Neuter |
| NOMINATIVE | he | she | it |
| POSSESSIVE | his | her | its |
| OBJECTIVE | him | her | it |

|  | Plural |
|---|---|
| NOMINATIVE | they |
| POSSESSIVE | their |
| OBJECTIVE | them |

**5C** In addition to the personal pronouns, there is a subclass called **possessive pronouns**, which substitute for a phrase consisting of a noun and another noun in the genitive or a noun and a personal pronoun in the possessive case. Thus instead of saying "Alice's essay won the first prize," we can say "*Hers* won the first prize"; instead of saying "Our car is a year old," we can say "*Ours* is a year old," and so on. There is a possessive pronoun corresponding to each of the personal pronouns: *I-mine; we-ours; you-yours; he-his; her-hers; it-its; they-theirs.* We realize without further illustration that possessive pronouns very often substitute for noun subjects and noun objects: "*Mine* was the last on the list"; "Somebody took *yours.*"

**5D**  The **relative pronoun** is a pronoun used to relate the clause in which it appears to an antecedent in another clause. The relative pronouns are *who, which,* and *that. Who* is used when the antecedent refers to a person; *which* when it refers to inanimate object or thing; *that* is used for antecedents referring to either persons or things.

> Andrew Jackson was a leader *who* represented the democracy of the frontier.

> This is the same law *which* the Congress rejected many years ago.

> Bob is a friend *that* I met many years ago.

*Which* is commonly used in non-restrictive clauses and frequently in long clauses with interrupting elements.

> The storm, *which* was almost a hurricane, passed through our state last night.

> It was a decision *which,* despite the opposition of the city council, made the mayor more popular than ever.

In other contexts *that* is the common form, though *which* is often used, especially in formal contexts.

> The car that you bought is a good one.

The relative pronoun *who,* unlike *which* and *that,* has special forms for the possessive (*whose*) and for the objective (*whom*) cases.

*Who, which,* and *what,* together with their compounds *whoever, whichever,* and *whatever* are used also as indefinite relatives. They are called indefinite relatives in constructions where they have no antecedent, as in "Do *what* you like," "*Whoever* comes will be welcome."

**5E**  The **demonstrative pronoun** is used to indicate the position of the user with respect to the things symbolized. *This* (plural: *these*) indicates something nearby or something of recent occurrence in the discourse.

> *This* is the book we were looking for.
> *These* are the best apples we have seen.

*That* (plural: *those*) is used to indicate something relatively distant from the speaker or something that has occurred earlier in the discourse.

*That* is the longest one.
*Those* were clever stories that he told last night.

**5F** **Indefinite** and **numeral pronouns** point out and indicate quantity. Some **indefinite** pronouns are: *some, any, all, many*. **Numeral** pronouns is a name sometimes given to numbers such as *two, five, seven* when these are used without following nouns.

*Some* still believe that the world is flat.
*All* are subject to the call of national duty.
*Two* were taken at one time.

**5G** The **interrogative pronoun** is used to ask a question. The interrogative pronouns are *who, which, what, whoever, whichever,* and *whatever*. Generally they are without antecedent, but they symbolize something present in the speech situation.

*Who* said that?
*Which* do you mean?
*Whatever* possessed him to do this?

**5H** The **intensive pronoun** is used to stress the meaning of an antecedent. Its function is to make a second reference to the thing symbolized by the antecedent for the purpose of emphasizing its identity. Intensive pronouns consist of certain of the personal pronouns combined with *-self* (plural: *selves*): *myself, yourself, himself, themselves*.

You *yourself* may be called.
Phyllis did all the work *herself*.

**5I** The **reflexive pronoun,** which is identical in form with the intensive, is used when the subject of a clause acts through the verb upon or in relation to itself. Thus we say "Tom Brown helped *himself*." instead of "Tom Brown helped Tom Brown."

Barbara found *herself* the center of attention.
We hurt *ourselves* by waiting too long.

**5J** The **reciprocal pronoun** is used to indicate a relationship between the members of a subject. The two groups *one another* and *each other* make up the reciprocal pronouns. The reciprocal pronouns show that the members of the subject are both subjects and objects of the action of the verb. Thus if we say, "In times of hardship, the neighbors helped *each other*," we mean that the neighbors both helped and were helped.

Lincoln and Douglas opposed *each other*.
The children laughed at *one another*.

### The Preposition

**6A**   The preposition is a part of speech used to show a connection between other grammatical elements. Often this connection is between two substantives: a house *by* the road; a place *in* history. In many instances, however, the preposition shows a connection between a verb and a substantive.

> They walked *across* the fields.
> He carefully placed the ball *on* the tee.

The substantive following a preposition may be one word, a phrase, or a clause.

> Margery was seated *on* a small chestnut horse.
> He said nothing *about* where the men were expected to lodge.

**6B**   The substantive following a preposition is always in the objective case. Thus, when the substantive is a pronoun, it will show the regular inflection for that case: *with her, to him, for us.*

**6C**   Most prepositions used to connect substantives with other substantives or with verbs convey some idea of spatial or temporal relationship. This may be seen from the following list of the more common prepositions.

| | |
|---|---|
| about | from |
| across | in |
| after | inside |
| against | into |
| among | of |
| at | on |
| before | out |
| behind | outside |
| beside | with |
| between | within |
| by | |

As a consequence, nearly all prepositional phrases having a substantive ending function as adjectives or adverbs.

> They bought a place *outside the city.*
> Leave the key *in the door.*

Prepositions may be word phrases: *apart from, in front of, alongside of, instead of, by means of.*

**6D**   Prepositional phrases may occur in a series.

> This is the end *of the attack on the mosquitoes.*

There is often the possibility of ambiguity in such series.

AMBIGUOUS: He spoke to the girl in the car.

This can mean that the girl was in the car and that he was not, or that both were in the car. Such ambiguities should be avoided in written English. (See "Placing Modifying Phrases," page 176.)

## The Conjunction

**7A** The conjunction is a part of speech used to show another kind of relationship between grammatical elements. Frequently the conjunction is used to join elements which have an identical function in the sentence, such as two or more subjects, objects, or verbs.

> Wheat *and* potatoes are the principal crops.
> They set out one morning to hunt rabbits *and* squirrels.
> Dust swirled *and* eddied in the streets.
> The investment provided a small *but* steady income.

**7B** Conjunctions used to join elements of equal grammatical function are called **coordinating conjunctions**. The coordinating conjunctions are *and, but, or, for, nor, yet, so.*

**7C** Another group of conjunctions is used to connect elements with elements of different grammatical function. These are called **subordinating conjunctions**, and they are used most frequently to connect dependent clauses with independent clauses.

> A bell rings *when* dinner is ready.
> The excitement died down *after* the election was over.
> He always found time for an hour of exercise *though* his day was crowded.

Among the most commonly used subordinating conjunctions are the following:

| | |
|---|---|
| after | since |
| although | than |
| as | that |
| as soon as | though |
| because | unless |
| before | when |
| even if | whence |
| if | where |
| in order that | whereas |
| provided that | while |

**7D** A small group of conjunctions, called **correlative conjunctions**, are used to join pairs or series of elements. These are *both . . . and, either . . .*

*or, neither . . . nor, not . . . but,* and *not only . . . but also.* (Very often the *also* of *but also* is omitted.)

> *Both* young *and* old can enjoy tennis.
> *Neither* love *nor* money could turn him aside from pursuit of his goal.
> He spoke *not only* to the father *but* (*also*) to the mother.

## Verbals

**8A**   Verbals are words which are derived from verbs, but which function as other parts of speech. There are three types of verbals: the **infinitive,** the **participle,** and the **gerund.**

**8B**   The **infinitive** is an "infinite" verb; that is to say, it is not limited as to number, person, mood, and so on. Consequently it can never take the place of a finite or limited verb, which has these properties. The infinitive is regularly made of the infinitive sign "to" and the simple form of the verb: *to go, to sing, to make, to hope.*

The infinitive may function as a noun, as an adjective, or as an adverb.

> *To win* the next game was important. (noun)
> Now is the time *to pray.* (adjective)
> They were afraid *to ask* for more. (adverb)

The infinitive also has the function of entering into combination with various auxiliaries when these are used to express modification of the action or state of being asserted by the verb. In such combinations the infinitive sign "to" is omitted.

> We must *go.*
> He *does* take chances.
> They could *make* a good showing.

"To" is omitted also when the infinitive is used after certain verbs, such as *watch, hear, dare, need.*

> We watched the plane *land.*
> We heard Marilyn *sing.*
> He did not dare *put* all his eggs in one basket.
> You need not *go.*

**8C**   The **participle** is a verbal used chiefly as an adjective. The present participle can always be identified by the *-ing* ending attached to the verb form: *walking, speaking, planning.* Past participles usually have an ending in *-ed* or *-d,* although a few English verbs have irregular past participle forms.

> The *singing* birds attracted the cat.
> A beggar *standing* on the corner asked John to stop.

A *dented* fender ruined the appearance of the car.
A *captured* animal must be handled carefully.

**8D**   The **gerund** is a verbal used as a noun, and hence is sometimes called a verbal noun. It is identical in form with the present participle and is distinguished from the participle solely by its function as a substantive.

> *Seeing* is *believing*.
> By *taking* care, one can avoid accidents.
> They witnessed the *changing* of the guard.

## Phrases

**9A**   Thus far we have considered the parts of speech in isolation. We realize, of course, that in actual utterances various parts of speech combine into larger groups which convey units of meaning. The most elementary of these groups is the phrase. A phrase may be defined as a group of words which serves as a single part of speech and which does not contain a subject and a predicate. We should observe carefully the latter characeristic, as it is the only distinction between the phrase and another element, sometimes no larger, called the clause. There are various kinds of phrases, some of which are listed here.

**9B**   A unit consisting of a verb and its auxiliaries is called a **verb phrase:** *is done, will have been seen, could have gone.*

**9C**   A group consisting of a preposition and a noun (with its modifiers) is a **prepositional phrase:** *in the garden, over the storm-tossed ocean.*

**9D**   A group consisting of a noun and its modifiers and any modifiers of the modifiers is called a **noun phrase:** *the bare trees, the very cold day.*

**9E**   A group consisting of a participle and its object and any modifiers of the participle and the object is a **participial phrase.**

> *Walking briskly,* he entered the room.
> *Seeing the unsatisfactory outcome of his efforts,* Edward tried a new plan.

**9F**   A group consisting of an infinitive and its object and any modifiers of the infinitive and the object is an **infinitive phrase.**

> *To read a book* in a few hours can be advantageous in college.

**9G**   A group consisting of a gerund and its object and any modifiers of the gerund and the object is a **gerund phrase.**

> *Sailing a boat* requires much skill.
> He enjoyed *running slowly along the shore.*

### Clauses

**10A**   The clause is the traditional name for a group of words with at least one subject and a predicate.

> Truth endures.
> The man picked up his hat and left.
> The cold wind blew as they turned toward home.

**10B**   A clause is said to be **independent** when it is complete in itself and does not need any other grammatical unit for its essential meaning. Independent clauses can be either complete sentences or parts of sentences.

> The man picked up his hat.
> The man picked up his hat as the woman signaled that it was time to go.

**10C**   A clause is said to be **dependent** when it is part of a larger grammatical construction. Dependent clauses are always *parts* of sentences.

> *When atomic power is made available for transportation,* some of our urban problems may be alleviated.
> He knew *what made the watch run.*

## SENTENCES

### Classification by Structure

**11A**   All sentences may be divided according to their structure into two types: the **simple** and the **composite.**

**11B**   The **simple sentence** is so called because it is a one-clause sentence, like those with which we introduced the definition of a clause: "Truth endures," etc. A sentence remains simple as long as it contains only one predication; it may compound the subject or the verb or both and still retain the one-clause structure.

> Tom and Gene were often at odds.
> He climbed higher and peered over the fence.
> Elephants and lions were captured and trained.

**11C**   In observing the nature of the dependent clause, we have noted one way in which the dependent clause can combine with another clause to form a composite type of sentence.

> The town looked fresh *as they sat at morning coffee in the square.*
> He pointed out *that government is the servant of the people who elect it.*

Sentences which consist thus of an independent clause and one or more dependent clauses are called **complex sentences.**

**11D** Sentences which consist of a combination of two or more independent clauses are called **compound sentences.**

> *The orchestra ceased playing, and the curtain went up.*
> *Years pass, and fashions change, but human nature remains the same.*

**11E** A sentence which consists of two or more independent clauses and one or more dependent clauses is called a **compound-complex sentence.**

> *Texas is the largest state in the United States; it is also the chief producer of oil, which is indispensable to modern industry.*

## Classification by Meaning

**12A** Sentences can also be classified on the basis of the kind of meaning which the sentence as a whole expresses. This is a semantic classification, inasmuch as it is made only with reference to the sense of the sentence.

**12B** A sentence which states something as a matter of fact is called a **declarative sentence.**

> Water is a solvent.
> Algebra is a branch of mathematics.
> Brussels is the capital of Belgium.

**12C** A sentence which asks a question is called an **interrogative sentence.**

> Were there any copies left?

**12D** A sentence which expresses an order or command is called an **imperative sentence.**

> Give me your attention.
> Follow carefully the directions given on the label.

**12E** A sentence which negates an assertion is a **negative sentence.**

> He did not want any more aid.

**12F** The declarative is often considered as a base sentence, and the negative, interrogative, and imperative sentences as derived from the declarative.

> He eats everything on his plate.
> He doesn't eat everything on his plate.
> Does he eat everything on his plate?
> Eat everything on your plate!

### Sentence Structure

**13A**   As we noted in 11A, all sentences may be divided according to their structure into two types: **simple** and **composite**. The simple sentence is so-called because it contains one predication (one assertion), although it may have a compound subject or a compound verb. (*Tom and Gene were often fighting. He climbed higher and looked over the fence.*) The major parts of all simple sentences are the **subject** and the **predicate**. The subject is the part about which the predicate makes an assertion; the predicate is the part which does the asserting.

Thus, a sentence consisting of a single subject and a single predicate may consist of only two words.

> Time passes.
> Birds fly.

**13B**   In most sentences, however, both subject and predicate contain more than one member. The subject is often accompanied by one or more **modifiers**.

> The *tall* man spoke.
> A *bright red* apple hung on the topmost bough.

**13C**   The predicate often contains an **object**. An object may be defined as a noun or noun equivalent which receives the action expressed by the verb.

> The rider seized the *reins*.
> The student opened the *book*.

**13D**   Objects are divided into **direct** and **indirect objects**. If the noun or noun equivalent receives the action of the verb directly, as in the sentence above, it is called a *direct object*. But if it receives the action only indirectly, it is called an *indirect object*.

> The teacher gave the *class* a long assignment.
> Please lend *me* your pen.

In these sentences, *long assignment* and *pen* are direct objects. But the noun *class* and the pronoun *me* receive the action of the verb indirectly and hence are indirect objects.

**13E**   When the predicate contains a verb used intransitively, or without an object, a different kind of element may be employed to complete the meaning of the sentence. This is the **complement** or "completer." Complements are classified according to whether they are substantives or adjectives.

**13F**  If the expression following the intransitive verb and completing the meaning of the sentence is a substantive, it is called a **predicate nominative.**

> These animals are *bears*.
> He looked every inch a *soldier*.

**13G**  If the complement is an adjective or an expression which can function as an adjective, it is called a **predicate adjective.**

> The children were *happy*.
> He seems *in trim*.
> The weeds grew *thick*.
> Progress was *slow*.

**13H**  In some predicates there is a second object which stands beside the regular object to complete its meaning in the sentence. This second object is called an **objective complement.**

> The Senior Class elected Raymond *president*.
> The company made him *chief purchasing agent*.

**13I**  In many sentences the predicate also contains modifiers of the verb and of the object and modifiers of these modifiers.

> He soon saw a new opportunity for a very lucrative business.

In this sentence, for example, *soon* modifies the verb *saw; new* modifies the noun *opportunity,* which is the object of the sentence; *for a very lucrative business* is a prepositional phrase also modifying the noun *opportunity;* within this phrase *lucrative* is an adjective modifying the noun *business;* and *very* is an adverb modifying the adjective *lucrative.*

**13J**  Noun phrases and prepositional phrases can occur in the simple sentence, in either the subject or the predicate.

> *The tall man in the dark suit* is the one.
> We need *more people with his vision*.

**13K**  The composite sentence contains more than one subject-predicate relation.

> While the men were talking in the living room, the women were in the kitchen doing the dishes.

> The contractors finished the job on time, but the company decided on some additions which made another week's work necessary.

**13L**  One type of composite sentence consists of a simple sentence which has been included in a larger structure. This **included sentence** has been traditionally called a **dependent clause,** or a **subordinate clause.** These names all stress that the included construction is a part of a larger grammatical construction and depends on that larger construction for the completion of its meaning. Further, the dependent clause, or included sentence, may function as a noun or as a modifier within the larger construction.

> That *anyone can make a mistake* is generally admitted. (Here the simple sentence *anyone can make a mistake* has been included within the whole sentence and is the subject of that sentence, functioning as a noun.)

> The teacher found that *some students had not studied the lesson.* (The included sentence is the object here.)

> Here is the place where *the collision occurred.* (The included sentence is a modifier.)

> Children grow excited *when Christmas approaches.* (The included sentence is a modifier.)

Such composite sentences are often called **complex sentences.**

**13M** Some grammarians consider participial, infinitive, and gerund phrases to be types of included sentences which have been reduced to phrases. Thus they would say that the sentence

> Walking along the street, John saw a dollar bill in the gutter.

is derived from two sentences:

> (1) John was walking along the street.
> (2) John saw a dollar bill in the gutter.

Similarly, what has traditionally been called an **absolute phrase** may be considered an included sentence which has been reduced and transformed. The connectives that normally link included sentences to the larger constructions in which they are found are missing in the absolute phrases; in addition, the verb is sometimes omitted. When the verb does appear, it occurs in participial form. Thus we might describe the following sentence

> They had decided, the day being fine, to go fishing in the bay.

as deriving from

> (1) They had decided to go fishing in the bay.
> (2) The day was fine.

The connective we might expect, *since, because,* or similar connective, does not appear before the included sentence, and the verb is changed to its participial form. The first of the following two examples is similar. In the second the verb has been omitted entirely.

> The last guest having departed, the doors were closed for the night.
> His papers in order, he was admitted without further delay.

**13N** A second type of **composite** sentence consists of two or more simple sentences. Such a sentence is often called a **compound sentence.**

The orchestra stopped playing, and the curtain went up.
Years pass and fashions change, but human nature remains the same.

**13O** Combinations of **complex** and **compound** sentences are sometimes called **compound-complex** sentences.

Texas is the largest American state; it is also the chief producer of oil, which is indispensable to modern industry.

Chicago is the metropolis of the Middle West; it is also an important center for the manufacture of steel, which is essential to modern industry.

Some maintain that history is a social science, but historians have generally denied that it is a science at all.

**13P** Complex, compound, and compound-complex sentences thus have much more complicated structures than simple sentences. In fact, we may consider that the simple sentence is the basic sentence in English, and that the other sentence types are *transformations* (by means of addition and combination) of the simple sentence.

## Detached Elements in the Sentence

**14A** Some sentences have, in addition to such normal members as subject, verb, object, complement, and modifier, elements which seem to be grammatically independent of the sentence unit.

**14B** The **appositive** is a noun or noun equivalent used to explain or amplify another noun or noun equivalent. The appositive regularly stands immediately after the noun or noun equivalent which it explains.

Mr. Adams, *our local representative,* will call at your office on Monday.
The streamliner *City of Los Angeles* leaves Chicago at 5:30 P.M.

**14C** The **vocative expression** is any word or combination of words used in direct address. Usually the vocative expression is a proper name. It may, however, be a common noun or phrase.

*Elizabeth,* do you remember where you hung my raincoat?
*Mr. Chairman,* I move that the meeting adjourn.
*You in the Ford convertible,* please back up a little.

**14D** The **interjection** is an expression used either to summon the attention of someone or to express feeling on the part of the speaker.

*Hey,* look where you're going!
*Oh,* I shouldn't be surprised by anything he says.

**14E**   There are, in addition to these well-defined elements, certain conventional introductory phrases which modify the sense of the sentence as a whole without having a grammatical relationship with it.

> *To tell the truth*, there were not many qualified applicants.
> *Generally speaking*, politicians and philosophers do not think alike.
> *Looking over the whole situation*, there seems little to fear.

## SOME PROBLEMS OF GRAMMAR AND SYNTAX

### Agreement of Subject and Verb

**15A**   A verb must agree with its subject in person and number. If there is a conflict between the form and the sense of the subject, the sense governs the number of the verb.

**15B**   A collective noun will be followed by a singular verb if the predication is about the group as a unit.

> The jury *was instructed* by the judge.

But the noun will be followed by a plural verb if the predication is about the members as individuals.

> After five hours of deliberation, the jury *were* disagreed.
> A number *are* unable to be present.

**15C**   If the subject is plural in form but symbolizes a single entity, the verb following is singular.

> Fifteen miles *is* too far to walk.
> Fifty thousand dollars *is* a lot of money.
> The sum and substance of the matter *is* that we accepted his offer.

**15D**   A compound subject is followed by a plural verb.

> Books and papers *were* on the desk.

**15E**   Expressions such as *together with, in addition to,* and *as well as* following a subject do not affect its number. If the subject is singular, the verb will be singular.

> Painting as well as music *was* part of the curriculum.
> The Saar, together with Alsace and Lorraine, *was* taken from Germany by the Treaty of Versailles.

**15F**   The number of the verb is not affected by the number of a predicate nominative. If the subject is singular, the verb will be singular.

> The topic of his lecture *was* snakes.
> The first part of the program *is* games.

**15G** If the two parts of a subject joined by *either . . . or* or *neither . . . nor* differ in number, the verb agrees in number with the nearer part.

> Either his friends or he *is* to blame.
> Neither he nor his friends *were* to blame.

Similarly, if the two parts of a subject differ in person, the verb following agrees with the nearer part.

> Either you or I *am misunderstanding* the text.
> Either we or she *has taken* the wrong turn.

**15H** The agreement of subject and verb is not affected by the grammatical number of the nouns intervening between the subject and the verb.

> The addition of more students, more activities, and more courses *makes* administering a school more difficult each year.

## Agreement of Pronoun and Antecedent

**16A** A pronoun agrees with its antecedent in person, number, and gender.

> George was young, but *he* was large for *his* age.
> The horses were halted, for *they* were beginning to show signs of fatigue.
> Marie was pretty, and everyone wanted to dance with *her*.

**16B** But the case of a pronoun is determined by its function. Thus a pronoun will be in the nominative case if it functions as a subject.

> A prize will go to *whoever* keeps the neatest room.

Similarly, it will be in the objective case if it functions as an object.

> *Whom* did you see in town?
> *Whomever* he met was likely to be asked for a loan.

When *who* occurs as object of a verb, educated speakers will generally use *whom* in writing, and often in speaking. When *who* occurs as object of a preposition, educated speakers will use *whom,* especially when the preposition immediately precedes the pronoun.

> To *whom* is he addressing the letter?

**16C** A verb following the pronoun *who* or *that* will be singular or plural depending on the number of the antecedent.

> She is one of those women who rarely *go* visiting.

The verb must be plural because the antecedent of *who* is *women.*

> Rex was one of those dogs *that learn* very quickly.

Here again the verb must be plural because the antecedent of *that* is *dogs.*

**16D**  The pronouns *anybody, anyone, everybody, someone, either,* and *neither* are regularly construed as singular. A pronoun having one of these as its antecedent must therefore be singular.

> Everyone must bring *his* own lunch.
> Neither of them was able to make *his* excuse sound very convincing.
> Has anybody lost *his* umbrella?

### Reference of Pronouns

**17A**  The antecedent of a personal pronoun should be unmistakable. Avoid especially pronouns whose reference is ambiguous.

AMBIGUOUS:  Roy told his professor that he didn't know much about mathematics. (*He* could refer either to *Roy* or his *professor.*)

CLEAR:  Roy said to his professor, "I don't know much about mathematics."

AMBIGUOUS.  Francis informed his friend that his money was gone. (The second *his* could refer to either *Francis* or *friend.*)

CLEAR:  Francis told his friend, "My money is gone."

**17B**  Within the same sentence avoid using a pronoun in the nominative case to refer to a noun in the possessive case.

FAULTY:  In Franklin's *Poor Richard's Almanac,* he says that a penny saved is a penny made.

SUGGESTED CORRECTION:  Franklin says in his *Poor Richard's Almanac* that a penny saved is a penny made.

**17C**  Be cautious about using a pronoun to refer to an antecedent which is only implied. Even the most careful writers sometimes use *this* to refer to the content of a preceding sentence or a preceding paragraph, but the use of *that* and *which* with such references is generally frowned upon.

DOUBTFUL:  He saved carefully, which enabled him eventually to start a business of his own.

BETTER:  He saved carefully, and his thrift enabled him eventually to start a business of his own.

DOUBTFUL:  They failed because they would take no one's advice, and that ought to teach them a lesson

BETTER:  They failed because they would take no one's advice, and the result ought to teach them a lesson.

### Verbals

**18A**  When a gerund is linked with a noun or pronoun in the genitive relationship, the noun or pronoun takes the genitive case form, in formal usage.

Mother objects to *my* lying in bed in the morning.
There is no doubt about the *people's* being tired of machine politics.

## Participial Phrases

**19A** Participial phrases must be clearly related to the remainder of the sentence in which they occur. Every sentence that contains a participle should also contain a noun which the participle can modify. If we consider the participle phrase to be derived from a simple sentence (He is walking to school > walking to school), we can say that the subject of that simple sentence and the subject of the completed sentence should be the same.

Harry was talking rather quickly.       ⟩ Talking rather quickly,
Harry moved toward the telephone. ⟩ Harry moved toward the telephone.

Carelessness with participial phrases results in the "dangling participle."

WRONG:   Being only nine years old, Christmas was an exciting time.
RIGHT:   Being only nine years old, Bobby found Christmas an exciting time.
WRONG:   Crossing the campus, many new faces were seen.
RIGHT:   Crossing the campus, I saw many new faces.

NOTE: There are certain exceptions to this rule in the form of participial phrases used as introductory expressions.

RIGHT:   Barring unforeseen difficulties, we should make rapid progress.
RIGHT:   Considering everything, his record is commendable.

**19B** The participial phrase cannot stand alone.

WRONG:   He has a very long day. Studying, working and commuting.
RIGHT:   He has a very long day, studying, working, and commuting.

## Sequence of Tenses

In writing complex sentences, it is often necessary to harmonize the time expressed by the verb of the principal clause with that expressed by the verb of the subordinate clause. Although there is no precise set of rules for doing this, the following principles may be helpful.

**20A** If the verb of a principal clause is in the past or past perfect tense, the verb in a subordinate clause will usually be in the past or past perfect tense.

He said that he *wished* to come.
He had been told that the neighbors *were* unfriendly.
She believed that she *had left* her purse at the drug store.

**20B**   If the verb of the principal clause is in any tense other than the past or past perfect, the tense of the verb in a subordinate clause is determined by the time that is being expressed.

> I think that he *will have arrived* by this time.
> We have felt that Mr. Wrenn *is* a conscientious worker.
> They will suspect that we *have stolen* a march on them.

**20C**   If the verb of a principal clause expressing desire or purpose is in the present tense, the verb in the following subordinate clause will be in the present subjunctive. If the verb in the principal clause is in the past tense, the verb in the following subordinate clause will be in the past subjunctive.

> Ration cards are issued so that everyone *may get* his fair share.
> Ration cards were issued so that everyone *might get* his fair share.
> We hope that there *may be* a large attendance.
> We hoped that there *might be* a large attendance.

**20D**   A verb used to express something that is permanently or generally true is usually in the present tense regardless of the tense of the verb of the leading clause.

> Eratosthenes knew that the world *is* round.
> He believed that honesty *is* the best policy.

## EXERCISES

**Exercise A**   *Agreement of Subject and Verb*
*Choose the correct form of the verb in the following sentences. Where you think both choices are possible, justify your decision.*

1. The company (has, have) declared the usual quarterly dividend.
2. The United States (is, are) considered a first-rate military power.
3. The committee (was, were) polled by the chairman.
4. Politics (was, were) the subject of the discussion.
5. There (was, were) only two stores in the village.
6. Neither they nor their victim (lives, live) to tell the story.
7. Either you or she (has, have) made an error.
8. Studying, together with working at a part-time job, (fills, fill) up his day.
9. Fireworks (has, have) been the cause of many tragedies.
10. Norman, as well as his brother, (is, are) fond of water sports.
11. Seven and seven (makes, make) fourteen.
12. The award of books, scholarships and other prizes (cost, costs) the school several thousand dollars each year.
13. The dinner and the entertainment afterward (take, takes) two hours.
14. The major part of the course (is, are) classroom drills.

15. His salary, as well as his income from stocks, (was, were) subject to taxes.

## Exercise B  *Number of Pronouns*
### *Choose the correct form in the following sentences.*

1. He is one of those people who (is, are) always in a hurry.
2. Somebody has left (his, their) car lights on.
3. She is one of those women who (plays, play) golf.
4. Everyone was told to keep (his, their) own score.
5. Shakespeare was one of those geniuses that (is, are) gifted from birth.

## Exercise C  *Case of Pronouns*
### *Choose the correct form in the following sentences.*

1. The letter was addressed to (whoever, whomever) it might concern.
2. The teacher always recognized (whoever, whomever) held his hand up first.
3. (Whoever, whomever) we choose as our President must be a native of this country.
4. With (who, whom) did you attend the graduation ceremony?
5. (Who, whom) did you decide to invite to the party?
6. Do you know (who, whom) will replace you as chairman of the committee?
7. The scholarship will be awarded either to George or (me, I).
8. After considerable searching we were able to prove that it was (they, them).
9. The director, his assistant, and (I, me) are responsible for the presentation of the play.
10. The organization owes a great deal to both Harrison and (he, him).
11. Prizes for service were given to the two oldest members, Frank and (I, me).

## Exercise D  *Reference of Pronouns*
### *Correct or make clear the reference of pronouns in the following sentences.*

1. Herbert told his father that his glasses were broken.
2. In Caesar's *Gallic Wars* he says that the Belgians are the bravest fighters.
3. Jack informed Carl that his name was on the honor roll.
4. He painted his own house, which took about a month.
5. In the morning paper it says that a new hurricane is threatening Long Island.
6. Jim liked to tinker with motors, which in the end gave him a good practical knowledge of mechanics.
7. She went to Hollywood as a young girl, which was the beginning of a fabulous career.
8. Evelyn often spoke to her mother about her lack of good clothes.
9. Mr. Leigh had traveled in Africa, which gave him an advantage in the discussion.
10. Mr. Fox told his son that he knew little of the matter.

**Exercise E**   *Verbals*
*Correct the errors in the use of verbals in the following sentences.*

1. Mrs. Gray objected to Sylvia talking so long on the phone.
2. He was surprised by everyone being so carefree.
3. Nobody knew about him leaving town.
4. The disagreement resulted in the men going on strike.
5. She shuddered to think of anybody being hungry.
6. While mowing the lawn, a golf ball was found.
7. Gazing intently at the horizon, a tiny speck came into view.
8. Marching solemnly in the parade, his big feet grew tired.
9. Opening the letter, a check fell out.
10. Seeing no chance of a promotion, the job was discouraging.
11. He accidentally dropped a match, causing the mixture to ignite.
12. He stayed up until two o'clock. Talking and joking with his brother.
13. John started work at the garage last month. This affecting his schoolwork considerably.

**Exercise F**   *Sequence of Tenses*
*Correct any errors in the use of tense in the following sentences.*

1. We hope that he might be present at the gathering.
2. Highways are carefully marked so that the tourist may have no difficulty in finding his route.
3. He knew that gasoline was dangerous.
4. Ben felt that he had mastered the lesson.
5. Chairs were provided so that no one may have to stand.
6. Ronald single-spaced the letter so that he might get it all on one page.
7. They had not forgotten that the sun rose later in the winter.
8. The chairman believes that the quota will be exceeded.
9. The lecturer began by pointing out that mathematics was essential to physics.
10. Everyone must register so that we may have a record of attendance.

**Exercise G**   *Adjectives and Adverbs*
*Choose the correct form in the following sentences.*

1. He will never finish his paper because he reads so (slow, slowly).
2. Michael is the most (worthy, worthiest) candidate for special honors.
3. He feels that he is much more (wise, wiser) after having been responsible for the whole summer program.
4. When two answers come from the machine, the operator has to decide (quick, quickly) what to do.
5. The heavyweight champion is known for punching (hard, hardly).
6. Although she has trouble organizing her material, she types it (perfect, perfectly).

# Punctuation

The marks of punctuation used according to rule are explanatory or inter-
pretive. They are not, as has been charged, so many arbitrary additions
serving only to make the writer's task more tedious or difficult. Some
marks of punctuation are needed to show when certain elements come to
an end. Others are needed to show the relationship of elements to each
other. Still others are needed to show the relative weight which is to be
given to an expression. A writer will sometimes use punctuation to indicate that he wants a passage to be read slowly. And sometimes he will use
it even to indicate his attitude toward what he is writing.

These facts show that punctuation is highly functional, because it
furthers definite purposes. A skillful writer intends his marks of punctuation just as seriously as he intends his words and phrases. He could not
convey his whole meaning without them. If we did not have the marks of
punctuation, we might have to employ words—as the word "stop" used to
be employed to end sentences in telegrams—to indicate terminations,
pauses, attitudes, and other factors important in the expression. The period, the semicolon, the comma, and other marks do this for us if we use
them according to their accepted significance. They help us to interpret
for the reader what we desire to say.

To a limited extent, it is possible to punctuate by "ear" or instinct.
We usually feel when a sentence has come to an end, and we usually sense
where a pause comes in its development. These feelings are not wholly
unreliable guides. However, there are many punctuation problems in
which sound or feeling will mislead us. Sometimes there will arise a real
question as to which of two marks should be used. To answer such a question we must be able to make a grammatical analysis of what we are saying, and then we must refer to the conventions of punctuation. These
conventions have grown up over a long period of time as the best general

333

ways of using punctuation meaningfully. The rules may not meet every problem, but they will help in the solving of even special problems. The value of a standardized punctuation is that when we punctuate according to accepted usage, the reader knows how to interpret.

Punctuation has, furthermore, some connection with the style of one's writing. A style which is involved and difficult will require proportionately more marks to be reasonably clear; one which is simple and straightforward will require fewer. But many college students tend to overpunctuate because they do not take time to analyze grammatically the sentences they are writing. A clear grasp of the grammar of sentences is the key to avoiding aimless punctuation and overpunctuation.

The following are the most widely accepted rules governing present-day punctuation.

# TERMINAL MARKS OF PUNCTUATION

Terminal marks of punctuation are used to end the sentence and certain other elements. These marks are the period, the question mark, and the exclamation point.

## The Period

**21A**  The period is used to end every statement.

This year's birds are not found in last year's nests.

**21B**  The period is used to end an imperative sentence unless the sentence is strong enough to call for an exclamation point.

**21C**  The period is used to end a polite form of the interrogative sentence to which an affirmative answer is expected.

Will the members of the committee please meet next Wednesday to consider the new proposal.

May we have your remittance not later than the tenth of the month.

## The Question Mark

**22A**  The question mark is used after an interrogative sentence.

Did he say eleven o'clock?
Is William on the program?

**22B**  A question mark in parentheses may be used to call attention to uncertainty as to fact, or to indicate an ironical attitude on the part of the writer.

Ptolemy was born in 367(?) B.C.
We engaged a room at their cheapest(?) rate.

NOTE: The question mark is not used after an indirect question.

Janet asked whether the firm had an opening for a stenographer.

## The Exclamation Point

**23A**  The exclamation point may be used after a sentence, phrase or word which is intended to express unusually strong feeling.

The keys had been left behind!
Pancakes and sausage for breakfast!
Ouch!

# INTERNAL MARKS OF PUNCTUATION

Internal marks of punctuation are used to set off words, phrases, clauses, and certain other elements within the sentence.

## Between Independent Elements

**24A**  The comma is normally used between the clauses of a compound sentence when they are joined by the coordinating conjunctions *and, but, for, or, nor, yet, so.*

The dinner was over at half past eight, and the guests then moved to the patio for coffee.

They had planned on going swimming if the weather was good, but since it was raining they decided on a party indoors.

Since *but, for,* and *yet* often occur between contrasting ideas, a comma before these conjunctions is particularly useful.

The channel was only seven miles wide, yet no one had swum it yet.

The comma can also prevent ambiguities which the word order of the compound sentence occasionally produces.

I loaned the bicycle to Frank, and his brother used it to deliver the papers. (Without the comma, *Frank and his brother* might be taken as a grammatical unit.)

When the independent elements are short, a comma is not usually used.

The loan was made and we bought the house.

**24B**  A series of short, independent clauses, with no connecting conjunctions, is occasionally separated by commas.

She wept, she screamed, she became hysterical.

**24C**   Independent clauses not joined by a conjunction in compound and compound-complex sentences are separated by a semicolon.

Good intentions are not enough; intelligence also is required.

The session had already lasted past midnight; it was a time when the members were growing restless.

**24D**   The semicolon is always used between independent clauses when they are joined by one of the conjunctive adverbs (*however, nevertheless, consequently, furthermore*) and sometimes between independent clauses joined by the coordinating conjunctions *and, but, for, nor, yet,* and *so* when the writer wishes to emphasize the break between the clauses, or when the clauses are long.

The sum was not large; however, they decided to make it do.

Burgoyne's army was suffering from desertion; furthermore the supply of food was running low.

Some works of genius may be the result of sudden inspiration; but the majority are the fruit of sustained labor.

We decided to cross the river by dark because of the danger of being spotted by the enemy force in daylight; and as a further precaution we changed our crossing point to one three miles south of the bridge.

NOTE: The semicolon separates elements of equal grammatical rank. Do not use a semicolon to separate an independent clause from a dependent clause, or a phrase from the rest of the sentence.

WRONG:   He took a train; though he usually traveled by air.
RIGHT:   He took a train, though he usually traveled by air.
WRONG:   They went to the beach at eight in the morning and remained there all day long until six o'clock; just to get a good tan.
RIGHT:   They went to the beach at eight in the morning and remained there all day long until six o'clock just to get a good tan.

## Setting Off Phrases and Clauses

**25A**   The comma is sometimes used after an introductory phrase. It is generally used after an introductory clause, unless the clause is very short.

In the first place, few are able to meet the requirements.

Unless relations between the two countries improve, there is little prospect of disarmament.

When prices rise the man on a fixed salary feels the pinch.

**25B**   The comma is used before non-restrictive phrases and clauses. A very important part of punctuation depends on recognizing the difference between restrictive and non-restrictive elements.

A phrase or clause is restrictive if it is essential to point out, limit, or identify, so that its omission would leave the main thought of the sentence incomplete. Because they are so closely related to the principal idea being expressed, restrictive elements are not set off by punctuation.

A man *of that character* can scarcely be trusted.
A job *in a big city* appeals to many young people.
This is the dog *which won the blue ribbon.*
Persons *who voted in the last election* need not register again.

An element is non-restrictive when it is merely added to give some further detail, or to express an afterthought. It is not needed to make clear the essential meaning of the sentence, and a comma is used to signify that its attachment is comparatively loose.

His clothing, *of faded blue denim,* suggested that he was a workman.

The party, *with its babble of voices and thickening cigarette smoke,* went on until midnight.

Jim passed only one course, *which was mechanical drawing.*

The redwoods, *which are the oldest of living things,* are found in California.

Note that the failure to use a comma before a non-restrictive relative clause changes the meaning of the entire construction.

Ralph sent a card to his girl friend *who lives in Pittsburgh.*
Ralph sent a card to his girl friend, *who lives in Pittsburgh.*

The meaning of the first sentence is that Ralph has more than one girl and that the card went to the one who lives in Pittsburgh. The second sentence means that Ralph has only one girl and that she lives in Pittsburgh.

A similar difference appears in the sentences below.

Mr. Johnson sold the car which had been damaged in an accident.
Mr. Johnson sold the car, which had been damaged in an accident.

**25C**   An appositive is set off by commas unless it is essential to identify the expression with which it is in apposition.

His new friend, Mr. Mayfield, called next day.
*But:* His brother Clyde is the most successful of the boys.
    The liner *President Madison* will dock at noon.

**25D**   The comma is used to set off certain types of parenthetical clauses which serve to give the source of information conveyed by the sentence. The parenthetical clause is enclosed in commas if its position is internal.

The President will spend Christmas at the White House, it was reported in Washington yesterday.

The enforcement of traffic laws, it was pointed out by the Department of Highway Safety, requires the cooperation of the public.

**25E**  Sometimes a comma is used to indicate an ellipsis (an omitted word or words in a construction).

> For some customers quality is the chief consideration; for others, price.

> In the older and more settled society of the East they might ask who was your grandfather; but on the frontier, never.

## Items in a Series

**26A**  The comma is used to separate words or phrases in a series.

> On the outdoor stands were displayed tomatoes, cabbages, carrots, radishes, lettuce, and other fresh vegetables.

> Among his followers were idealists working for a cause, self-seekers bringing an axe to grind, and ordinary citizens impressed with the need of a change.

NOTE: In a series of this kind it is best to use a comma before the *and* which introduces the final member. Although this comma is frequently omitted in newspaper style, there are situations in which it serves to prevent confusion.

**26B**  A series of dependent clauses is separated by commas.

> If he has a goal in view, if he is willing to work, and if he mixes well with his fellows, he will probably succeed.

**26C**  If two or more coordinate adjectives precede the substantive they modify, they are separated by commas.

> It was a wicked, causeless action.
> Clear, blue, sparkling, the sea stretched away to our right.

It is important to note, however, that if the adjectives preceding the substantive are not coordinate—that is to say, if they express qualities of very different kinds—they are not separated by punctuation.

> Mrs. Beckett was a nice old lady.
> Ray had bought a fine new fishing rod.

**26D**  The semicolon is used to separate a series of clauses or phrases which contain internal punctuation.

> The message said that the men were safe, owing to a fortunate occurrence; that they had been taken from their ship, the *Rover;* and that, in all probability, they would reach San Francisco on Friday.

> The Yankee has been characterized by ingenuity, which has made him an inventor; by impatience with traditions, which has made him an experimenter with institutions; and by a pragmatic philosophy, which has made him content to judge his work by its consequences.

**26E**  Sometimes the comma is used to enforce or call attention to a contrast of items.

> The recipe calls for meal, not flour.
> The victims were numbered not in hundreds, but in thousands.

# OTHER USES OF PUNCTUATION

## The Comma

**27A**  The comma is used after the name of a person when the name is followed by a degree or title.

> Theodore Davis, Ph.D.
> Lucille Smith, R.N.
> James S. Palmer, Editor
> William P. Watson, Attorney-at-law

**27B**  The comma is used to separate the parts of an address.

> Los Angeles, California          Hillsboro, New Hampshire
> The postmark showed that it had been mailed in Chicago, Illinois, a week before.

**27C**  The comma is used between the day of the month and the year in dates.

> February 16, 1952

**27D**  The comma is used after the greeting in personal or informal correspondence.

> Dear Mary,                    Dear Cousin Bob,

**27E**  The comma is used after a vocative expression.

> Louise, have you seen the movie at the Strand?

**27F**  The comma is used before a short or informal quotation.

> Mr. Myers remarked to his son, "When you are my age you will see things differently."

> The next question was, "What are the principal exports of Cuba?"

## Quotation Marks

**28A**  Quotation marks are used to enclose all matter which is directly quoted.

> He said to his companion, "I'll meet you in about twenty minutes."

"The play was interesting," remarked Mabel, "but I was disappointed in the last act."

Then he read from the *Book of Proverbs:* "Wealth gotten by vanity shall be diminished; but he that gathereth by labor shall have increase."

Single quotation marks are used to enclose a quotation which appears within another quotation.

"Everyone said that Victor had 'missed the boat' by not taking the chance."

**28B**   Quotation marks are sometimes used to enclose a term which is technical or otherwise not familiar, or which is used in a humorous or ironical sense.

Physical measurement of molecules can be made by using an "ultra-centrifuge."

That was his idea of a "peaceful" solution.

**28C**   Quotation marks are used to call attention to a word or phrase which is used apart from its normal signification, or as an instance of a word or phrase.

The word "nice" has an interesting semantic history.
Now we come to the much-abused term "liberalism."

By "assuming the responsibilities of marriage" they evidently mean working harder and making more money.

**28D**   Quotation marks are regularly used to enclose the titles of short stories, essays, chapters, articles, and short poems.

Have you read Stuart Chase's "The Luxury of Integrity"?
The line was from Tennyson's "Locksley Hall."

NOTE: The titles of books, of long poems, and of periodicals are generally put in italics. In a typewritten manuscript, they should be underlined.

Donald Davidson's *The Attack on Leviathan* is a defense of regionalism.
Satan is a principal character in *Paradise Lost.*
Her first story was accepted by the *Atlantic Monthly.*

**28E**   The comma and the period are always placed inside quotation marks.

"No," he said. "I do not remember ever having seen him."

**28F**   If a question mark, semicolon, or exclamation point belongs to the quoted part, it goes inside the quotation marks. If it does not belong to the quoted part, it goes outside.

He began by asking, "How would you like to go to Los Angeles?"
"Be quiet!" Betty said impatiently.
Did you hear him say, "I would never vote for Johnson"?

## The Colon

**29A** The colon is used before a series which is long or formal.

The following schools participated in the study: the University of California, the University of Chicago, Harvard University, Ohio State University, Princeton University, the University of Michigan, and Yale University.

**29B** The colon is used to introduce a quotation which is relatively long or formal.

Turning to his notes, the mayor said: "There is no doubt that the city is faced with a crisis through the growing tendency of individuals and businesses to move to the suburbs. Figures for last year show an 8% decline in the assessed value of real estate within the city's corporate limits."

Arthur then quoted the lines from Longfellow's "The Building of the Ship":

> Thou, too, sail on, O Ship of State
> Sail on, O Union, strong and great!
> Humanity with all its fears,
> With all the hopes of future years,
> Is hanging breathless on thy fate!

**29C** The colon is sometimes used before a clause which is an adjunct to the preceding clause.

Music has been called the most perfect of the arts: it is the art to which all the other arts aspire.

**29D** Sometimes the colon is used before an element which marks an important change of meaning or emphasis in the sentence.

That he was not a great poet is admitted: some have maintained that he was not a poet at all.

He felt that he had yielded enough: from now on there would be no more concessions.

## The Dash

**30A** The dash is used before an abrupt change in the sense of a sentence and before an important change in the construction.

Peering around the corner into the darkness, he saw—nothing.
The facts of the matter are—but what is the use of going into all this?

**30B**   The dash may be used before an element which sums up more or less compactly the meaning of a sentence.

> Behind his polite manner, his solicitude for others, his talk of the general welfare, one thing stood out—he wanted power.

**30C**   Dashes may be used to enclose parenthetical matter which deserves to be set off with more emphasis than marks of parenthesis denote.

> The newspaper—there is only one paper in Central City—took up the matter editorially.

> She wanted to talk about one thing—namely, her children.

## Marks of Parenthesis

**31A**   Marks of parenthesis are used to set off matter which appears as an explanation, commentary, or afterthought.

> Each peasant was to be given four hectares (about ten acres) of land.

> The next piece on the program (Debussy's "Afternoon of a Faun") came just before the intermission.

> His old friend Ed Smith (his only friend, if the truth were known) came to help him out.

**31B**   When marks of parenthesis are used within a sentence, the parenthetical element is not followed by a mark of punctuation unless punctuation is otherwise called for at that point.

> The amount of money involved (about $16.00) was hardly worth all the anxiety.

> Until he pays what he owes (about $16.00), he cannot receive further credit.

**31C**   If the element enclosed in marks of parenthesis is a full and separate sentence, it is followed by a period before the second mark.

> The manager was in a bad mood. (The team had just lost four straight games.) In desperation he decided to try the rookie pitcher.

## Brackets

**32A**   Brackets are used to enclose matter which is inserted by someone other than the writer (usually the editor) to clarify or complete the meaning of a passage. Brackets are therefore always a sign that the item they enclose does not appear in the original.

> He declared that this scandal [the Teapot Dome issue of 1924] would rock the country to its foundations.

The allusion to the Ides of March [among the Romans a fatal or inauspicious day] was understood as a threat.

Brackets always signify something interpolated from the outside. A writer makes use of marks of parenthesis to enclose matter of his own which is explanatory or incidental.

# MECHANICS

## Capitals

**33A**  The beginning word of each sentence and of each element punctuated as a sentence is capitalized.

The game was played in perfect weather.
Bravo! A hole in one.

**33B**  Normally the initial word of every line of verse is capitalized.

That time of year thou mayst in me behold
When yellow leaves, or none, or few do hang
Upon those boughs which shake against the cold,
Bare ruined choirs where late the sweet birds sang.

**33C**  All proper names and most proper adjectives derived from them are capitalized.

Great Britain, Caesar, the Taj Mahal
Canadian, Machiavellian, Christian

**33D**  Common nouns are capitalized when used as personifications.

There they worshipped at the shrine of Fortune.
Then comes Summer with her ripening grain.

**33E**  Common nouns which combine with a proper noun to constitute a specific proper name are capitalized.

the Mediterranean Sea, the Mississippi River, the Gulf Stream, the White Mountains

**33F**  Titles when accompanied by a proper name are capitalized.

In the next car rode President Wilson.
The case was referred to Attorney-General Clark.
The question was raised by Chancellor Bowman.

**33G**  All principal words in the titles of books, articles, and plays are capitalized.

*The Life of Reason*
"Human Nature and the Social Sciences"
"The Taming of the Shrew"

**33H**   The names of historical epochs and of important historical events are generally capitalized.

| | |
|---|---|
| the Renaissance | the Norman Conquest |
| the Reign of Terror | the Crusades |
| the Industrial Revolution | the Peninsular Campaign |

**33I**   The points of the compass are capitalized only when they are used as names of definite geographical areas.

Helen spent a year in the West.
Anti-slavery sentiment was growing in the North.
*But:* Five miles farther on, the road turned north.

**33J**   The names of people and of languages are always capitalized.

| | |
|---|---|
| the Romans | Latin |
| the Indians | French |
| the Germans | Slavic |

**33K**   The first word of a direct quotation is capitalized.

James Madison wrote in *The Federalist:* "There are two methods of curing the mischiefs of faction: the one, by removing its causes; the other, by controlling its effects."

NOTE: When a directly quoted sentence is interrupted by an expression such as "he said," do not capitalize the first word of the second part.

"The reason people do such things," he said, "is that they don't know better."

## Italics

Italics is a term meaning a kind of printer's type. In handwritten and typewritten manuscripts expressions which should be italicized are underlined.

**34A**   The titles of books, periodicals, and long poems are italicized.

*Vanity Fair,* the *Reader's Digest,* the *Iliad*

The title of a newspaper is italicized but the name of the city in which it is published is not, unless it is an integral part of the title.

the New York *World Journal Tribune*
the Louisville *Courier-Journal*

**34B** Foreign words and expressions which are still regarded as foreign are italicized, but since acceptance and use of foreign words and expressions vary from group to group, each writer will know the needs of his audience. Some dictionaries indicate foreign words and expressions by putting a double bar before them, but recent editions have begun omitting such indications.

> *pro bono publico*
> *Weltanschauung*

**34C** Words, letters and numbers referred to as such are italicized.

> The coordinating conjunctions are *and, but, for, or, nor, yet,* and *so.*
> Dot your *i*'s and cross your *t*'s.
> Eliminate the *3*'s and *5*'s from each set.

**34D** The names of ships and airplanes are italicized.

> The *Excelsior* was launched in May, 1951.
> Lindbergh made his famous transatlantic flight in the *Spirit of St. Louis.*

**34E** Words and expressions to which special emphasis is given may be italicized. It is well, however, not to overindulge in this practice. Too much reliance upon italics for emphasis is a stylistic weakness.

> Albert *knew* that he had locked the house carefully.

## Abbreviations

**35A** The titles Mr., Mrs., and Dr. are always abbreviated when used with a name.

> We called on Mr. and Mrs. Partington.
> They summoned Dr. Forman.

**35B** The names of titles and degrees are abbreviated when they are used following a name.

> Peter Stirling, M.P.
> W. D. Chamberlain, Jr.
> Dean of the faculties was Homer Clark, Ph.D., D. Litt., D.C.L.

**35C** The abbreviations A.M. (also a.m.) (*ante meridiem,* before noon), and P.M. (also p.m.) (*post meridiem,* after noon) are used when time is being designated.

**35D** The following abbreviations are regularly used in formal writing.

> A.D. (*Anno Domini,* in the year of our Lord)
> B.C. (Before Christ)

*e.g.* (*exempli gratia*, for example)
etc. (*et cetera*, and others)
*i.e.* (*id est*, that is)
No. (number)
*viz.* (*videlicet*, namely)

St. Augustine died in 430 A.D.
Caesar invaded Britain in 55 B.C.

There had been earlier evidences of dissatisfaction with British rules, *e.g.*, Bacon's rebellion.

He was asked to give his name, address, phone number, church preference, etc.

CAUTION: Do not use the abbreviation *etc.* merely to avoid the effort of filling out your thought. It should be used only when a further listing of items would be pointless.

Mr. Anderson is an experienced businessman, *i.e.*, one who knows what it is to meet a payroll every month.

His ticket was No. 27.

Robert had been carried away by his new discovery, *viz.*, free verse.

Footnotes, bibliographies, dictionaries, encyclopedias, and manuals often follow special systems of abbreviations, the key to which is ordinarily provided in the work itself. The abbreviations explained above are for general use.

## Numbers

**36A**   Figures are used for dates, street and room numbers, telephone numbers, volume and page numbers, hours given with A.M. and P.M., and decimals.

The Clayton Anti-Trust Act was passed October 14, 1914.

Her family moved to 312 Elm Tree Lane.

He had given his phone number as Plaza 3-4100.

This interesting observation is found in Tocqueville's *Democracy in America*, Vol. II, p. 142.

The convention was called to order at 9:30 A.M.

The rainfall for the month was 2.4 inches.

**36B**   Numbers of less than 100 are usually spelled out; numbers of more than 100 are expressed in figures.

Last term twenty-eight students made the honor roll.
The entering class showed an increase of 139.

**36C**  If, however, a passage contains a group of numbers, figures should be used even though the numbers are less than 100.

> When they compared results, Gerkhe had 42, Jones 27, Newman 25, and Robbins 38.

**36D**  Never begin a sentence with a figure.

> WRONG:  1,000 men formed the division.
> RIGHT:  One thousand men formed the division.

**36E**  The writing of numbers in both figures and words is confined to legal and commercial papers and letters.

> LEGAL PAPER STYLE:  The undersigned agrees to pay the sum of one thousand dollars ($1,000) within six (6) months.

## The Apostrophe

**37A**  The apostrophe followed by an *s* is used to indicate the genitive form of singular nouns.

> a man's clothing
> the student's record

**37B**  The apostrophe only is used to indicate the genitive form of plural nouns ending in *s*.

> the ladies' section
> The flowers' names were difficult to spell.

**37C**  Some Biblical, classical, and common names ending in an *s* or *z* sound form the genitive by adding the apostrophe alone.

> Jesus' parables          Ulysses' voyage
> Aeneas' fate             James' car

**37D**  To indicate the genitive form of compound words and of pairs having joint possession, add the apostrophe followed by *s* to the final word.

> His mother-in-law's house
> Reagan and Brown's general store

CAUTION: Do not overlook the distinction between the contraction *it's* (it is) and the possessive pronoun *its*. Possessive pronouns never take the apostrophe: this is *yours;* that is *theirs; its* appearance was novel.

**37E**  The apostrophe is used to indicate a contraction and sometimes to indicate the omission of numbers.

It's about time!
Julia didn't care what they said.
The stock market crash of '29 was a shock to most Americans.

**37F**   The apostrophe followed by an *s* is used to form the plural of figures and letters, and of words when attention is to be called to their status as plural forms.

How many *2's* are in the series?
He had an odd way of forming his *f's*.
There are too many *that's* in your sentence.

**37G**   The apostrophe followed by a *d* may indicate that the word or expression is being used arbitrarily as a verb in the past tense.

The boss OK'd his expense account.

## The Hyphen

**38A**   The hyphen is used between the parts of some compound words.

the runner-up
an aide-de-camp

**38B**   The hyphen is used between most compound modifiers when they precede the substantive.

an ill-starred enterprise
an industry-wide strike
a behind-the-times proposal

**38C**   The hyphen is used after certain prefixes, such as *all, ex, pan, self,* and *trans* (in some usages).

an all-American tackle
ex-Governor Sandford
a pan-German movement
a self-explanatory rule
a trans-Siberian journey

**38D**   The hyphen is used with compound numbers ranging from twenty-one to ninety-nine.

**38E**   The hyphen is used to prevent confusion with another word of similar form.

It became imperative to re-form the lines.
The new work was indeed a re-creation.

## Ellipsis Dots

**39A**  Ellipsis dots are used to indicate an omission in a quoted passage. If the omission occurs within a sentence, three dots are used. If it occurs at the end of a sentence, or if an entire sentence or more is omitted, four dots are used.

> Mr. Chalmers remarks in *The Republic and the Person:* "The historical fact is that during the Twenties and Thirties . . . men of letters, philosophers and others interested primarily in ideas were announcing principles which countenanced and even supported the pacifism and complacency of popular thought."

> The critic Edmund Wilson has written of Edith Wharton: "Her work was, then, the desperate product of a pressure of maladjustments; and it very soon took a direction very different from that of Henry James. . . . James's interests were predominantly esthetic: he is never a passionate social prophet; and only rarely . . . does he satirize plutocratic America."

## EXERCISES

*In the following exercises supply necessary punctuation or correct mechanics as appropriate.*

### Exercise A   *The Punctuation of Compound Sentences*

1. St. Louis and Chicago were at one time rivals in size the city on the Great Lakes however was destined to become the transportation center of the nation.
2. He must have been successful for he appeared next day wearing a broad smile.
3. Snow and ice are hazards to traffic they can also cause failures in telephone service.
4. One was lost and two were broken but the rest arrived in fairly good condition.
5. Many persons have the ambition to be writers however few realize the sacrifices which a writer must undergo.
6. He learned that the town had a public library and he became a steady borrower of biographies and histories.
7. Sometimes she dreamed of going abroad at other times she thought of retiring to the country but always she put off the decision.
8. The volume of sales was somewhat larger nevertheless the net income was reduced by higher operating expenses.
9. He walked up the steps and opened the door then he switched on the living room light.
10. General Custer fought in the Civil War but he is best known for his stand against the Indians on the Little Big Horn.
11. Some books should be studied carefully others deserve little more than a casual inspection.

12. New England and Virginia were the seedbeds of the American Revolution and both contributed able leaders to the movement for independence.
13. Mr. Allison regularly arose at seven o'clock he arrived at his office promptly at nine.
14. They studied maps they sent off for travel booklets they even inquired the cost of a passage to Europe.
15. Few men have captured the imagination of their time as did the poet Byron he expressed its mood of romantic pessimism.
16. He wasted no time on those already persuaded his efforts were all directed at those who had not made up their minds.
17. A young person is tempted to follow intellectual fashions for he has not learned the importance of being himself.
18. Norman was always well dressed yet he never seemed to have any money.
19. The purpose of fiction is not simply to entertain it is to present a truthful picture of human life.
20. Common sense is not a very common quality and those who possess it are usually sought after.
21. Mathematics befuddled him and he could never learn a foreign language but he could do anything with his hands.
22. George kept a careful record of expenses thus he knew at the end of the month exactly where he stood.
23. The Grand Canyon is a stupendous natural wonder few people can gaze into those depths without a sense of awe.
24. Commuting between New York and San Francisco was not exactly his ideal of a life nevertheless this was about what the job required.
25. Mr. Jones liked to think of himself as an investor accordingly he always bought the *Wall Street Journal*.

## Exercise B   *Punctuation of Restrictive and Non-restrictive Elements*

1. He carefully set aside those which he expected to use next day.
2. Mammoth Cave which is located in Kentucky is now part of a national park.
3. He seemed to the children with his tales of foreign lands the most fascinating man they knew.
4. Ben told everyone to pull when he gave the signal.
5. O. Henry the author of *The Four Million* showed that one can see romance even in a great city.
6. A man whom he had known in the army stopped him on the street.
7. A cheer went up as Herman broke the tape at the finish line.
8. The theory of single tax of which Henry George was the leading exponent holds that taxes should be levied solely on property.
9. He who hesitates is lost.
10. The old building opposite the courthouse was damaged by fire.
11. Enrico Fermi who has been called the architect of the atomic age was born in Italy.
12. Edwin with his usual pleasing manner showed up at every social occasion.

13. People advanced in years love to reminisce about the past.
14. Mr. Hawkins who was cashier at the bank also taught Sunday school.
15. These are the only ones that look ripe.
16. The siege of Troy which lasted for ten years is the subject of the *Iliad*.
17. Next morning they started as early as they could.
18. Mr. Wright who is the town's oldest inhabitant walks to work every day.
19. A man of varied interests finds his days filled with activity.
20. Columbus who thought that he had found the mainland of India called the native Americans Indians.
21. A man with that much money is expected to give to charity.
22. He liked to attend Westerns which took his mind off his troubles.
23. New York which is America's largest city is made up of five boroughs.
24. As usual there was only one choice of dessert which was tapioca pudding.
25. The old barn with its smell of hay and harness was a favorite playing spot for the children.

## Exercise C  *Punctuation of Series*

1. The garden became a favorite spot for robins redbirds and the ubiquitous sparrow.
2. He took algebra which he liked history which he at least found interesting and Latin for which he could not see any possible use.
3. Belching chimneys grimy roof tops and rows of drab houses are the usual signs of an industrial city.
4. People admired him for his easy gay confident air.
5. Everyone considered Mr. Byers a dull young man.
6. They began business in a little store on the corner, where they sold tobacco candy chewing gum and postcards.
7. At her father's table she heard little but talk of party politics candidates caucuses and elections won or lost.
8. The grass turned brown the creeks grew shallow and soon the whole region was faced with a drought.
9. How hard money is to acquire how easy it is to lose and how little it does to insure happiness were lessons he had learned.
10. The oldest institutions of higher learning in the United States are Harvard William and Mary and Yale in that order.
11. Words words words were all that came out of the assembly.
12. Winners from this district include John R. Stevens, 112 Riverview Drive, Peoria, Ill. Marvin A. Lambert, 345 South Main, Kenosha, Wis. Paul B. Hayes, 1078 East Seventh St., Indianapolis, Ind. and Alfred Suderman, 380 Fairview, Des Moines, Iowa.
13. On her table was the usual disarray of cosmetics pin cushions mirrors and ribbons.
14. Flies gnats and especially mosquitoes made the outing somewhat less than completely enjoyable.
15. He tasted he smiled he asked for some more.
16. Both candidates seemed to be promising peace prosperity and universal happiness.

17. Young personable and enthusiastic he appeared well suited to the job.
18. The donations were mostly in nickels and dimes.
19. Mr. Weber was a connoisseur of books and of rare old wines.
20. In she came with a pot of strong steaming hot coffee.

## Exercise D   *Punctuation of Quoted Material*

1. How are you feeling today? he asked Mr. Barnes. First rate replied the old gentleman.
2. Rising to his feet the chairman asked Does everyone have a copy of the new resolution?
3. The agricultural policy of the present administration Congressman Smith declared in an address yesterday penalizes the farmer at the expense of the wage earner.
4. He turned to her with a startled look and said Did you put the keys in your purse?
5. This is always the way it happens complained Lucy Whenever we want to go anywhere it rains.
6. Howard began to write thoughtfully The political institutions of this country depend for their existence on the consent of the people.
7. He recalled the cry that inspires all Texans Remember the Alamo.
8. The teacher asked how many students had read the lesson.
9. How much is this hat inquired the brisk young man of the clerk.
10. They never inquired whether he was a Democrat or a Republican.
11. Lincoln gave the following advice to young men desiring to become lawyers The leading rule for the lawyer as for the man of every other calling is diligence. Leave nothing for tomorrow which can be done today.
12. Do you remember where you put my overshoes he asked. Have you looked in the closet downstairs she replied. I have looked there just now he said but I did not see them. Well, they were there the last time I cleaned the house she added.
13. What said Mr. Blevins to his little nephew. Cake and watermelon too!
14. How did you like the show inquired his companion. Well enough he replied but I couldn't understand how the heroine could fall for that sort of fellow.
15. Going, going, gone, sang out the auctioneer.
16. He could remember only a few lines of Poe's *The Raven*.
17. The word bungalow is of East Indian origin.
18. He ended by asking How many of you would like to be in that situation?
19. Trying to understand the meaning, Ned looked up the term oxymoron.
20. He wrote in a postscript Can you tell me whether the remark War is hell is attributed to General Sherman?

## Exercise E   *Punctuation of Possessives*

1. A good days pay for a good days work was the slogan of the company.
2. The whole neighborhood had heard about the Adamses new car.
3. In the eighth grade the students study Brown and Sharpes *Grammar of English*.

4. The family prepared for the son-in-laws visit.
5. The controversy over states rights is one of the central themes of American history.
6. At the end of five years the property was theirs.
7. Although he meant well, he got in everybodys way.
8. Womens styles change every year.
9. Please stop at Smith and Turners and pick up a package for me.
10. The soldiers uniforms were worn to tatters.
11. The old song had lost none of its appeal.
12. The cat is theirs, but the dog is ours.
13. James undertook to recite Moses commandments.
14. The commander-in-chiefs presence had a visible effect on morale
15. Chester thought he could borrow someone elses notes.

## Exercise F *Capitals, Abbreviations, and other Mechanics*

1. Stephen A. Douglas was born in Vt., but he moved to Ill., where he became known in politics as the little giant.
2. Every student is held for 4 years of english and some for 3 of math.
3. They are a proud people who wont accept charity.
4. Coming from the east, he could not understand why people in the southwest were so concerned about water.
5. Norma spoke to Jean sotto voce because she knew that the others were listening.
6. Mr. Gibson is a broker ie one whose business it is to bring sellers and buyers together.
7. The President Taft was launched on June the fifteenth, 1955.
8. The item appeared on page seventeen of last Monday's New York Times.
9. Bill guessed that the score would not be over fifteen (15), but he had not taken into account the strength of the wolverines.
10. High above the Chicago Board of trade building stands ceres, the goddess of grain.
11. Whenever her emotions were aroused, her conversation was likely to be punctuated with oh's and ah's.
12. 100 police were assigned for protection when the all important meeting was held in New York.
13. Robert A. Miles, junior, was the name of the new instructor in spanish, and he had taken an apartment at one hundred and eighteen maple drive.
14. He had never been below the mason-dixon line, and a trip to Maryland was for him a visit to the south.
15. The prof. reminded the class that Ibsen had written a number of plays, of which *ghosts* was but one.
16. Rep. Shannon carried his district by a plurality to twenty two thousand four hundred and sixty five in a total vote of one hundred and twelve thousand two hundred and ninety seven.
17. Address all inquiries to Mister Walter Brown, Pres., Appliance Manufacturing Company, Washington, Indiana.
18. The west has always been a favorite setting for stories of adventure and violence, and the american cowboy is now known the world over.

19. It was found after experimentation that the ideal proportion of nitrate for this type of fertilizer is six and eight tenths per cent.
20. He mentioned an article which appeared on page sixteen of last week's saturday evening post.
21. A sentence with too many ands may suffer from over-coordination.
22. Starting with the French Rev. in seventeen eighty nine, a spirit of revolt spread over Europe and altered many ancient institutions despite the overthrow of napoleon at Waterloo.
23. A well to do business man, Mr. Robertson was a member of 3 or 4 civic clubs and president of the chamber of commerce.
24. He quoted the sentence as follows, omitting one clause: The use of history is to make men critical of the past.
25. If we can judge by the number of Ph D s on the faculty, Wilson college deserves a high rating, said president Miller.

# Spelling

Spelling today is standardized, and habitual misspelling is a handicap for anyone. College papers are usually marked for misspelling, and in business correspondence a misspelled word is considered a serious error.

Some people learn to spell almost as easily as they learn to breathe; others have difficulty in achieving even a passable correctness. The differences are due to a number of things: how much time the individual spends in contact with printed matter; whether his memory is chiefly visual, aural, or motor; how seriously he takes the problem of spelling; and others. For these reasons no one remedy can be prescribed for all poor spellers. The student should analyze the source of his difficulty and then follow the procedure that seems best adapted to correct it. The rules given below are not guaranteed to transform every poor speller into a good one. But applied conscientiously, they will certainly produce some improvement.

1. *Try to improve your memory of how the written or printed word looks.* The best spellers seem to be those with "photographic" memories, who take a picture of the word as it appears on the printed page. Not everyone is born with a good visual memory, but memory can be trained and specialized for specific tasks. You may be surprised, if you make a real effort, how far you can educate your memory to retain certain things. Try looking at words as you would look at anything of which you need to gain a clear impression.

2. *Write out the words which you persistently misspell.* Print the letter or letters which give the most trouble in large form. For example:

aCCoMModate     repEtition
privIlege        sepArate

Then pronounce the word out loud, giving special emphasis to the troublesome part. In this way you are calling upon your aural memory to assist your visual; you are remembering partly by sound. Keep a list of these words and go over them until you have learned to spell the chief offenders in your vocabulary.

3. *Learn to distinguish between words which are much alike in sound or form.* Consult a dictionary carefully as to their meanings and make use of this knowledge to keep them distinct. Some examples are *accept, except; affect, effect; allusion, illusion; born, borne.* These and others will be found in the *Glossary.*

4. *Learn a few of the more general rules governing English spelling.* Although most of these rules have exceptions, and rules never made a first-rate speller anyhow, they will guide you in important instances to a choice between right and wrong.

**a.** A noun ending in *-y* preceded by a consonant changes the *-y* to *-i* and adds *-es* to form the plural.

army, armies     lady, ladies
copy, copies     party, parties

**b.** Most words ending in silent *-e* drop the *-e* before a suffix beginning with a vowel.

advise, advisable    move, moving
educate, educating    prepare, preparing
mine, mining     write, writing

EXCEPTIONS: In a few words the final *-e* is retained in order to prevent mispronunciation: hoeing, shoeing, singeing.
The *-e* is retained if the suffix begins with a consonant.

debase, debasement   enlarge, enlargement
confine, confinement   fate, fateful
excite, excitement    like, likeness

After *-c* or *-g*, if the suffix begins with *-a* or *-o*, the *-e* is retained to indicate a soft sound for the *-c* or *-g*.

change, changeable   notice, noticeable
advantage, advantageous  service, serviceable

**c.** Words ending in *-ie* generally drop the *-e* and change *-i* to *-y* before the suffix *-ing.*

die, dying     tie, tying
lie, lying     vie, vying

**d.** Most words with the letters *-ei* or *-ie* pronounced *ee* are spelled *-ie* except after *-c.*

believe   conceit   EXCEPTIONS: leisure,
grievous   perceive   neither, seize, weird
relieve    receive

**e.** Words of one syllable, and words accented on the last syllable, when they end in a single consonant preceded by a single vowel double the consonant before suffixes beginning with a vowel.

| | |
|---|---|
| cut, cutting | confer, conferring |
| man, manning | equip, equipped |
| run, runner | occur, occurrence |
| stop, stopping | submit, submitted |

5. *Keep a dictionary handy.* Few people ever get beyond the stage of needing to consult one. A good dictionary will give you a more complete list of spelling rules and will advise you when two spellings of a word are permissible (*e.g.*, adviser, advisor; judgment, judgement; traveler, traveller).

## A LIST OF WORDS OFTEN MISSPELLED

| | | | |
|---|---|---|---|
| abbreviate | architecture | candidate | cooperate |
| absence | arctic | can't | corollary |
| absorption | argument | catastrophe | corps |
| accept | ascent | cavalry | corpse |
| access | assassin | cellar | correlate |
| accessible | assent | cemetery | council |
| accident | assistance | characteristic | counsel |
| accidentally | athlete, athletics | chauffeur | counterfeit |
| accommodate | author | chimney | crisis |
| accumulate | average | choir | criticism |
| achieve | awful | Christian | criticize |
| acknowledge | | client | curriculum |
| acquaintance | balance | cloths | |
| acquitted | balloon | clothes | dairy |
| address | bare | colonel | deceit |
| aerial | baring | column | deceive |
| affect | barrel | commence | decent |
| aggravate | battalion | committee | decision |
| all right | bear | comparative | defendant |
| alley, alleys | bearing | comparison | descent |
| ally, allies | believe | compel, compelled | desert |
| already | benefit | competitive | desirable |
| altar | benefited | complement | dessert |
| alter | biscuit | compliment | diary |
| altogether | born | conceive | disappoint |
| always | borne | condemn | disastrous |
| amateur | Britain | condescend | disease |
| among | bureau | confidential | dissipate |
| analyze | bureaucracy | connoisseur | doesn't |
| apparatus | business | conscience | |
| apparent | | conscious | earnest |
| appearance | calendar | conspicucus | economics |
| appointment | Calvary | continuous | efficient |
| appreciate | campaign | convenient | eligible |

eliminate
embarrass
employee
engineer
environment
equal
equally
equip, equipped
equivalent
especially
exaggerated
exceed
exhibit
exhilarate
existence
experience
extraordinary

familiar
fascinate
February
finally
financier
foreign
forfeit
formally
formerly
forty
friendly
fulfill
fundamental

gauge
genius
government
grammar
grievous
guarantee

handkerchief
harass
height
heroes
hindrance
hope
hoping
hygiene
hypocrisy

illiterate

illusion
immediately
incident
incidentally
indispensable
individual
inevitable
ingenious
ingenuous
innocent
intelligent
intercede
interfere
irresistible

laboratory
legitimate
leisure
library
license
lightning
livelihood
lose

maintain
maintenance
maneuver
mathematics
medicine
miniature
minute
miscellaneous
mischievous
Mississippi
mosquitoes
muscle
mutilate
mysterious

naïve
necessary
Negroes
niece
noticeable
nowadays

obedience
occasion
occasionally
occur

occurrence
official
omission
opinion
opponent
opportunity
optimist
origin
outrageous

pageant
pamphlet
parallel
parenthesis
parliament
pastime
peaceable
perform
permanent
perseverance
personnel
Philippines
physical
picnic
picnickers
playwright
politician
possession
potatoes
precede
precedence
precious
prejudice
president
priest
principal
principle
privilege
proceed
procedure
professor
prominent
prophecy
prophesy
psychology

quantity
questionnaire
quiet
quite

realize
receipt
receive
recommend
refer
referred
reign
relieve
religious
repetition
representative
resistance
restaurant
rhythm

sacrifice
sacrilege
sacrilegious
scarcely
schedule
science
secede
secretary
seize
separate
sergeant
siege
similar
simultaneous
sincerely
skillful
society
sophomore
stationary
stationery
statistics
statue
stature
strategy
strenuous
studying
succeed
supersede
suppress
syllable
symmetrical
synonym

temperament
temperature

| | | | |
|---|---|---|---|
| temporary | truly | unnecessary | vengeance |
| tendency | typical | until | villain |
| therefore | tyranny | usual | |
| thorough | | usually | weather |
| tragedy | unanimous | | weird |
| transferred | unconscious | valuable | whether |
| translate | undoubtedly | vegetable | writing |

# A Glossary of Usage

This glossary lists words which present recurrent usage problems. The judgments noted are consistent with the best available dictionaries and usage studies. But it should be noted that usage changes continuously and varies somewhat from one area of the country to another. A good desk dictionary should be used for guidance on words and expressions not included here.

The following labels have been used:

ACCEPTABLE: used in conversation and writing of educated people.

UNACCEPTABLE: not used in either conversation or writing of educated people.

COLLOQUIAL: used in conversation of educated people and in informal writing.

FORMAL: limited to formal context in speech and writing.

DIALECT: limited to certain geographical areas.

JARGON: limited to certain social (labor, business) groups.

Certain other self-explanatory labels such as VAGUE, INACCURATE, PRE-FERRED, and the like have been introduced when they seemed usefully descriptive of the principal objection to the usage.

**A, An.** The first of these two forms of the indefinite article should be used before words beginning with a consonant sound or with the sound of *y* or *w;* the second before words beginning with a vowel sound.

ACCEPTABLE: a book, a history, a task, a union, a once-forgotten story.
ACCEPTABLE: an end, an image, an honor, an umpire.

360

**Absolutely.** *Absolutely* usually means *entirely, completely.* It is used colloquially in the sense of *very* or *much.*

COLLOQUIAL: Linda was absolutely terrified.
ACCEPTABLE: His figures are absolutely correct.
ACCEPTABLE: The water showed absolutely no trace of contamination.

**Accept, except.** These words are sometimes confused because of their similarity of sound. *Accept* is a verb which means *to receive, to take or admit willingly. Except* may be either a verb or a preposition depending on its function in an utterance. As a verb, it means *to leave out, to omit, to make an exception of.* As a preposition it means *excluding.*

ACCEPTABLE: The union accepted the terms offered by the management.
ACCEPTABLE: He excepted military heroes from his list of benefactors of humanity.
ACCEPTABLE: Everyone except David arrived in time.

**Admit, admit of.** *Admit* means *to allow to enter; admit of* means *to be capable of, to be open to.*

ACCEPTABLE: This ticket admits you to any performance.
ACCEPTABLE: The rule admits of only one exception.

**Advice, advise.** *Advice* is used only as a noun; *advise* only as a verb.

ACCEPTABLE: He resolved to follow his instructor's advice next time.
ACCEPTABLE: Mr. Remington advised us not to put all our eggs in one basket.

**Affect, effect.** *Affect* is a verb which means *to influence, to modify, to change. Effect* is used both as verb and noun. As a verb it means *to accomplish, to bring about as a result.* As a noun it means *a result, the thing accomplished.*

ACCEPTABLE: A war affects everyone's life.
ACCEPTABLE: The Citizens League effected several reforms in municipal administration.
ACCEPTABLE. The Industrial Revolution had many social effects.

**Aggravate.** The meaning is *to make worse, to intensify.* Colloquially it may mean *to tease* or *annoy.*

COLLOQUIAL: Tommy likes to aggravate his sister.
ACCEPTABLE: A shortage of food aggravated the sufferings of the people.

**Ain't.** This form is considered unacceptable by most educated people. It is advisable not to use it except in dialogue or humorous writing. The acceptable forms are *aren't* for the first and second persons and *isn't* or *aren't* for the third person.

ACCEPTABLE:　Aren't I a taxpayer?
ACCEPTABLE:　Isn't the train on time?

**All-around.** The acceptable form is *all-round;* the meaning is *extending all round, developed in the round.*

ACCEPTABLE:　He soon became an all-round mechanic.

**All right.** The expression should be written as two words, not *alright.*

**All together, altogether.** The first expression means *all in one place, all acting in unison.* The second expression is an adverb meaning *completely, entirely.*

ACCEPTABLE:　All together the men put their shoulders to the wheel.
ACCEPTABLE:　Ben was not altogether at fault.

**All the farther.** A dialect form for *as far as.*

DIALECT:　This was all the farther we could go by automobile.
ACCEPTABLE:　This was as far as we could go by automobile.

**Allow.** *Allow* means *to permit, to allocate* or *apportion.* It is used in the sense of *to think* or *consider* only in dialect.

ACCEPTABLE:　Everyone is allowed to express his opinion.
ACCEPTABLE:　She allowed a certain amount each week for carfare.
DIALECT:　He allowed that good weather had helped the crops.

**Allusion, illusion.** An *allusion* is an indirect reference which does not name or mention specifically. An *illusion* is a false or deceptive appearance to the sight or the imagination.

ACCEPTABLE:　The audience recognized his allusion to the story of the prodigal son.
ACCEPTABLE:　A mirage is an illusion produced by heated air.

The corresponding verb forms are *allude* and *illude.*

**Along the line of.** It is preferable to use *in, in the field of, in the sphere of, in respect to,* or some other more concrete expression.

VAGUE:　He was a specialist along the line of biophysics.
BETTER:　He was a specialist in the field of biophysics.
VAGUE:　Along the line of international law there is much to be done.
BETTER:　In the sphere of international law there is much to be done.

**Already, all ready.** These are two different expressions. The first is an adverb, which means *previously* or *before.* The second consists of two words and signifies that whatever is being described is in a state of readiness or preparation.

ACCEPTABLE:　The children have already gone to bed.
ACCEPTABLE:　The soldiers are all ready.

**And etc.** This expression is a tautology, since *etc.* is an abbreviation of *et cetera,* meaning *and other things.*

**Amount, number.** *Amount* is used with mass nouns. *Number* is used with count nouns.

ACCEPTABLE: A large number of students attended the rally.
ACCEPTABLE: The amount of gas in the tank wouldn't get them to Toledo.

**Anecdote, antidote.** *Anecdote* means a story with a special point. *Antidote* means *a counteractive agent to a poison, a remedy.*

ACCEPTABLE: He told an anecdote of Davy Crockett.
ACCEPTABLE: Whiskey was long supposed to be an antidote for snake bite.

**Angle.** This is colloquial for *point of view.*

COLLOQUIAL: The advertising executive is always looking for a new angle.
FORMAL: The advertising executive is always looking for a new point of view.

**Ante-, anti-.** *Ante-* is a Latin preposition meaning *before. Anti-* is a Greek preposition meaning *against, opposed to.* Be sure to distinguish these in attaching them as prefixes.

ACCEPTABLE: Some of the remains go back to ante-Roman times.
ACCEPTABLE: Mr. Jarman was suspected of anti-democratic tendencies.

**Anyways, anywheres.** Dialect for *anyway* and *anywhere.*

**Apt, liable.** *Apt* means *fitting, suited to, having special ability for. Liable* means *legally subject to* or *exposed to the danger of.*

ACCEPTABLE: Donald proved apt at arithmetic.
ACCEPTABLE: The speaker used an apt quotation from Shakespeare.
ACCEPTABLE: Pedestrians who jaywalk are liable to a fine of $10.

*Liable* in the sense of *likely* or *probable* is colloquial.

COLLOQUIAL: It is liable to rain this afternoon.

**Around.** Colloquial for *approximately, about, near.*

COLLOQUIAL: It cost around ten dollars.
ACCEPTABLE: The bank is asking approximately $12,000 for that house.
COLLOQUIAL: His father is arriving around eight o'clock.
ACCEPTABLE: We can leave in about ten minutes.

**As.** Not considered acceptable when used in place of *whether* or *that.*

UNACCEPTABLE: I don't know as he will come.
ACCEPTABLE: I don't know whether he will come.

*As* is often a confusing connective, for it can mean *because, at the time that, during the time that, when,* and so forth.

CONFUSING:  As the negotiations were nearing an end, some of the delegates remained in Zurich for the weekend.

BETTER:  Because the negotiations were nearing an end, some of the delegates remained in Zurich for the weekend.

BETTER:  During the time that the negotiations were nearing an end, some of the delegates remained in Zurich for the wekend.

**At.** Unacceptable when used with *where*.

UNACCEPTABLE:  Herbert didn't know where he was at.

ACCEPTABLE:  Herbert didn't know where he was.

**Awful.** This word, in formal contexts, means *dreadful, terrible*. In colloquial contexts, it may mean *bad. Awfully,* in colloquial contexts, may mean *very* or *much.*

COLLOQUIAL:  Her dress is awful.

COLLOQUIAL:  Prices are awfully high.

ACCEPTABLE:  A tornado is an awful sight.

**Back of.** This expression is colloquial for *behind, in back of.*

COLLOQUIAL:  The clerk was back of the counter.

ACCEPTABLE:  The clerk was behind the counter.

**Bad, badly.** Do not use *badly* after linking verbs such as *look, seem, feel, taste.* These verbs are always followed by the adjective form *bad,* which is understood as applying to the subject of the sentence.

UNACCEPTABLE:  What makes the coffee from the laboratory taste so badly?

ACCEPTABLE:  What makes the coffee from the laboratory taste so bad?

**Badly** should be used only when it has the function of an adverb.

ACCEPTABLE:  Cousin Sue loves to talk, but she hears badly.

ACCEPTABLE:  He thumbed through the badly worn book.

**Being as, being as how.** These expressions are never conjunctions. Do not use them in place of *because* or *since.*

UNACCEPTABLE:  Being as he was slow, he fell behind the others.

ACCEPTABLE:  Because he was slow, he fell behind the others.

**Beside, besides.** Do not confuse *beside,* which means *by the side of,* with *besides,* which means *in addition to.*

ACCEPTABLE:  Beside the walk was a border of flowers.

ACCEPTABLE:  Besides his regular duties, he was expected to raise money.

**Between, among.** As a general rule, *between* is used when only two objects are referred to. *Among* is used in referring to more than two.

ACCEPTABLE:  This was supposed to be a secret between Laura and Catherine.

ACCEPTABLE:  The work was divided among the members of the fraternity.

*Between* may be used with reference to more than two if a reciprocal relationship is to be stressed.

> ACCEPTABLE: Prosperity depends on commerce between the nations of the world.

**Born, borne.** *Born* is the past participle form of *to bear* only when it means to be brought into existence by birth. For all other senses use *borne*.

> ACCEPTABLE: Washington was born in 1732.
> ACCEPTABLE: The tree had borne no fruit for two years.
> ACCEPTABLE: Mr. Andrews had borne a heavy load of responsibility.

**Bust, busted.** Unacceptable forms of *burst*.

**Calvary, cavalry.** *Calvary* is a proper name designating the place where Christ was crucified. *Cavalry* means troops mounted on horses.

**Can, may.** In formal contexts, *can* is preferred for capability and *may* for permission, probability, or likelihood.

> FORMAL: Books may be taken from the library for a period of two weeks.
> COLLOQUIAL: Books can be taken from the library for a period of two weeks.
> COLLOQUIAL: Can I add more salt to the solution?

**Cannot help but.** The *but* is usually regarded as unnecessary; its use in this expression is to be avoided in written English.

> COLLOQUIAL: We cannot help but admire their courage.
> ACCEPTABLE: We cannot help admiring their courage.

**Can't hardly.** Unacceptable.

> UNACCEPTABLE: They can't hardly make ends meet.
> ACCEPTABLE: They can hardly make ends meet.

**Canvas, canvass.** *Canvas* is a noun meaning a type of heavy cloth. *Canvass* is both noun and verb. As a noun it means a solicitation or a systematic examination. As a verb it means to solicit or to examine systematically.

> ACCEPTABLE: Canvas is a material often used for awnings.
> ACCEPTABLE: The *Daily Star* canvassed the voters for their opinion on the proposed city ordinance.

**Capital, capitol.** *Capital* designates the city; *capitol* designates the building in which the legislative branch of the government meets.

> ACCEPTABLE: Washington, D.C., is the capital of the United States.
> ACCEPTABLE: The dome of the Capitol shone in the morning light.

**Case.** The expression *in the case of* is often unnecessary.

> WORDY: In the case of China, it hasn't been admitted yet.
> BETTER: China hasn't been admitted yet.

**Casual, causal.** *Casual* means *incidental, occurring without design. Causal* means *pertaining to cause.*

> ACCEPTABLE: He knew Mr. Robertson's views only from casual conversation.
> ACCEPTABLE: A causal analysis may lead to a different conclusion.

**Climactic, climatic.** *Climactic* is the adjective form of *climax; climatic,* of *climate.*

> ACCEPTABLE: The climactic event of the week was the Junior Prom.
> ACCEPTABLE: Extensive climatic changes occurred during the glacial period.

**Clothes, cloths.** *Clothes* means *garments; cloths* means *woven fabrics.*

**Complected.** Dialect. Standard form is *complexioned.*

**Complement, compliment.** *Complement* means *that which completes something else; compliment* means *an expression of praise* or *approval.*

> ACCEPTABLE: A complement of twelve men would bring the company to its normal size.
> ACCEPTABLE: Mary received many compliments on her new dress.

**Conscience, conscious.** *Conscience* is a noun meaning *sense of moral rightness; conscious* is an adjective meaning *aware.*

> ACCEPTABLE: The affair never troubled his conscience.
> ACCEPTABLE: For the first time Peter was conscious of being a grown man.

**Contact.** *Contact* is a noun meaning a *meeting* or *junction.* Its use as a verb in the sense of *get in touch with* is considered colloquial, though it is becoming frequent in writing.

> COLLOQUIAL: In Dallas he contacted Mr. Davis, who promised to show him the whole area.

**Contemptible, contemptuous.** *Contemptible* is applied to things that deserve contempt. *Contemptuous* is applied to persons or things showing contempt.

> ACCEPTABLE: Cowardice is contemptible.
> ACCEPTABLE: His contemptuous attitude made him unpopular.

**Continual, continuous.** *Continual* means *continuing at intervals. Continuous* means *continuing without break or interruption.*

> ACCEPTABLE: The speaker had to deal with continual interruptions.

ACCEPTABLE: Rivers and creeks had been swollen by a continuous rain of twelve hours.

**Could of.** A spelling mistake for *could have.*

ACCEPTABLE: Frank could have made higher grades than he did.

**Council, counsel.** *Council* means *a group or assembly which meets to deliberate. Counsel* as a noun means *advice* and as a verb means *to give advice.*

ACCEPTABLE: The leader called a council of war.
ACCEPTABLE: He had always gone to his father for counsel.
ACCEPTABLE: His father counseled him not to accept the first job that was offered.

**Crazy about.** Colloquial for *likes,* is *enthusiastic about.*

COLLOQUIAL: Betty is crazy about ice cream sodas.
ACCEPTABLE: Betty likes ice cream sodas.

**Credible, creditable.** *Credible* means *capable of being believed. Creditable* means *praiseworthy, conferring credit upon.*

ACCEPTABLE: The story of his African adventure, though extraordinary, is credible.
ACCEPTABLE: At the track meet Johnnie turned in a very creditable performance.

**Criterion.** *Criterion,* meaning a standard or test, is a singular form. The usual plural form is *criteria.*

ACCEPTABLE: The criteria for admission to a university have changed considerably in the last ten years.

**Cute.** *Cute* is colloquial when used in the sense of *attractive, pretty.* It is an overused word and should be avoided in writing.

**Data.** Plural form of *datum,* "piece of evidence (fact, figure, picture, and so forth) on which conclusions, inferences may be based." Very formal usage treats *data* as a plural.

FORMAL: Those data were collected by scientists.

Less formal usage treats data as a singular.

ACCEPTABLE: The data was collected by scientists.

**Deal.** When used in the sense of a transaction, an arrangement, an agreement, or a treatment of someone, it is colloquial.

COLLOQUIAL: Renting that summer house would be a good deal.
COLLOQUIAL: He didn't get a very good deal from that professor.

**Desert, dessert.** *Desert* means *an arid, unpopulated tract of land;* also, *that which is deserved as reward or punishment. Dessert means a food served as the last course of a meal.*

> ACCEPTABLE:   There are deserts in California.
> ACCEPTABLE:   The villain in the melodrama got his just deserts.
> ACCEPTABLE:   Apple pie was the favorite dessert.

**Different from, than.** Either is permissible, but American usage prefers *different from*.

> ACCEPTABLE:   The idea of general education is different from that of vocational training.

**Disinterested, uninterested.** *Disinterested* means *impartial, not showing favor. Uninterested* means *taking no interest, indifferent to.*

> UNACCEPTABLE:   Students who are disinterested in their work seldom make high marks.
> ACCEPTABLE:   Students who are uninterested in their work seldom make high marks.
> UNACCEPTABLE:   Henry sought the opinion of some uninterested person.
> ACCEPTABLE:   Henry sought the opinion of some disinterested person.

**Disremember.** An unacceptable form of *do not remember*.

**Don't.** This is a contraction of the plural form *do not*. Never use it with a singular subject.

> UNACCEPTABLE:   Don't he keep up with the news?
> ACCEPTABLE:   Doesn't he keep up with the news?

**Due to.** Formal usage has insisted that *due to* be used only in adjectival constructions. Accordingly, "He failed due to laziness" is condemned because "due to laziness" functions here as an adverbial phrase modifying "failed." But "His failure was due to laziness" is approved because in this construction "due to laziness" functions as a predicate adjective following the linking verb "was." In formal writing it is best to avoid the adverbial "due to" construction and to use instead "because of" or "owing to."

> COLLOQUIAL:   The game was postponed due to rain.
> ACCEPTABLE:   The game was postponed because of rain.
> COLLOQUIAL:   Due to the number of applicants, the work of selection proceeded slowly.
> ACCEPTABLE:   Because of the number of applicants, the work of selection proceeded slowly.

**Each other, one another.** These words are reciprocal pronouns. In precise writing, use *each other* when referring to two; *one another* when referring to more than two.

> ACCEPTABLE:   The two men had known each other since childhood.
> ACCEPTABLE:   The members of the team depend on one another.

**Else's.** When *else* is used with an indefinite pronoun (anybody, somebody) in the genitive case, it takes the apostrophe and -*s*.

    ACCEPTABLE:   He took little interest in anybody else's problems.

**Emigrate, immigrate.** *Emigrate* means *to move out. Immigrate* means *to move in.* Correspondingly, *emigrant* refers to a person who is leaving a country; *immigrant* to a person who is coming in to take up residence in a country.

    ACCEPTABLE:   His ancestors emigrated from Europe about the middle of the eighteenth century.

    ACCEPTABLE:   His ancestors immigrated to Pennsylvania about the middle of the eighteenth century.

**Enthuse.** A colloquial form for *to be enthusiastic.*

    COLLOQUIAL:   The people were enthused by reports of victory.

    ACCEPTABLE:   The people were enthusiastic over reports of victory.

**Equally as good.** The *as* has no function. Write *equally good.*

    ACCEPTABLE:   This brand costs less than the other, but it is equally good.

**Except.** See *accept.*

**Everywheres.** Dialect for *everywhere.*

**Extra.** Colloquial when used to mean "very" or "unusually."

    COLLOQUIAL:   That was an extra hard exam.

**Fact.** Often an unnecessary word, especially in such expressions as *due to the fact that* (because), *except for the fact that* (except that), *in the fact that* (if).

**Factor.** Like *fact,* this is often unnecessary.

    WORDY:   Some of the factors which a university student has to consider very carefully during his first year at school are his expenses and his use of his time.

    BETTER:   During his first year at school, a university student has to consider his expenses and his use of time very carefully.

In very precise usage this word means *a constituent* or *one of the elements contributing to a result.* Some writers try to avoid using *factor* to mean *feature* or *aspect* and they would consider the following sentence to be inaccurate. *The visitor dwelled on the factors of American life which had impressed him.*

**Farther, further.** In formal usage, *farther* is used to indicate spatial progression; *further* to indicate non-spatial progression, or something additional in thought or idea. Informally *further* is often substituted for *farther*.

ACCEPTABLE: They drove thirty miles farther before stopping for the night.

ACCEPTABLE: The demand for kitchen appliances is expected to increase further.

**Fewer, less.** Use *fewer* when referring to count nouns, *less* when referring to mass nouns.

ACCEPTABLE: Figures show that fewer students are enrolled than last year.

ACCEPTABLE: The Department of Agriculture has asked farmers to sow less wheat.

**Firstly.** No longer used. *First* is preferred.

First, there is the legal aspect of the question.

NOTE: *Secondly, thirdly,* and so forth are still used.

**Fix.** Colloquial when used to mean *trouble, predicament.*

COLLOQUIAL: His carelessness about dates had gotten him into a fix.

ACCEPTABLE: His carelessness about dates had gotten him into trouble.

*Fix* is dialectal when used as a verb meaning *to prepare, make ready.*

DIALECT: We found them fixing to leave town.

ACCEPTABLE: We found them preparing to leave town.

**Forbear, forebear.** *Forbear* is a verb meaning *to abstain from, to avoid. Forebear* is a noun meaning a *forefather.*

**Forceful, forcible.** *Forceful* means *possessing or showing force. Forcible* is used to describe something effected or accomplished by force.

ACCEPTABLE: Mr. Wiggins made a forceful argument.

ACCEPTABLE: The burglar had made a forcible entry into the apartment.

**Formally, formerly.** *Formally* means *in a formal manner; formerly* means *previously.*

ACCEPTABLE: He was formally introduced to Miss Jones.

ACCEPTABLE: Students were formerly required to attend chapel.

**Former, latter.** *Former* and *latter* are used when only two things are involved. When there is need to refer to more than two, use *first* and so on to *last.*

ACCEPTABLE: Kelly, Johnson, Dahlberg, and Smith were competing, and the first drew the best position.

**Funny.** *Funny* means *laughable, comical.* It is colloquial when used to mean *odd, eccentric.*

COLLOQUIAL: He had a funny habit of taking off his glasses and putting them on again.

**Good.** *Good* is never used as an adverb.

UNACCEPTABLE: I did good on the chemistry test.
ACCEPTABLE: I did well on the chemistry test.

**Got, gotten.** Both are recognized past participle forms of the verb *to get.*

ACCEPTABLE: He had got his sister a present.
ACCEPTABLE: He had gotten his sister a present.

**Guess.** *Guess* means *to conjecture, to pick one of a set of alternatives.* It is colloquial when used in the sense of *suppose, think.*

COLLOQUIAL: I guess Mr. Atkins has a new automobile.
ACCEPTABLE: The general correctly guessed that the enemy would move against his left flank.

**Had better, better.** *Better,* a reduced form of *had better,* is frequent in conversation.

COLLOQUIAL: The State better change its educational system quickly.
ACCEPTABLE: The State had better change its educational system quickly.

**Hadn't ought.** To form the past negative of *ought,* we add *not* (followed by the infinitive) in formal usage.

FORMAL: He ought not to have gone so far.

Normally we usually avoid this construction and use *shouldn't.*

ACCEPTABLE: He shouldn't have gone so far.

*Hadn't ought* is an unacceptable past negative formation.

UNACCEPTABLE: He hadn't ought to have gone so far.

**Hanged, hung.** When this verb means death by hanging, its forms are *hang, hanged, hanged.* When it means to fasten or suspend something, the forms are *hang, hung, hung.*

**Hardly, scarcely.** These words are negative in sense and the addition of a second negative is considered unacceptable.

UNACCEPTABLE: She couldn't hardly believe her eyes.
ACCEPTABLE: She could hardly believe her eyes.

**Have got.** The use of *have got* is considered colloquial for *have.*

COLLOQUIAL: He's got three offers.
ACCEPTABLE: He has three offers.

**Healthy, healthful.** *Healthy* means *possessing or enjoying health; healthful* means *promoting health.*

ACCEPTABLE:   She had healthy children.
ACCEPTABLE:   The climate is mild and healthful.

**Historic, historical.** *Historic* means *famous in history,* or *epoch-making. Historical* means pertaining to history.

ACCEPTABLE:   The Monroe Doctrine was a historic step in American foreign policy.
ACCEPTABLE:   He gathered many historical facts about the settlement of Kentucky.

**If, whether.** *Whether* is preferred to *if* after verbs such as *ask, say, know, doubt.*

ACCEPTABLE:   I don't know whether this is the right size.

**Immigrate, emigrate.** See *emigrate.*

**In, into.** *In* refers simply to location inside, *into* refers to movement toward the inside. In conversation *in* is often substituted for *into.*

COLLOQUIAL:   The equipment fell in the river.
ACCEPTABLE:   Mr. Bosworth's office is in the next room.
ACCEPTABLE:   He wiped his feet carefully before going into the house.

**In back of.** See *back of.*

**In regards to.** Unacceptable. Write *in regard to* or *as regards.*

**Individual, party.** *Individual* should be used to refer to a single person as distinguished from a class or group. To refer to a number of people, *persons* or *people* may be used. *Party* refers to a person or persons in legal language and in some special contexts (*a party of four* at a restaurant).

UNACCEPTABLE:   None of the individuals in the elevator were injured in the fall.
ACCEPTABLE:   None of the people riding in his car were injured.
ACCEPTABLE:   What the new regulation means to the individual will be explained later.
UNACCEPTABLE:   Who was that party I saw you with last night?
ACCEPTABLE:   Mr. Gilbert appeared in court as one of the parties to the suit.

**Indulge.** When *indulge* is used to mean *to take part,* it is not considered good usage.

UNACCEPTABLE:   They indulged in a party before the exam.

**Infer, imply.** These cannot be used interchangeably. *Infer* means *to deduce as a conclusion, to conclude on the basis of evidence. Imply* means *to hint at, to express indirectly.*

ACCEPTABLE:   Bob inferred from the article that the author was a Democrat.

ACCEPTABLE:   His statement implied that the situation was deteriorating.

**Ingenious, ingenuous.** *Ingenious* means *clever, resourceful. Ingenuous* means *simple, free from deceit.*

ACCEPTABLE:   Ralph had an ingenious plan for meeting the difficulty.

ACCEPTABLE:   She was too ingenuous to be at ease in sophisticated society.

**Irregardless.** Unacceptable. Write *regardless.*

**Is when, is where.** Considered awkward in writing.

UNACCEPTABLE:   Racketeering is where money is extorted by illegal interference or the threat of violence.

ACCEPTABLE:   Racketeering is the practice of extorting money by illegal interference or the threat of violence.

**Its, it's.** Keep these distinct by remembering that the apostrophe signifies the omission of a letter. *Its* is a possessive pronoun; *it's* is a contraction of *it is.*

**Kind, sort.** In formal English these expressions should not be used with plural pronouns and verbs.

UNACCEPTABLE:   These sort of men make good soldiers.

ACCEPTABLE:   This sort of men makes good soldiers.

ACCEPTABLE:   This kind of book is appealing to boys.

**Kind of, sort of.** Colloquial when used to mean *slightly, somewhat. Somewhat* is used in formal contexts.

COLLOQUIAL:   He returned with his enthusiasm sort of dampened.

ACCEPTABLE:   He returned with his enthusiasm slightly dampened.

**Kind of a, sort of a.** Colloquial.

COLLOQUIAL:   Tom protested that he was not that kind of a man.

ACCEPTABLE:   Tom protested that he was not that kind of man.

**Latter.** See *former.*

**Lay, lie.** *Lay* (past tense: *laid*) is a verb used transitively. It means *to cause to lie down* or *to place in a position. Lie* (past tense: *lay*) is used intransitively and means *to recline, to take a position of rest.*

ACCEPTABLE:   She laid the sewing basket on the table.

ACCEPTABLE:   The tree lies where it fell.

ACCEPTABLE:   On Sunday afternoons he lay down for a nap.

**Learn.** *Learn* is never used in the sense of *teach* with an indirect object.

UNACCEPTABLE:   He learned his brother how to drive the car.

ACCEPTABLE:   He taught his brother how to drive the car.

ACCEPTABLE:   He learned how to drive the car.

**Leave.** *Leave* means *to depart, to take leave of, to let alone.* It is colloquial when used in the sense of *allow* or *let.*

> COLLOQUIAL:   We had better leave them go their own way.
> ACCEPTABLE:   We had better let them go their own way.
> ACCEPTABLE:   When he was grown, he decided to leave the farm.

**Liable.** See *apt.*

**Lick.** Lick is colloquial when used in the sense of *beat, overcome, defeat.*

> COLLOQUIAL:   State licked their opponents, 27–7, last Saturday.
> ACCEPTABLE:   State defeated their opponents, 27–7, last Saturday.

**Lie.** See *Lay.*

**Like.** Colloquial when used as a conjunction introducing a clause. Use *as if* or *as though.* But distinguish between *like* used as a conjunction and *like* used as a preposition in a prepositional phrase.

> COLLOQUIAL:   He acted like he was the owner.
> ACCEPTABLE:   He acted as if he were the owner.
> ACCEPTABLE:   Harry walks just like his father.

**Loan.** In preferred usage *loan* is a noun. The verb is *lend.*

> COLLOQUIAL:   The bank will loan him a thousand dollars.
> ACCEPTABLE:   The bank will lend him a thousand dollars.

**Loose, lose.** *Loose* is used as both verb and adjective. As a verb it means *to untie, to set free;* as an adjective it means *in a free or unfastened state. Lose* is a verb only.

> ACCEPTABLE:   He loosed the yelping dogs.
> ACCEPTABLE:   A loose collar added to his disheveled appearance.
> ACCEPTABLE:   Joyce always loses her fountain pen.

**Lot, lots of.** Colloquial for *many, much, a large amount.*

> COLLOQUIAL:   He gets a lot of business from tourists.
> ACCEPTABLE:   He gets a large amount of business from tourists.

**Mad.** In literary usage, *mad* means *insane.* In less formal and colloquial usage it means *angry.*

> LITERARY:   Abandoned by his wicked daughters, King Lear goes mad.
> COLLOQUIAL:   Charles was mad at the policeman for giving him a ticket.

**May of.** A spelling mistake for *may have.*

**Maybe, may be.** *Maybe* is an adverb meaning *perhaps. May be* is a modal form of the verb *to be.*

> ACCEPTABLE:   Maybe conditions will improve next year.
> ACCEPTABLE:   It may be necessary to review the lesson.

**Might of.** A spelling mistake for *might have*.

**Moral, morale.** Moral (normally used in the plural) means *a principle of social conduct, a social convention.* It means also *the lesson of a story or an event.* Morale means *spirit, determination, enthusiasm for an undertaking.*

> ACCEPTABLE: It is expected that a political candidate will be a man of good morals.
> ACCEPTABLE: The moral of the story is that one should never procrastinate.
> ACCEPTABLE: The morale of the troops was greatly improved by victory.

**Most.** In some dialects, the adjective *most* is used as an adverb.

> DIALECT: Dinner is most ready.
> ACCEPTABLE: Dinner is almost ready.

**Muchly.** Unacceptable. Use *much*.

**Myself, yourself, himself.** In conversation these intensive pronouns are often substituted for the personal pronouns, but this substitution is not acceptable in writing or in formal contexts.

> COLLOQUIAL: They gave the prize books to Johnson and myself.
> ACCEPTABLE: They gave the prize books to Johnson and me.

**Nice.** A word of general approval, meaning *attractive, agreeable, pleasant,* which is so overused that it is of little value in precise writing.

**No account.** Dialectal for *worthless, without value.*

> DIALECT: This cigarette lighter is no account.
> ACCEPTABLE: This cigarette lighter is worthless.

**Nowheres.** Dialect for *nowhere*.

**O.K.** A colloquial expression meaning *correct* or *approved*. It should not be used in formal English.

**Only.** In written English when *only* is used as a restrictive modifier, it should be placed next to the expression it modifies.

> COLLOQUIAL: He only saw his wife and children.
> ACCEPTABLE: He saw only his wife and children.
> COLLOQUIAL: He only had one year of high school.
> ACCEPTABLE: He had only one year of high school.

**Off of.** The *of* is superfluous.

> ACCEPTABLE: It was lucky that Jerry knew how to swim when he fell off the pier.

**On to, onto.** *On to* consists of an adverb and a preposition. It is correct in such expressions as "Turn on to the next page." *Onto* is a preposition.

ACCEPTABLE:   The men jumped onto their horses.

**Outside of.** *Outside of* used for *except* is considered colloquial.

COLLOQUIAL:   Outside of the people in his home, no one knew of his success.

ACCEPTABLE:   Except for the people in his home, no one knew of his success.

**Per.** *Per* is a Latin preposition meaning *through, throughout, during, on a basis of.* In formal writing it is best to confine its use to Latin expressions.

ACCEPTABLE:   The rainfall is 36 inches per annum.

ACCEPTABLE:   The per capita consumption of dairy products increased slightly last year.

**Percent, percentage.** *Percent* means *number of units out of each hundred* and is used following a figure or number. *Percentage* has the more general meaning of *a portion, a fraction.*

ACCEPTABLE:   Thirty percent of the men were rejected.

ACCEPTABLE:   A large percentage of the men were rejected.

**Personal, personnel.** *Personal* is an adjective meaning *pertaining to a person. Personnel* is a noun meaning *those persons who make up the membership or staff of an organization.*

ACCEPTABLE:   The letter was for Mr. Sykes' personal attention.

ACCEPTABLE:   The personnel of the bureau had been increased.

**Phenomenon** (plural: *phenomena*). *Phenomenon* as used in science means *any observable thing, fact,* or *occurrence.* In a sense generally current today it means something *abnormal, extraordinary,* or *wonderful.* The plural form is often used with a singular verb in informal usage. (See *Data.*)

**Piece.** Dialect for *short distance.*

DIALECT:   I will travel a piece with you.

ACCEPTABLE:   I will travel a short distance with you.

**Plenty.** *Plenty* is a noun meaning *an abundance, a great deal.* It is not used as an adverb in written English.

COLLOQUIAL:   He was plenty anxious to come.

ACCEPTABLE:   He was very anxious to come.

ACCEPTABLE:   He has plenty of material for the job.

**Practicable, practical.** *Practicable* means *feasible, capable of being put into practice. Practical* means *useful.* When applied to persons, *practical* means *capable of getting results, able to deal effectively with ordinary matters.*

> ACCEPTABLE: Lighter-than-air craft are practicable, but they have not proved very practical.
> ACCEPTABLE: As a practical man, he knew the value of advertising.

**Precede, proceed.** *Precede* means *to come before. Proceed* means *to move forward, to carry on.*

> ACCEPTABLE: Spring precedes summer.
> ACCEPTABLE: The court proceeded to pass sentence on the defendant.

**Principal, principle.** *Principal* is both noun and adjective. As a noun it means *the chief official of a school, a person chiefly liable in a legal proceeding,* or *a sum of money drawing interest.* As an adjective it means *chief, primary, most fundamental. Principle* is a noun only. It means *a fundamental truth, belief, or law.*

> ACCEPTABLE: Mr. Anderson is the principal of Lakeside High School.
> ACCEPTABLE: These bonds are guaranteed as to interest and principal.
> ACCEPTABLE: The principal export of Brazil is coffee.
> ACCEPTABLE: He undertook to learn the principles of public speaking.

**Proposition.** In logic *proposition* means any statement which can be affirmed or denied. In more general usage it means something offered or proposed. It is colloquial when used to mean *job, undertaking.*

> FORMAL: "Four score and seven years ago our fathers brought forth on this continent a new nation dedicated to the proposition that all men are created equal."
> ACCEPTABLE: The proposition that the two businesses be merged was discussed with interest.
> COLLOQUIAL: Protecting the Mississippi Valley against floods is a difficult proposition.
> ACCEPTABLE: Protecting the Mississippi Valley against floods is a difficult job.

**Proved, proven.** Both are past participle forms of *prove,* but *proved* is in more common use.

**Put across.** Colloquial when used to mean *impart, make understood,* or *carry out, accomplish.*

> COLLOQUIAL: The teacher knew his subject, but he couldn't put it across.
> ACCEPTABLE: The teacher knew his subject, but he couldn't impart it.

**Quote.** Often used as an informal substitute for *quotation.*

**Raise, rise.** *Raise, raised, raised* is transitive.

> ACCEPTABLE: They raised their children strictly.

*Rise, rose, risen* is intransitive.

> ACCEPTABLE:  On the horizon, smoke was rising slowly.

**Real.** Often used colloquially for *very* or *really*.

> COLLOQUIAL:  That building was real old.
> ACCEPTABLE:  That building was very old.

**Reason is because.** A clause introduced by *because* is adverbial and should not be used as a predicate nominative in writing. Use a noun clause such as *reason is that*.

> COLLOQUIAL:  The reason Jack failed is because he never prepared his lessons.
> ACCEPTABLE:  The reason Jack failed is that he never prepared his lessons.

**Reckon.** Dialectal when used to mean *think, guess, suppose*. In formal usage *reckon* means *to calculate, to determine*.

> DIALECT:  I reckon he will arrive in a short while.
> ACCEPTABLE:  The position of the ship is reckoned at each noon.

**Respectfully, respectively.** *Respectfully* means *with respect, courteously*. *Respectively* means *with reference to each in the order given*.

> ACCEPTABLE:  Joseph always treated his elders respectfully.
> ACCEPTABLE:  John Webster and Marvin Jones were elected president and secretary respectively.

**Reverend, honorable.** In formal usage these expressions should not be used with the surname alone. They should be used with the full name or with a title and the surname, and should be preceded by *the*.

> ACCEPTABLE:  The Reverend Charles A. Davis will conduct the service.
> ACCEPTABLE:  The Reverend Dr. Smith is a member of the board.
> ACCEPTABLE:  The Honorable Theodore Harris, Representative of the Third District of Illinois, will be the principal speaker.

**Right.** Dialectal for *very*.

> DIALECT:  It was a right difficult journey.
> ACCEPTABLE:  It was a very difficult journey.

**Right away.** Colloquial for *immediately*.

**Rout, route.** *Rout* means *a disorderly flight*. *Route* means *a course to be traveled, a way*.

> ACCEPTABLE:  General Greene put the enemy to rout.
> ACCEPTABLE:  Their route took them through the Mohawk Valley.

**Same.** The use of *same* in place of the personal pronouns *it, they* and *them* is confined to business communications.

> JARGON:  We have noted your request and are pleased to comply with same.

**Same as.** Colloquial for *just as, in the same way that.*

> COLLOQUIAL:   He has to make a living the same as you do.
> ACCEPTABLE:   He has to make a living just as you do.

**Seeing as how.** Unacceptable for *because* or *since.*

> UNACCEPTABLE:   Seeing as how he was late, I gave him an extra ten minutes.
> ACCEPTABLE:   Since he was late, I gave him an extra ten minutes.

**Set, sit.** The verb *set* is always used with an object except in a few expressions such as "the sun sets" and "a hen sets." It means *to cause to sit,* or *to put in position or order. Sit,* which is seldom used with an object, means *to be seated.*

> ACCEPTABLE:   James set the parcel on the table.
> ACCEPTABLE:   Diana set the alarm for seven o'clock.
> ACCEPTABLE:   Father sits in his favorite chair.

**Shall, will.** *Will* is becoming the common form for all persons. *Shall* is still used in formal contexts (speeches, poetry, and so forth) and for emphasis (*You shall go to the dentist, young man!*). Shall is also used in the first person in interrogatives (*Shall I begin now?*).

**Shape up.** Colloquial for *develop satisfactorily.*

**Should of.** A spelling mistake for *should have.*

**Show up.** Colloquial for *appear, arrive.*

**Sight, site, cite.** The noun *sight* means *view, appearance. Site* means *location* or *seat. Cite* is a verb meaning *to refer to* or *to quote.*

> ACCEPTABLE:   Her first sight of the Rocky Mountains was thrilling.
> ACCEPTABLE:   Chicago was the site of the Columbian Exposition.
> ACCEPTABLE:   The speaker cited figures showing the decline in immigration.

**So.** *So* is a colloquial, usually feminine, form when used to mean *very.*

> COLLOQUIAL:   The weather is so hot today.
> ACCEPTABLE:   The weather is very hot today.

When *so* is used to introduce a sentence it is considered colloquial usage. This is true whether the sentence occurs by itself or if it is included as part of another sentence.

> COLLOQUIAL:   The opera began so they could not continue their conversation.
> ACCEPTABLE:   Since the opera began, they could not continue their conversation.
> COLLOQUIAL:   The construction was poor. So the building collapsed.

ACCEPTABLE: Because the construction was poor, the building collapsed.
COLLOQUIAL: He ordered the tickets in advance; so they did not have to wait in line.
ACCEPTABLE: He ordered the tickets in advance; consequently, they did not have to wait in line.

When used in clauses of result or purpose, *so* is considered colloquial. Use *so that* in writing.

COLLOQUIAL: They checked the list carefully so no one would be overlooked.
ACCEPTABLE: They checked the list carefully so that no one would be overlooked.

**Some.** The use of *some* as an intensive is considered colloquial.

COLLOQUIAL: That was some party!

**Somewhat of, something of** are considered colloquial expressions.

COLLOQUIAL: Next day, Bill found himself somewhat of a hero.

**Somewheres.** Dialect for *somewhere*.

**Specie, species.** *Specie* means *gold and silver coin*. *Species* (plural: *species*) means *class* or *kind*.

ACCEPTABLE: The foreign creditors asked that the debt be paid in specie.
ACCEPTABLE: He found a new species of tomato.
ACCEPTABLE: There are many species of flowering shrubs in the Great Smoky Mountains.

**Statue, stature.** *Statue* means a modeled figure or image. *Stature* means *height;* figuratively used, it means *ability, capacity*.

ACCEPTABLE: In the public square was a statue of General Washington.
ACCEPTABLE: He was an impressive man of great stature.
ACCEPTABLE: Few men are of sufficient stature to be president.

**Such.** When used as an intensive it is a colloquial, often feminine usage.

COLLOQUIAL: They had such an expensive trip.
ACCEPTABLE: They had a very expensive trip.

**Suit, suite.** *Suit* means *an article of clothing*. *Suite* (pronounced *swēt*) means *a number or series of things*, as a *suite* of rooms.

**Suspicion.** *Suspicion* is used only as a noun. The verb is *suspect*.

ACCEPTABLE: We suspected that he knew the truth already.

**Sure.** Colloquial when used for *surely*.

**Swell.** An overused, colloquial form for *very good*. See *Nice*.

**Than, then.** Spelling problem. *Than* is the conjunction (*He's taller than his brother*); *then* is the adverb (*Then he spoke for the first time*).

**That . . . that.** Avoid the redundant repetition of *that* following an intervening clause.

> UNACCEPTABLE: I believe that when a person is twenty-one years old that he should be able to make his own decisions.
>
> ACCEPTABLE: I believe that when a person is twenty-one years old he should be able to make his own decisions.

**There, their, they're.** Note the spelling differences between *there* (*He's there now. There is a tower not far from here*), *their* (*They spent their funds last year*), and *they're* (*they are*).

**This here, that there, these here, those there.** Unacceptable forms of *this, that, these, those.*

**Transpire.** *Transpire* means *to become known.* It is used to mean *happen* in much writing, but some writers disapprove of this usage.

**Thus.** *Thus* is an adverb. It has no *-ly* form in standard English.

> ACCEPTABLE: Do it thus.

**Treat, treat of.** *Treat of* is more common when the meaning is *deal with a subject, discuss.*

> ACCEPTABLE: This work treats of the French and Indian War.

**Try and.** Colloquial for *try to.*

> COLLOQUIAL: The nations involved must try and settle their differences.
>
> ACCEPTABLE: The nations involved must try to settle their differences.

**Unique.** *Unique* (from the Latin *unicus,* meaning *one*) means *sole* or *only.* In formal usage it is applied to a thing which is the only one of its kind. Since it does not admit of a comparison, do not use it with *more* or *most.*

> COLLOQUIAL: Allen had the most unique experience.
>
> ACCEPTABLE: Allen had a unique experience.
>
> ACCEPTABLE: Franklin D. Roosevelt had the unique record of being elected four times to the presidency.

**Uninterested.** See *Disinterested.*

**Wait for, wait on.** *Wait for* means *to delay, to wait until something occurs. Wait on* means *to serve. Wait on* is used dialectally for *wait for.*

> ACCEPTABLE: We decided to wait ten minutes for Jimmy.
>
> ACCEPTABLE: Mr. Perkins waited on us in the book department.

**Ways.** Dialectal for *way.*

DIALECT: She felt a long ways from home.
ACCEPTABLE: She felt a long way from home.

**Where.** In expressions like *read where, see where,* and so forth, is colloquial for *read that, see that,* and so forth.

COLLOQUIAL: I see where the Senators have lost another game.
ACCEPTABLE: I see that the Senators have lost another game.

**Without.** Unacceptable when used as a conjunction.

UNACCEPTABLE: A student cannot participate in sports without he passes his courses.
ACCEPTABLE: A student cannot participate in sports unless he passes his courses.

**Would of.** A spelling mistake for *would have.*

**You, one.** In less formal style, *you* is often used as an indefinite pronoun in place of the formal *one*. It may give the style a touch of intimacy or a certain degree of concreteness. The important thing is to be consistent in the use of *one* or *you* and to avoid the confusion that results from abrupt shifting back and forth.

UNACCEPTABLE: You will find in this work many references to early American inventions. One will be impressed by the resourcefulness of the pioneers in dealing with primitive conditions.
ACCEPTABLE: You will find in this work many references to early American inventions. You will be impressed by the resourcefulness of the pioneers in dealing with primitive conditions.

# Index

# Index

385

*Plenty,* 376
Plurals of nouns, 306
Point of view, in description, 71–75; in narration, 93–96
Possessive pronoun, 313
*Post hoc, ergo propter hoc,* 156–157
*Practicable, practical,* 376–377
*Precede, proceed,* 377
Predicate adjective, 323
Predicate, of sentence, 322–323
Predicate nominative, 323
Premises, in syllogism, 120ff.
Preposition, defined, 316; listed, 316
Prepositional phrase, 316–317, 319
*Principal, principle,* 377
Process, exposition of, 54–58
Profile, writing of, 103–104
Pronoun, defined, 312; agreement with antecedent, 327–328; demonstrative, 314; indefinite and numeral, 315; indefinite relative, 314; intensive, 315; interrogative, 315; personal, 313; possessive, 313; reciprocal, 315; reference of, 328; reflexive, 315; relative, 314; for transitions in paragraph, 224
Proper noun, 306
Proportion, in theme, 15–16
*Proposition,* 377
Propositions, recognizing, 106–107; structure of, 107–108; supporting, 113–114; types of, 108–111
*Proved, proven,* 377
Punctuation, exercises in, 349–353; internal marks of, 335–339; nature of, 333–334; rules for, 339–343; terminal marks of, 334–335

Question, begging the, 155–156; complex, 156
Quotation marks, rules for use of, 334–335, 339–341; colon before, 341; comma before, 340; to enclose words and phrases, 340; with titles, 340
Quotations, direct, 282–284; comma before, 339
*Quote,* 377

*Raise, rise,* 377–378
*Real,* 378
*Reason is because,* 378
Reciprocal pronoun, 315
*Reckon,* 378
Reference of pronouns, 328
Reference books, in library, 274–277
Reflexive pronoun, 315
Relative pronoun, 314
Repetition, in transitions, 17–19, 225
Research paper, gathering materials for, 272–281; selecting material for, 281–282; specimen, 289–301; suggested

topics for, 288–289; writing procedure for, 282–288
*Respectfully, respectively,* 378
Restatement, in transitions, 17–19
Restrictive elements, no punctuation of, 336–337
*Reverend, honorable,* 378
Rhetoric, relation to logic, 134–136
Rhetorical analysis, of sentences, 192–200
Rhetorical patterns, of sentences, 180–192
Rhetorical syllogism (*see* Enthymeme)
Rhythm, 195
*Right,* 378
*Right away,* 378
*Rout, route,* 378

*Same,* 378
*Same as,* 379
Scale, of description, 76–77
*Seeing as how,* 379
Selected readings, 383–664
Semicolon, rules for use of, 338; between independent clauses, 336; separating elements containing internal punctuation, 338
Sentence, defined, 163; balanced, 170–171; classification by meaning, 321; classification by structure, 320–321; complex, 171–174; compound, 169–170; detached elements in, 325–326; exercises on, 198–200; expletive construction of, 185–186; grammatical patterns of, 168–179; included, 323–324; incomplete or fragmentary, 165–167; length, 189–192; loose and periodic structure of, 182–185; modifiers in, 174–179; order, 180–182; parallelism in 188–189; passive voice in, 186–188; rhetorical analysis of, 192–200; rhetorical patterns of, 180–192; simple, 168–169; structure, 322–325; topic, 202–206
Sentence structure, 322–325
Sequence, of tenses, 329–330
*Set, sit,* 379
*Shall, will,* 379
*Shape up,* 379
*Should of,* 379
*Show up,* 379
*Sight, site, cite,* 379
"Signpost" terms, 17
Similitude, arguments from, 142–143
Simple sentence, 168–169; defined, 320, 322
Simplicity, related to clarity, 20
Sketch, writing of, 102–103
Slang, nature of, 32–33
*So,* 379–380
*Some,* 380
*Somewhat of, something of,* 380
*Somewheres,* 380

# Correction Chart